ECOLOGICAL RESISTANCE MOVEMENTS

The Global Emergence of Radical and Popular Environmentalism

BRON RAYMOND TAYLOR, EDITOR

STATE UNIVERSITY OF NEW YORK PRESS

GE
140
.E26
1995

Published by
State University of New York Press, Albany

For information, address State University of New York
Press, State University Plaza, Albany, N.Y., 12246

Production by E. Moore
Marketing by Theresa Abad Swierzowski

Library of Congress Cataloging-in-Publication Data

Ecological resistance movements : the global emergence of radical and
    popular environmentalism / Bron Raymond Taylor, editor.
        p.   cm. — (SUNY series is international environmental policy
    and theory)
        Includes bibliographical references and index.
        ISBN 0-7914-2646-7 (pbk. : alk. paper). — ISBN 0-7914-2645-9
    (alk. paper)
        1. Environmental degradation—Social aspects.   2. Environmental
    degradation—Political aspects.   3. Deep ecology.   I. Taylor, Bron
    Raymond,   II. Series.
GE140.E26   1995
363.7—dc20   94-39374
                                                                  CIP

10 9 8 7 6 5 4

For

ANDERS BRONSON,

KAARIN ELISABETH,

AND

KELSEY ERIN

Choose wisely

CONTENTS

Acknowledgments   xi

Introduction: The Global Emergence of Popular
    Ecological Resistance   1
    Bron Taylor

PART I. POPULAR ECOLOGICAL RESISTANCE
IN THE AMERICAS

1. Earth First! and Global Narratives of Popular
    Ecological Resistance   11
    Bron Taylor

2. With Liberty and Environmental Justice for All:
    The Emergence and Challenge of Grassroots
    Environmentalism in the United States   35
    Bob Edwards

3. Bread and Soil of Our Dreams: Women, the Environment,
    and Sustainable Development—Case Studies   56
    from Central America
    Lois Ann Lorentzen

4. Profits, Parrots, Peons: Ethical Perplexities in the
    Amazon   70
    Heidi Hadsell

PART II. POPULAR ECOLOGICAL RESISTANCE
IN ASIA AND IN THE PACIFIC

5. International Native Resistance to the
New Resource Wars   89
Al Gedicks

6. Visitors to the Commons: Approaching Thailand's
"Environmental" Struggles from a Western
Starting Point   109
Larry Lohmann

7. Grassroots Environmental Resistance in India   127
Vikram K. Akula

8. Popular Environmentalists in the Philippines: People's   146
Claims to Natural Resources
Emma Porio and Bron Taylor

PART III. POPULAR ECOLOGICAL RESISTANCE IN AFRICA

9. Grassroots Resistance to Dominant Land-Use   161
Patterns in Southern Africa
Yash Tandon

10. *Luta*, Livelihood, and Lifeworld in Contemporary Africa   177
Ben Wisner

PART IV. POPULAR ECOLOGICAL RESISTANCE IN EUROPE

11. Have a Friend for Lunch: Norwegian Radical Ecology
Versus Tradition   201
David Rothenberg

12. Between Moderation and Marginalization:
Environmental Radicalism in Britain   219
Wolfgang Rüdig

13. Popular Resistance and the Emergence of Radical   241
Environmentalism in Scotland
*Brendan Hill, Rachel Freeman, Steve Blamires,
and Alastair McIntosh*

PART V. CONCLUDING REFLECTIONS ON THE GLOBAL
EMERGENCE OF POPULAR ECOLOGICAL RESISTANCE

14. Postmodern Environmentalism: A Critique of
    Deep Ecology   259
    Jerry A. Stark

15. In Search of Gaian Politics: Earth Religion's Challenge   282
    to Modern Western Civilization
    Daniel Deudney

16. In Defense of Banner Hangers: The Dark Green Politics
    of Greenpeace   300
    Paul Wapner

17. The Effectiveness of Radical Environmentalists   315
    *Sheldon Kamieniecki, S. Dulaine Coleman, and
    Robert O. Vos*

18. Popular Ecological Resistance and Radical
    Environmentalism   334
    Bron Taylor

References   355

Contributors   407

Index   411

Acknowledgments

I am grateful to many people for helping with this volume. Lois Lorentzen, Alan Durning, and the editors of *the Ecologist*, and possibly others whom I have forgotten, made helpful suggestions regarding contributors. Sheldon Kamieniecki deserves special recognition as series editor for substantive ideas throughout this process, as well as exceptional mentoring over the past several years. I owe special thanks to several of the contributors. Often with heroic promptness, Lois Lorentzen, Al Gedicks, Bob Edwards, and especially Jerry Stark read my chapters. Stark provided especially detailed and timely copyediting, as well as sound advice throughout this project. And no doubt my own analysis in this book would have been weaker without the regular and cogent critique of Bob Edwards. Larry Lohmann and Heidi Hadsell also added perspectives that shaped in important ways the framework for this volume.

On the home front, Cindy Schultz revolutionized the efficiency of the Department of Religious Studies and Anthropology, thus freeing me from many time–consuming tasks, and Michele Lorenzini, Vicki Simon, and Lisa Frei provided conscientious and competent research assistance. I am grateful to the Faculty Development Board at the University of Wisconsin, Oshkosh, for its flexibility and willingness to fund my research, and to my departmental colleagues for supporting one who does not easily fit into traditional disciplinary categories. I am especially grateful to and amazed by my wife Beth, whose energy, empathy, and good humor made this book possible.

Finally, I wish to acknowledge and thank those within the international deep ecology movement who have granted interviews, and especially those who have helped facilitate the research in other ways. My gratitude is profound, even though I cannot list all of you here. Jaspar Carlton deserves special credit for speaking of the "ecological resistance," providing a term which found its way into the rubric of this volume.

INTRODUCTION:
THE GLOBAL EMERGENCE OF
POPULAR ECOLOGICAL RESISTANCE

Bron Taylor

In the waning decades of the twentieth century, ecologists have both described and predicted the collapse of natural ecosystems and widespread species extinction. Meanwhile, social scientists argue that the ecological deterioration detailed by these ecologists fuels the social conditions of famine, refugee displacement, ethnic rivalry, and violent social conflict (Homer–Dixon 1991; Homer–Dixon, Boutwell and Rathjens 1993; Kaplan 1994). Some even observe that such calamities erode the legitimacy and power of nation–states, often in direct proportion to their inability to resolve problems of environmental decline (Lipschutz and Conca 1993; Lipschutz and Mayer 1993; Rosenau 1990, 1993; Habermas 1983). Meanwhile, grassroots environmental organizations have proliferated and have become increasingly assertive. This development has further escalated social conflicts related to environmental decline.

This book is about grassroots environmental groups who are fighting against environmental degradation. Some of these groups, like those in the international deep ecology movement, hope to overturn the anthropocentrism of Western civilization, an orientation they regard as a central cause of environmental problems (Devall and Sessions 1985). Others emerged from a variety of oppositional political movements (anticolonial, national independence, antinuclear, Marxist, feminist, Gandhian, etc.) as activists recognized the importance of ecological issues to their interests and objectives. Many of these groups have only recently assumed an "environmental" character. Still others, whose members were initially motivated by reformist environmental concerns, were radicalized by their experience of public indifference and organized corporate and governmental resistance to their ecological efforts.

These ecological resistance movements express a variety of critical ideas and employ a range of tactics which sometimes, in one way or another, appear to be "radical" or "militant." But the diversity of these movements makes it difficult to find an adequate umbrella term of reference for them. Uncritically labeling all these groups "radical" or "militant" can be misleading. Many of these groups eschew such labels.[1] Still, definitions are important. Although they often contain biased presuppositions which can lead an inquiry astray, without them, it is difficult to focus an inquiry. Perilous though it may be to begin with an umbrella term for the movements examined in this volume, some term of reference is required.

We refer to these groups inclusively as *popular ecological resistance movements*, a phrase inspired by Latin American social scientists who refer to nonmiddle–class, peasant, indigenous peoples and participants in underground economies. Yet we expand upon this definition to include populist environmentalists (who may be from middle–class backgrounds), such as members of the U.S.–based "environmental justice" movement and the "back–to–the–land" movements in Western countries such as Australia, the United States, and Ireland (Tovey 1993). Any single term of reference for the diverse movements explored in this volume will be problematic. Indeed many of the specific chapters struggle with questions about how we should conceive of these movements. Nevertheless, as the chapters unfold, what we mean by the term *popular ecological resistance* will become clearer. (We do not mean, for example, that all these movements are well liked or enjoy widespread support; often they are not even well known.)

This book focuses exclusively upon popular environmental resistance movements because of the dearth of scholarly attention paid to them. One reason for this lack of attention is that many such groups have recently formed, or have only recently assumed an environmental agenda. Moreover, analysts tend to focus upon well–established and mainstream environmental movements. Another reason for the lack of attention may be the tendency of social scientists to focus on the politics within and between nation–states. For these reasons, and perhaps others, ecological resistance movements have not received the scholarly attention one might otherwise expect.

FOUR LINES OF INQUIRY

This volume pursues the description and interpretation of these movements along four central lines of inquiry. The first illuminates these movements as much as possible through firsthand observations and interviews, often supplemented by documentary research.[2] The second examines these movements in the light of social-movements theory. The third discusses in a more theoretical way the philosophical and moral views represented by some movement participants. The fourth attempts to assess the impacts and prospects of the movements described in this volume.

1. A Descriptive Tour of Ecological Resistance

The central goal of the descriptive line of inquiry has been to understand and represent these diverse movements on their own terms. Specifically, *we set out to describe movement participants' own perceptions about their ecological predicament, their understandings of the cause(s) of their predicament, and their proposed prescriptive remedies.* We also endeavored to hold in abeyance any assumptions that these movements might be similar. Instead, we hoped to allow generalizations to emerge from our collaborative observations, rather than attempting to use observations to prove preconceived theoretical ideas.

In section 1, we begin our descriptive tour of ecological resistance in the Americas. Chapter 1 analyzes the spiritual politics of Earth First! and the tendency of some "radical environmentalists" to view the global proliferation of grassroots environmental activism as an outbreak of deep ecology. This chapter poses problems that the following contributions help answer. Next, Bob Edwards examines the "environmental justice" movement. He illustrates, among other things, the increasing role ethnic minorities are playing in environmental activism in North America. Lois Lorentzen then introduces us to homegrown "eco–feminism" of women's environmental movements in Central America, and Heidi Hadsell leads us to an agrarian community of river dwellers far up the Amazon River in Brazil, who are struggling to overturn unsustainable resource exploitation in their region.

In section 2, we begin a voyage to Asia and the Pacific through Al Gedicks's discussion of indigenous environmental resistance. Using case studies of such movements in Canada, the United States, Ecuador, and then in Malaysia, Gedicks stresses the central role indigenous communities are increasingly playing in struggles over resources and land practices. Next, Larry Lohmann discusses Thai social movements which have captured the imagination of Western environmentalists and cautions sympathizers not to view such movements uncritically through Western lenses. Vikram Akula focuses on the diverse popular environmental movements of India, while Emma Porio and I discuss grassroots struggles for resources in the Philippines which increasingly have assumed an "environmental" character.

In section 3 we continue on to Africa. Here the contributions of Yash Tandon and Ben Wisner paint a landscape where struggles for independence, democracy, women's rights, and land increasingly blur with environmental concerns into social movements that are both old and new. Here again we learn how very different environmental movements in less affluent countries can be from those found in Western countries.

Finally, in section 4, we wander north to Europe. Here David Rothenberg provides a good feel for the essence of deep ecology, which has its origins in Norway. He simultaneously explores the increasingly violent conflict between the Norwegian government and the militants of the Sea Shepherd Conservation Society, who sink whaling ships and otherwise interfere with Norwegian efforts to resume whaling. Next, Wolfgang Rüdig offers a history of the emergence of and obstacles to ecological radicalism in Britain, while Brendan Hill and colleagues introduce us to a little known movement in the Scottish Highlands where Celtic renewal and nationalism are linked to the quest for land rights, ecological restoration, and various forms of ecological radicalism.

2. Ecological Resistance and Social-Movement Theory

A second line of inquiry uses current social movement theory to explain the dynamic interplay of macrostructural, organizational, and cultural factors in the emergence, development, and impact of popular ecological resistance movements. Macrolevel analysis considers broad changes in the structure of economic and political relations and the incursions of state and corporate power into formerly private spheres of life (Melucci 1989; Offe 1985). Social-movement theory attends to how the structures of everyday life, culture, indigenous forms of organization, and shifting structures of protest traditions influence the emergence, activities, and impacts of social movements (McAdam, McCarthy and Zald 1989; Morris and Mueller 1992). It also examines how such factors influence the tactics such movements choose and the narratives they produce. A number of this volume's contributors weave this line of inquiry into their analysis by considering whether the case studies add meaningfully to current discussions of social-movement theory.[3]

3. The Challenge to Modernity

A third line of inquiry examines the manner in which popular ecological resistance movements challenge the philosophical, moral, and religious underpinnings of modern society. Found especially in the final, "Concluding Reflections" section, the contributions by Dan Deudney and Jerry Stark focus most specifically on these matters, providing competing perspectives about whether the philosophical and moral claims posed by deep ecology and other forms of nature mysticism are promising or compelling. These chapters especially help to bring into focus personal questions regarding what sort of environmental ethics and politics we should endorse.

4. The Impacts and Prospects of Ecological Resistance Movements

A forth line of inquiry examines the impacts, prospects, and obstacles facing ecological resistance movements. Most of the case studies provide some analysis along these lines, but the final three chapters especially prioritize such assessment. Paul Wapner analyzes the international influence of Greenpeace, while Sheldon Kamieniecki and his colleagues focus on the effectiveness of radical environmentalism. At the end of the volume I also discuss the impacts and prospects of these movements, as well as trends and tendencies that can be discerned among them. Specifically, I suggest that patterns in the perceptions of movement participants about the causes of their environmental predicaments, and commonalities among their prescriptions, make it possible to label these diverse movements "radical," if this is understood in a limited and qualified way.

Because these movements have received so little scholarly attention, this volume places a premium on careful description. There has been no effort to impose a single analytic lens or point of view. Indeed, several chapters disagree about fundamental issues, others pose their own research questions and raise new theoretical issues, and still others urge analytic caution by addressing difficulties in comprehending or generalizing about these movements.

The case studies assembled in this volume are not exhaustive. Nor have we fully discussed every issue in social theory or environmental philosophy raised by them. Nevertheless, this volume provides an unusual and complementary balance between description and theory, supplying insights from a variety of disciplinary perspectives.[4] Moreover, the rich descriptive data the contributors have provided can be mined for additional theoretical purposes and arguments by others. But perhaps the greatest contribution of this volume is that it offers those who embark on this global tour of popular ecological resistance a unique opportunity: to think afresh about a variety of pressing ecological, political, and moral issues that are raised by the emergence of these movements.

NOTES

1. For example, in an uncritical and unqualified way, some observers label all these movements "radical environmentalism." By providing in–depth description and analysis of a variety of these movements, the present volume serves as an antidote to such oversimplifications.

2. This is the "grounded theory" approach described by Charmaz (1983), Emerson (1983), and Glazer and Strauss (1967).

3. I wish to thank Bob Edwards for clarifying social movement theory for this nonspecialist.

4. The distinction between description and theory is useful, but often overdrawn. Descriptive work always involves an interpretive dimension and theoretical premises.

PART I
POPULAR ECOLOGICAL RESISTANCE
IN THE AMERICAS

Chapter 1

EARTH FIRST! AND GLOBAL NARRATIVES OF POPULAR ECOLOGICAL RESISTANCE

Bron Taylor

We tell and hear stories. They awaken feelings in us. Thinking in response, we ponder the meaning of narratives. Is there a fable here, a moral lesson, a call to action? Personal stories can fuse with the broader narratives of communities and cultures—often unconsciously and uncritically—especially in social contexts characterized by little cultural diversity. But more often, integrating personal and cultural narratives is a difficult personal process. There are many stories. Which ones move us? Which make sense?[1]

The stakes are high in battles over narratives. These battles, and the stories themselves, shape our individual and collective identities, and thus our character. They tell us how we should live and how we should relate to others. Questions such as Who am I? How and with whom do I fit in? Where is my community? and What is the good life? are often if not usually resolved in narrative.

Since my undergraduate days, I have been moved often by what Roger Betsworth calls "outsider" stories. First, by "Liberation theology" with its story of Christians acting to promote *earthly* peace and justice. This spin on Christianity was striking in its deviance from the dominant, otherworldly Christian stories with which I was well acquainted; it also repudiated the close association between the church and political power that has dominated the last millennia and a half. Liberation narratives, which explain inequality as the consequence of oppression also contradicted central U.S. narratives, including the Gospel of Success and the Enlightenment story of progress—both of which assume that hard work yields individual success and material prosperity—and claim that these consequences constitute the good society (Betsworth 1990).

Further exploration uncovered more stories and introduced additional, incompatible claims into the contestation. Complicating matters further, since factually irreconcilable stories still move people emotionally (sometimes even the same individuals!), it became obvious that affect and intuition were not sufficient grounds for choosing between competing narratives. It seemed, therefore, that competing claims would have to be arbitrated rationally, that only careful reasoning could help sort out which stories made sense. Nevertheless, moral sentiments *are* connected to emotions and intuitions, to our capacity for caring. Consequently, we need to find an approach that can reconcile narratives presented to us with our own personal experiences, as well as an approach that recognizes the connections between the reflective and the affective dimensions of moral experience.[2]

My own experience has been that we can discover new insights by seriously considering the contending claims of competing narratives. For example, by researching liberationist claims I gradually became convinced that (1) multilateral "aid" often exacerbates the plight of the poor by promoting cash-crop "monocultures" that, in turn, lead to food exports to affluent consumers while depriving subsistence foods to local populations; (2) huge "development" schemes such as hydro-electric dams displace rural peoples and destroy vast areas capable of sustaining them (Goldsmith 1983; McDonald 1993); and (3) such agricultural practices and development projects are intimately related to the world's declining biological diversity (Hayter 1985; Rich 1994). I was initially skeptical of such claims, since they contradicted (or at least qualified) a narrative with which I was much more familiar, that of the United States generously assisting less affluent nations.

As valuable as specific insights might be, however, even more significant is what I have learned about the value of outsider voices *per se*. Even when mistaken, they can raise important questions and focus attention on issues demanding thoughtful scrutiny. Sometimes they expose selfish interests and self-deceptions camouflaged in the dominant narratives of the politically powerful (Betsworth

1990). Outsider voices can carry valuable knowledge that guardians of the world's dominant narratives prefer would remain little-known. For example, relevant to this volume's themes, protests by native Americans over how Euro-Americans came and destroyed indigenous cultures and ecosystems can counter tendencies within the Euro-American culture toward unmerited feelings of superiority, while simultaneously demanding respect for native peoples and Mother Earth. In such ways, outsider voices can kindle moral imagination, obliging us to consider moral claims completely outside our own frames of reference.

By engaging strange voices and deviant stories in conversation, and by making moral decisions in response, we can deepen understanding and build moral character. The initial step in such engagement is often the most difficult: the painful act of listening.

This book contains many stories of ecological resistance and reflections about them. The seeds for this volume were planted in 1978 when I first read Edward Abbey's *The Monkeywrench Gang*, a novel about a band of fed-up environmentalists who resorted to sabotage in an effort to halt and reverse the destruction of a desert they loved. Abbey was an anarchist whose stories pitted freedom-loving individuals against the dehumanizing and earth-destroying forces of an authoritarian, bureaucratic, and obsessively prodevelopment society. I first read it as fiction. But Abbey was romanticizing the exploits of an already emerging ecological guerilla force that, in 1980, took form as the ecological resistance movement known as Earth First![3] Recognizing Earth First! as an outsider voice, in 1989 I decided to conduct field and documentary research, first to understand the movement as a historical and social phenomenon, and second to consider its moral, ecological, and political claims.

In this chapter, I first provide an interpretation of the key moral, ecological, and political claims articulated by participants in the Earth First! movement. I then describe perceptions shared by many Earth First!ers about grass-roots movements around the world which they consider to be kindred movements of ecological resistance. In this way, I introduce Earth First!'s own narrative as well as other narratives of ecological resistance originating in diverse contexts around the world. My purpose in describing such narratives is not to endorse or promote them. Rather, toward the end of this chapter, I use the claims and perceptions embedded in these narratives to pose problems for us to consider throughout this volume. By studying the Earth First! movement and agonizing over its claims, I have deepened my own understanding of the moral, ecological, and political dimensions of contemporary environmental controversies. Even if we end up disagreeing with them, examining outsider claims and narratives can enhance our own understandings.

EARTH FIRST!: A NEW STORY OF ECOLOGICAL RESISTANCE[4]

Earth First! announced itself in the early 1980s with a series of humorous protests. For example, activists illegally unfurled a plastic "crack" down the face of Glen Canyon Dam, symbolically "liberating" the Colorado River. But soon the actions turned more serious as activists struggled to prevent destructive enterprises in wilderness areas. They blockaded logging roads, sometimes with activists chained to machinery or buried up to their necks[5] or perched precariously high atop wooden "tripods." Activists conducted multiday "tree-sits" to prevent felling. Various forms of "night work," "ecotage," or "monkeywrenching"—movement parlance for sabotage intended to thwart environmental destruction—increasingly accompanied the civil disobedience campaigns.

Activists viewed ecotage as economic warfare against those who would destroy wilderness areas. By vandalizing equipment; pulling up survey stakes; driving metal, ceramic, or quartz spikes into trees; and so on, practitioners hoped to halt the destruction by making it unprofitable (Foreman and Haywood 1987). Meanwhile, they took their message across North America: through guerilla theater, where activists dressed in animal costumes conducting mock trials of human corporate criminals; through poetry and song at demonstrations, in the courts, and in jails; through "road shows" (touring public presentations), often involving spellbinding storytelling woven into science-based arguments about the ecological importance of wilderness; and through the creative invention of ritual processes designed to evoke and deepen what they considered proper human perceptions of the sacrality of the natural world (Taylor 1993). Less well known is their strategy of "paper monkeywrenching"—the threat or actual filing of administrative appeals and lawsuits by individuals and small groups of activists. Scattered around the country, often self-taught, but increasingly sophisticated both legally and scientifically, such activists have been among the most effective North American campaigners for biological diversity.[6]

In myriad ways these activists lived out their narratives of ecological rebellion, sometimes weaving their resistance into a larger evolutionary story. For example, in words originally expressed by the Australian Earth First!er John Seed, "I am the rainforest, recently emerged into consciousness, defending myself."[7] This idea became a movement slogan when popularized by Earth First! cofounder Dave Foreman. It suggested that ecological resistance is an evolutionary expression of self-defense, a necessary adaptation for reharmonizing the human and nonhuman worlds.

Other movement stories have assumed nearly mythic significance, especially Aldo Leopold's wilderness epiphany about the intrinsic value of the nonhuman world, gained as he witnessed the "green fire" die in the eyes of a wolf he had shot.[8] This story is strikingly similar to the description by Paul Watson[9] of the day his gaze met that of a harpooned whale he was trying to save. Looking into that whale's eye revealed, Watson recounts, an "intelligence . . . that spoke wordlessly of compassion . . . , that communicated [that he knew] what we had tried to do." From this experience, Watson received his commission: "On that day I knew emotionally and spiritually that my allegiance lay with the whales . . . over the interests of the humans who would kill them" (Watson 1993b).[10]

Finally, in addition to these classic tales, there is a growing body of narratives about heroic environmental activists. Those engaged in ecological resistance, especially those injured or martyred, are often honored in poetry and song.[11]

DEEP ECOLOGY AND THE MORAL CLAIM OF EARTH FIRST!

With such tactics and legitimating stories, activists of the Earth First! movement have advanced moral, ecological, and political claims which constitute the three essential pillars of Earth First!'s ethics. Their *moral claim* is that nonhuman life is valuable, even apart from its usefulness to human beings. Every species has "intrinsic worth," and each should be allowed to fulfill its "evolutionary destiny." To this, many Earth First!ers add, humans are no more valuable than other species. This is a proposition posed dramatically, if implicitly, by those acts of ecotage risking human injury or death.[12] This simple form of the moral argument has become known as *deep ecology*, a term coined in 1973 by Norwegian philosopher Arne Naess, but quickly adopted by Earth First!ers in the early 1980s. The terms *biocentrism* (for life-centered), and increasingly, *ecocentrism* (for ecosystem- centered), expressed the conviction that all ecosystems should be allowed to flourish, that humans should not impede such flourishing, and that when possible they should restore the natural preconditions for such flourishing.[13] This biocentrism is contrasted with anthropocentrism, that is, a human-centered approach to the environment.

Accepting arguments like those advanced by Toynbee (1972) and White (1967), most Earth First!ers blame the major religious monotheisms of the West for fueling the anthropocentrism they generally believe is the main cause of the human destruction of nature. In contrast, what animates most Earth First!ers are their own spiritual experiences in nature which convince them of the interrelatedness and sacrality of all life.[14] Such experiences are the foundation of most deep ecological arguments about the intrinsic value of species and ecosystems. However, some activists believe it is counterproductive to their cause to discuss such underpinnings (Taylor 1995a).

A SCIENTIFIC ARGUMENT FOR DEEP ECOLOGICAL URGENCY

Based on their reading of the ecological sciences, Earth First!ers add the *ecological claim* that we are in the midst of an unprecedented, anthropogenic extinction crisis, and consequently, many ecosystems are presently collapsing. This is the second pillar of Earth First's ethics, and provides an essential underpinning and rationale for militancy. Without this claim there is no basis for urgency, no reason for people with deep ecological moral senti- ments to risk their freedom or disrupt their private lives.[15] If accu- rate, such ecological analysis reveals a wide gap between fact and value, between what is and what ought to be: ecosystems that *ought* to be flourishing are being destroyed by human action. This intro- duces the realm of politics, the necessary arena for strategy over how to bridge gaps between what *is* the relationship between humans and nature and what such relations *ought* to be.[16]

POLITICAL ANALYSIS AND THE CALL TO RESISTANCE

Deep ecological moral perceptions combined with ecological urgency do not by themselves enjoin specific political strategies or tactics. The argument for such tactics requires political analysis. The heart of Earth First!'s *political claim* is either that democracy in the United States is a sham, thoroughly thwarted by corporate economic power, or, even if not a complete sham, the democratic political system is so distorted by corporate power and regressive human attitudes that it cannot respond quickly enough to avert the escalating extinction catastrophe. Moreover, Earth First!ers would argue that, in light of nature's intrinsic value, governing processes that disregard the interests of nonhumans are illegitimate.

Many Earth First!ers add to such critiques the ecofeminist contention that androcentrism and patriarchy play important roles in ecological destruction. Many agree that human hierarchy is also a key factor, drawing on social ecology or other anarchistic critiques. Few Earth First!ers would suggest, however, that either androcentrism or hierarchy fully explain environmental degradation. Nevertheless, virtually all of today's Earth First!ers believe patriarchy, hierarchy, and anthropocentrism reflect related forms of domination that destroy the natural world. Most Earth First!ers agree that all such domination must be overcome if humans are to reharmonize their lifeways within nature.[17]

Such political analysis provides the third essential pillar of Earth First!'s radicalism. Without it, in a formally democratic society, it is difficult to argue persuasively that illegal tactics are morally permissible. By asserting either that democratic procedures never existed, or that they have broken down, or that they camouflage domination, these activists argue that illegal tactics are morally justifiable.

These three claims lead to the assertion that the current situation—morally, ecologically, and politically—is so grave that tactics considered objectionable by most are instead necessary and even obligatory. Such analysis, in turn, provides for a continuum of tactics that roughly parallel these three claims. Some Earth First!ers prioritize efforts to change anthropocentric human attitudes by developing ritual processes that are believed to awaken nature spirituality in urbanized humans. Others prioritize the use of scientific knowledge to argue for biological diversity in legal and policy-making venues, sometimes through Earth First! spin-offs such as the Alliance for a Paving Moratorium, the Biodiversity Legal Foundation, or the Wildlands Project.[18] Still others prioritize more aggressive political action, using a variety of provocative tactics to resist destructive enterprises, to publicize ecological injustices, and ideally, to precipitate the overturning of the intrinsically destructive industrial state.[19]

Differences about priorities and tactics sometimes contribute to tensions within the movement. Nevertheless, most Earth First!ers believe that the struggle for biodiversity must be fought on all three of these related fronts—promoting spiritual awakening, ecological education, and fundamental political change. Most respect the work of those whose priorities differ from their own.[20] All agree, as well, that the reharmonizing of life on earth, requires the *international* expansion (and renewal) of deep ecological perceptions and actions.

INTERNATIONAL ECOLOGICAL RESISTANCE AND RADICAL ENVIRONMENTAL SOLIDARITY

Earth First!'s first symbolic act involved creating a memorial to the Apache indian chief Victorio, whose last-ditch, armed resistance to the European conquest symbolized to them the struggle to preserve ecologically harmonious lifeways in North America. From that moment on, Earth First!ers have celebrated ecological resistance movements wherever they could be found. Popular environmental movements are interpreted as kindred movements in different cultural garb, particularly when they appear to be motivated by nature-based spirituality,[21] and Earth First!ers try to act in solidarity with such groups.

Among the most notable expressions of such solidarity are the United States-based Rainforest Action Network (RAN), and the Australia-based Rainforest Information Center (RIC). The latter was founded in 1983 by John Seed, an Australian environmental activist introduced to Earth First! in the early 1980s by poet and counterculture visionary Gary Snyder.[22] Seed liked what he saw in the Earth First! journals Snyder showed him. Soon he was in the United States, participating in road shows that, in 1983 and 1984, established thirty rainforest action groups. Soon afterward Mike Roselle (an Earth First! cofounder) and Randall Hayes (another activist drawn to Earth First! in the early 1980s) formed RAN. Their initial goal was to coordinate the efforts of these groups. A 1985 strategy conference led, in turn, to the 1986 formation of the World Rainforest movement, now based in Penang, Malaysia, which serves as an international umbrella network for rainforest activism.[23]

Most prominent among the struggles celebrated (and often supported) by Earth First!ers and their compatriot solidarity activists are those engaged in by (1) people believed to live sustainably (esp. forest dwellers and indigenous peoples), (2) those animated by nature spiritualities deemed similar to deep ecology, and (3) those who have become especially militant, employing civil disobedience, ecotage, and (rarely) violence against the agents of destruction.[24] A brief survey of the movements that have drawn the greatest attention of Earth First! and RAN provides a rudimentary sense of the scope and nature of the ecological resistance, and the solidarity activism, that is unfolding internationally.

Substantial movement attention has focused on the struggles of Amazonia's Seringueiros (peasant rubber tappers) and indigenous peoples, who formed their own Forest People's Alliance in 1987 to defend themselves and their forests against colonizers (see Hecht and Cockburn 1989:183, cf. 160–63, 180–83).[25] In the eyes of movement activists, the struggle of these groups, who promote "extractive reserves" (setting aside the forest for small-scale gathering, hunting, and rotating small-plot agriculture) is clearly radical. Extractive reserves presume "communal land ownership [and thereby attack] private property and hence capitalism" (Hecht and Cockburn 1989:181–82). Moreover, their tactics are often militant, including nonviolent, usually illegal, land occupations, as well as sporadic and desperate armed attacks on miners, loggers, or other settlers.[26]

Dispatches from a 1989 alliance-building meeting of nearly a thousand delegates from twelve Amazonian tribes illustrate Earth First!'s fascination with such "kindred" resistance movements. This meeting was held in Brazil at Altimira, near the site of a series of dams planned for the Xingu and Iriri rivers, which are tributaries of the Amazon. During one session, a Kayapo woman threatened with a machete an attending Brazilian official. Reporting for the *Earth First!* journal, Sea Shepherd director Benjamin White quoted her as threatening, "You build this dam, we will go to war, and you will die." White implied that the Indians were deep ecologists at heart and likened their indigenous attitudes to Earth First's no compromise stance. "Unlike the typical language of moderation, conciliation and defeat of North American liberals" White wrote, "the

Indians' statements reflected their years of armed struggle and unwillingness to compromise" (1989).[27] Another article reported that nature spirituality fueled their resistance, quoting one native leader, "It is necessary to respect our Mother Nature. We advise against destroying the forests. For a long time, the white man has offended our way of thinking and the spirit of our ancestors. Our territories are the sacred sites of our people, the dwelling place of our creator" (Swikes 1989; see also Pearce 1991:133–34, and Hecht and Cockburn 1989:212–13).

The struggle of the Ecuadorian Huaorani against oil exploration and extractive colonizers (see Gedicks, this volume) has similarly received recurrent attention. For example, the *Earth First!* journal mentioned how, in 1987, one group of Huaorani, the Tagaeri, killed a nun and a bishop who were trying to proselytize and pacify them, thereby promoting the objectives of the oil companies.[28]

The most common tactics employed by solidarity activists involve Amnesty International-style letter-writing campaigns on behalf of people involved in ecological struggles and boycotts attempting to halt consumption of products whose production causes deforestation. Virtually every issue of RAN's *World Rainforest Report*, the *Earth First!* journal, and *Wild Earth*—the three most influential radical environmental journals in the United States— contains updates of various resistance campaigns, urging readers to write letters applying pressure on officials. Boycotts of various sorts are ongoing and sometimes successful. For example, RAN led a successful boycott against Burger King, claiming it was importing beef raised on rainforest-cleared land. More important is the tropical timber boycott promoted since 1989 by Earth First!, RAN, and numerous other groups.[29] One priority of these efforts has been to halt the export of unsustainably harvested timber from Sarawak in Malaysia.

The effort to save the rainforest upon which these people depend has led to other innovative tactics. One involves clearing three to four-meter wide corridors through the forest and replanting them with native palm trees in order to demarcate and thereby protect Huaorani territory that the Ecuadorian government previously, but without adequate enforcement, had promised would remain inviolable. Such corridors prevent "accidental" colonization—no one can claim ignorance of the boundary. John Seed of the RIC steered funds raised in the United States toward such efforts, including four thousand dollars from the Foundation for Deep Ecology[30] (Seed 1994).[31] By 1993, with the assistance of solidarity activists, the Huaorani had planted 100,000 native palm trees in corridors 130 kilometers long. They further demarcated the boundary by erecting metal signs reading "Huaorani territory," marked with crossed spears.[32]

John Seed's passion to save the rainforests was not initially motivated by concern for forest dwellers. Now he finds himself deeply involved in indigenous human rights struggles. Once the battle for the rainforest brought him into close proximity to its peoples, he realized that without defending the people who had lived sustainably in it, the forest itself could not be saved. He is amused by the ironies of certain strategic innovations, such as cutting down portions of the rainforest to save it and its people.[33]

The reason for this sense of irony is that Seed and other radical environmentalists have also become involved in "eco-forestry," sponsoring logging with *wokabout somils*. These portable saws are carried into the forest and used to cut and mill logs. This type of logging eliminates the need for the roads, road building, and heavy equipment, that cause most of the destruction associated with large-scale commercial logging. The idea is to reduce the impact of logging while increasing local incomes, thereby eroding the incentive for local people to support industrial forestry. Seed has also sought funds to purchase *wokabouts* for ecoforestry projects in Papua New Guinea (PNG) and the Solomon Islands (Seed 1990). In 1993 in PNG, such "ecoforestry" tactics were reported by RAN to be well underway (Belcher and Gennino 1993:33), leading Seed to solicit additional funds from the United States for another innovation, "to train participants in the care and use of waterbuffalo" for hauling the sawn timber from locations far from roads (Seed 1994).[34]

The resistance to logging by the Penan and Iban tribes in Sarawak has probably drawn more radical environmentalist attention and solidarity action than any other popular ecological resistance movement. Given their willingness to risk arrest, it is not surprising that their resistance captures the radical environmental imagination. In a typical pattern, the rebellion of these traditionally nomadic, foraging peoples was fueled by the devastation of their land base by logging. In 1982, "the [more] assertive Iban tribe blew up twenty-five bulldozers and logging trucks after loggers refused to leave their lands," repeating such tactics four years later (Scarce 1990:151). In 1987, the Penan began a series of antilogging blockades which they have sustained well into the 1990s. These blockades were initiated on the advice of Bruno Manzer, a Swiss citizen who had been living among the Penan since 1984 (Snow 1994).[35] By 1993, U.S. funds to feed the blockaders were being funneled to them through John Seed and his allies.

The blockades have inspired an international campaign to boycott Sarawakian timber (see Gedicks, this volume). Within the limits of their usually meager resources, Earth First!ers and other radical environmentalists have launched direct efforts to halt the export of forest products and to stimulate international outrage over the destruction of these forests and peoples. In 1989, thirteen international activists arrived in Sarawak, including Earth First! activists from the United States, the United Kingdom, Australia, and Sweden, and a woman from Robin Wood, a German radical environmental faction founded in 1982. Their objective was to champion the Penan and Dyak resistance. Six of them eventually locked themselves to sixty-foot cranes, preventing for one day the loading of timber. Others spirited photographs out of the country for international distribution (Wilson 1991).[36] Earth First!, RAN, the RIC, Greenpeace, and Friends of the Earth, along with numerous smaller groups, have repeatedly demonstrated in protest of tropical timber imports into the United States, the United Kingdom, Australia, Germany, and Japan. The boycott has reduced Malaysian timber exports, especially to Europe, and to some degree in the United States.[37]

Reporting on the indigenous resistance in Sarawak, Earth First! again attends to the nature-based spirituality of the Iban and the Penan, implying that they share deep ecological perceptions: "As nomadic people [the Penan] need the forest for their food, medicines, and spiritual identity. . . . They joined together [in these blockades] to speak for the ancient trees, for all life in the jungle and for their grandchildren" (Caruso and Russell 1992; Penan Leaders 1993).

No country has experienced greater diversity of popular ecological resistance than the Philippines. The struggle of the Kalinga and the Bontoc peoples to prevent a dam threatening to inundate their burial grounds and villages, and another struggle by farmers in the San Fernando province to stop or control logging, have gained international attention (see Porio and Taylor in this volume, Broad and Cavanagh 1993, ch. 4; Durning 1992).

Another indigenous struggle in the Philippines, this time against an energy project threatening a sacred mountain, has drawn the attention of *Earth First!* A solemn intertribal blood pact to defend their land, "even to the last drop of blood," was made among the indigenous Lumad communities in 1989. Further threats of armed rebellion were articulated the following year: "We are willing to take up arms, if necessary, to defend our rights to survive as a people of mother earth" (Broad and Cavanagh 1993:34; cf. Durning 1992:5–6, 38–39). Once again, a discussion in *Earth First!* linked the resistance of the Bagobo elders (who come from one of the Lumad groups) to their nature spirituality. The Bagobo view themselves as "the stewards of the mountain," reported the journal, "engaged by the spirits to protect the ecological and spiritual sanctity of the lands" (Fay and Barnes 1989).[38]

Earth First! has also closely followed the native Hawaiian and environmentalist resistance to geothermal projects, which traditionally religious Hawaiians believe will injure Pele, the Hawaiian volcano goddess, whom they fear will retaliate (Faulstich 1990). This resistance has led to mass demonstrations, including one resulting in 133 arrests (RAN 1990). After the withdrawal of the geothermal development company, *Earth First!* proclaimed, "Pele's power is still strong" (Pele Defense Fund 1994).[39]

Many other struggles are discussed in *Earth First!* including those of the Karen, Karenni, and Moi in Myanmar (formerly Burma). These tribes have become so desperate in their efforts to preserve their teak forests that they have threatened to attack the loggers directly.[40] Strictly nonviolent movements, such as the Gandhian Chipko "tree hugging" movements of India, are also considered kindred movements (see McRae 1994; Akula in this volume; Taylor et al. 1993:72–76; Schelling 1991; Berreman 1989; and Shiva 1988).[41]

Earth First!ers also believe (or at least hope) that radical ecological resistance is proliferating in the industrial world. The rebellions in eastern Europe are viewed as ecologically motivated (Scarce 1990: 141). Further evidence is found in the emergence of Earth First!-style actions in Czechoslovakia in opposition to the Gabcikovo dam project (see Kolenka 1993) in England where activists claim significant victories in resisting road building and in Switzerland where there have been violent anti-automobile demonstrations.[42] And great hope is derived from the Celtic renewal and ecological resistance movements of Scotland, Wales, and Ireland (see e.g., Oxford Earth First! 1993; Burbridge and Torrance 1993; McIntosh, Wightman and Morgan 1994; and Hill et al., in this volume). Even more militantly, in the fall of 1993 the Earth Liberation Front announced that it had established twenty clandestine cells which had already caused damage costing over 2 million British pounds to England's "earth rapers." The "elfs" proclaimed that they had emerged from the British EF! movement (which had not engaged previously in ecotage) and claimed they had coordinated "earth nights" across several continents on pagan holidays. They invited synchronized sabotage during the Halloween holidays (ELF 1993).

Any overview of Earth First!'s international efforts must mention the export of the *road show* strategy to Europe, and as of this writing, the founding and support of Institutes for Deep Ecology (by this and similar names) in England, Germany, Poland, and Russia.[43] Such institutes of "applied deep ecology" are rapidly becoming centers for Earth First!-style political resistance and for promoting spiritual awakening of reverence and compassion for the natural world. Toward this latter end, the Council of All Beings and other newly developed ritual processes are regularly conducted throughout Europe, especially in the aforementioned countries.[44] Such evangelical strategies will likely expand the deep ecology movement in Europe, as they have in the United States.

In North America, the early 1990s witnessed increasing efforts by Earth First!ers to act in solidarity with this continent's indigenous nations. Such solidarity is expressed through support of groups such as the Apache Survival Coalition, which has been resisting telescope construction desecrating an ecologically sensitive mountain in Arizona, and the Coalition for Nitassian, which is comprised of Innu and Cree indians and nonindian solidarity activists who have been resisting Hydro Quebec's hydroelectric dam projects (see Gedicks in this volume). Such groups multiplied rapidly in the 1990s.

Meanwhile, several new international environmental umbrella groups were formed in the late 1980s and early 1990s, including the Indigenous Environmental Network,[45] the Arctic to Amazonia Alliance,[46] and the Native Forest Network.[47] Each has had significant involvement from Earth First! activists. Each is committed to native peoples and the biological integrity of the regions in which they live. Each hopes to nurture the recently evolving but fragile alliances between Indians and environmentalists in North America.

CRITICAL QUESTIONS ARISING FROM NARRATIVES OF ECOLOGICAL RESISTANCE

The preceding overview has introduced diverse narratives of resistance, from the outlines of Earth First!'s own stories, to accounts of international environmental resistance *viewed primarily through the perceptions and hopes of Earth First! activists*, supplemented by scholarly treatments where available and relevant. Through international networks of solidarity and resistance, diverse stories merge into a cross-cultural narrative about the global emergence of popular ecological resistance.

For those prone to environmental romanticism, it is easy to be swept up by such narratives where good triumphs over evil and communities of humans and nonhumans find their way back to an Edenic harmony. Those willing to risk physical harm or personal liberty to right wrongs and confront us with a moral challenge deserve a fair hearing before they are incarcerated and we turn away indifferently. This book allows these storytellers to pose their questions. It also brings us full circle to the existential questions posed at the outset of this chapter: Do these stories move us? Do they make sense?

But these stories also raise further questions not usually pondered by those wrapped up in them. For example, Do the storytellers assume facts not in evidence? Do they exaggerate their claims to conform them to their hopes? Is popular ecological resistance rapidly spreading across the planet? Is it significantly and increasingly animated by deep ecological spiritual sentiments, biocentric ecology, and radical politics? Or rather, are Earth First!ers and their kindred spirits projecting their own presuppositions and hopes onto movements that, although engaged in struggles with significant ecological dimensions, are neither deep ecological or even self-consciously environmentalist?

WHAT IS RADICAL ENVIRONMENTALISM?

The perceptions and hopes of such radical environmentalists pose an even more basic question that has inspired the inquiry in this volume: What is radical environmentalism? Moreover, we can rightly wonder whether, when discussing movements emerging from very different cultural and ecological environments, such terms of reference themselves promote or hinder understanding.[48]

When I began research exploring international grassroots "environmental" movements, I did so in part because I wanted a comparative reference point for understanding what I was discovering in the North American Earth First! movement. I wanted to know whether Earth First!-style activism was unique to the industrialized world or was increasing around the world. As I learned more about the international movements that Earth First! tended to celebrate, it was *not* obvious to me that their perceptions were accurate, that kindred forms of an international radical environmentalism were actually emerging. There seemed to be significant discontinuities between activist narratives and perceptions and other accounts of the same movements. Gaps in scholarly analysis exacerbated the difficulty of assessing such discontinuities. Clearly these phenomena deserved much closer scrutiny than most had heretofore received. Moreover, it was obvious that advancing our comprehension of contemporary ecological resistance would best be accomplished through an interdisciplinary and international effort. Such realizations led to an earlier collaboration (Taylor et al. 1993) that has culminated in this volume.

I hope that this chapter has evoked some of the curiosity that has inspired this collaborative inquiry. The reader can compare the type of ecological resistance described in this chapter with those described in the subsequent case studies and ponder the variety of scholarly questions these diverse narratives pose. In the final chapters we will survey the global panorama of ecological resistance conveyed in these pages, reflect on the impacts of these movements, consider the viability and prospects for those resistance movements that are animated by various forms of nature spirituality, and reflect on what if any patterns among them make it possible to speak of the international emergence of a global environmental radicalism. I also hope we will allow these narratives to pose their questions and claims directly to us as individuals—that we do not get so wrapped up in the fascinating effort to understand these movements as social phenomena that we lose sight of the high stakes, real-life dramas these case studies present. The struggles described in these pages matter. They are life-and-death struggles, and they demand a personal response.

NOTES

1. For those confronted with a host of competing narratives at the increasingly multicultural university, choosing narratives can be an especially difficult task. Today's universities not only expose students to more stories than previously, but it is presumed less often that Western culture provides the best and most compelling stories. Consequently, battles over narratives have become increasingly divisive—witness, for example, the "war" over multicultural education (Hunter 1991:197–224). To a great extent such debates are about which stories should be taught at all and which, if any, will be privileged.

2. For this discussion I am indebted to Gilligan (1982) and Daniel Maguire (1978) who persuasively contend that caring and our affective lives have been undervalued in Western moral thought, to Steven Toulmin (1970) for his discussion of the place of reason in ethics (and Hare's "emotivist" critique of ethics that purports to be reason based, to which Toulmin is responding) and to David Tracy (1978) for his suggestion that we seek a "critical correlation" between tradition (which I take to be our contending narrative traditions rather than any particular one), our own experiences, and reason.

3. See Zakin (1993), esp. 41–63, for a brief history of some of the earliest resistance that Abbey fictionalized.

4. Any discussion of Earth First! is necessarily interpretive and oversimplified. The movement is pluralistic and constantly changing. One could focus on, defend, or criticize any of one or more movement streams. I could choose, for example, to focus on the most troubling ideas and actions of its activists. This is the approach of movement adversaries. But this too often devolves into "straw-man" analysis—tarring an entire movement with the unthoughtful or distasteful statements or actions of a few. A better approach—one that provides a greater opportunity for learning—is to pose movement contentions in their own strongest ways, afterward scrutinizing them.

As one who has done extensive field work and textual study of this movement, it is obvious to me that far too much attention has been given to certain statements by Edward Abbey, David Foreman and Christopher Manes (1987, 1990). Some of these statements certainly deserve criticism, as Dave Foreman has admitted (Bookchin and Foreman 1990). But such statements do not represent the movement as a whole and for all time. I trace much of the "straw-man" problem to analysis which depends exclusively on texts. Such dependence leads to preoccupation with ideas and controversies that have appeared in print, which in turn has led to serious misunderstandings of the movement. An example is Guha's 1989 critique of radical environmentalism which, as George Sessions notes, "erroneously asserts [that radical environmentalism] has little or no interest in the issues of restructuring society to achieve ecological sustainability and social justice" (Sessions 1993b). Another problem is how some early but inaccurate characterizations of Earth First! such as those found in Stuart McBride's *Outside* magazine article (1983), are perpetuated by later writers who tend to portray this movement as a group of fed-up, nature-loving, cowboy-redneck "buckaroos" (Zakin 1993).

5. By burying themselves up to their necks in the road they make it impossible for vehicles to pass without killing the activists. Moreover, removing them without injury is a time-consuming process.

6. At the center of this strategy is Jaspar Carlton, who founded the Biodiversity Legal Foundation.

7. This formulation is from a 5 November 1992 interview with Seed in Eastern Minnesota. For other versions, see Seed et al. (1988), 36, 6; and compare Foreman (1990). Seed stressed that, although he put this idea in words that caught on, the idea it expressed had been percolating in the counterculture for some time, for example, in the writings of movement "elders" such as Gary Snyder and Joanna Macy.

8. See Leopold (1948) for the original story. The wolf story is mythologized repeatedly in movement lore, song, and poetry. Virtually every road show has some song or prose reference to this event. And since 1990, the recitation of this story in song serves as an important climax at tribal wilderness gatherings as activists are urged to "dig down deep" and find the "wild green-fire within" to empower them for eco-battles.

9. Watson is captain of the Sea Shepherd Conservation Society, which sometimes calls itself the "navy" of Earth First! and is best known for sinking whaling ships.

10. The Sea Shepherds now claim credit for sinking or scuttling five whaling vessels, one in Lisbon, two in Iceland, and two in Norway (SSCS 1991; Watson 1993a; SSCS 1994). In the summer of 1994, the Norwegian navy unsuccessfully attempted to apprehend a Sea Shepherd ship planning to interfere with Norwegian whaling. Sea Shepherds accused the Norwegians of shooting at and using depth charges against them.

11. For example, Judi Bari and Darryl Cherney were bombed for their efforts to halt the destruction of old growth ecosystems in the northwestern United States. Bari suffered permanent injuries. Cherney celebrates her

spirit of resistance in song. Other people who have suffered martyrdom, such as practitioners of wicca (witchcraft), indigenous peoples, and those who have resisted the enclosure of the commons, are also honored in song and poetry.

12. Overwhelmingly, but not exclusively, such risks have accrued to the activists themselves.

13. I am aware that some supporters of deep ecology, such as George Sessions, Arne Naess, and Warwick Fox (who prefers the term *transpersonal ecology* to deep ecology), desire a more nuanced description of deep ecology than the description provided here. My objective, however, is to look at this movement "on the ground," not as it appears in the discussions of movement intellectuals. It is the popular sense of deep ecology that unifies movement activists (to the extent they can be unified, given their diversity).

14. Elsewhere I have discussed in more detail the spirituality, politics, and divisions within this movement (Taylor 1991, 1994). More recently I have argued that many of the strongest wilderness advocates in the past century, and most Earth First! activists today, can accurately be labeled "pagan environmentalists" (Taylor 1995a). Nevertheless, many Earth First!ers prefer to avoid this label, given the long history of persecution faced by real and imagined practitioners of such nature-based spirituality.

15. Many within the so-called "New Age" movement share deep ecological intuitions about the intrinsic value and sacredness of all species. But they may not share the ecological apocalypticism or the political analysis of the radical vanguard of the deep ecology movement. Consequently, they remain politically quiescent.

16. See, for example, the eightfold deep ecology platform developed by Arne Naess and refined with George Sessions, quoted in Jerry Stark's contribution to this volume.

17. My perception here is based on extensive field work and illustrates that the ongoing criticisms of Earth First! by social ecologists, ecofeminists, and many others are based on portraits that were simplistic to begin with in the early years of Earth First! and which became increasingly so as those with deep ecological moral sentiments adopt ecofeminist and social ecological perspectives. Even in its earliest incarnations, Earth First! had great, although not perfect, affinity with the anarchistic premises of social ecology. Ecofeminist perspectives were imported into the movement somewhat later but have been nearly as influential.

18. The Wildlands Project, initiated by Dave Foreman (after disassociating himself from Earth First!) in close consultation with Reed Noss

(who in 1994 became editor of *Conservation Biology*), is an innovative effort to develop a comprehensive wilderness recovery strategy for North America. See Foreman and Davis (1992), and for a brief overview, see Taylor (1995b).

19. Some are not optimistic that human agency can produce this desired result. They think industrial society will collapse of its own ecologically unsustainable weight (Wolke 1989; see Taylor 1994: 194–95).

20. For more detailed analysis of some of these tensions, see Taylor (1994).

21. A good example of such celebration is the summary of "Radical Environmentalism's International Face" in Scarce (1990:139–59).

22. They met as a result of their common interest in Buddhist practice. Snyder, a Pulitzer Prize-winning poet considered a movement elder by many Earth First!ers, had himself been drawn to "the energy" of Earth First! in the early 1980s. While fond of many present and past Earth First!ers, he remains critical of ecotage and some Earth First! demeanor during protests. He is concerned that movement "theater" too often becomes counterproductive and distracts from the deep ecology message (interview with Gary Snyder, 1 June 1993, Davis, California).

23. In collaboration with *The Ecologist*, probably the most influential international journal of human ecology (the way human culture influences the environment), the World Rainforest movement now publishes scholarly research exploring rainforest issues. See, e.g., Colchester and Lohmann (1993).

24. One practical reason biodiversity activists should be especially concerned about indigenous peoples is that they "occupy . . . 12–19 percent of the earth's land surface [although] they have officially sanctioned rights to use, at most, 6 percent. In effect, indigenous peoples tend more of the earth than do all park and nature reserve authorities, which together manage 5 percent of the globe's land" (Durning 1992:28).

25. In 1980, the Indians themselves organized the Indigenous Peoples Union.

26. Warriors from different tribes have killed loggers and miners found in their traditional forest areas (Hecht and Cockburn 1989:140,143), and similar incidents have reportedly continued in recent years. However, the violence faced by forest dwellers is much more common, continuous, and widespread.

27. He implied that they are deep ecologists by suggesting that, to their credit, they "never began debating the nuances of deep ecology"

(White 1989). The implication was that they do not need to—they just live it. Interestingly, White acknowledged that they did not consider themselves environmentalists and that they seemed to resent the presence of northern environmentalists. Nevertheless, he said they were interested in the possibility of the Sea Shepherd sailing up the Amazon with supplies to draw international attention to their struggle.

28. Although reported here (Gordon 1991) in a dispassionate tone, such news is greeted with enthusiasm by some Earth First!ers.

29. See the special edition insert in *Earth First!* 1989 (vol. 9, no. 7). The issue includes reports on resistance and deforestation in Indonesia, Thailand, Malaysia, and Burma, discusses the United States role in the international timber trade; and calls for a consumer boycott of all tropical timber products. For RAN's updated overview of deforestation in Southeast Asia and a directory of resistance groups in these countries and their international supporters, see Belcher and Gennino (1993).

30. This foundation was funded by Doug Thompkins, an accomplished mountain climber and co-founder of Esprit corporation. When his marriage ended, he sold his interest to his wife, eventually endowing the Foundation for Deep Ecology with 150 million U.S. dollars. The foundation has poured resources into dozens of grass-roots deep ecology efforts, including major support for Dave Foreman's Wildlands Project. In a new twist for the Sierra Club's strategy of publishing beautiful wilderness pictures to engender support for wilderness, with Thompkins' support, it published *Clearcut: The Tragedy of Industrial Forestry* (Devall 1993). This coffee table book weaves together pictures of devastated landscapes, scientific analyses of the ecological impacts of clearcutting, and deep ecology poetry and philosophy. Arne Naess told me that Thompkins' "conversion" to deep ecology has to be considered a movement watershed, and that it occurred when Thompkins read one of Naess' publications (interview with Arne Naess, 27 May 1994, Killarney, Ireland).

31. Four activists from the RIC were arrested in 1991 for helping these Indians demarcate their territory (Gordon 1991).

32. This from a 25 March 1993 letter from Jonathan Miller of the *Centro de Investigation de los Bosques Tropicales* (CIBT) to John Seed. The letter indicates that demarcation "of the Napo-Galeras sacred jaguar mountain" would soon begin. The RIC also provided a $2,100.00 grant to support a similar demarcation strategy in the Galeras Mountain region of the Andes, which had been legally protected in 1987 by the government of Ecuador but again without adequate enforcement. The RIC has also assisted financially the relocation of colonists from indigenous land and, in some cases, has sought to purchase rainforest for indigenous stewardship.

33. Unless otherwise indicated, John Seed's reflections are drawn from a 5 November 1992 interview in eastern Minnesota.

34. However, Seed told me by e-mail on 29 June 1994, that the eco-forestry initiative in the Solomon Islands had evaporated, and to his knowledge, had come to a standstill in PNG also. Interestingly, radical environmental entrepreneurs have initiated two separate sustainable forestry cooperatives in northern California.

35. In December 1992, Manzer and several Japanese activists held a fast in solidarity with the Penan in Japan trying to promote a boycott of Sarawakian timber and force concessions from Japanese timber officials (Snow 1994).

36. This action was controversial. Some local activists complained that the action played into the Malaysian government's hands by reinforcing their argument that the resistance was caused by "Western eco-imperialists" (Lockhead 1992), an argument rejected by one of the North American Earth First! organizers (Jagoff 1992b).

37. Citing the *Far Eastern Economic Review*, RAN reported that imports of Malaysian wood had fallen 11 percent in Europe (Belcher and Gennino 1993:29). An update from RAN printed in *Earth First!* claimed a minor victory in 1993 when Warner Brothers Studios announced they would no longer use tropical timber in set construction (RAN 1993). To gauge the breadth of the international solidarity campaign, see especially the mission statements of the international NGOs listed in Belcher and Gennino 1993:75–95. For stories of Earth First! blockades of ships carrying tropical timber in the United States and the United Kingdom, see Jagoff 1992a and Meese 1992.

38. Alan Durning, a Filipino scholar at the Worldwatch Institute, argues that "amid the endless variety of indigenous belief, there is a striking unity on the sacredness of ecological systems" (1992:29). If true, this helps explain why Earth First!ers have little trouble finding evidence of nature-beneficent spirituality in indigenous resistance movements.

39. The Hawaiian sovereignty movement has assumed a militant environmental posture, blaming tourism for many cultural and ecological woes and opposing tourist development schemes throughout the 1990s. As Mililani B. Trask, prime minister of the Sovereign Nation of Hawai`i told me, "Environmental issues are now a part of nation building because the land we're fighting for is toxified." For Trask, the struggle for self determination is inseparable from environmental struggle, because to put ourselves and our children first, "we have to put the Earth first . . . because we're related to her" (interview 24 May 1994, Killarney, Ireland). During a meeting on indigenous issues at the conference we were attending, Trask told

the assembly that it was time to hold a war council, carefully develop a plan, and criticize it, so we can save the children and the earth.

40. For an excellent but brief country-by-country overview of the deforestation and environmental movements in Southeast Asia, see Belcher and Gennino (1993).

41. For an example of *Earth First!* solidarity with Chipko-style movements in India, see the article on the resistance to the Tehri Dam (Nachowitz 1989).

42. Interview with Kraig Klungness and Katie Scarborough of the "Roadfighting Strategy Project" (an offshoot of the Alliance for a Paving Moratorium), 25 May 1994, Killarney, Ireland.

43. Joanna Macy, who had established strong links with the European antinuclear movement through her "despair and empowerment" work during the cold war era, and more recently through her "nuclear guardianship" efforts (a vigil to keep track of the era's dangerous radioactive by-products), is the individual most responsible for the spread of deep ecology in Europe. According to John Seed, she is the primary architect of the Council of All Beings (Seed et al. 1988), which she and John Seed have led numerous times in Europe. More recently, she has focused on leading advanced training in "applied" deep ecology in Europe (interview with Kathleen Sullivan, of the U.K.'s Institute for Applied Deep Ecology, 26 May 1994, Killarney, Ireland).

44. For discussion of this ritual process, see Taylor (1993, 1994:190–92).

45. Founded by native Americans in 1990 at a Dilkon, Arizona, conference fiscally sponsored by Greenpeace and several native American environmental organizations.

46. This was founded by Erik Van Lennup in 1987 to build international support for the cultural and ecological survival of indigenous peoples and their environments.

47. The Native Forest Network was founded in the early 1990s to do for the temperate forests what RAN was trying do for rain forests, namely, provide a network to increase the effectiveness of temperate forest activists. It has rapidly become the coordinating center for over a dozen temperate forest campaigns internationally.

48. A related question is Who the radical environmentalists are? Those who ask deep ecological questions, like Naess and his progeny? Those who employ extralegal tactics? Those who would displace Western religious, philosophical, or scientific attitudes toward nature with the pri-

mal spiritual perceptions of indigenous peoples or with religions originating in the Far East? Those who would reject Enlightenment rationality, or philosophical liberalism, because they link "the good" (culture or society) with economic growth and individual license to exploit nature? Those who wish to "go to the root" of the environmental crisis by returning to or defending pre-industrial, agrarian or forager lifeways? Those who wish to overturn property relations and monocultures through land reform and the restoration of the commons (communally controlled and managed lands)? These are types of radicalism that can be kept in mind while reading the subsequent chapters of this volume.

Chapter 2

WITH LIBERTY AND ENVIRONMENTAL JUSTICE FOR ALL: THE EMERGENCE AND CHALLENGE OF GRASSROOTS ENVIRONMENTALISM IN THE UNITED STATES

Bob Edwards

INTRODUCTION

The worldwide observance of Earth Day in 1990 inspired a wave of reflection and commentary on the state of the U.S. environmental movement and its prospects for the future. Several types of interpretations were articulated. The "environmental decade" of the seventies had been a time of tremendous growth both in the popularity and in the influence of the Washington-based environmental mainstream. By the 1980s the political context of environmental action had changed dramatically. Domestically, the political climate of the Reagan years had constricted opportunities for environmental action, prompting the mainstream movement to choose a more cautious approach and a narrower agenda (Gale 1986). At the same time the emergence of transnational concerns over global warming, ozone depletion, and rainforest destruction opened new possibilities in the international arena. While the mainstream movement pursued global issues and waged insider Washington battles, thousands of local environmental protests erupted around the country.

The emergence of a grassroots movement comprised of those most affected by environmental degradation inaugurated a new chapter of environmental action in the United States. If the mainstream environmental groups effectively redefined environmentalism during the 1980s by emphasizing the management of environmental policy on an issue-by-issue basis (Gottlieb 1993), the grassroots groups are doing just the opposite in the 1990s. The grassroots groups were intensely critical of the environmental mainstream for compromising too quickly with the Reagan administration, for cooperating too closely with polluting industries, and for inattention to grassroots concerns.

By the early 1990s grassroots challenges had developed two centers of gravity: the deep ecology of groups like Earth First! and thousands of local, state, and national groups coalescing in a movement for environmental justice.[1] Though many Earth Day commentators acknowledged the latter's existence, few understood either the diversity of its roots or the significance and depth of its challenge. The environmental justice movement of the early 1990s has assimilated environmental issues into a comprehensive vision of democratic process, civil rights, and social justice. This chapter traces its origins and development, examines the environmental justice framework, compares it to the mainstream movement, and considers its future prospects.

Environmental Justice

The unifying insight of environmental justice recognizes that neither the costs of pollution nor the benefits of environmental protection are evenly distributed throughout our society (Morrison and Dunlap 1986; Bryant and Mohai 1992). Uneven distributions of "socially acceptable" environmental hazards and their long-term corrosion of health and life quality stem from inequalities of socioeconomic and political power. Such inequalities underlie a broad range of environmental problems from overpopulation, resource depletion, environmental degradation, and degree of direct exposure to hazardous materials. Those who live or work in close proximity to the source, storage destination, or waste stream of environmental contaminants bear most of the burden and risks associated with their production. By contrast, the economic benefits of industrial production are concentrated among wealthier groups whose communities are insulated by distance from direct daily exposure. Questions of who pays and who benefits from contemporary policies of economic growth, industrial development, and environmental protection are at the heart of the environmental justice agenda (Bullard 1993).

Across the nation, low-income people, regardless of race, and people of color, regardless of economic status, are more likely to suffer poor health and quality of life due to environmental degradation. Numerous studies have found that those who live in close proximity to noxious facilities are disproportionately people of color or of low income, and race has been found to be the stronger indicator of the two (Mohai and Bryant 1992).[2] In economically distressed communities promises of new jobs associated with the siting of hazardous facilities or threats of job loss associated with their closing are not easily dismissed. Many residents reluctantly accept long-term health risks in exchange for the prospect of short-term economic benefit. Many who would leave cannot. Low-income families cannot afford to "vote with their feet" and move away from a high risk place of residence. Mobility options of even middle-class people of color are still constrained by racial segregation in housing (Massey and Denton 1993). No one prefers to work in or live and raise children downstream from hazardous facilities, though out of necessity many do.

TRIBUTARIES OF ENVIRONMENTAL JUSTICE EMERGENCE

The process by which locally unwanted land uses (LULUs) are sited in the first place tends to follow a path of least political resistance. More often than not that path leads to politically orphaned, low-income and minority communities lacking the political clout to prevent it. Environmental justice is a movement of numerous constituencies whose interests have been neglected in recent decades.[3] Urban community groups seeking to improve living conditions and protect public health are one vital strand.[4] Current manifestations of century-old grassroots resistance by Appalachians to the political and economic domination of that region by external interests illustrates a type of regional tributary.[5]

The focus of what follows, however, will attend to its two major tributaries. Perhaps the most widely publicized was made from scratch by the thousands of local groups organized to confront perceived risks to the health and well-being of their families and communities.[6] By contrast, a second major tributary emerged from communities of color, extending long-term struggles against racial discrimination into the environmental policy arena.[7] By the mid-1990s these tributaries converged into a loosely structured nation-wide network whose diversity enhances its political significance. However, differences in experience and resources led them to follow divergent paths of emergence and mobilization during the 1980s.

MOBILIZING FROM SCRATCH: TOUGH WOMEN AGAINST TOXICS

Environmental justice activists generally do not come from the highly educated and professional ranks that provide so many members for the mainstream environmental groups. Many even resist being called "environmentalists." "On the whole, these citizens come from the most alienated and passive ranks of society, middle America, where politics seems remote and pointless" (Greider 1992:167). More often than not, women with little or no prior political experience lead local antitoxics groups (Krause 1993). They are not motivated by political ideology, aesthetics, or avant garde eco-philosophy. Rather, this self-described "movement of house-wives" has organized around a variety of local issues ranging from waste dumps and incinerators and workplace exposure to air pollution and ground water contamination out of concern for the health and well-being of their families and communities.

The conflict at Love Canal culminating in the permanent relocation of over five hundred households by the summer of 1981 proved both catalyst and prototype for the emergence of antitoxics groups nationally. Love Canal had the dramatic elements of a great story—a heroic everywoman, Lois Gibbs, leading her neighbors in a victorious struggle to protect children and community from irresponsible corporations, indifferent bureaucrats, and arrogant scientists—and garnered extensive media coverage. Members of local groups struggling in isolation all over the country read the numerous feature articles in popular magazines and saw the 1981 TV movie "Lois Gibbs and Love Canal."

By the time the TV movie aired, Gibbs had used her federal relocation payment and what CBS paid for the rights to her story to move to the Washington area and found the Citizens Clearinghouse for Hazardous Wastes (CCHW). Working on a shoestring out of Gibbs's basement, CCHW sought to expand the network of contacts she made during the conflict at Love Canal. For the first few years CCHW did little more than respond to hundreds of calls from other "Love Canals" around the country.

Variations of the Love Canal scenario—decades of highly toxic waste dumping by a chemical subsidiary of Occidental Petroleum, construction of a school and hundreds of homes on the site with the full knowledge of public officials, gradual discovery by residents of severe health consequences, a four-year fight to get official acknowledgement of a link between the waste dump and health impacts, and the organized use by residents of confrontational tactics to force action from public officials—have been replayed hundreds, if not thousands, of times since.[8] In 1994, with twelve staff members and a $900,000 annual budget, CCHW works to assist grassroots groups in their local efforts while continuing to build the network nationally. According to CCHW the environmental justice network with which they communicate extends to over eight thousand organizational and twenty-seven thousand individual contacts.[9]

BRIDGING CIVIL RIGHTS AND ENVIRONMENTALISM

By contrast, the other major tributary of environmental justice did not mobilize from scratch. Rather, its source is found in the deep waters of the civil rights movement and centuries of resistance among communities of color. African American environmental mobilizations have been facilitated by skilled activists, black elected officials, and a national network of advocacy organizations flowing directly from the civil rights movement.[10] The civil rights movement of the 1950s and 1960s had a profound impact on later social movements, including mainstream environmentalism.[11] Yet, during the "environmental decade" of the seventies, activism in the black communities continued on civil rights, social justice, and "built environment" issues like community development, affordable housing, and lead poisoning.[12] However, when environmental campaigns against industrial polluters and hazardous waste facilities did emerge, the leaders of pre-existing social justice groups were consistently out front making it happen (Bullard and Wright 1987).

The first nationally significant environmental protest by African Americans took place in Warren County, North Carolina, in 1982. Thirty-two thousand cubic yards of soil contaminated with PCB-tainted oil which had previously been dumped illegally along roadways around the state were to be disposed of in a Warren County landfill. In a siting process more politically expedient than scientific, state officials chose the Warren County site in spite of a water table only five to nine feet below ground (Bullard 1990). Protesters in Warren County engaged in a civil disobedience campaign during which they blockaded roads with their bodies and filled local jails with over four hundred arrested protesters.

Though unable to stop the landfill, the Warren County protest attracted the participation of prominent black leaders and elected officials, and church and civil rights organizations. One participant was Congressman Walter Fauntroy who upon his return to Washington commissioned the U.S. General Accounting Office (USGAO) to study the question of race and hazardous facility siting. The USGAO found evidence of racial discrimination in the siting of such facilities (USGAO 1983). At the urging of other Warren County protesters, the United Church of Christ's Commission for Racial Justice, in a departure from its typical protest strategy, initiated an extensive national study of race and toxic waste. They found the racial composition of a community to be the strongest predictor of hazardous waste site location (UCC 1987). Racially discriminatory aspects of such siting decisions have been a major impetus to black environmentalism. The crowning event of this mobilization, thus far, took place in Washington D.C. in the fall of 1991. Over six hundred grassroots activists from around the country participated in the People of Color Environmental Leadership Summit. They met to network, set a national agenda, and develop movement strategy for the 1990s.

In one sense the African American community came late to environmental action, but arrived with hard won and substantial political resources and protest savvy. These enabled their environmental efforts to mobilize quickly without the substantial investments of time and energy needed to first build movement infrastructures and communication networks. By contrast the anti-toxics tributary was made from scratch primarily by women who had little or no prior political experience and whose communities offered no long-standing advocacy traditions for them to tap. Local antitoxics protests had begun at least as early as the late 1960s, but lacked an organizational infrastructure, communication networks, and sympathetic elected officials comparable to those in the civil rights community. Local antitoxics struggles remained isolated until the presidential campaign of 1980 when the national media spotlight fell briefly, but intensely, on Love Canal and a national network began to be built. For many of these same reasons, each tributary followed different paths in framing environmental justice.

COLLECTIVE ACTION FRAMES AND GRASSROOTS ENVIRONMENTAL ACTION

Collective action frames are narrative maps guiding movements toward their goals. Frames include interpretations of the injustice or immorality of specific social conditions, an attribution of blame for them, some kind of action agenda for solving them, and a motivation for taking that action (Snow and Benford 1988; Gamson 1992). They are interpretative symbolic schemes socially constructed by movements to orient their actions in an ever-shifting political, social, and cultural context. Because the social and political landscape is dynamic and fluid, movement frames evolve over time as groups revise them in light of changing circumstances and accumulating experience. In some cases, experience can discredit a frame so thoroughly that it is discarded altogether. "For example, it has been amply documented that many [antitoxics] activists begin with assumptions of fairness about the political and regulatory process in the United States, as well as a naive faith in science as unbiased and 'above' politics. As a result of their experiences, this frame's validity is shattered" (Čapek 1993:7). In other instances collective action frames are extended to integrate new issues into an existing advocacy tradition. This was the case when the civil rights frame was extended to include environmental racism.

FROM NIMBY TO ENVIRONMENTAL RACISM

Like many early black environmental actions, Warren County began as a narrowly focused NIMBY (Not in My Backyard!) style protest to prevent a LULU (Locally Unwanted Land Use). However, the discriminatory aspects of the siting process quickly led to a "put in black people's backyard" interpretation of the state's choice of Warren County for a facility that no one in North Carolina wanted

(Bullard 1990:5). While crafting a statement for the press conference releasing the United Church of Christ's *Toxic Waste and Race in the United States* study, Ben Chavis (who later became national director of the NAACP) struggled for a way to capture the essence of the report's findings. He labeled it "environmental racism."[13]

Framing the siting and exposure issue as a new form of racism proved a stroke of genius. Almost overnight environmentalism became accessible to wide segments of the African American community, churches, and civil rights organizations. Quickly traditional civil rights and social justice frameworks were extended to include environmental concerns. In the process blacks redefined environmentalism and provided a powerful and overarching narrative capable of unifying a range of life quality grievances in communities of color.

The resulting agenda, broadened to include the input of native Americans, Asian-Americans, Hispanics, and other peoples of color was formalized in the statement of purpose and call to action drafted by delegates to the People of Color Environmental Leadership Summit (Kerr and Lee 1993). The seventeen "Principles of Environmental Justice" are quite comprehensive, covering a range of ecological, social, political, cultural, and strategy issues. Their import conveys a radical critique of the global status quo. The preamble conveys the sense of the statement:

> We the people of color, gathered together at this multinational People of Color Environmental Leadership Summit, to begin to build a national and international movement of all peoples of color to fight the destruction and taking of our lands and communities, do hereby re-establish our spiritual interdependence to the sacredness of our Mother Earth; to respect and celebrate each of our cultures, languages and beliefs about the natural world and our roles in healing ourselves; to insure environmental justice; to promote economic alternatives which would contribute to the development of environmentally safe livelihoods; and, to secure our political, economic and cultural liberation that has been denied for 500 years of colonization and oppression, resulting in the poisoning of our communities and land and the genocide of our peoples, do affirm and adopt these Principles of Environmental Justice. (UCC 1992)

It's Hard to Get from NIMBY to NOPE!

With no resonant movement traditions to draw on, antitoxics groups have had to struggle to get from NIMBY to NOPE (Nowhere on Planet Earth). When a child is sick with a rare disease, misfortune is the likely interpretation. However, the discovery of widespread and equally extraordinary private misfortunes within the same community poses a collective problem. The subsequent linking of the community's health problem to chemical compounds trespassing into homes or contaminating drinking water is a grievance capable of unifying a NIMBY-style, defensive protest. In the course of local conflicts, groups often became aware of other communities where similar problems were occurring. Members of one group visited others to learn from their experience, join in protest actions, or show solidarity, believing that one community's solution should not become another's nightmare. In the process ties developed, connections were made and the issues began to be framed as larger than local.

However, groups do not change their agendas simply because some of their members change their minds. Quite a gap exists between the recognition of the macro context of local problems by some members of a grassroots group and the adoption by the group of a larger than local environmental justice frame. As anti-toxics groups either win or lose the specific local campaigns that got them going in the first place, a difficult and complex transition begins. Some groups disband entirely, others lay dormant until another pressing local issue arises, while still others shift to nonpolitical goals unrelated to environmental justice. This process of organizational attrition removes less radical groups from the movement as it develops over time. Groups that take on a larger than local orientation and become more radical, lose members. Some members drop out because of pressing personal obligations, like caring for terminally ill relatives or supporting a family after the death of a spouse. Others quit as long-standing political differences resurface as the group's initial NIMBY orientation wanes. Processes of attrition by which more conservative individuals leave groups and less politicized groups leave the movement contributed to the radicalization of the remaining groups, and the movement as a whole, as it developed through the 1980s. For example, each of the twenty to thirty grassroots groups of a regional network in central Appalachia lost members in their transition from NIMBY to NOPE. As one activist recalled, "about 10 groups that used to be real strong have disappeared, but the rest are leaner, meaner, and madder than ever."

Attrition helps explain how this tributary radicalized so quickly, but not what started that process in the first place. Angered initially by a profound sense of violation at having their very homes transformed into health hazards, activists get "madder and meaner" as they encounter bureaucratic indifference, political double-speak and scientific equivocation. Firsthand experience with how government scientists, industry lawyers, and politicians all too often respond to ordinary citizens can be a powerful organizing tool. Attempts to get accurate and accessible information about a local situation are often ignored or deferred indefinitely. In public hearings grassroots activists are allowed to express themselves before official bodies, but are seldom taken seriously. Often their concerns are met with disdain. Repeated experiences like these have convinced them that they have been orphaned politically and are being treated like second-class citizens.

After finding no polite way to get their concerns addressed, grassroots groups turned to a politics of "rude and crude" confrontation with specific officials. They have concluded that, for now, people must fight for what they believe should be rights for all. Besides having to fight for safe homes and workplaces, they find they must also fight for accurate and accessible information about their situation, fight to participate in making decisions that affect their lives, fight for clean up and compensation, fight to make corporations act responsibly, and fight to get government to enforce existing environmental laws (CCHW 1993:60). A profound sense of betrayal by the democratic institutions of American society pervades this movement. That the "People's Bill of Rights," put forth by a self-described "movement of housewives" seems radical, indicates that segments of the middle class are understanding things about American democracy the black community has known for centuries.[14]

DIFFERENT PATHS TO ENVIRONMENTAL JUSTICE

The problem definition of the African American environmental frame has shifted and broadened from blocking LULUs, to environmental racism, to the globalized vision of the People of Color Environmental Leadership Summit. However, other aspects of their framing have remained rather stable. The causal attribution of institutional racism, the repertoire of nonviolent direct action, litigation and electoral tactics, and human rights rationale resonate deeply with the civil rights movement of the 1950s and 1960s. Subsequent experiences of African American environmental justice groups have not forced them to discard the collective action frame of the civil rights movement. Rather, the heritage and tradition of that movement and its narrative framework have been updated and extended to encompass environmental justice.

By contrast, local antitoxics groups emerging around the country traveled a more winding road to the environmental justice frame. Many grassroots activists describe their own early involvement as naive. "Generally, people at first have a blind faith in government. So when they go to the EPA or the state agency and show them there is a problem, they think the government will side with them. It takes about a year before they realize the government is not going to help them. They see the agencies studying them to death. That's when they become really angry—radicalized."[15] As local antitoxics groups became politicized, their entire collective action frame—problem definition, tactical repertoire, and social change strategy—radicalized dramatically throughout the 1980s. The wisdom of these experiences is cumulative for the movement as a whole, and its national organizations and leadership are building working relations with popular environmental organizations internationally. However, most newly organized local groups still begin as NIMBYs and must find their own way to NOPE, a process facilitated by the national network.

MOVEMENT STRATEGIES AND TACTICS: WE'LL NEVER WIN IF WE PLAY BY THEIR RULES!

By the 1990s both major tributaries of environmental justice had converged toward a common frame despite following quite different narrative paths to get there.[16] By contrast, both recognized early on that going through channels or engaging in polite protest would not bring results. The dominant template in American culture for such "politics by other means" continues to be the repertoire of confrontational, disruptive, direct action tactics pioneered by the civil rights movement. From a durable base of local, state, and national organizations, the grassroots movement has developed a varied and sophisticated tactical repertoire and an outsider political strategy.

Getting accurate and accessible information has been an enduring problem among grassroots groups. Consequently, a number of research tactics have been developed to help empower local groups. Community health surveys conducted by grassroots groups document the extent of health problems within a community. They are also an effective way to help define a problem as collective or social and not merely personal or private. This type of bootstrap epidemiology is supplemented by corporate research into the history, ownership, subsidiaries, and wider operations of specific corporate polluters or disposal firms. Activists have also developed extensive expertise on the workings of local, state, and federal regulatory processes.

Litigation is a common movement tactic. Groups have filed restraining orders to block the operation of facilities and sued polluters for damages. Residents of Fernald, Ohio, discovered that radioactive material from a nearby nuclear facility had contaminated their water supply. When the Fernald Residents for Environmental Safety and Health (FRESH) learned that plant operators and Department of Energy officials had known of this but concealed it, they successfully sued the United States Department of Energy. The legal odyssey of the Yellow Creek Concerned Citizens (YCCC) of eastern Kentucky may be more typical. After twelve years of legal action against the Middlesboro Tanning Company for dumping toxic waste into the creek that fed their water supply, the case has still not come to trial. Ironically, the strongest part of their case was brought under "nuisance" statutes, in the same area of law one would use to stop trespassing or prevent neighbors from incessantly playing loud music. The core of their strategy lies outside environmental law because proving a direct link in court between a particular toxic substance and high rates of miscarriage, birth defects, and cancer among residents is difficult.[17]

Formidable technical and procedural obstacles impede grassroots efforts to work through established political and legal channels. Litigation is a long, expensive, and tedious process that local groups must support with limited means. It may be a relatively effective way to gain compensation for loss, but movement leaders express misgivings about it as an effective social-change strategy. Larry Wilson of the Yellow Creek Concerned Citizens and the Highlander Research and Education Center put it this way: "We're playing by their rules. The system was invented by the people who are poisoning us. The rules say they get to argue over how much cyanide they can put in our coffee, how much poison they can put out before they have to take responsibility for it. That's not a system we can ever win in."[18]

CONFRONTATIONAL TACTICS AND MEDIA COVERAGE

Grassroots groups have found the outsider politics of rude and crude confrontation far more effective than the polite protest of going through channels. Such tactics are not new to grassroots environmental resistance in the United States. In the 1950s the development of strip mining sparked two decades of grassroots resistance by Appalachians trying to end it by direct action.[19] Opposition was motivated by people's love of the mountains and the tight connection between their way of life and the land. Resistance was most fierce in the coal fields of eastern Kentucky where in 1967 and 1968 residents stood before bulldozers, destroyed $2 million worth of mining equipment, and in one case traded shots with mine employees in an effort to keep their land from being stripped (Bingman 1993).[20] By 1972 groups like Mountain People's Rights and the Appalachian Group to Save the Land and People were waging an aggressive civil disobedience campaign against strip-mine operators.

In the 1980s grassroots groups used similar tactics. Lauri Maddy of Rose Hill, Kansas, handcuffed herself to the governor's chair for four hours. Declaring herself a "hazardous waste," she hoped to make him as uncomfortable in his environment as chemically contaminated drinking water made her family in theirs (Community Environmental Health Program 1992). Grassroots groups have used impolite protest to gain media attention and publicity. Confrontations are often personalized, directed at specific officials, rather than at faceless agencies. Personalizing makes it harder for responsibility to be concealed behind a veil of bureaucracy. Activists have blockaded landfills, delivered large samples of toxic waste to state legislative bodies, and seized control of hearings turning them into community interrogations of public officials. They have marched, boycotted, held Mother's Day "die-ins," mock funerals, and at times have "blown up" public hearings by disrupting the proceedings so thoroughly that official decisions they considered harmful to their communities could not be made.

Grassroots environmental justice groups have used confrontational tactics quite effectively to gain media coverage and put pressure directly on specific power holders. Though the media can be used effectively by activists, its attention is fickle and moves quickly on to new stories (Downs 1972; Ryan 1991). National media coverage of Love Canal proved crucial for building the movement's internal network, but as Lauri Maddy suggests, it is an unreliable political lever: "Even though national and international media picked up [my] story, and the Governor promised me the moon, nothing changed" (Community Environmental Health Program 1992). Veterans of direct action opposition to strip mining came to a similar conclusion. Mary Beth Bingman summed it up: "Confronting an issue as complex as strip mining in a region with a seriously depressed economy requires careful organization and a long-term strategy. Most early anti-strip organizations did not have either. We had hoped our action would be a catalyst, but we had not laid the foundation."[21]

Over the last ten years the grassroots movement has recognized the limitations of polite protest, litigation, media attention, and confrontational tactics. Even confrontation is not an effective social change strategy unless its use grows from a base of strong organizations capable of mounting sustained pressure for change over the long haul. Without an enduring base, the movement can resist environmental injustices, but it will not win.

"PLUGGING THE TOILET," A CRUDE BUT EFFECTIVE STRATEGY

At a rally in Warren County, North Carolina, in 1982, William Sanjour, then chief of the EPA's hazardous waste implementation branch, spelled out the challenge to the movement in its starkest terms. "Landfilling is cheap. It is cheaper than the alternative. The people who like to use landfills such as chemical industries are very powerful. No amount of science, truth, knowledge or facts goes into making this decision. It is a purely political decision. What they listen to is pressure."[22]

In the years since, the movement has taken up this challenge. In a speech sponsored by the Susquehanna County Pennsylvania Environment Day in 1988, Lois Gibbs described the pressure point of their strategy.

The moral of the story is that the only way we can fight these situations is by fighting politically. We cannot fight scientifically alone. We cannot fight legally alone. The solid waste and hazardous waste fights across this country are being waged every single day and our theory of how to cure this country of this vulgar problem is to plug up the toilet. Stop the landfills and incinerators from being sited. When the toilet overflows, then they will decided to do something. (Ferraro 1988)

By blocking the opening of new disposal facilities, landfills, incinerators, deep-well injection, and "waste to energy" plants, they plan to raise the cost of business as usual to prohibitive levels. The strategy resembles past efforts by antinuclear power groups that jammed up authorization, permit, siting, and environmental-impact processes so much that delays raised costs to the point that nuclear power was no longer profitable.[23] The beauty of this strategy is that whether NIMBY or NOPE, groups that "plug a toilet" contribute to the pressure, regardless of their level of commitment to environmental justice.

The movement for environmental justice wants to reframe the policy debate over hazardous waste and shift the public agenda away from its current preoccupation with regulating waste disposal toward reducing waste production at the source. They want industry to shoulder the full social, health, and ecological costs of their products, including waste products, because that would create a strong economic incentive for nontoxic alternatives. However, they currently have limited access and input into the legislative and regulatory politics that could mandate the changes they advocate. What they do have is substantial negative power in thousands of communities around the country. Since 1984, when CCHW launched its Landfill Moratorium Campaign, such negative power has prevented the opening of new hazardous waste sites. In 1990 the recipient of the last landfill operating permit issued, Browning-Ferris Industries, announced its intention to leave the hazardous waste business (Greider 1992:169).

The grassroots movement has succeeded in raising the stakes, making it more difficult and expensive for irresponsible industries to pass the costs of chemical contamination on to those who live further down the waste stream. They have done so without passing any new legislation, engaging in the legal and scientific debates over regulatory policies, or entering electoral politics. Over the last ten years the grassroots movement may, as some activists are fond of claiming, have "done more than all those pinstriped eco-lobbyists in Washington put together." Besides pursuing different political strategies and tactics, the contrast in constituencies, collective-action frames, and base of power between the grassroots and mainstream environmental movements is quite stark.

THE ENVIRONMENTAL MAINSTREAM

Earth Day 1970 is widely viewed as the birthday of the U.S. environmental movement. Hundreds of thousands of people, many current or recent college students, participated in events around the country. With the mass participation in Earth Day still fresh on their minds, Congress passed a series of major environmental legislation and a complex environmental regulatory system developed in Washington. By the end of the decade the popularity of environmental causes had grown significantly, but grassroots actions typical of Earth Day had faded away. The movement's center of gravity had shifted to Washington, and environmental organizations became increasingly professionalized, sustaining themselves on a combination of foundation grants, product sales, and direct-mail fundraising. Membership often consisted of little more than sending in an annual fee. The vast majority of their members were college educated, middle class and white. Board members and staff were predominantly male. The mainstream's core constituency and leadership are centered precisely in the segments of American society least likely to experience environmental injustice.

During the "environmental decade" of the seventies, mainstream groups gained clout by developing legal and scientific expertise as well as insider lobbying savvy (Gottlieb 1993; Mitchell 1986). Their policy-relevant research and expertise provided access to the process of implementing legislation and developing procedures for managing environmental policy. However, the election of Ronald Reagan in 1981 brought a forthright effort to undo the environmental policy gains of the seventies. The largest Washington D.C.–based groups formed the Group of Ten to focus the mainstream agenda and develop coordinated efforts to resist the environmental deregulation efforts of the Reagan administration.[24] Lobbying battles raged inside the Washington policy establishment, and the points of conflict were legal, scientific, and highly technical. During the 1980s, mainstream environmentalism became less a movement than a highly professionalized lobbying adjunct specializing in the provision of legal and scientific expertise to Washington policy makers (Gottlieb 1993:124). By the end of the 1980s the fever pitch of conflict had subsided and the mainstream groups had grown considerably in both membership and resources.[25] However, the environmental regulatory programs were in a shambles (McClosky 1990:83). A decade of lackluster and underfunded enforcement had reduced EPA programs to "hollow laws," potent symbols in campaign-trail competitions, yet utterly lacking the substance to compel compliance from polluters.[26]

SIGNIFICANCE AND PROSPECTS OF ENVIRONMENTAL JUSTICE

By Earth Day 2000 the grassroots movement will have had an enduring impact on the environmental movement as a whole. Already the environmental constituency has been broadened. No matter how much the mainstream may recoil from grassroots rhetoric, tactics and demands, their lobbying position will be enhanced by it. During the late 1960s the activities of radical black organizations and urban riots, led to increased acceptance and facilitation of "reasonable" civil rights activism (Haines 1984). Similarly the confrontational actions of the AIDS Coalition To Unleash Power (ACT UP) and Queer Nation helped legitimate more "reasonable" AIDS related advocacy of groups like Gay Mens's Health Crisis. This dynamic also corresponds to the intentions of certain Earth First! activists (Manes 1990; Foreman 1991). The presence of the radical grassroots flank clamoring beyond the Washington beltway is shifting the center of the environmental policy debate. Mainstream groups are paying serious attention to grassroots concerns and their policy proposals appear more "reasonable" by comparison. Of at least equal importance, grassroots efforts to "plug the toilet" appear to have raised the costs of disposal enough for waste producers to begin considering source reduction alternatives.

The base of support and core constituencies of the environmental justice movement lie outside the profile of mainstream environmental groups. Collectively, communities of color make up a substantial, vital and politically sophisticated segment of the movement. Most grassroots leaders are women. Women are also well represented on the staffs and boards of the movement's "larger than local" groups. In striking contrast to the mainstream movement, the environmental justice movement has been quite successful in forging ties with working class constituencies and segments of organized labor. Its issues resonate in isolated rural areas as well as blighted urban ones. There is little question that this movement is the most vital and diverse grassroots movement in the United States today. By all estimates it is growing rapidly in size, scope, sophistication and clout. "As those who are most at risk join the environmental movement and expand its definition, their participation also broadens the possibilities for social and environmental change" (Gottlieb 1993:306).

NOTES

1. Despite increasing cooperation between deep ecologists and environmental justice groups in recent years and their common usage of direct action, sometimes including illegal tactics, their differing origins and development merit separate attention.

2. Mohai and Bryant (1992) reviewed fifteen reports published since 1971 that have analyzed the relationship of income and/or race to exposure to environmental hazards. These examined exposure to air pollution, solid waste, noise, and hazardous waste, the consumption of chemically contaminated fish, and the risk of rat bite. Both race and income were consistently found to predict increased exposure. Of the nine reports identifying the most important predictor, six cited race, and three cited income.

3. See Greider (1992) for a detailed treatment of this concept across a range of issues during the 1980s.

4. See Urban Environmental Conference, Inc. (1985).

5. Appalachia is not the only regional tributary contributing to the environmental justice movement. For example, in the southwest groups like the Southwest Organizing Project and the Southwest Network for Environmental and Economic Justice have grown out of long-term grassroots struggles unique to that region. A rich regional literature portrays Appalachia as an "internal colony" of the United States, a domestic "third world," where indigenous groups have resisted the economic and political domination of outsiders for decades (Lewis et al., 1978; Gaventa 1980; Corbin 1981; Fisher 1993; Gaventa et al., 1992). Much of the resistance has centered around issues of land ownership, destruction, taxation, and use (Gaventa and Horton 1984). For an analysis of inner cities as "internal colonies" see Blauner (1969).

6. Numerous case studies and analytic studies of this tributary exist. Regarding Love Canal, see Levine (1982). For detailed analyses of other cases, see Freudenberg (1984); Edelstein (1988); Brown and Mikkelson (1990); and Setterberg and Shavelson (1993). For treatments written by

movement participants, see Gibbs (1982); Cohen and O'Connor (1990); and Community Environmental Health Program (1992).

7. For a comprehensive overview of various communities of color mobilizing against environmental racism, see Bullard, ed. (1993), and Bryant and Mohai (1990). For specific treatments of black environmentalism, see Bullard and Wright (1992), and Bullard (1990).

8. This account emphasizes the political aspects of the grassroots movement for environmental justice. However, there are profound social and psychological impacts bourn by residents of contaminated communities. The daily struggles with uncertainty and terminal and debilitating diseases place tremendous stress upon both activists and nonactivists alike. For detailed analysis of problems of linking health impacts to specific chemical contaminants, see Brown and Mikkelson (1990). For detailed treatment of technical conflicts between grassroots groups and state and federal agencies, see Edelstein (1988).

9. Undoubtedly, many of these eight thousand groups have ceased operations, but the estimated size of the movement is consistent with other social movements during the 1980s. For example, the 1987 edition of *Grassroots Peace Directory* listed approximately 7,700 U.S. groups working for peace. Approximately 35 percent of those still active in 1988 had ceased operations by 1992 (see Edwards and Marullo 1994).

10 . According to the League of Conservation Voters, the "Congressional Black Caucus had the highest average of support for conservation issues of any group surveyed. The other groups in descending order were House Democrats, Senate Democrats, Congresswomen, House of Representatives, Senators, House Republicans and Senate Republicans" (Davis 1990:59). Caucus members like then Del. Walter Fauntroy of the District of Columbia were instrumental in commissioning numerous federal studies related to the siting of hazardous waste facilities and other questions pertinent to environmental justice concerns.

11. See Humphrey and Buttel (1982) on environmentalism; Evans (1980), and Ferree and Hess (1985) on the women's movement; and McAdam (1982), and Snow and Benford (1992), on subsequent movements generally.

12. The term *built environment* has been used in reference to urban areas and other physical infrastructures that form the proximate "environment" of most humans. It is constructed by humans and insulates them from the natural environment, wilderness, or nature. Recently it has been argued that the built environment has subsumed "nature." No place or habitat on earth has escaped the impact of human intervention or technol-

ogy. For a classic statement see Ellul (1964). For a popular, nontechnical account see McKibben (1989).

13. Environmental racism is racial discrimination in environmental policy making; in the enforcement of regulations and laws, in the deliberate targeting of communities of color for toxic waste disposal and siting of polluting industries; in the official sanctioning of the life-threatening presence of poisons and pollutants in communities of color; and in the history of excluding people of color from mainstream environmental groups, decision making boards, commissions, and regulatory bodies (Chavis 1993:3).

14. The preamble to the "People's Bill of Rights" reads as follows:

> People in this country have the right to be safe and secure in their homes and workplaces. We have the right to bring up our children and live our lives free from harm imposed by toxic substances that have been brought into our communities, neighborhoods, workplaces, schools and farms by others without our knowledge and without our consent. We have the right to clean air, clean water, uncontaminated food and safe places to live, work, and play. We have the right to action and to public policy which will restore to us that which has been taken away and to stop the needless and unjustifiable attack on our lives, families, homes, jobs, and future that come from the imposition of toxic substances in our environment. (CCHW 1993:59)

15. Lois Gibbs of CCHW quoted in Greider (1992:167).

16. The conceptualizations of environmental justice put forth by both tributaries are very similar and highly compatible, despite differences of emphasis. Compare the "Principles of Environmental Justice" (UCC 1992) with the "Toxic Bill of Rights" (O'Connor 1990:22–24) or "People's Bill of Rights" (CCHW 1993:59–60). For a somewhat different interpretation of the environmental justice frame, see Čapek (1993).

17. Interview with YCCC attorney Todd Leatherman and YCCC leaders Larry and Sheila Wilson on 15 May 1993, Arlington, Virginia.

18. Larry Wilson of the YCCC, and codirector of the Environmental Program at the Highlander Research and Education Center quoted in Greider (1992:166).

19. Traditional deep mine operations dig several hundred feet into the earth to tunnel along a seam of coal and haul it back to the surface. By contrast, strip mining digs down, usually hundreds of feet from the surface, to expose an entire seam of coal. In the process it denudes the land and displaces vast amounts of dirt often depositing it in nearby stream beds. Besides the obvious destruction of the land, strip mining causes excessive

erosion and flash floods and fills stream systems with silt, all of which have a devastating impact on downstream communities and livelihoods.

20. In Kentucky the "broad form deed" enabled mine operators to own the coal beneath the land while others owned and lived on the surface. In numerous court challenges to the broad form deed the rights of mine operators were recognized over and above those of the surface owners whose grandparents had sold mineral rights when deep mining was the only method known. In 1989 the Kentucky state constitution was amended to ban the broad form deed. This happened in large part because of a ten-year campaign by Kentuckians for the Commonwealth (KTFC), a statewide social and environmental justice organization (Zuercher 1991).

21. Quoted from Bingman (1993:28).

22. Quoted from Bullard (1990:38).

23. Some of the most effective Earth First! actions have followed a comparable strategy, which they refer to as "paper monkeywrenching."

24. The Group of Ten consisted of the CEOs of the National Wildlife Federation, Izaak Walton League, National Audubon Society, National Parks and Conservation Association, Sierra Club, the Wilderness Society, Natural Resources Defense Council, Environmental Defense Fund, Environmental Policy Center, and Friends of the Earth. By the end of the 1980s the group had ceased formal operations, in part because old strategic tensions re-emerged in the Reagan aftermath and because grassroots pressure made the affiliation too costly for groups like Sierra Club and Friends of the Earth (see Gottlieb 1993:118–24).

25. However, the more anti-establishment groups among the D.C.-based environmental mainstream, like Friends of the Earth, the Environmental Policy Institute, Environmental Action, and the Environmental Task Force, declined during the Reagan years as more radical, grassroots groups drained away supporters (McClosky 1990).

26. For a general analysis, see Edelman (1977), for a detailed treatment of specific cases during the 1980s, see Greider (1992).

Chapter 3

BREAD AND SOIL OF OUR DREAMS: WOMEN, THE ENVIRONMENT, AND SUSTAINABLE DEVELOPMENT— CASE STUDIES FROM CENTRAL AMERICA

Lois Ann Lorentzen

When I started working with the mothers' clubs in the Catholic church, it was the first time I realized that we women work even harder than the men do. We get up before they do to grind the corn and make tortillas and coffee for their breakfast. Then we work all day long taking care of the kids, washing the clothes, ironing, mending our husbands' old rags, cleaning the house. We hike to the mountains looking for wood to cook with. We walk to the stream or the well to get water. We never sit still one minute. We give the children medicine if they're sick. . . . I must admit that sometimes I get so overwhelmed by the odds against us that I break down and cry. I see our children dying of hunger and the ones that live have no jobs, no education, no future. I start to wonder if it (the struggle) is worth it. But whenever I have these doubts, whenever I start to cry, I put my hands into fists and say to myself, "Make your tears turn into anger, make your tears turn into strength." (Alvarado 1987: 51–52, 143)

The words of Honduran activist Elvia Alvarado graphically depict the work of many of the world's women as they provide for the daily sustenance of others. Increasingly, this role in the day-to-day meeting of basic needs has led to environmental activism as women make the link between environmental degradation and increased difficulties in providing the basics of food, fuel, and water for their families. Women participating in popular environmental movements in El Salvador and Honduras, especially those women most affected by environmental degradation due to their critical roles in providing subsistence, are gaining important insights into "alternative" development models and new understandings of environmental ethics. The meaning of sustainable development is shaped by particular historical, economic, and social conditions. Popular ecological resistance movements in Central America often spring from religious commitments, as evidenced by Elvia Alvarado's indebtedness to the mothers' clubs started by the Catholic church. This and other forms of "radical Catholicism" claim that Christianity must align itself with the "lowest of the low," with those most oppressed and exploited in society.

El Salvador faces the highest level of environmental degradation in the Americas. Of the natural vegetation of El Salvador, 80 percent has been eliminated, less than 3 percent of the original forest remains (and only 1 percent of original sea level forests), and 77 percent of the soil is severely affected by erosion and low soil fertility, acidified by pesticides and chemicals (CESTA brochure 1993). Throughout Central America, agrochemicals banned in their countries of origin are widely used.

The human price for this level of environmental damage is extraordinarily high. The ecological crisis, or "ecocidio" as some call it, manifests itself as an economic, social, and political crisis, resulting in epidemics, hunger, death, and disease. In El Salvador, agricultural production has been halved in the last twenty five years, and one-fifth of the population does not have enough food. Of those under five years of age, 80 percent are malnourished, and nearly 20 percent of all deaths are of children under one year of age. Intestinal sicknesses are common, causing, along with infectious diseases, half of all deaths. High concentrations of DDT have been found in both cow and human milk. Forty-six percent of the population is without access to potable water, and three-quarters are without sanitary services (CESTA brochure 1993). Migration from the country to the city has heightened environmental problems in urban areas.

The high level of natural resource degradation found throughout Central America occurs for reasons similar to those in many less-developed countries. Extensive cultivation of land for export crops to satisfy the needs of external markets, rapid population growth, intensive crop cultivation and overgrazing, lack of environmental regulation of industries, use of destructive agrochemicals, and so on, all play their part.

In the case of El Salvador, a brutal civil war greatly exacerbated the environmental crisis. The scorched-earth policy pursued by the military resulted in the destruction of forests. This policy is also referred to as "draining the lake to kill the fish." In order to isolate guerrilla fighters, everything in an area was killed—people, animals, vegetation. Use of chemicals and bombs in this process destroyed ground vegetation and contaminated the soil. Great internal migration was also caused by the war. Similarities between Vietnam and El Salvador suggest that the land will take fifty years to recuperate from war-inflicted damage (Urbino and Santamaria 1989: 118).

As Daniel Faker graphically demonstrates, environmental problems in Central American are greatly exacerbated by this recent history of war and militarization. The United States supported counterinsurgency programs in El Salvador and Guatemala; Honduras was militarized as a base for operations in other countries; the United States funded the "contra" war in Nicaragua, and U.S. troops invaded Panama in 1989. Ecological conditions needed for subsistence in hundreds of villages in the region were destroyed as a direct result of militarization. The discussion of popular ecological resistance which follows must be understood in the light of decades of wars in which the United States generally assisted in repressing popular organizations which challenged elite holders of economic and political power (Faber 1993).

ECOFEMINISM IN EL SALVADOR

This is a quote from Salvadoran poet Claribel Alegria's "Documental":

> The virgin coffee
> dances in the shed
> They strip it,

rape it,
stretch it out on the patios
it gives itself up to the sun.
As the dark warehouses brighten,
you can see malaria,
blood,
illiteracy,
tuberculosis,
misery
reflected in the golden coffee . . .
Country etcetera,
country wound,
child,
sob,
obsession.
(Translated by Lynne Byer in Angelsey 1987, 161)

Alegria links violence to the earth with violence to women. Virgin coffee becomes a metaphor both for land and for women who are stripped and raped to brighten, with gold or cash perhaps, the dark warehouses. Exploitive development policies which abuse land and women are further linked to illiteracy, poor health, and suffering children. Salvadoran ecofeminists contend that the impact of environmental degradation affects women differently because by being linked conceptually with nature, women are part of the same dominated and exploited ecosystem (Canas 1991: 8). This is by no means an essentialist position. Central American ecofeminists don't think that women are by nature more like the land. When activist Rosario Acosta likens the sterilization of the land to the sterilization of women, she claims that the way women and nature are perceived is formed by an export-driven model of economic development (Acosta 1993). In this model of economic and social development, both women and the land are viewed as objects available for appropriation. Although the ecological problem affects all, women are hit especially hard given their underrecognized and often uncompensated domestic work.

The embracing of ecofeminism by sectors of the environmentalist movement is not a mere "translating" of notions articulated in more affluent countries. When Rosario Acosta was asked if she was influenced by North American and European feminists she explained, "We do not want your [feminist] theory" (Acosta 1993). It is the lived experience of providing food from a damaged environment that has generated feminist methodology and activist strategies. Women are found on the forefront of environmental movements in Central America because they are directly involved with family sustenance, rarely because they have been influenced by feminist theory from more affluent countries.

As food providers and producers, women are especially dependent on a healthy environment. Eroded land produces less food, and more malnourished children. Forests and trees are necessary for fuel, food, and fodder. Increasing deforestation requires hours spent in basic fuel gathering and food production. The traditional diet of beans and corn, rice, and tortillas is undermined as intensive marketing of processed foods like bread and soft drinks increasingly occurs.

Women bear the brunt of child care and care for the sick and elderly and are especially affected by contaminated water. As Alma Carballo of CESTA (Centro Salvadoreno de Tecnologia Apropriada) notes, when polluted waters increase the incidence of cholera, "Who deals with this at the hospital?" (Carballo 1993). Birth defects and contaminants in mothers' milk have increased throughout Central America due to pesticides and chemical fertilizers. Those most affected by the death of the land have the least access to it. Only 2 percent of Salvadorans, for example, own 60 percent of the arable land (Lemus 1993). Figures for Honduras are comparable.

FROM CARETAKING TO ACTIVISM

The labor of caretaking and providing sustenance depends on a healthy environment. As a peasant woman notes, "Somos la raiz donde se sostiene un pueblo para crecer" (We [women] are the root which sustains a people's growth) (Canas 1991: 6). Given this understanding, the involvement of women in popular ecological resistance is not surprising. Activities range from mainstream political organizing and promotion of sustainable development projects, to more militant sorts of actions.

The National Coordinating Committee for Salvadoran Women (Coordinadora Nacional de la Mujer Salvadorena—CONAMUS), founded in 1986, is one of El Salvador's oldest women's organizations. CONAMUS has consistently struggled to include women in the development process. CONAMUS organizes women at the base level, sponsoring, for example, health programs emphasizing the use of natural products. In the Department of Chalatenango, an area under guerilla control during most of El Salvador's civil war, fruit trees have been planted in areas with adequate water, and trees which provide firewood and berries for soil retention have been planted in more arid areas (Ramirez 1993). In 1991, an entire issue of *Palabra de Mujer*, CONAMUS's quarterly publication, was devoted to ecofeminism after extensive internal discussion regarding women and the environment in Central America. CONAMUS was part of Mujeres '94, a coalition of women's organizations shaping a political platform for the March 1994 elections. A significant portion of the platform was devoted to women, the environment, and development (Vasquez 1993).

The Union of Salvadoran Workers (UNTS) sponsors projects training women in alternative health, nutrition, and use of natural medicinal plants. The rejection of western industrial medicine and use of natural medicinal plants has also been extremely important in popular health movements both in El Salvador and in Honduras. Health clinics in remote villages, generally run by women, often provide training in the use of natural medicines. UNTS executive committee member Rosario Acosta and others are strong critics of the government's model of economic development, claiming it is influenced by foreign investment and capital accumulation rather than sustainability (Acosta 1993). The return to use of natural medicinal plants encouraged by UNTS and other groups reflects this move to local sustainability and away from models coming from more industrialized nations.

Use of herbal remedies, while seemingly benign, is one reason women's environmental groups are considered politically radical. This perception occurs for two reasons. The return to natural medicines is a woman-controlled movement. It is peasant women who know the healing qualities of local plants, and they pass this knowledge on to their daughters. Rural villages often have a midwife who is also a healer or *curandera*. It is also a clear protest against present Salvadoran health services as well as against a model of economic development which adopts mechanistic western medicine. The movement is thus perceived, correctly, as a woman-controlled initiative struggling against government interests, thus radical.

The Salvadoran Center for Appropriate Technology (Centro Salvadoreno de Tecnologia Apropiada—CESTA) has mounted the most sustained campaigns related to women and the environment, with staff members such as Alma Carballo devoted to women and development. CESTA projects include solar kitchens, nutrition and soy programs for women, traditional medicine projects, fruit dehydrators, water purifiers, mills for grinding flour which use bicycles for energy generation, and alternative technologies consciously designed for women. CESTA sponsors projects coordinated with Nora Vamegas, the director of the Secretariat of Women at National University, in which students from the physics, engineering, medicine, and economic schools design environmentally sustainable development projects.

Most remarkable is that all CESTA members are trained in gender theory in order to continually affirm the centrality of the problem of gender in development. Again, this gender analysis is homegrown. When Mercedes Canas was recently asked if she noticed differences between feminism in Europe and in Central America, she answered that due to historical processes she noted substantial dissimilarities (Ueltzen 1993:160–61). It is interesting that U.S. feminism did not even enter the rather lengthy discussion! Salvadoran and Honduran feminists are more likely to look to their compatriots in Latin America. Most women's organizations participate, for example, in the annual Encuentro Latinoamericano Feminista. Although almost all women's organizations I visited had an Australian, Swedish, German, or North American woman working with them, these women were always in support positions.

THE STRUGGLE FOR LAND

It is often the case that popular environmental movements emerge over battles concerning who owns and/or controls land (Taylor et al. 1993:1). Central American women's environmental activism fits this trend. The Salvadoran group Women for Life and Dignity (Mujeres por la Dignidad y la Vida—DIGNAS) has mounted an aggressive campaign since the end of the civil war to obtain land for women. A document presented by DIGNAS to the Thirteenth Congress of the Communist party and to COPAZ, the group responsible for land transfers mandated by the United Nations following the civil war, harshly criticizes the discriminatory practices of the land transfers. Ironically, DIGNAS has found itself in peacetime battling with male members of the popular movement who support the postwar granting of land tenure almost exclusively to men (although women often worked the land as men went to war).

In Honduras, women's groups led by Elvia Alvarado staged massive protests against the United States–based Stone Container Company which had been given rights by the Honduran government to exploit the forest. The government eventually reversed this policy in 1987. Women's groups in Honduras have been involved in the fight for land through staging marches, sit-ins, hunger strikes, and "land recoveries." As Elvia Alvarado states: "We don't call them land takeovers or invasions. No, we call them land recoveries. You read in the paper, campesinos invade such and such a piece of land . . . not true . . . . We don't invade land, we recover land that belongs to us which has been invaded by the big landowners or the foreign companies . . . by what right did they take the land from our families to begin with?" (Alvarado 1987:89).

An innovative demonstration over land was led recently by Maria Mirtala Lopez of El Salvador. Currently, the most heated battle over land use centers around a piece of land called "El Espino." El Espino is both an ecological reserve and home to an agricultural cooperative. El Espino's location, on the edge of rapidly growing San Salvador, makes it an obstacle to the expansionist plans both of the government and of economic interests. Government plans for El Espino include rescinding all decrees passed in the 1980s which protected El Espino, making part of the land available for urban development, converting another section of the land into a Disneyland-style park, and allowing the El Espino cooperative to live in the remainder. A coalition of environmental groups, women's groups, and the cooperative struggled for years to keep the property and to preserve the ecological equilibrium of this tiny remnant of forest.

In a recent visit to San Francisco, California, Maria Mirtala Lopez told a class on gender and development of a demonstration that she, the women's movement, and the youth movement had recently staged in an endangered section of El Espino. A month-long fiesta and dance was celebrated. Bulldozers and soldiers were met by people dancing, drinking beer, and eating. As bulldozers changed directions, so did the dancers. As Lopez said, "This demonstration was very good for our figures—I've never danced for a month before!" (Lopez 1994). In frustration, the bulldozers and soldiers finally left the area, leaving the battle to be staged in the courts.

RADICAL CATHOLICISM AND ENVIRONMENTAL RADICALISM

Clearly women's involvement in ecological resistance is linked to their family roles. The articulation of a moral rationale rarely is that of pure self-interest, but of family and community protection. Another often unrecognized dynamic animating these movements is religion (Taylor et al. 1993:4). Radical Catholicism as articulated by liberation theologians such as Salvadoran Jon Sobrino demands that faith commitment is expressed in praxis or struggle with and for the most oppressed. For liberation theologians, God takes sides in history, exercising a "preferential option for the poor" and Christians should too. Christians are to actively engage in the work of the Kingdom of God, an earthly labor which involves changing unjust social structures. Environmental activists suggest that social sin is not merely the poverty and exploitation of people but also the contamination of resources. Ricardo Navarro, director of CESTA and founding member of the Salvadoran Ecological Union (UNES), suggests that denying food to people through unjust economic and social structures is no more of a social sin than polluting rivers through the excessive use of pesticides, which also cause death (Navarro 1990:99). For activists such as Navarro, the violation of nature is essentially a religious offense. When the nineteen members of UNES met in 1991 to prepare the document *Propuesta del Cerro Verde* (Green Hill Proposal), they explicitly called on the churches to denounce environmental degradation as a serious affront against the creator. They further recommended that ecological committees be formed in each parish or church to promote "conversion" to ecological community (UNES 1990). For a new group of radical Catholics, faith must grow from the perspective of a profoundly damaged environment, just as it identifies with the most vulnerable humans. Central American theologian Ingemar Hedstrom suggests that a Central American liberation perspective must interpret the preferential option for the poor to mean a preferential option for life (Hedstrom 1990:120).

Although this may sound like the birth of an anti-anthropocentric environmentalism arising within some Central American churches, most activists are quick to reject biocentric notions. Many agree with Ramachandra Guha's claim that "the anthropocentrism/biocentrism distinction is of little use" in understanding third-world environmental degradation (Guha 1989:71). Women and the environment must "travel together," claims Isabel Vasquez, director of CONAMUS. The central issue for peasant women environmental activists is survival. Concern for the land is linked with survival for humans—nature is not viewed as a separate space but as home.

Increasingly, activists are also realizing that the poor are disproportionately women. Alma Carballo of CESTA claims that the environmental problem affects poor people the most and the poorest of the poor are women (Carballo 1993). "Liberating" those most oppressed might easily involve, for example, increasing access to water and fuel for women. The liberation of the most oppressed—women—is thus intimately tied to the liberation of the land. Liberation theologians suggest that the poor have an "epistemological privilege." Knowledge about sustainable development might then come from the "lowest of the low," from "those who care for others without being cared for themselves" (Curtin 1993:12). Of course, peasants divorced from their land may have lost important knowledge about how to live sustainable lifestyles. Yet they know intimately the cost of the failures of development models imported from more affluent nations. This knowledge combined with eco-sciences and lessons from traditional lifeways merges to create a popular environmental movement and epistemology "from below."

The perspective of liberation theology articulated above is acted out very concretely. Representatives of CRIPDES will claim that women have been marginalized at all levels—politically, in the household, and environmentally—and are in the process of initiating women-centered projects (Pineda 1993). The women's organization DIGNAS sponsors groups for women which engage in "Reflection on our life conditions from faith . . . a feminist reading of the Bible intending to transform oppressive faith into a liberating faith" (DIGNAS brochure 1993). DIGNAS works with women in Christian base communities throughout El Salvador in sustainable agricultural work. The emphasis on sustainable development is seen as part of the fight to better the quality of life for women demanded by a reading of the Bible based in liberation theology.

Radical Catholicism may play a role in more militant groups as well, such as those of Elvia Alvarado. Alvarado's activism began when the church started mothers' clubs for women. In the process, the church offered an analysis of their oppression as well as workshops on food, nutrition, cooperative work, agriculture, and so on. Alvarado says that the "mothers' clubs had opened my eyes to another world, a world where people tried to change things. I wanted to take what I had learned and share it with others" (Alvarado 1987:11). From these mothers' clubs grew peasant associations aggressively involved in land take-overs, protests, hunger strikes, and sit-ins. For Alvarado, this is part of faith commitment. She states: "I don't think that God says, 'Go to church and pray all day and everything will be fine.' No. For me God says, 'Go out and make the changes that need to be made and I'll be there to help you.' The story of Christ proves we can make change if we fight hard enough and if we never lose faith in what we're fighting for" (Alvarado 1987:30).

WHERE ARE THE MEN?

There is certainly male involvement in environmental movements in Central America. However, generally only the women's organizations are making the connection between the poor treatment both of women and of nature, and the most vocal environmentalists and ecofeminists are women. In the offices of CONAMUS, DIGNAS, and so on, you will see no men. The situation is complicated for Central American ecofeminists. Canas points out that a major difference between European and Central American feminists is that those from Central America tend to be working in other parts of the popular movement, as well as in specifically ecofeminist causes (Ueltzen 1993:161). Thus, feminists work within the broad-based popular movement while constantly struggling with men within the movement. In spite of Rebeca Palacios's powerful position as a guerrilla commander during the civil war, she states, "Es terrible la gran solidaridad masculina!" (The male solidarity is terrible) (Ueltzen 1993:185). The Human Rights Commission of El Salvador concludes that Central Americans need "to make visible the existing inequalty between the sexes, the product of a male-oriented and patriachal culture and socialization process . . . the problem is an ideological one, at the root of the population's very structure, in the distribution of work and power" (Human Rights Commission of El Salvador 1993:7).

Women's environmental movements in Central America not only have minimal participation by men, they often encounter resistance, even from the men of the popular movement. In preparation for the March 1994 elections in El Salvador, the major women's organizations staged Mujeres '94 (Women 1994), a massive initiative to introduce women's issues into the political debates and platforms. The "Platform of Salvadoran Women" included demands for land for women, respect for the environment and women, development policies that addressed the needs of women, and free and voluntary motherhood. A call was made for development models in which women participate as agents and for the promotion of technologies which are targeted at women and do not damage the environment. An entire section of the document was devoted to the demands of peasant women for land (Muheres 1993). Yet when the author visited El Salvador as an international observer during the March 1994 elections, there was no mention made of the document by either the right or the left.

Women are almost completely excluded from access to land in spite of provisions in the Peace Accords signed after the civil war which guaranteed pieces of land to people who had worked it. As noted earlier, DIGNAS has mounted an active campaign to obtain land for women. As part of this campaign they have severely criticized the Communist party and the Faribundo Marti Liberacion Nacional (FMLN—the coalition party of the left) for their discriminatory interpretation of the land transfers mandated by the United Nations. A male member of the FMLN explained to me that the lack of land transfers to women was a cultural problem, rather than a problem of gender discrimination. This analysis is not shared by the women's movement. Following a long conversation with Isabel Vasquez of CONAMUS in which she spoke of all the types of resistance they faced as they did their work, she said she was motivated by "the resistance itself" (Vasquez 1993).

LESSONS FROM CENTRAL AMERICAN WOMEN'S ENVIRONMENTAL ACTIVISM

What is learned from the struggles of women environmentalists in El Salvador and Honduras which can be applied in other parts of the world?

The following are but a few lessons learned from the Central American reality:

1. Liberation theology provides a powerful religious rationale for placing together the concerns for social justice, gender equality, and environmental sustainability. Liberation theology has been articulated in contexts other than Latin America, and

although cultural variations exist, the theme of concern for the "lowest of the low" remains constant. Theologians should, as is beginning to emerge in Central America, link social transformation and calls for justice with concerns about gender and the environment. Religious groups might also provide models of consciousness raising and cooperative work.

2. The Central American experience graphically demonstrates that the ideology which authorizes oppression based on race, gender, physical abilities, and so on, is the same ideology which legitimates the domination of nature. In the case of Central America, the grotesquely unequal ownership of land has been the primary symbol of this multifaceted domination.

3. Both liberation theology and women's organizations suggest an epistemology in which women who are most closely linked to sustenance are considered the development experts. Economic models which count the unwaged, noncommodity production of the domestic and subsistence activities of women should be favored. Women who deal directly with food, fuel, and water crises should be political forces in their resolution. Ecological scientists and peasant women should join forces to combine the best of indigenous ecological developmental knowledge with the insights of contemporary ecological science.

4. The organization of women into their own autonomous organizations is critical and should be integral to any process of political/social/economic transformation. The challenge to discriminatory land policies of both the Salvadoran left and the Salvadoran government only occurred through the efforts of groups such as CONAMUS and DIGNAS.

Popular ecological resistance by women's groups in El Salvador and Honduras stems from the need to provide basic family and community sustenance. The focus often revolves around land. The movements are part of larger popular movements which resist mainstream models of economic development for the region, believing that the industrial growth pursued by more affluent countries results in decreased access to the land for peasant and other marginalized groups. Resource scarcity grew dramatically during war times, yet women who fought during the war now find themselves battling the patriarchy both within and without the popular movement as they fight for land tenure.

El Salvador is a country in transition, reeling out of a brutal civil war and suffering severe environmental degradation. Honduras suffers from similar struggles concerning land ownership and use of the environment. The voices of environmental activists, liberation theologians, and especially women who are religiously, philosophically, and concretely through their activism linking concerns about gender, the land, and justice, speak powerfully of sustainable ways of living on the planet and with each other. As an eight-year-old girl from Palomera, El Salvador, put it, "I am thinking of a future full of much fruit, much happiness, many flowers, and bird songs."

Chapter 4

Profits, Parrots, Peons: Ethical Perplexities in the Amazon

Heidi Hadsell

Introduction

Certainly since Rio '92 but also preceding it, the term *sustainable development* has attracted considerable attention. The term has a number of attributes which recommend it, among them its broad and vague character, qualities which help keep groups with very different, even opposing, interests and values in roughly the same conversation.[1]

Despite its grounding in concrete situations of environmental degradation and the muffled panic occasioned by the growing awareness of the depth, scope, and complexity of environmental destruction, the ethical discussion of sustainable development quickly becomes abstract. We develop and organize our thought around ethical principles, middle axioms, core values, religious ideals, and definitions, all intended at some point to guide action. It is important to think carefully and abstractly about the issues of sustainability, and there is validity in the arguments regarding the precise meaning of the term *sustainable development*, particularly in relation to understandings of sustainability by communities differing according to geography, religion, ethnicity, class, and so on. However, such debate can lose touch with the actions it is intended to guide and with the agents who must do the acting. Therefore, it is imperative to return frequently to concrete groups, big and small, dealing with concrete elements of sustainable development, and to specific agents of sustainable development, in order to test the efficacy and adequacy of our ethical reflection. Happily, this effort at intentionally touching base also widens the nature of the ethical conversation and expands the partners included in it.

The following is a discussion of an agricultural community in the backwaters of the Amazon, a community of people who are situated at the base of their political and economic pyramid and thus seldom if ever included in any kind of public conversation. This community (like many others similar to it) has embraced sustainable development as its central organizing principle. It has thereby become an agent of sustainable development, carrying out what it sees as, and what undoubtedly in fact is, a life and death struggle.

I describe this community in Brazil and its particular understanding of and active pursuit of sustainable development both to touch base and to learn from this concrete level of engagement in sustainable development. While I arrive at no fully formed conclusions, this exercise makes it amply clear that understandings of sustainable development are inevitably contextual, conditioned both by concrete situational factors such as the resources available for organization, social mobilization, and action,[2] and by ideological commitments and world views prior to and larger than the idea or practice of sustainable development itself.

ITACOATIARA AND BEYOND

It is a five-hour bus ride from Manaus to the lumber town of Itacoatiara, situated where the road ends at the Amazon River. After several more hours up river by boat one comes to a small community on the banks of an island in the river. From the river only the crude wooden church and community meeting hall are visible, and except for individual houses scattered about the community, house and church are all there is to this tiny outpost of humanity. It is a community of people known in these parts as *ribeirinhos* or "river dwellers." The people who live here are basically farmers. They tend the soft and fertile ground which the river exposes as it recedes during the dry season. They supplement their farming activity by fishing in the river and in the small lakes the receding waters of the river leave during the dry season.

While many in the community have been in the area for generations, others are more recent arrivals, propelled by economic forces beyond their ken, mostly having to do with land issues, particularly the concentration of land ownership elsewhere in Brazil and the national and international exigencies of agribusiness in Brazil and abroad. The simplicity of the subsistence farming the *ribeirinhos* are engaged in and the smallness of its scale contrast sharply with the size and the sophistication of the agribusiness enterprise of Brazil. The *ribeirinhos* farm primarily so they themselves can eat, and they fish to supplement their farming. They may occasionally and with difficulty produce a small surplus, and even more occasionally, with even greater difficulty, find a way to get it to a market somewhere nearby.

The *ribeirinhos* have, over generations, brought their farming techniques and their agricultural crops with them into the Amazon. They have also brought their habits of fending for themselves, accustomed as they are to being buffeted about by people and economic forces far more powerful than they are themselves.

The time it takes to get there, the hours on the bus and on the river, the footpaths instead of roads, the dugout canoes and crude farming tools, the absence of electricity or even the smallest of comforts, and the pleasure the inhabitants take from having visitors and the time they spend with them lend to this community the appearance of remoteness. It seems an eddy in the march of time, not even loosely connected to life in the rest of Brazil, as removed from the market as it is from the means of mass communication.

The impression of remoteness is, however, illusory. For the presence of the market grows steadily throughout the region and has begun to impinge on the life of these *ribeirinhos*.[3] Indeed it is the full-scale arrival of the market economy and the imposition of its logic on them that is pushing the *ribeirinhos* toward environmental questions, forcing them to grapple daily with a host of issues leading inexorably to the same realization that people are coming to all around the globe, namely, that they cannot survive living and producing as they do, that their way of life is not sustainable.

The Disappearing Fish

The immediate challenge to the way of life of the *ribeirinhos* is not directly related to their own agricultural and fishing activities.

Rather the threat comes via the fishing activities of others. Like their farming techniques, the fishing techniques the *ribeirinhos* use are simple. Their agricultural techniques are nonmechanized, and for fishing they use only rods, hand held nets, and sometimes spears. They fish primarily in order to supplement what they are able to grow to eat or the livestock they are able to maintain.

While the *ribeirinhos* fish in the Amazon itself, in the dry season, when the waters of the river recede, they favor the small lakes that form in the wake of the receding water. As the water recedes, the fish from the river are trapped and are the most plentiful and the easiest to catch.

For generations this community and many others like it, fishing for themselves and perhaps for a small surplus, have found the fish abundant and easily caught. It is easy to understand why. The communities are small, they fish only in order to eat, and their simple technologies mean that they catch relatively few fish.

However in the last decade or so the relationship between these river communities and the supply of fish available to them has begun to change. The agents of change are the commercial fishing boats which have appeared in the region and which, unlike the *ribeirinhos*, are operating under the market logic of profit and loss in a region geographically removed from their own communities and within a perspective on time that extends only a few short years.

Not surprisingly, the fishing boats, which are both Brazilian and foreign, find the same advantage to the inland lakes left by the receding waters of the Amazon as do the *ribeirinhos*. However, unlike the *ribeirinhos*, the commercial fishermen have the technology to take advantage of the trapped fish in ways that the river dwellers never dreamed possible.

The commercial fishermen force their way into the inland lakes with high-powered fishing boats. Using finely woven nets so that few fish will escape, however small, the commercial fishermen customarily take all the fish they find in their nets, including those that they will later sell, those caught by the nets that by virtue of size or type they will not even attempt to sell, and those that, in order to make room for more lucrative fish found later, they will throw back dead into the river.

This predatory commercial fishing leaves the lakes virtually empty of fish, and the *ribeirinhos* are now finding that their own fishing is far more difficult. They are obliged to spend more time fishing to catch many fewer fish, in a process which results in less time available for farming, their principle subsistence activity. Their diet is thus poorer in protein.

The commercial boats arrive, take the fish, and then move on to other lakes or return to the cities to sell their fish in national and international markets. The *ribeirinhos* are not so mobile. They stay where they are and confront lakes empty of fish and a way of life that is increasingly unviable. Eventually, if this continues, these communities will die, the people in them scattering in search of survival elsewhere.

The *ribeirinhos* do not want their community to die, however, and they know that prospects elsewhere for survival are just as slim if not more so. Their survival, they have already realized, is closely connected to saving the fish in the lakes. They have, in other words, begun to tackle the question of sustainable development.

The *ribeirinhos*, in a document signed in May 1992 by representatives of a number of river communities, state:

> During the decade of the 80s, due to the diminution of fish we began a struggle in defense of fishing and of the restocking of fish in the lakes and rivers. The ever greater presence of big fishing, of predatory practices, of the enormous waste of fish, left us no other alternative. The communities where we live began to organize themselves into local committees with the aim of impeding the invasion of lakes and guaranteeing the preservation of fish.[4]

THE STRUGGLE: A DESCRIPTION

The struggle of the *ribeirinhos* to save the lakes depends not only on a common perception of the root of their difficulties but also on the community's ability to organize itself. If their life is to be sustainable, they must discover the steps to make it so. Their first step must be to organize themselves so that they can somehow impede the invasion of the lakes by the commercial fishing fleets.

The Realization of Moral and Political Rights

The self-organization of the *ribeirinhos* has first and foremost a political objective. The ecological objective is secondary and will be achieved only as a result of political organization. The central political struggle of the *ribeirinhos* is to agree among themselves to claim a moral and political right to control their own natural resources, namely, the fish in the lakes which they have traditionally believed were theirs. The assertion of this right must be preceded by the general realization among them that they do indeed have such moral and political rights. This realization itself is often very difficult to achieve because the peasants have endured and internalized decades of authoritarian rule and social and economic hierarchy which have led them to assume that they essentially have no rights at all.[5]

The moral assertion of their rights by the *ribeirinhos* must subsequently be followed by the actual grasp of control over their lakes.[6] This control, in the absence of public officials willing to work with it, is the community's own responsibility. Thus in addition to organizing itself politically, the community must take steps on its own to guard the lakes day and night to impede the entrance of the commercial boats.

As the *ribeirinhos*'s involvement in the preservation of the lakes deepens, other elements of political life inevitably become apparent. The community has embarked on a process of the discovery of its rights, and in this light begins to wonder about other elements included in the rights of citizenship. It begins, for example, to question the role of its elected officials and the police. The struggle becomes a learning experience first and foremost in political terms that may be generalizable to other issues in the future.[7]

The Transformation of Social Relationships

If they are to succeed in changing their relationships with nature so that they may preserve the fish in the lakes, the first thing the *ribeirinhos* must be able to do is to change their relationships with each other (through organization), with the commercial fishermen (through seizing control of their own lakes), and eventually, in order to be successful over the course of years, with local and regional political authorities (through exercising whatever political influence they can muster). It is clear that the relationship of the *ribeirinhos* with nature is inseparable from their relationships with each other and with other relevant social actors.[8]

The immediate aim of the transformation in these social relationships is environmental, specifically, the preservation of the fish in the lakes. The *ribeirinhos* realize that stopping the commercial fishermen from depleting their lakes is just the first step. They can no longer simply assume fish will always be abundant, nor can they realistically assume that they can banish all outside fishing boats from their lakes once and for all. Their long-term strategy of survival therefore requires long-term management of the resources in their lakes. They plan to structure their lakes so that roughly one lake in every three is used for propagation of fish, one is used for their own fishing—but not for commercial use—and one is reserved for the use of the commercial boats, controlled by the *ribeirinhos* under the existent legal guidelines which regulate the size of nets, the fishing seasons, and so forth.

The Role of the Commisao Pastoral da Terra (CPT)

The *ribeirinhos'* grasp of their situation—both politically and ecologically—is aided by the political and theological input of the CPT. Similarly, their ability to organize is greatly enhanced by the presence of the CPT. Although the *ribeirinhos* are themselves responsible for their own decisions and organizations, it is clear that both in terms of their comprehension of their situation in relation to their lakes and in terms of organizational capacity, they are far beyond where they would have been without the theoretical and organizational resources of the CPT.

The CPT is a creation of the Organization of Brazilian Bishops founded in 1975. The CPT was founded in response to the growing conflicts over land throughout Brazil, including the Amazon, and the involvement of the Catholic church in many of these conflicts. The CPT is composed of priests, nuns, and lay people who work with people involved in land issues in various communities scattered throughout Brazil. Its mission is primarily that of *assessoria*, or assistance in the organizations of peasants and workers formed around land issues, as well as other related issues. The CPT lends legal assistance when land issues end up in court, technical assistance to farmers (or *ribeirinhos* and the like), and organizational know-how and moral support related simply to its presence in the workers' lives.[9] (In Brazil the CPT is known primarily for its militant work with landless peasants in such efforts as land invasions.) The CPT is an important part of the web of political, labor, and non-governmental organizations that work with rural and urban poor in Brazil, often known in sociological parlance as mediators.[10]

The resources the CPT brings to the struggle are ideological,[11] technical, and to a lesser extent financial. The nature of these resources varies, depending on the specific CPT office and its staff and on the issues and people of each given situation.[12] Generally speaking, however, the ideological tools of the CPT are those of liberationist Catholicism. By this I mean, briefly, a Catholicism that views the affirmation that God is especially concerned with the poor and the oppressed to be a central theological affirmation found at the core of Christianity. This Christianity is marked by a this-worldly eschatology requiring Christian involvement in historical projects of political and economic justice by and for the excluded. Toward this end it takes as a central ethical task the responsibility to facilitate political and economic education and analysis, as well as transformative action, both by the poor themselves, who are viewed as primary historical agents, and by others, who act in solidarity with the poor and the excluded.[13]

The values stressed by this liberationist Christianity, which is one wing of Brazilian Catholicism, are those that center on economic and social justice. These values stress group solidarity, the participation and inclusion of all in groups and in group decisions, and, together with a suspicion if not of material wealth itself at least a distrust of what wealth acquisition requires in terms of cooperating with and benefiting by oppressive and unjust structures.

The religious identity and self-understanding of the CPT, which is the wellspring of the commitment of CPT staff, blends with and is not easily separable from political perspectives characteristic of the Brazilian left.[14] These are perspectives that differ somewhat from each other but that share an awareness of and strong critique of the extreme class divisions in Brazil, and of economic and political institutions that function for the benefit of a small minority of the population, and often for the profits of foreign enterprises, but towards the detriment of the vast majority who live at the margins of political and economic life. This current generation of the left is related to the left that the military coup of 1964 aimed at silencing and comprises the coalition that in 1989 came within several million votes of electing a Socialist president from the Partido dos Trabalhadores—(Worker's party—PT).[15]

From the perspective of the CPT, the poverty and political and economic powerlessness of communities such as that of the *ribeirinhos* described here is unjust, unnecessary, and unacceptable, and therefore must be confronted and indeed transformed. The attempt to control the lakes and to save the fish in these lakes is viewed as part of the transformative process. The primary agents of transformation, according to the CPT, are and must be the poor themselves—in this case the *ribeirinhos*. The CPT views its role as secondary, consisting of simple assistance and solidarity.[16]

In August 1993, the author attended a meeting in the community of *ribeirinhos* focused on its participation in the regional campaign begun by the CPT to save the lakes. At this meeting there were no outside mediators present, but the presence of the CPT was unmistakable in the well-trained leadership of the community, the emphasis on the importance of the solidarity of all the members of the community, and in the natural blend of biblical study and theological reflection with political analysis, opinions, and organization.

The meeting itself was an exercise in the practice of democracy, as the reluctant and the normally silent (such as the women) were encouraged to speak and to share their own experiences. It was also aimed at the formation of political consciousness, as the leadership connected the struggle to save the lakes with the disinterest and ill will of many local politicians and contrasted it with the support of the PT. The meeting was also an opportunity for theological reflection, beginning as it did with a Bible study to which the conversation returned throughout the afternoon. Each of these elements, important in and of itself, contributed to the immediate goal of the meeting which was to maintain and extend the community participation in the struggle to save the lakes.

The meeting began with a Bible study of Genesis 1:26–30, led by the current leader of the local base community. The peasant, drawing upon his training as a base community leader and his participation in CPT educational and organizational events as well as fine pedagogical instincts, argued that God has given humanity creation to use, much as a friend loans someone something precious for that friend to use, expecting it back in the same state in which it was loaned. That is, God expects us to use and to care for creation, and eventually to return it in the state in which it was given to us.

The Bible study set the theme for the afternoon, and provoked a lively discussion of the text and, later, of the campaign to save the lakes. It also provided religious motivation for the preservation of the lakes and, since most of the participants at the meeting were Catholics, it also implicitly lent the authority of the church to the campaign.[17]

In addition to the ideological and analytical resources offered by the CPT to communities of *ribeirinhos*, it also offers organizational experience and expertise. The value of organizational experience may not be apparent at first to such groups as the *ribeirinhos*, but it quickly becomes so. Even the most basic knowledge of how to call and run meetings, how to keep track of what was decided, how to choose leaders, and how to vote, is precious for those who have never had access to such activities.

Similarly invaluable is knowledge of and access to the networks in which the CPT functions. These are networks which hold the possibility for new alliances, wider solidarity, and insights into other local issues and concerns. The campaign to save the lakes is itself a regional campaign created and spread to many communities by the CPT, but also carried by other political and non-governmental organizations which are allies of the CPT. In this campaign the mediation between local, often isolated, communities and regional, national, and even international networks and alliances accomplished by the *assessores* of the CPT is quite clear.

Finally, although modest, the financial resources of the CPT are, compared to those of peasants like the *ribeirinhos*, considerable. The *assessores* of the CPT, religious, technical, legal, or what have you, are employed not by the peasants themselves but by the Catholic church. The *assessoria* the peasants receive is a resource they do not have to buy, and indeed could never afford. Similarly, the peasants benefit from local and regional CPT offices both as places to gather and to hold meetings and as places housing valuable and scarce equipment such as telephones and sometimes copiers or fax machines. The cars, vans, boats, or other means of transportation used by the CPT are equally valuable and scarce, as is the training the peasants themselves receive in campaigns.

The *assessores* of the CPT also hold the keys to invaluable information in the areas of science, government, and law. Here they mediate between sophisticated and not easily available scientific knowledge of, for instance, the effects of the depletion of fish on the lakes and the peasants who are living these effects, but who without the benefits of science cannot fully comprehend the present trends or events, or intervene intelligently. In another type of mediation, the *assessores* may demystify government and its rules and procedures, helping peasants discern which part of which government body is the relevant one for a given question or complaint and just how to approach the appropriate officials.

In the case of the *ribeirinhos* an international network has, through the CPT and its allies, provided a concept—that of sustainable development—the use of which has made it possible to grasp both the forces impinging on its livelihood and some possible forms of action to take in self-protection against them. The concept of 'sustainable development' has also provided the center around which the *ribeirinhos* have been able to organize and against which they can measure their failures and successes.

In addition to all of these resources which the CPT offers, one must add the more amorphous but equally potent power of presence. The mere presence of the CPT provides a kind of attention, an affirmation from relative outsiders, that people like the *ribeirinhos* have never experienced before. CPT presence in a community gives a sense that one is being attended to and that one matters. It is also important that the enemies of those with whom the CPT works— the holders of large tracts of land, commercial fishermen, local political hierarchies, and so forth—that they are being watched by those who, by virtue of education and regional and national social and religious connections, count; consequently, they can no longer act with total impunity.[18]

In these ways the mere presence of the CPT in a town or city can subtly shift at least the perception of the balance of power. This sense of presence is essential in terms of morale in the struggle as the individual and the community develop solidarity.

In short, the CPT, having enjoyed the benefits of education and organizational experience and possessing ideological motivation, with the authority and resources of the Catholic church behind them, are an invaluable resource for the *ribeirinhos*. Indeed, the CPT and the few other organizations such as political parties willing to work with and represent them, may be the only chance the *ribeirinhos* will have to stay where they are and preserve their way of life and their lakes. They may make the difference between success and failure.

It is in the life of communities like that of the *ribeirinhos* that the meaning of sustainable development gains life and substance. In this case, in the service of the *ribeirinhos* in defense of their community and way of life, the *assessores* from the CPT have made the concept of 'sustainable development' available. They have been the mediation between an international concept very much in vogue and a small group of farmers for whom this concept, rightly used and interpreted, can be remarkably empowering. In mediating, they have been able to help breathe life into the concept of 'sustainable development,' which they have taken down from the shelves of abstraction and put in service of this community.

Concluding Reflections

We learn with and from the *ribeirinhos* that while sustainable development is an economic process, as well as a process that depends on technical and scientific expertise and innovation, first and foremost, at least among peasants such as the *ribeirinhos* in Brazil, it is a political process. As is amply demonstrated by this case study, to move toward sustainability requires for communities like the *ribeirinhos* a shift, often a major one, to occur in the existent balance of political forces. For the *ribeirinhos* to effectively carry out a project in sustainable development has meant first of all an assertion of the simple right to have enough to survive. This in turn has required a transformation of identity (from a peasant with no rights to a community with rights) and of relationships in the social ecology in which they live.

To assert that sustainable development is a political process is to underline the extent to which sustainability expresses human relationships and not simply relationships of humans with nature. In this sense it is a moral concept par excellence. The *assessores* and the peasants themselves are first and foremost moral actors who view the struggle to save the fish in the lakes as primarily a moral struggle, aimed at the transformation of the social world in which they live.

The possibility of actualizing anything that even approaches sustainable development depends on a complex relation of factors, as the peasants themselves have discovered. In ethical debate about sustainable development we have focused on the meanings of the term, and not enough attention has been given either to the agents of projects of sustainable development or to the larger ideologies that provide motivation sufficient to put sustainable development into practice in concrete situations.

The case of this community of *ribeirinhos* demonstrates that in order to start a process in motion whose goal is sustainable development—which in this case means, very modestly, maintaining a subsistence way of life with community control over key resources both for its own sustenance and for the long-term preservation of those resources—the presence of mediators such as the *assessores* of the CPT was fundamental.

The *assessores* of the CPT are invaluable to the *ribeirinhos* both because they possess the requisite organizational and technical expertise to mount a campaign to save the lakes and because they possess the ideological motivation (in the form both of political ideals and commitments and of religious values and beliefs) compelling enough to impart to the *ribeirinhos* a sense of agency and power, as well as certainty as to the justness of the cause. Their ideological motivation also sustains both the CPT and the *ribeirinhos* in the face of sure defeats and uncertain victories. Indeed, it seems correct to conclude that the continued and sustained involvement of the *ribeirinhos* themselves in their struggle will depend as much on the depth of their own grounding in political and religious ideals and values as upon the encouragement they derive from whatever minor successes they manage along the way.

Their ideological grounding, as in the case of the *assessores*, will help carry the *ribeirinhos* through the certain defeats that await them and help connect their understanding of their struggle to save the lakes with larger political and religious visions. Indeed, broad ideological vision and commitments color the very meanings given to sustainable development by groups and communities. Here the understanding of sustainable development is subsumed under the liberationist assumptions and values the CPT and the *ribeirinhos* have brought to it, values which are widely shared in large sectors of the Brazilian Catholic church as well as in the political parties of the left. These are values that inform many struggles and social movements in Brazil, a large percentage of which do not have to do with the preservation of the natural environment.

While the immediate goal is the preservation of the lakes, it is a goal viewed as legitimate both by the CPT and by the *ribeirinhos* with whom they work, by virtue of its relation both to the ongoing struggle of the *ribeirinhos* for mere survival in an unjust economic and political hierarchy, and to their further empowerment that they may begin to transform this crushing reality.

To ponder the chances of success of the campaign to save the lakes is to ponder not only the organizational abilities of the CPT but also the ability of all small grassroots organizations such as those in Brazil to counter the seemingly inexorable forces of the market economy.[19] Currently, the *ribeirinhos* are fighting the commercial fishing boats. Even were they to win this battle, the next battle looms on the horizon and may well be with the lumberjacks or the miners and the economic and political interests they serve. Eventually, the battle may even be with federal ecology laws themselves, which have been used more than once to move peasants out of the way of large capital.[20]

One of the strengths of the CPT is its comprehension of the market economy's impacts. According to the logic of the market, peasants such as the *ribeirinhos* can only be viewed as anachronisms, carrying on an unprofitable way of life, who, when face to face with the forces of modernization and capital accumulation, must surrender to the inevitable.

Countering this market calculus, but not underestimating its strength, the CPT, with the *ribeirinhos*, asserts the intrinsic value of person and community, insists on the practice of justice and of meaningful political participation and the right to control and to preserve the fish for their own sake as God's gift, because they help sustain and nurture human life. These are core elements of the concept of 'sustainable development' shared by many all over the world, but affirmed here in a given context. Together they form an idea which contains considerable political potency. Here the link with liberationist Christianity and with invaluable resources in the form of the CPT adds to its potency, as the campaign to save the lakes, essentially a defensive act, becomes also a campaign to empower the peasants, an offensive strategy aimed directly at the human social world.

NOTES

1. One definition of sustainable development is that of the United Nations Commission on Environment and Development (UNCED). In 1987 UNCED defined sustainable development as "a process of change in which exploitation of resources, the direction of investments, the reorientation of technology development, and institutional change are all in harmony and enhance both current and future potential to meet human needs and aspirations" (The World Commission on Environment and Development, *Our Common Future* [Oxford, New York: Oxford University Press, 1987], p.46).

2. In terms of thinking about organization and social action I am greatly aided by the work of Charles Tilly on collective action and resource mobilization. His careful analyses both of historical and of contemporary moments of collective action are very helpful and act as a constant reminder that collective action depends on concrete resources as well as compelling ideas. See especially Charles Tilly, *Class Conflict and Collective Action* (Beverly Hills and London: Sage Publications, 1981).

3. For example, the lumber industry is increasingly active in this region, and because it does not replant what it logs, it expands constantly.

The town of Itacoatiara is the home of two lumber mills of considerable size owned by European companies. The lumber mills use the river both for the transport of logs and for their storage. According to a labor organizer in one of the mills, while the workers have many issues of contention with the owners of the mills, the ecological issue as such—the destruction of forests caused by the mills—is not currently one of them.

4. "Carta dos Ribeirinhos do Amazonas" [Letter of the *ribeirinhos* of Amazonas], signed in Manaus on 29 May 1992, bearing the letter head of the Commisao Pastoral da Terra Regional Amazonas e Roraima (The pastoral land commission of the regions of Amazonas and Roraima).

5. There has been some interesting work done on the authoritarian culture of Brazil, related to political and economic patterns in Brazil reaching back hundreds of years, reinforced by recent years of dictatorship and expressive of continual, underlying class conflict. For a discussion of this authoritarian culture see the work of Roberto Da Matta, especially his book *Carnavals, Bandits et Heros* (Paris: Editions du Seuil, 1983), now in English, entitled *Carnavals, Bandits and Heros*. This work contains a particularly interesting chapter entitled "Do You Know Who You Are Speaking To?" which is especially pertinent here.

6. The likelihood is high that the *ribeirinhos* are basically squatters on what has been empty and now is increasingly contested land. The lakes do not legally belong to the communities. However, each community has a number of what become inland lakes within its informal boundaries which it has used as if it were the owners.

7. The "Carta Dos Ribeirinhos do Amazonas" demonstrates both the political content the *ribeirinhos* themselves attribute to the process of sustainable development and the manner in which the effort to save the lakes is itself a political education. The letter affirms that sustainable development is an integrated process with economic, social, political, and educational elements. It concludes that "Sustainable development for us *ribeirinhos* demands the articulation of all of these dimensions in a process in which the organized communities of the lakes and rivers are the political subject which guarantees regional development combined with the full respect for the nature of the Amazon ("Carta Dos Ribeirinhos do Amazonas," May, 1992).

8. The *ribeirinhos* see this element clearly, expressing it in their letter as follows: "We place ourselves together with the indigenous peoples, as the fundamental subjects of the cause of environmental protection and for the defense of life in the Amazon region" ("Carta Dos Ribeirinhos do Amazonas," May, 1992).

9. The literature on the CPT is growing in Brazil, but little exists to date in English. For those who read Portuguese, see especially the small body of literature on the land conflicts in Araguaia in the southern Amazon region, including two books written by a priest who has been closely involved: Ricardo Rezende Figueira, *A Justica do Lobo, Posseiros e padres do Araguaia* (Petropolis: Editora Vozes, 1986) and Ricardo Rezende Figueira, *Rio Maria, Canto da Terra* (Petropolis: Editora Voz, 1992).

10. There is ample literature in Brazil both on urban and on rural grassroots social movements, probably because of the high degree of organization in grassroots Brazil. A key reference point in this literature has been Paul Singer and Vinicius Caldera Brandt, eds., *Sao Paulo: O Povo em Movimento* (Petropolis: Vozes, 1980).

11. I use the word *ideological* in the broad sense, to refer to the realm of ideas and beliefs, including religious beliefs, political world views, and so on. It is not used here in a pejorative sense, nor is it meant to imply "wrong" ideas.

12. By viewing the CPT as a resource I am following the insights of Charles Tilly and the school of thought known as "resource mobilization" mentioned above. See Charles Tilly, *From Mobilization to Revolution* (New York: Random House, 1978).

13. I am not attempting to be definitive here, rather to summarize several key elements in liberationist thought that motivate and guide CPT cadres' actions and values.

14. For interesting background on the Catholic church and politics in Brazil see Scott Mainwaring, *The Catholic Church and Politics in Brazil, 1916–1985* (Stanford: Stanford University Press, 1986).

15. Interestingly, in 1994 the same candidate, Luis Ignacio da Silva (or Lula) is, according to the *New York Times*, the current front-runner for the October presidential election. See "For the Nations of the Western Hemisphere, Renewed Growth," *New York Times*, 3 January 1994.

16. This is a point that in my experience people working for the CPT never fail to stress, both for theological reasons—the poor and the oppressed comprising the center of God's care and concern—and for political and sociological reasons, following the Marxist insistence that the workers are or will be the agents of transformation in Capitalist economies. This stress on the agency of the poor is also an implicit reply to charges made by the many enemies of the CPT and the movements they work with, that the CPT workers are outside agitators stirring up trouble where none had existed before.

17. Later in the same meeting the Catholic flavor caused some discomfort when a small group of Seventh Day Adventists entered who had heard about and were interested in joining the struggle to save the lakes. It was clear from their demeanor and from what they eventually said that they viewed both the meeting and the campaign as being essentially by and for Catholics. Once they expressed their fear the Catholic majority rushed to affirm the importance of the unity of all. Testimony from a variety of participants and scriptural quotations ensued designed to underline the essential unity of all, both in the struggle to save the lakes and in their Christian beliefs.

18. The impresion of watching and therefore inducing others to follow the law, or at least to be more careful when breaking it, is used by many human rights groups. The letter campaigns of Amnesty International are a well-known example. While their mere physical presence can indeed be very helpful in situations of conflict such as those one finds all over the Amazonian region, the CPT workers often put themselves at great risk by being present. This is the same risk to life and limb the peasants carry when participating in movements such as the campaign to save the lakes.

19. The underlying cause of the defensive battles such as the struggle to save the lakes described here is, of course, the rapid expansion of capital into the Amazonian region over the last several decades. For a number of interesting articles that examine various facets of this Capitalist expansion in the Amazon, see Marianne Schmink and Charles Wood, *Frontier Expansion in Amazonia* (Gainesville: University of Florida Press, 1984).

20. This has happened in various regions of Brazil both in and outside of the Amazon and has to do with laws being unevenly enforced, so that those who by virtue of power and wealth ignore the laws, while the poor and the powerless find that the ecology laws have become one more weapon used against them. For a description of one instance of this dynamic see Heidi Hadsell and Robert Evans, "Is President Collar Green?" *Christian Century* (November, 1991).

PART II
POPULAR ECOLOGICAL RESISTANCE IN ASIA AND IN THE PACIFIC

Chapter 5

INTERNATIONAL NATIVE RESISTANCE TO THE NEW RESOURCE WARS

Al Gedicks[1]

Over the past three decades multinational corporations and development-oriented governments have waged resource wars against native peoples (Anthropology Resource Center 1981; Gedicks 1993). From the Amazon Basin to the frozen stretches of northern Saskatchewan, to the tropical forests of Southeast Asia and central Africa, energy, mining, logging, hydroelectric, and other megaprojects have uprooted, dislocated, and even destroyed native communities. But this assault has met significant resistance from both the native rights and the environmental movements. At the 1977 International Non-Governmental Organizations Conference on Discrimination against Indigenous Populations in the Americas, the delegates recommended that the United Nations Committee on Trans-National Corporations "conduct an investigation into the role of multinational corporations in the plunder and exploitation of native lands, resources, and peoples in the Americas" (International Indian Treaty Council 1977:24). With considerable information about these costly and destructive projects at hand, native people and their allies began planning counterstrategies.

This chapter examines four cases of the new resource wars that are on the cutting edge of international native resistance to resource colonization. In each case, corporate and governmental attempts to gain access to cheap energy, minerals, or timber on native lands has been met with fierce resistance from native peoples.

GROWING NATIVE RESISTANCE TO DAMS: JAMES BAY II, QUEBEC, CANADA

Certainly one of the most serious threats to native peoples comes from the damming of rivers to generate hydroelectric power. From the Amazonian rainforests to the Canadian subarctic region, the insatiable demand for cheap energy has threatened to literally submerge the lands of tribal hunters and gatherers. One of the largest projects, and one which has generated fierce resistance among the Cree and Inuit Indians, is located in northern Quebec, on the shores of James Bay.

Here the Cree and Inuit are fighting Hydro-Quebec, a $50-billion utility that is wholly owned by the Quebec government. Robert Bourassa, the Quebec prime minister and original mastermind of the James Bay project, sees hydropower as the key to the province's economic and political independence from Canada. Northern Quebec, he wrote in a 1985 book, *Power from the North*, is a "vast hydroelectric project-in-the-bud, and every day millions of potential kilowatt hours flow downhill and out to the sea. What a waste!" (Bourassa 1985:4).

James Bay Phase I, which was constructed without an environmental impact assessment, has already flooded 4,425 square miles of land. The entire project includes 9 dams, 206 dikes, 5 major reservoirs, and a diversion of 4 rivers (LaDuke 1993:14). Now Hydro-Quebec wants to spend 12.6 billion Canadian dollars to tap hydropower on the Great Whale River, which flows into Hudson Bay. The entire James Bay project will generate, at peak output, some twenty-seven thousand megawatts of power, equivalent to about thirteen Niagara Falls.

The costs of the project would fall heavily both on the region's native people and on the delicate ecosystems that the natives depend upon for their economy and culture. The series of dams, water diversions, and hydroelectric projects planned for James Bay Phase II, would flood an area roughly twenty-seven hundred square miles in a subarctic region where ten thousand Cree and five thousand Inuit have hunted and trapped for thousands of years. Even now, over 40 percent of the Cree make their living off the land (Masty 1991:14).

One of the unforeseen results of the first phase of the James Bay project on the La Grande River was the contamination of the fish with mercury in the impounded areas. The massive flooding caused the death of plant material, which produced bacteria that transformed naturally occurring mercury in the soil and vegetation into toxic methylmercury. The mercury moved up the food chain to the fish and ultimately to the Cree, who depend on the fish for their diet. Two-thirds of the Cree in areas affected by the first phase of the project suffered from mercury exposure that exceeded World Health Organization standards (Gupta 1993:50). In classic blame-the-victim style, the Cree have been told to restrict their consumption of several species of fish throughout the La Grande River drainage.

The Cree and the Inuit living in northern Quebec were never consulted about the James Bay project. They learned about the project from news reports. By that time, planning was already well underway. The Cree had to act quickly if they were going to resist the damming of rivers that would flood the land where they hunted, fished, and trapped. While the Cree and their consultants were preparing their legal case against the project, others in the James Bay Committee were organizing a grassroots opposition movement which brought together hunting and fishing groups, various Indian organizations, and a host of environmental and conservation groups (McCutcheon 1991:52–53).

The Cree asked the superior court of Quebec to order a halt to further construction of the James Bay project because it would damage their lands and destroy their way of life. The superior court ordered a halt to all construction on the La Grande project, but the Quebec appeals court overturned the ban, arguing that construction was too far along to stop and that the needs of millions of the province's energy consumers outweighed the concerns of a few thousand natives. While the Cree and Inuit lost the battle to stop Phase I of the James Bay project, they acquired invaluable political experience, organizational skills, and a network of non-native American experts and advisers to help them wage the battle against Phase II.

A critical part of the campaign against Phase II was the opposition to Hydro-Quebec's marketing strategy to export electricity to the United States. The Cree and Inuit developed an extensive and sophisticated international network of support groups that targeted the electrical export contracts in Maine, Vermont, and New York. This network included the Sierra Club, the National Audubon Society, the Natural Resources Defense Council, Greenpeace, and Earth First! They have also established contact with the Kayapo Indians of Brazil, who have been fighting large hydroelectric projects in their territory (Turner 1991:55). In the spring of 1990, a delegation of the Cree and Inuit paddled down the Hudson River to New York City on their specially made *odeyak*—half canoe, half kayak. They stopped at numerous points along the way to bring their urgent message to a U.S. audience. Hydro-Quebec had sold this project to U.S. utilities as "cheap and clean." But, according to Whapmagoostui Chief Robbie Dick, "It's not cheap for us. When you turn on your switch, you're killing us" (cited in McCutcheon 1991:186). Through videos and other media events, like the fall 1991 "Ban the Dam Jam" rock concerts in New York City, the Cree and Inuit have brought international attention to their battle. Far from framing it as a Canadian issue, the Cree and Inuit have emphasized the crucial role that international energy contracts play in the destruction of their cultures and ecosytems. Seven U.S. utilities in New York and New England have entered into long-term contracts to purchase power from Hydro-Quebec. "Our aim," says Matthew Mukash, a Whapmagoostui council liason officer who holds a degree in political science, "is to kill contracts in the United States" (cited in Thurston 1991:58).

Grassroots opposition led to the cancellation of contracts in Maine and Vermont. In New York City, Jeffrey Wollock of the Solidarity Foundation helped found the James Bay Defense Coalition, comprising some twenty-four environmental and native rights organizations. The coalition's objective is to get the state to cancel the $19 billion New York Power Authority (NYPA) contracts. The NYPA is Hydro-Quebec's largest export customer. This may prove to be the Achilles heel of the entire project because Hydro-Quebec has borrowed heavily to finance construction.

In August 1991, after meeting with Matthew Coon-Come, grand chief of the Cree of Quebec, New York Governor Mario Cuomo announced that NYPA would postpone finalizing its contracts with Hydro-Quebec while the state reviewed the economic and environmental impacts of the contract. In March 1992, Governor Cuomo announced that New York state was cancelling a twenty-year contract to buy power from Hydro-Quebec. His energy advisers "calculated that signing the Quebec contracts would actually be slightly more expensive for New York consumers than relying on conservation and other energy sources" (Verhovek 1992:1). This turnaround was a confirmation of many of the economic arguments the Cree and their allies had been making for years. In challenging Hydro-Quebec's export contracts, the James Bay Defense Coalition exposed the erroneous economic assumptions of the project to public scrutiny.

While Governor Cuomo's announcement was a major victory for the native rights and environmental coalition opposed to James Bay II, this is not the end of the battle. Hydro-Quebec is determined that Phase II will proceed regardless of the financial uncertainties, and the Cree will continue to argue their case in the courts, environmental hearings, mass media, and international forums. They will also use direct action if necessary. In the spring of 1991, six hundred Cree blockaded a construction site on the La Grande River, stopping work for hours. In the spring of 1994, on the occasion of Hydro-Quebec's fiftieth anniversary, the Native Forest Network organized a series of demonstrations on three continents in solidarity with the Cree, Inuit, and other indigenous people who are threatened by the company's hydroelectric schemes in Quebec, India, China, and Guyana. Demonstrations occurred in several U.S. cities, in Australia, and in various cities across Europe (*The Ecologist* 1994:1).

Hydro-Quebec's response to the growing opposition has been to expand and re-arm its private security force. Quebec Crees, Greenpeace, and a number of environmental and religious organizations blasted the governmental corporation for this repressive move and cited a recently leaked Hydro-Quebec document which outlines a plan for "advanced investigatory powers" to protect the corporation's interests from opponents. The report singled out natives as a force to be reckoned with and a group capable of using violence in the pursuit of its goals (La Duke 1993:14). Cree representative Romeo Saganash called the proposal "a threat to the development and the preservation of the right of the Cree to voice their positions in the province of Quebec" (cited in La Duke 1993:14).

On November 18, 1994, Quebec Premier Jacques Parizeau announced that James Bay II was being shelved indefinitely. "We're not saying never but that project is on ice for quite a while" (*Associated Press* 1994). Whatever the outcome, the Cree and the Inuit have demonstrated that native people are capable of blending the assertion of treaty rights to their land and resources with the most innovative and militant forms of environmental activism to challenge the most powerful institutions of a large nation-state.

BLOCKADING THE LOGGERS: NATIVE RESISTANCE
TO DEFORESTATION IN MALAYSIA

There are about 250 million native peoples worldwide, many of whom live within or on the margins of tropical rainforests in Southeast Asia, Central and South America, and central Africa (Burger 1990:18). They depend upon the forests for their food, medicines, clothes, and building materials. However, the extensive and accelerating exploitation of the rainforests for timber, minerals, oil, hydroelectric energy, cattle ranching, and plantation agriculture makes them "the most seriously threatened habitat of indigenous peoples" (Burger 1987:45).

At present, Malaysia is the country where deforestation is most rapid. The highest rate of commercial deforestation in the world, encompassing some 2,100 acres per day, occurs in the Malaysian state of Sarawak, in the northwest part of the island of Borneo. Over the past quarter century, some 30 percent of Sarawak's unique tropical forests have been logged (Chartier 1987:65). The rainforests of Sarawak are also home to 220,000 tribal peoples collectively known as Dayak. They include the Iban, Kayan, Kelabit, Kenyah, Kejaman, Punan Bah, Tanjong, Sekapan, Lahanan, and Penan peoples. The fiercest resistance to logging on native lands has come from the Penan, one of the few remaining nomadic hunting and gathering rainforest tribes in the world.

In 1983, Malaysia accounted for 58 percent of the total world export of tropical logs. Eighty percent of the timber is sold to Japan where it ends up as throwaway packing crates and disposable construction forms for pouring concrete. The remaining 20 percent goes to Europe, the United States, Singapore, and Korea (RAN 1989:29). By 1985, Sarawak accounted for 40 percent of Malaysia's total log production. The government of Sarawak routinely grants logging licenses to timber companies without any notice to the native peoples who have lived on these lands for at least fifty thousand years. Under *adat*, or customary law, anyone who occupies or cultivates the land is entitled to its use. This customary right to land, as practiced by the natives, is recognized in the Sarawak Land Code (SAM 1988:65). Nonetheless, the timber companies have concessions to 60 percent of the forest area of Sarawak. Between 1968 and 1984 the area considered communal forest shrunk from 303 square kilometers to only 56 square kilometers (SAM 1998:69).

Forest concessions are routinely given in areas within traditional village boundaries. It is not unusual for the native people to wake up in the morning and see bulldozers and chainsaws leveling their farms, desecrating sacred ancestral burial grounds, and opening roads through their property. Top government officials hand out logging concessions to friends, relatives, and political allies. The granting of logging concessions has become "a means of creating a class of instant millionaires, and nearly every member of the state assembly has become one" (Davis 1993:26). Little wonder that when native communities apply to the government for communal forest reserves to protect the land around their settlements they are routinely denied, while the same forest is opened up to the timber companies. James Wong, Sarawak's minister for the environment and tourism, is also the owner of one of Malaysia's most prosperous logging companies, Limbang Trading, which controls over 300,000 hectares of timber concessions in Sarawak. Robin Hanbury-Tenison, the president of Survival International, once asked Wong whether he was concerned about the likely climatic effects of deforestation. Wong replied, "We get too much rain in Sarawak. It stops me from playing golf" (Hanbury-Tenison 1990:29).

To extract the great mahogany trees and the other valuable woods, bulldozers tear up entire forests, washing vast amounts of earth and topsoil into the river system. The most pervasive effects of logging in hilly terrain is "the reduced water-holding capacity of the land and increased erosion from rain. Many plant and animal species, at all levels of the food web are affected or destroyed as a result" (Hanbury-Tenison 1990:67–68). Thousands of natives are being forced off the land and into the towns where they face slum housing, malnutrition, unemployment, alcoholism, and prostitution.

In February 1987, the Penan, whose way of life is entirely dependent on the forest, appealed to the state government:

Stop destroying the forest or we will be forced to protect it. The forest is our livelihood. We lived here before any of you outsiders came. We made our sago meat and ate fruit of the trees. Our way of life was not easy, but we lived it in contentment. Now the logging companies turn rivers into muddy streams and the jungle into devastation. The fish cannot survive in

dirty rivers and wild animals will not live in devastated forests.
. . . If you decide not to heed our request, we will protect our
livelihood. We are a peace-loving people, but when our very
lives are in danger, we will fight back. This is our message.
(Chartier 1987:65)

When the authorities ignored their appeals, the Penan decided
to erect barricades across logging roads. The barricades consisted of
logs and the bodies of hundreds of men, women, and children standing across the logging roads, blocking the timber lorries from getting
through. The Penan were soon joined by other Dayak tribes and
members of environmental groups. The blockades began in March
1987 and involved several thousand native people from over thirty
communities in the Baram and Limbang districts where the logging
was heaviest. The timber industry was paralyzed for several months
because the timber lorries couldn't move.

As long as the blockades were in effect the government was
losing potential timber revenues. The Dayaks were soon faced with
whole platoons of heavily armed, paramilitary police who forced
them at gunpoint to dismantle their blockades. In November 1987,
forty-two Penan and Kayan blockaders were arrested. The
Malaysian government also invoked its emergency Internal Security Act to close down three national newspapers, ban public rallies,
and arrest 103 citizens, including prominent environmentalists,
lawyers, and tribal rights activists (RAN 1988:5). Among those
detained was Harrison Ngau, a Kayan who works with Sahabat
Alam Malaysia (SAM, or Friends of the Earth, Malaysia). SAM had
been in the forefront of organizations appealing to the federal and
state governments of Malaysia and Sarawak to protect the lands,
forests, and resources of the Dayaks.

The arrests provoked worldwide protests to the International
Commission of Jurists in Geneva, Switzerland. In January 1988, the
government released all but 33 of the 145 activists jailed in the
November sweep. After the arrest of the blockaders, however, the
government passed a law which prohibits the setting up of blockades on logging roads. Violation of the law carries a two-year jail
term and a fine of six thousand dollars. In February 1988, 71 of the
arrested Penan met and decided that the new law was unjust
because it denied their legally recognized customary land rights.
"We are the owners preventing outsiders from coming onto our

property," they said. "We are not doing something wrong on other people's property" (RAN 1989:30).

In the meantime, the logging companies were working twenty-four hours a day with the help of floodlights. This renewed assault resulted in a series of blockades and new arrests, bringing the total arrested since 1987 to three hundred. Using a network of environmental and human rights groups, SAM organized an international campaign to draw world attention to the April 1989 trial of the forty-two Penan and Kayan blockaders. In North America, the Rainforest Action Network organized extensive showings of the video *Into Darkest Borneo*. News updates on the Penan struggle were also made available on the EcoNet computer network.

Survival International and the International Union for the Conservation of Nature and Natural Resources intervened to pressure the Sarawak government to recognize and uphold the Dayak people's rights to their lands and to withdraw the licenses of the logging companies working on native property. Because most of Sarawak's timber exports go to Japan, demonstrations were organized at Japanese embassies around the world during World Rainforest Week in October 1988. In April 1989, SAM hosted the World Rainforest Movement Meeting in Penang, Malaysia. More than a dozen organizations were in attendance, from Indonesia, the Philippines, Thailand, India, Japan, Australia, Canada, Great Britain, and the United States. Participants drafted an emergency call to action for the forests, their people, and life on earth. Included in this declaration was a call to ban all imports of tropical timber and wood products from natural forests (WRM 1989:78). With all the international publicity focused on the Sarawak government's treatment of the Dayak blockaders, the prosecution decided to withdraw all the charges against the forty-two Penans and Kayans arrested in October 1987.

Despite the legislation against obstructing the flow of traffic on logging roads, the blockades went up again in May 1988 and continued through the fall of 1989. By the end of the fall, four thousand Dayaks had shut down logging in nearly half of Sarawak (Davis 1993:30). After each wave of arrests the government would escalate the repressive force used to dismantle the blockades. In September 1993 a combined force of three hundred people, including soldiers, police, forestry officials, and employees of the Samling Timber Company, arrived at the Penan Long Mobui blockade in forty-five vehicles, including cars, tractors, lorries, and bulldozers. According to a Penan eyewitness,

> All our huts were torn down with chainsaws and burned. Our rice fields were bulldozed, and five tear-gas bombs were thrown in the midst of men, women, children and elderly people. When we were disabled by the tear gas, the police and soldiers went on to destroy our barricade which we had been guarding for nine months. The police had shields and helmets and they hit us without pity. Some of us bled and fell unconscious. One very sick six-year-old child, who had just come back from the hospital in town, died soon afterwards." (*Earth First!* 1993:1, 25)

The next day Malaysian police and air force came back in search of the protest leaders. They set fire to the huts where they believed the leaders were hiding.

While the Malaysian government seeks to improve its international image by providing Malaysian timber to help rebuild the historic Globe Theater in London, the Penan are desperately trying to get the international community to recognize the connection between the tropical timber trade and genocide. The situation of the Penan remains of paramount concern to a variety of international human rights and environmental organizations, but much more pressure must be applied against the Malaysian government and against Malaysian consulates and embassies around the world. The blockades continue.

BIG OIL INVADES THE ECUADORIAN AMAZON RAINFOREST

The Amazon region of northeast Ecuador, known as the "Oriente," consists of over 13 million hectares of tropical rainforest lying at the headwaters of the Amazon River network. The region contains some of the most biologically diverse rainforests on earth as well as a considerable number of endangered species. According to tropical ecologist Norman Myers, the area "is surely the richest biotic zone on Earth," and "deserves to rank as a kind of global epicentre of biodiversity" (Myers1988). The area is also home to some 350,000 to 500,000 people, including eight groups of native people, as well as recent colonists from Ecuador's coastal and highland regions (Kimerling 1991:31). The native peoples include the Shuar,

Achuara, Quichua, Cofan, Siona, Huaorani, and Secoya. Since the late 1960s, they have had to defend their lands and communities against oil drilling, road construction, and the invasion of colonists who pour into the jungle along oil company roads. In 1967, the *New York Times* reported that "a vast helicopter operation, believed to be second only to that in Vietnam, is rushing oil-drilling rigs and supplies into the rugged northern region of Ecuador" (cited in NACLA 1975:29). This massive invasion was led by the Texaco-Gulf consortium, with the help of a 1.4 million hectare concession from Ecuador's military junta (1963–66). In 1972, Ecuador enacted legislation which created a state oil corporation, now called "Petroecuador," and replaced the concession system with "association contracts" between its state company and foreign oil companies. The government then became a profit-sharing partner in oil production rather than being paid in royalties (NACLA 1975:35). Oil production now accounts for 70 percent of Ecuador's exports, and oil revenues finance the nation's massive $12.4 billion foreign debt obligations (Parlow 1991:36). Neither the Ecuadorian government nor the oil companies recognize the rights of native peoples who have lived in the rainforest for thousands of years. "In some cases," reports Survival International, "oil wells have been placed actually within lands which have been already properly titled to Indian communities—making conflict inevitable" (1987:1).

As the oil companies continue to build roads into the jungle, they are accompanied by army escorts. Both Arco and Unocal have been using armed Ecuadorian military to defend their sites from native peoples protesting the invasion of their homelands (RAN 1991:4).

In 1983, the government gave the Huaorani title to a 67,000-hectare reserve and the right to hunt in another 250,000-hectare forest reserve known as Yasuni National Park. The park is one of the most valuable natural reserves in the world and was declared a "world biospheric reserve" by the United Nations Educational, Scientific, and Cultural Organization. Despite repeated promises to protect Huaorani land rights, the government has failed to demarcate Huaorani lands or to prevent oil exploration in the park. Indeed, Survival International, which has been campaigning for Huaorani land rights since 1982, has charged that "some so-called conservation zones were created deliberately to keep areas clear of settlers so that oil extraction can take place unhindered" (1987:1).

In the fall of 1990, the Ecuadorian government opened up the last refuge of the Huaorani to oil development. Conoco Ecuador, a subsidiary of the U.S.-based Dupont Corporation, is most interested in blocks sixteen and twenty-two, which cover 900,000 acres of rainforest. Much of this falls within the boundaries of Yasuni National Park. Conoco was the corporation that financed the government's preliminary management plan for the park. Not surprisingly, the plan allows more than half of the area to be available for industrial use. There are no provisions for recognition of Huaorani land rights.

The controversy over the Yasuni National Park has become the focal point for an international battle involving Conoco, the Ecuadorian government, the Confederation of Indian Nations of the Ecuadorian Amazon (CONFENIAE), and North American environmental and human rights groups, including the Natural Resources Defense Council (NRDC), Cultural Survival, the Rainforest Action Network, Friends of the Earth, and the Sierra Club Legal Defense Fund. The latter group filed a complaint on behalf of the Ecuadorian Indian Federation to the Inter-American Commission on Human Rights, arguing that drilling on native lands constitutes a human rights violation (Parlow 1991:33).

On 11 October 1991, Conoco announced it was pulling out of oil development in the Yasuni National Park. That same day the Maxus Energy Corporation, an independent oil company from Dallas, Texas, announced it was taking over the Conoco project. The Rainforest Action Network, in conjunction with an international coalition of native, environmental, and human rights organizations, responded with a campaign targeting Maxus, ARCO, Occidental, and other U.S.-based oil companies operating in the Oriente. At the same time, one of the most well organized Indian movements in the hemisphere has put increasing pressure on the Ecuadorian government to recognize native land rights.

In April 1992, fifteen hundred natives from Ecuador's Amazon rainforest walked 140 miles to Quito, the country's capital. There they negotiated with the government for titles to about 13,000 square miles of ancestral lands. "The urgency we have is that the Amazon Indian peoples (in Ecuador) have already lost almost the majority of our traditional territory," said Leonardo Viteri, coordinator of the Organization of Indigenous Peoples of Pastaza (Steller 1992). The Indians received title to their lands, but the government retained mineral rights to the lands and shows no sign of slowing down the oil rush. "The Indians must understand that Ecuador lives off oil," said Diego Bonifaz, who was President Rodrigo Borja's chief negotiator with the Indians (Associated Press 1992).

While the Ecuadorian government and the oil companies would like the Indians to believe that oil exploitation is the only possible path to development, this view is emphatically rejected by (CONFENIAE): "we the indigenous peoples say that development which destroys our rivers, our land and our lives is not real development" (Pandam 1994:x). Over the past twenty years, the international oil industry, led by Texaco together with Ecuador's national oil company, has placed some 330 wells and pumping stations in the jungle and extracted 1.5 billion barrels of Amazon crude from the Oriente. More than 12 million acres of forest have been consumed in this process.

In 1991 Judith Kimerling of the Natural Resources Defense Council brought the issue of oil company complicity in the destruction of the rainforest to public view with the publication of *Amazon Crude.* Among the environmental costs she documented: 16.8 million gallons of oil spilled from the Trans-Ecuadorian Pipeline alone; more than 4.3 million gallons of toxic wastes (including 3,000 gallons of crude oil per day into waste pits) spilled or discharged every day into the environment without treatment, contaminating countless streams and rivers; and 2.35 million cubic feet of gas burned without any emission control whatsoever (1991:31). Jacob Scherr, a senior attorney with the Natural Resources Defense Council called the Ecuadorian Amazon basin "an environmental free-fire zone" (Ellison 1992). In June 1992, Texaco withdrew from Ecuador and turned over its operation to the Ecuadorian government.

In October 1993, five native groups from the Oriente filed a billion-dollar lawsuit against Texaco, alleging damage to the rainforest from the company's oil operations. "Texaco's oil drilling in the Ecaudorian Amazon has created a catastrophe worse than the Exxon Valdez," said Joseph Kohn, a Philadelphia lawyer representing the tribes. "Texaco has essentially ruined what once was one of the most pristine forests in the world, with calamitous results for the inhabitants of the region" (Mokhiber 1993:15).

The lawsuit says that the environmental damage caused by Texaco has brought with it a public health crisis. In April 1993 the Center for Economic and Social Rights (CESR), a New York–based health and human rights group, sent a team of doctors, scientists, and lawyers from Harvard University to the Oriente. They found that sections of the rainforest are now so contaminated that Indians and colonists living there are exposed to high risks of cancers and neurological and reproductive problems. Water studies found that "drinking water, bathing and fishing water, and produced water (untreated toxic wastes) samples contained levels of toxic oil constituents many times greater than" the safety guidelines set by the United States Environmental Protection Agency (1994:16, 20).

David Dickson, a Texaco spokesperson from the company's White Plains, New York, office, called the allegations in the complaint "outrageous and categorically untrue." He said that the company "consistently operated under sound industry practices and complied with all Ecuadorean laws" (Maull 1993). But Cristobal Bonifaz, a lead attorney for the native groups, charges that rather than pump unmarketable crude oil back into the wells, as is customary in the United States, Texaco dumped millions of gallons of crude oil into man-made lagoons in the region, causing massive contamination. "In an effort to gain greater profits, Texaco deliberately implemented drilling practices which had as their built-in waste disposal mechanism the constant dumping of crude oil into the environment," Bonifaz said (Mokhiber 1993:15).

RAN has launched a consumer boycott and is encouraging people to cut up their Texaco credit cards and send them to the oil giant's corporate headquarters in Westchester County, New York. In April 1994, RAN organized a three-day protest of Texaco's plunder and pillage in Ecuador and Burma. Demonstrators, including Ecuadorian and Burmese natives, marched from Wall Street to White Plains and then to the company's Harrison, New York, headquarters. More than two dozen police were called in from surrounding towns, and nine demonstrators were arrested as they chanted "Texaco Must Go" (Lipka 1994). Less than a week later, in an unprecedented decision, a U.S. district court judge in New York ruled that the native groups had a right to argue their case against Texaco in a U.S. court. Whatever the eventual outcome of the case, the native peoples of Ecuador have demonstrated that those who are directly affected by the operations of multinational corporations can no longer be excluded from corporate and governmental decision-making processes.

EXXON MINERALS/RIO ALGOM VS. W.A.T.E.R.
(WATERSHED ALLIANCE TO END ENVIRONMENTAL RACISM)

In 1975, Texas-based Exxon Minerals Company discovered one of North America's largest zinc-copper sulphide deposits adjacent to the Mole Lake Sokaogon Chippewa Reservation near Crandon, Wisconsin. Situated at the headwaters of the Wolf River in Forest County, the underground shaft mine would disrupt far beyond its surface area of 866 acres (about one-tenth of which is wetlands). Over its lifetime, the mine would generate an estimated 60 million tons of wastes—an amount equivalent to the twelve Great Pyramids of Egypt. When metallic sulphide wastes have contact with water or air, the potential result is sulphuric acids and high levels of poisonous heavy metals like mercury, lead, zinc, arsenic, copper, and cadmium. After a decade of facing strong local opposition, Exxon withdrew from the project in 1986 but returned in September 1993 to announce its intention to mine with a new partner—Canada-based Rio Algom—in their new Crandon Mining Company.

The planned mine lies on territory sold by the Chippewa Nation to the United States in 1842, and directly on a twelve-square-mile tract of land promised to the Mole Lake Sokaogon Chippewa in 1855. Treaties guaranteed Chippewa access to wild rice, fish, and some wild game on ceded lands. The Mole Lake Reservation (formed in 1934) is a prime harvester of wild rice in Wisconsin. The rice is an essential part of the Chippewa diet, an important cash crop, and a sacred part of the band's religious rituals (Vennum 1988; Gough 1980). Any contamination or drawdown of water would threaten the survival both of fish and of wild rice. The Chippewa were not reassured when Exxon's biologist mistook their wild rice for a "bunch of weeds." Exxon's own environmental-impact report blandly mentioned that "the means of subsistence on the reservation" may be "rendered less than effective" (Exxon 1983:316).

If Exxon could have limited the conflict over the mine to a contest between itself and the Sokaogon, the construction of the mine would be a foregone conclusion. Multinational mining companies have a long record of overwhelming native peoples whose resources they have sought to control. In each case, the corporation has sought to reduce its political and financial risks by limiting the arena of conflict so that the victims are completely exposed to the reach of the corporation but only one tentacle of the corporation's world-wide organization is exposed to the opposition (Nader 1982:9).

The nature of the proposed mine, however, posed a number of environmental and social threats that were of major concern to non-native residents, environmental groups, sports and fishing groups, and other native American tribes. The nearby Menominee, Potawatomi, and Stockbridge-Munsee nations would be severely affected by the mine pollution and the social upheaval brought by new outsiders. With Mole Lake, they formed the Nii Win Intertribal Council (Nii Win is Ojibwe for "four"). The Oneida nation also joined the tribal opposition. All five tribes are working in alliance with environmental and fishing groups within a campaign called "WATER." (Watershed Alliance to end Environmental Racism). The Wisconsin conflict over treaty spearfishing pitted Chippewas against some white fishermen from 1985 until the anti–native American protests ended in 1992 (Whaley and Bresette, 1993). Now the mining conflict finds native Americans and some non-native American fishing groups on the same side, opposing an outside threat to the same resources. Trout Unlimited's Wolf River chapter says that "the mine as proposed would be a threat to the Wolf River as a trout stream" (1994).

Even before Exxon/Rio Algom filed its notice of intent to seek mining permits for the Crandon/Mole Lake mine, the WATER campaign announced a statewide emergency rally to stop the proposed mine at the state capitol in Madison. In March 1994, over four hundred people from all around the state rallied at the state capitol and listened as Frances Van Zile, an *Anishinabekwe* (Chippewa woman) spoke about the role of women as the "keepers of the water" in her culture:

> This isn't an Indian issue, nor is it a white issue. It's everybody's issue. Everybody has to take care of that water. The women are the ones who are the keepers of that water. I ask all women to stand up and support that and realize that if it wasn't for the water none of us would be here today because when we first started out in life, we were born in that water in our mother's womb. And I'll bet you everybody here turned on that water today to do something with it. And that's what they're going to pollute. That's what they're going to destroy. I'm not going to have any more wild rice if that water drops down three feet from the mine dewatering. That is important

to my way of life—to all Anishinabes' way of life. And they're taking that away—they're going to destroy our way of life.

Following the rally at the state capitol, demonstrators marched to the headquarters of the Wisconsin Department of Natural Resources and to the Wisconsin Manufacturers and Commerce Association. The latter is one of the chief lobbying organizations for the mining companies as well as for the mining equipment manufacturing industry in Milwaukee. By its physical presence, the WATER campaign intended to put corporate and governmental decision makers on notice that the resistance to this mine project could reach into the centers of corporate and governmental power.

Sokaogon Chippewa tribal members Fred Ackley and Frances Van Zile dramatically illustrated this determination to confront corporate decision makers when they attended Exxon's annual shareholder meeting in Dallas, Texas, the following month. With the assistance of the Sinsinawa Dominican Sisters of Wisconsin and six other religious congregations who own Exxon stock, the Sokaogon Chippewa were able to challenge Exxon on its own home turf. The Chippewa and the religious congregations specifically asked Exxon to provide a report to stockholders on the impact of the proposed mine on indigenous peoples and on any sacred sites within indigenous communities. The resolution also called upon Exxon to disclose "the nature of and reason(s) for any public opposition to our Company's mining operations wherever this may occur" (Exxon 1994:16). The resolution received 6 percent of the vote, or 49 million shares. Most shareholder resolutions of this type receive less than 3 percent of the vote. While the resolution was defeated, the Sokaogon Chippewa won enough votes to reintroduce the resolution at next year's meeting.

In all of these activities, the Sokaogon Chippewa are developing a multifaceted counterstrategy to Exxon's ecologically and culturally destructive mine plans. Through intertribal organization, alliance building with environmental and fishing groups, mass demonstrations, shareholder resolutions, and mass media publicity, the Sokaogon hope to increase the political and financial risks of the project for Exxon and Rio Algom. This was the reason why the Sokaogon and Nii Win Intertribal Council invited the Indigenous Environmental Network (IEN) to hold their fifth annual Protecting Mother Earth Conference on the Mole Lake Reservation in June 1994.

Previous IEN conferences brought together community-based indigenous activists from throughout North America, Mexico, Central and South America, and the Pacific Islands to work together, share information, and support each other in struggles to protect indigenous lands from contamination and exploitation. The network's previous efforts have helped grassroots activists defeat a five thousand-acre landfill on the Rosebud Reservation in South Dakota, and a proposed incinerator and an asbestos landfill on Diné (Navajo) land (Selcraig 1994:47). "This is to put Exxon and (Wisconsin) Governor Tommy Thompson on notice that we can bring people up here to stop the mine," said Bill Koenen, an IEN National Council member and a Mole Lake band member (Maller 1994). On the last day of the conference, over three hundred native and nonnative people tresspassed onto the Exxon mine site and conducted a spiritual ceremony. Exxon called the Crandon police, but no arrests were made. The police were reluctant to interrupt the ceremony. Later that day, a citizens' review commission representing a cross section of Wisconsin civic leaders heard testimony from native people who came from Alaska, Colombia, Ontario, and New Mexico to provide evidence about the impact of Exxon and Rio Algom's activities on native cultures and the environment. The panel, chaired by Wisconsin Secretary of State Douglas LaFollette, will compile a report that will be disseminated to the media, governments, and the public.

The Exxon/Rio Algom permit review process will take up to three years before any decision can be made. In the meantime, the Sokaogon and their allies will use every opportunity to strengthen this international alliance and win new allies by exposing the corporate and environmental track records of Exxon and Rio Algom.

CONCLUSION

The previous case studies of native resistance to the new resource wars have several common themes. First, native peoples are increasingly facing threats to their very survival as they try to preserve traditional land ownership and usage patterns against the onslaught of the industrialized world's insatiable demand for resources. Second, as native groups defend their land and cultures they invariably draw upon their own spiritual traditions which emphasize their sacred duty to protect the environment for future generations. As the Sokaogon Chippewa case illustrates, this spiritual dimension of resistance frequently means that women play a very prominent role in resistance movements.

Third, these native traditions are frequently blended with an increasingly sophisticated use of legal, lobbying, international networking, mass media, shareholder campaigns, and direct action tactics in conjunction with environmental, church, conservation, and human rights organizations to slow down, mitigate, or block destructive resource-extractive projects. Fourth, native people and their allies have achieved some impressive, if not decisive, victories in many cases. They have successfully targeted electricity export contracts in the James Bay struggle, brought an unprecedented lawsuit against Texaco for reckless environmental practices in the Ecuadorian Amazon, and forced Exxon's withdrawal from the mine-permit process in the mid-1980s. Fifth, none of these victories has been decisive. Exxon withdrew from the Crandon/Mole Lake project in the mid 1980s only to return with a new partner in the 1990s. Sixth, temporary victories are frequently met with increasing levels of violence and repression by multinational corporations and development-oriented governments determined to gain access to resources on native lands. Hydro-Quebec has beefed up its private security force and targeted the Cree for intensive surveillance. And the Malaysian security forces are now razing Penan villages to the ground to try to break the resistance of the logging blockaders.

Seventh, despite these setbacks, native peoples, in conjunction with a wide variety of nongovernmental organizations, have established an important principle of conduct in resource extractive projects, namely, that native groups have the right to participate in the decision-making processes that affect their lands and culture. The most recent draft of the United Nations Universal Declaration of the Rights of Indigenous Peoples makes explicit provision for this right (1989). As native peoples and their allies continue to develop their organizational and resistance capabilities in the coming decade we can anticipate the focus of the debate to shift from *how* this or that project will be developed, to *who* will be involved in the decision-making process. From the perspective of the multinational corporations, this is indeed a radical challenge to their way of doing business in many parts of the world.

NOTES

1. This article is a revised, updated, and abridged version of chapters 1 and 3 in *The New Resource Wars: Native and Environmental Struggles against Multinational Corporations* (Boston: South End Press, 1993).

Chapter 6

VISITORS TO THE COMMONS: APPROACHING THAILAND'S "ENVIRONMENTAL" STRUGGLES FROM A WESTERN STARTING POINT

Larry Lohmann

THE WESTERN DISCOVERY OF THAI "ENVIRONMENTALISM"

Two decades ago, it was possible for people in the industrialized West to perceive environmentalism as a Western or Western-originated phenomenon. Those days are now over. Today, newspapers, books, and trade journals in North America and Europe are full of references—sometimes worried, more often laudatory—to all sorts of Southern "environmentalists": Brazilian defenders of the Amazon, Kenyan tree planters, Argentinian antinuclear activists, Filipino advocates of alternative agriculture, and Indian tree huggers and antidam demonstrators. Confrontations between Southern activists and the World Bank or transnational mining or manufacturing firms in courts, streets, and universities are meanwhile increasingly being reported in the Western press as "environmental disputes." Among many progressive groups in the West, the image of third world farmers, too, is gradually changing from one of pitifully passive, ignorant creatures in dire need of Western tutelage about resource management to one of people with detailed, nitty-gritty, everyday environmental awareness gleaned from lifetimes of struggle to ensure themselves and their descendants supplies of flowing water, forest products, and fertile soil.

Westerners' discovery of Thai "environmentalism" may well have played some small part in these changes of perception. In 1988, many environmental campaigners in industrialized countries were heartened by a stunning victory achieved by the residents of Kanchanaburi province in alliance with Bangkok intellectuals, conservationists, students, and newspapers in forcing the Thai government to cancel the Nam Choan hydroelectric dam, which would have flooded the heart of the largest contiguous area of intact forest in mainland Southeast Asia. In the following year, in the wake of nationwide protests against timber concessions, catastrophic logging-related flooding in the south of the country, and timber agreements with Burma, logging was banned nationwide. The first such national ban to be instituted in an Asian country, the new law immediately and dramatically reduced timber removals from the country's forests. Thai farmers' demonstrations against the spread of commercial eucalyptus plantations beginning in the late 1980s have proved more difficult to understand for those outside observers to whom all tree planting sounds like a good thing, but have also attracted interest from Northern environmentalists who share a concern over ecologically dangerous monocultures.

The new awareness in the West of "environmental" action and thinking in Thailand and other Southern countries is in many ways a useful antidote to the common Western picture of the South as self-destructive and irrational, inhabited largely by mindlessly proliferating "slash and burn" agriculturalists and tinpot dictators, lacking brains, knowledge, initiative, and creativity, and in general too poor and downtrodden to be concerned about the environment. This awareness also helps reassure Western environmentalists, many of whom have only slowly begun to increase their contacts with third world colleagues, that they have many allies abroad. It may even be helping, in some cases, to reinforce the message that most of the people who are striving to preserve land, air, forests, and water live in the south and not in the overproducing, overconsuming industrialized societies.

But before toasts are proposed to a new era of global green consciousness and action, it would perhaps be prudent to back up for a moment and ask *why* Westerners are suddenly noticing, and celebrating as "environmental," various social movements in the south. Such movements, after all, have been around for a long time. In Thailand, for example, what would today be called "environmental" conflicts—which typically have pitted ordinary villagers against central authorities over rights to, and degradation of, forests, land, and water—date back to well before the Thai words for "environment" and "environmentalist" (sìngwâêtláwm and náksìngwâêtláwm, terms which appear to be literal translations from the English) entered common usage. Contemporary battles over the centralization of control of forests under the Royal Forest Department and its concessionaires are continuations of a conflict which began nearly a century ago; depletion of coastal fisheries has been an issue between small fisherpeople and trawler operators for decades; and strife over rural water pollution from mills and commercial plantations existed long before "nature" and "ecology" became all the rage.

It is true, of course, that such battles may be sharper and more visible to outsiders today than they were in the past. In a context in which the "escape hatch" once provided to ordinary people by the forest frontier has disappeared, growing trends toward centralization of control of land and water under the state and the world market—through dams and diversion projects, commercial trawling, forest zoning plans, the expansion of industrial parks, and so on—are provoking increasingly open conflicts between central authorities and local people over the issue of the ownership of farmland, forests, rivers, and fisheries. Yet the essential characteristics of the struggles have not changed radically.

Many of the country's more recent political conflicts, too, while they may look from outside to reflect an abrupt flowering of Thai "enviromental consciousness," are generally seen by the participants as involving more longstanding concerns. When, in April 1973, military officers were discovered to be using government equipment to hunt rare animals in an untouched forest near the Burmese border, for example, the issue was seized upon by activists not only because it was an outrage against "nature" but also because it was a symptom of the broader abuses of the dictatorship of the era; in this guise, the incident helped fuel the resentment that resulted in the student-led democratic overthrow of the government in October 1973. When the student movement later forced the government to withdraw mining concessions in southern Thailand which had been illegally given to the Union-Carbide-dominated Thailand

Exploration and Mining Company, the issue was seen within the country largely as one of nationalism and anti-imperialism, and not simply "environmentalism." Similarly, an incident in July 1986, in which a mob of local residents burned down a nearly completed factory in Phuket set up to process tin-mining residues into tantalum, was not, as it has sometimes been portrayed, an instance of North American–style "ecotage," but rather stemmed from public fears of loss of tourism income due to pollution, as well as complex rivalries between different corporate and political groups (Hirsch and Lohmann 1989). And the current struggle over commercial *Eucalyptus camaldulensis* plantations, like the agrarian struggles of the 1970s in which the word *environment* was never mentioned, is essentially a conflict over land rights. What farmers object to about the plantations is not simply the biological properties and effects of the Australian tree, nor even the fact that its proliferation in Thailand is partly to secure fiber supplies for heavy Japanese consumption of pulp and paper, although both of these are certainly issues, but rather that the expansion of eucalyptus plantations usurps farmland, pastures, and community forests they consider to be theirs and on which they rely for a livelihood (Lohmann 1991b; 1993a).

The lack of radical novelty in the Thai movements which now commonly go under the name *environmentalist* suggests that the surging interest which Westerners display in "Thai environmentalism" may say as much about the current state of the debate in the West—and the West's attempts to represent, assimilate, and subvert other societies—as about Thailand. To Northern governments and corporations, Thai and other third world "environmental" movements are of growing interest because they reveal potential threats to resource access or investments and suggest opportunities for export of new "green" products and services. To some Western environmental lobbyists, Thai "environmental" movements are another constituency to "represent." To UN agencies, they offer an excuse for expanding funding and staff for environmental programs. To some Western academics, information about Thai and other third world "environmentalism" is, among other things, valuable intellectual raw material for shaping into essays or debating points which will impress teachers or colleagues in new environmental studies departments in universities. To some Western greens, discovering "environmentalism" in Thailand and elsewhere in the South is important because it seems to demonstrate the "universality" of ecological politics or helps to deflect the criticism that environmentalism is middle class. To more self-consciously political Westerners, "Thai environmentalism" may be an appealing idea because it suggests new paths toward international movement cooperation on social issues generally.

This is not to say that Thai villagers and middle-class activists have not also played an active part in the discovery of Thai "environmentalism" by the West. Indeed, they have been only too willing to emphasize or construct environmental aspects of their movements—for both domestic and foreign audiences—on occasions when this has proved politically advantageous. In the struggle against logging concessions and eucalyptus plantations it has not been uncommon to see farmers' organizations concerned with ensuring access to local forests, appropriating environmentalist language even in their names (for example, *chomrom anurák thammacháât* [nature conservation club]). Thai social movements have also occasionally liaised, when this bears fruit, with urban-based conservation organizations—some of them Northern—although they are constantly wary lest foreign liaisons discredit them with a nationalistic Thai public.

Academic ecological science, while it has never motivated, dominated, or determined the direction of a social movement to defend forests or rivers in Thailand, also often plays an important subordinate role, as a counter to the usually questionable claims of government or corporate experts. In the recent campaign over the World Bank–supported Pak Mun hydroelectric dam in Ubon Ratchatanee province, for example, local villagers' concerns about the dam's effect on local fishery livelihoods were buttressed by the testimony of internationally respected independent experts on the fauna of the Mekong River system, who helped demolish the Bank's amateurish reassurances about the dam's likely effects on the little-studied but immense biodiversity of the system. (Woodruff et al., 1993).

Over the past five years, too, nearly all Thailand's voluntary organizations committed to rural development and human rights have come to present environmental work as one of their main concerns. To some extent this is due to a genuine change in the nature of that work. The pace of corporate and state takeover of land and river valleys for projects ranging from irrigation dams to tourist resorts, as well as the rising toll of pollution from power plants, commercial salt mining, sugar and pulp mills, and other industrial installations, has driven these organizations to focus more and more on campaigns to get the state to recognize local rights to water and land and less and less on (for example) the promotion of rice banks or credit groups. However, in another, more fundamental sense, these voluntary organizations are doing what they have always done. They are not taking up the standard of a new environmentalist philosophy which has burst upon a startled Thailand from the West, but rather are continuing to try to support rural peoples in their battles against oppression and exploitation.

WESTERN DICHOTOMIES

Whatever motivates Western discussions of Thai "environmentalism," and whatever they are used for, they are inevitably couched in language which owes a good deal to Western concepts and Western experience. This is only natural. All interpretations must begin somewhere, and people brought up in highly industrialized societies, including the writer of this chapter and most of its readers, can only start, like everyone else, with the frameworks and models which they know and which have proved useful in familiar contexts. As philosopher Hilary Putnam inquires wryly in another context, "We should use somebody *else's* conceptual scheme?" (cf. Taylor 1985).

To Western industrialists and environmentalists alike, a number of dichotomies seem almost inevitable in any description of environmental action. These include the following. Society is dominated either by the *state* or by the *market*. Land management, to avoid anarchy, must be either *public* or *private*. Attitudes toward nature are either *anthropocentric* or *ecocentric*. Actions tend to be inspired either by *religious and moral* or by *self-interested* motives. Policies can favor either *jobs* or *environment*, and environmental action can be either *pragmatic* or *radical*. Countries are either *overpopulated* or *underpopulated*. Environmental action is based on putting ecological *theory* (which may include religion, objectives, techniques, or science) into *practice* through first laying out a plan or set of laws and then implementing them. This action can be either *legal* or *illegal*, *militant* or *nonmilitant*.

Not all Western environmentalists, of course, take all of these dichotomies for granted. But most will unreflectively assume the validity of at least a few of them. Thus it is not uncommon for North American environmentalists to presume without thinking that their counterparts in Thailand must be faced with the job of "reconciling livelihood and environment," or to suppose that the task for environmentalists in a country without strong central authority like Laos is one of helping the government and the private sector establish firmer control over how land, forests, and water are used. Other American environmentalists may find it natural to assume that (say) the divisions in India's Chipko movement are parallel to the anthropocentric/ecocentric distinction familiar in Western industrialized societies, or that the major religions originating in India express moral sentiments which are "shared by the philosophy now called 'deep ecology'" (Taylor et al. 1992). The presupposition, in short, is likely to be that the societies, cultures, and individuals of less industrialized nations, as well as their environmental movements, are in many important respects similar to their counterparts in the West.

There is nothing inherently wrong with this assumption. Indeed, as mentioned above, as a first move in dialogue with members of other societies it may be unavoidable. The application to Southern countries of the dichotomies that I have mentioned, however, can provoke resistance among those whom they are supposed to describe (MacIntyre 1988:385). This has proved to be the case in Thailand as well as elsewhere in the south. Western activists who lecture their Thai counterparts on the need to take a "scientific" or a "market" approach to environmental problems, for example, or to "apply Buddhism" to them, or to "take overpopulation seriously," or to "stop being so confrontational with the state," or to act as Westerners' lieutenants in initiatives to change international institutions, may find themselves quietly dismissed by many of their Thai counterparts as contemptuous, ignorant, or politically naïve. Cooperation between the two sides may suffer as a result.

Western environmentalists who are interested in understanding and building solidarity with Thai social movements, by contrast, will learn to recognize and take seriously Thai hesitations about, or objections to, being described by the dichotomies I have mentioned. They will not treat these dichotomies as universal, and will thus not automatically assume that Thai "environmentalism" must be (for example) either anthropocentric or ecocentric, or either militant or non-militant. Nor will they insist that resistance to the use of these dichotomies must be due to disagreements over semantics, stubbornness, or inability to see the light. Rather, they will devote time to learning where and when to drop or modify these dichotomies. In the process they may be able to find out how to cooperate with their Thai counterparts in a more practically effective way.

In what follows, I will consider briefly why Thai activists might find certain of the Western dichotomies I have mentioned to be of limited use to them, and in what directions a more acceptable approach might lie.

DICHOTOMIES OF LIMITED RELEVANCE

Some Western dichotomies used to describe Thai "environmentalism" are based on assumptions which, while not necessarily false, seem to me nevertheless to be less than crucial to many Thai movements, to impose systems of thought which many Thai activists might find unfruitful, or to imply criteria of success and failure which many Thai analysts may not share.

The distinction between legal and illegal action, for example, is probably on the whole less important for movements in Thailand than for those in the United States or in European countries. This is due largely to the fact that, in Thailand, orally mediated customary norms involving personalized structures of authority and obligation often carry greater moral weight than written statutes. In some cases in which a community feels that its informally recognized rights to land or water have been ignored, it will take action regardless of the law, often in some confidence of a sympathetic public reaction. By the same token, it may strongly censor actions which are not formally illegal. Judges may meanwhile try to head off acrimonious litigation through avuncular efforts at informal compromise, and official study commissions may be appointed never to be heard from again. Many high officials and notables, for their part, regularly and openly flout the laws whether they are building tourist resorts in protected areas, polluting rivers, or dealing in drugs. Perhaps the best index of the significance (or lack of it) of the legal/illegal distinction in Thai "environmental" politics is the fact that approximately 11 million rural residents, or between 15 and 20 percent of the country's people, are officially classified as "illegal squatters" because they are living on land which has been gazetted as National Reserve Forest. While this legal fact is often dragged out as a pretext for threatening or evicting particular communities whose land is coveted by the plantation industry or the Royal Forest Department, no one has yet suggested putting the 11 million in jail.

The Western militant/non-militant distinction is also mis-leading when applied to contemporary Thailand. Since the beginning of the 1980s, no Thai movement which outsiders would call "environmental" has identified itself by means of a word which could be translated as "militant." This is not because such movements never display what Westerners would call "militant tactics." They do—often as a last-ditch and politically double-edged response to persistent trickery or brutal ploys on the part of the police, the army, or other bureaucracies. Indeed, Western observers misled by stereotypes of "Oriental passivity" are often dazed at the extent of openly defiant public action in Thailand in defense of land, as farmers rip out eucalyptus saplings in commercial plantations, lie down in front of bulldozers to prevent a village in a national park from being destroyed, or organize mass marches on Bangkok to protest eviction plans. But in a context in which flexibility, community feeling, and popular legitimacy are at a premium, such movements do not and cannot tie themselves to a strategic notion as rigid, abstract, and morally suspect as "militancy." During the country's current water shortage and the resulting opportunistic information blitz by the government about the supposed necessity for high-tech river management, even mere slogans such as "no more dams" can discredit the activists who adopt them because of their unreasonable militant ring in the ears of the Thai public.

The widespread Western presupposition that environmental action consists in first identifying on a theoretical basis "what has to be done" and then "getting others to understand and join in" has also, I think, proved an obstacle to Westerners' attempts to come to grips with Thai movements. Such an academic, top-down conception ignores the fact that much environmental knowledge and action, in Thailand as elsewhere, is locally specific, dependent on a constant, fluid interplay between theory and practice, and embedded in the democratically evolving practices of ordinary people. It also ignores the fact that no neutral conceptual framework or physical forum exists in which all sides can agree on "what has to be done." In disputes about Thai forests, for example, any particular conceptual or physical arena—"science," parliament, a subdistrict council meeting, the national Forestry Sector Master Plan, the Royal Forest Department, the main national forestry faculty, or a seminar arranged by environmental organizations—will favor some interest groups over others. Indeed, such arenas are typically chosen precisely so that certain groups can get an advantage over others. To insist that a discussion on forests be conducted exclusively in the terms of academic science, for example, tends to disadvantage and disempower ordinary villagers. This is not only because they may have difficulty arguing using its terminology, and because to appeal to science is to delegitimize local (often unwritten) knowledge, but also because dividing the world among forestry, limnology, agronomy, geology, demography, and so forth automatically encourages a centralized, bureaucratic approach at odds with local subsistence interests. In particular, it directs attention to a fuzzy picture of the aggregate production of discrete, countrywide sectors (forestry, agriculture, mining) instead of to a sharply focused picture of the highly localized, integrated forest conservation-irrigation -pasturage–rice farming–fruit growing systems to which many villagers are accustomed and in which distinctions between sectors are difficult to make (Lohmann forthcoming). By the same token, the frequently heard Western suggestion that social movements protesting dams or plantations have an obligation, before they take action, to propose "alternatives" which meet conditions Westerners consider important—such as satisfying national or international electricity or pulp demand—is misplaced when addressed to villagers and other activists in Thailand who do not recognize the validity or importance of those conditions.

The related notion that environmental action is to be evaluated according to how well it achieves some narrow, preset theoretical or technical goal also violates the sense of many Thai activists of what is important. The Nam Choan dam struggle is considered successful, for example, not only because it stopped a dam, but also because it helped build new political alliances and democratizing strategies among varied groups which have been crucial in other "environmental" battles since. Similarly, the simplistic claim frequently made by Western observers that the 1989 logging ban has failed because some illegal logging still takes place, or because Thai sawmills and furniture factories are now being fed with timber from Burma, ignores the way in which the ban has legitimated the political struggle which led up to it, provided a precedent for bans in other countries, and supplied local villagers with a court of appeal which it will be difficult for private firms or the government to undermine in the future.

So far, I have discussed dichotomies whose significance for Thai "environmental" activism is merely dubious. Other dichotomies—between state and market, public and private, jobs and environment, pragmatism and radicalism, and anthropocentrism and ecocentrism—are based on assumptions which, in Thailand, seem quite straightforwardly false. To ask Thai activists Are you pragmatic or radical? anthropocentric or ecocentric? in favor of free enterprise or in favor of government intervention? is thus often to put them in the position of the defendant in the hoary joke who is asked by the prosecuting attorney, And when did you stop beating your wife? Instead of answering the question, defendant and activists are each likely to want to challenge the premises which underlie it. It is with this last sort of dichotomy that I will be mainly concerned in the rest of this chapter.

RESISTING THE STATE-MARKET AND PUBLIC-PRIVATE DICHOTOMIES

Western and Japanese aid agencies, when they come to Thailand, typically presuppose that the main actors who will be able to implement solutions to the country's environmental problems are the government and the private sector (Lohmann 1991a; cf. Ferguson 1990). Thus a Forestry Master Plan for Thailand financed by FINNIDA, the Finnish bilateral aid agency, suggests that deforestation can be checked only by dividing forests into essentially two categories: those which are managed for commercial production, and those which are off limits to human interference. Although the plan recognizes some rights of rural communities to use forests for subsistence goods, the communities are envisaged essentially as temporary lieutenants of commercial interests, first to be "organized and instructed" by government and corporate representatives, then to be gradually moved to the cities as they are assimilated into the market system and lose their land to commercial interests (Jaakko Pöyry Oy 1993). Similarly, the proposed Global Environmental Facility program for conserving the Thung Yai Naresuan Wildlife Sanctuary near the Burmese border (the site of the defeated Nam Choan dam) assumes almost automatically that, if the sanctuary is to be protected, thousands of residents belonging to the Karen ethnic group must be evicted from it in order to ensure that it comes under the total control of government forest rangers (MIDAS et al. 1993). In the same vein, Caroline Sargent, a forester with the British-based International Institute for Environment and Development, laments in a recent book that the 1989 logging ban brought about a state of affairs in which there were "no longer loggers to defend the forests and prevent encroachment on forest land which was held under concession—and thus the natural forest continues to diminish" (Sargent and Bass 1992:20). This focus on, and faith in, the resource management of the public and private sectors is not confined to members of the international environmental establishment. Even unofficial environmentalist visitors to Thailand often make a beeline for bureaucracies or policy think tanks such as the National Environment Board, Thai Development Research Institute, or Royal Forestry Department on the assumption that, even given the failures of such institutions in the past, that is where the action is and where the new, more successful plans which will save the country's environment will originate.

Many Thai villagers and activists find such assumptions questionable. They point out that while in many Western countries it may be the case that stewardship of land, water, and forests rests overwhelmingly either with governments or with individual private owners and companies integrated into a monetized and centralized modern market system, this is not the case in much of Thailand. Here, a third type of authority, that of the village community exercising its own type of stewardship over common land, forests, and water, is also important; and it is the undermining of this authority by state or market that typically results in disorder and degradation (*The Ecologist* 1993).

One example of such commons regimes is the mǔang fǎai rice irrigation/forest conservation system used in most regions of northern Thailand (Chatchawan and Lohmann, 1991). In this system the local community builds (and periodically adjusts and rebuilds) a small reservoir and canal system to conduct water from a hill forest through rice fields in the valley below. Both the forest and the canal system are preserved and maintained as a unit by the community as a way of ensuring a minimum rice crop for everyone each year, through a complex system of organization of labor and time which relies on constant face-to-face discussion, homegrown materials, and local enforcement and mutual adjustments. Such commons can be found throughout Thailand, ranging from various kinds of community forests, which provide free vegetables, fruit, game, fodder, bamboo, and firewood as well as burial grounds, to communal pastures used for grazing cows and buffaloes; to coastal fisheries (Pinkaew and Rajesh 1992; Sanitsuda 1990).

Such commons regimes cannot be run from afar by the state since their maintenance requires highly flexible, democratic responses to local circumstances and needs and is finely dependent on local knowledge, materials, personalities, and senses of responsibility (Apffel Marglin and Marglin 1990; Apffel Marglin and Marglin 1994). Nor can they be run by a private corporation, since they are oriented toward community subsistence and cooperation rather than the profit maximization of individuals considered apart from the community. Here it is instructive to look at the answer which a Karen villager in a remote part of Chiang Mai recently gave to a foreign consultant who put a hypothetical choice to him about how to manage a local pine forest—used by the villagers for many years mainly for subsistence—for commercial gain. Two of the choices the consultant suggested were, first, for individual families to be assigned rights to separate forest plots, and second, for government officials to oversee the management of the forest as a whole. The villager rejected the consultant's entire approach. First, he objected to the manner in which the choice was put to him. If such matters were to be considered, he said, they could only be considered as a community, not through approaches to people like him as individuals. Second, he said, putting the forest in the hands of discrete individuals would destroy community cooperation and thus the forest itself. Putting the forest in the hands of government officials would lead to power imbalances, corruption, and again the destruction of the forest. The way to preserve the forest, the villager maintained, was to leave it defined by the local people's customary relationship to it.

Indeed, commons regimes such as müăng făăi, as Thai activists and villagers point out, have generally proved to be more effective in Thailand in protecting what Westerners call the "environment" than either the state or the private sector. The Royal Forest and Irrigation Departments, for example, prodded by foreign agencies, timber firms, and the export economy, have presided over nearly a century of inefficient water use and degradation of forests and land—degradation which accelerated precipitously after 1960 as state control was extended over more and more of the countryside. *Pace* Caroline Sargent, timber concessionaires never "defended the forests and prevented encroachment." Few, if any, ever observed regulations calling for rotational cutting or prevention of clearance. (In Indonesia, similarly, a study by a Jakarta-based environmental organization found that no more than 22 of 578 timber concessionaires followed state forestry rules [Durning 1994].) State promotion of commercial agriculture for export, meanwhile, has resulted in the clearance of tens of thousands of square kilometers of forests for upland crops such as corn, cassava, and pineapple in the space of a few decades. Even the state's policy of demarcating protected areas, in effect since the 1960s, has often resulted in degradation, when villagers are evicted from protected areas to which they are well-adapted and forced to pursue more ecologically destructive careers elsewhere. Mǔǎng fǎǎi, on the other hand—to take only one example of commons regime—has resulted in the preservation of forests in most areas of northern Thailand, as well as a consistently frugal and sustainable use of available water, for upwards of seven hundred years. Small wonder, then, that it strikes many activists and researchers who are acquainted with the facts on the ground as ludicrous that power over forests and land is so seldom entrusted to village communities and is instead turned over to the government and its concessionaires, often following the advice of international agencies, as being the "only shows in town."

Much of what might be labeled by outsiders as "environmentalist" resistance, too, has been led not by government officials nor by urban-based intellectuals, but by commoners with firsthand experience of what is happening to their land and commons. When, for example, in the 1970s and 1980s, farmers began to block logging roads and march on local government offices in protest against timber concessions which the Royal Forest Department had given out to local companies, their objective was not to save rare bird species nor halt global warming nor gain commercial profit from the forests themselves, but rather to safeguard part of the commons they relied on for water, vegetables, mushrooms, medicine, firewood, and game. The attempt of Ubon Ratchatanee villagers to stop the Pak Mun dam, similarly, was rooted partly in fears, later proved justified, that the project would result in a decline in household fish catches in the Mun River (Project for Ecological Recovery 1993). None of this is to suggest that the state has not taken positive steps to safeguard land, forests, and water. The logging ban is one example, and a recent decision to curb roadbuilding in protected areas another. But when such steps have been taken, they have invariably followed and not preceded popular action.

Resisting the Jobs-Environment and Pragmatism-Radicalism Dichotomies

It is not surprising that Thai villagers and activists find the jobs-enviroment and pragmatism-radicalism dichotomies which seem common sense to many Northern environmentalists to be often inappropriate or incomprehensible when applied to Thailand. They point out that to a majority of Thais, secure livelihood depends not, as it does to a majority in North America or Europe, on the availability of permanent paid employment in the industrial, service, or state sectors, but rather on the sustained availability of local land, water, and forests to rural communities. In Thailand, the commercial forces which are damaging the "environment" are thus also destroying, in a sense, "jobs." For every temporary construction job created by dam construction, for example, several farming and fishing livelihoods may be permanently lost. Similarly, even if northeastern farmers wanted jobs on the plantations which threaten to replace their farms, they would not be able to find nearly enough of them year-round to make up for the subsistence losses plantations entail (Lohmann 1991b). For rural Thais, then, there is not necessarily anything "pragmatic" about acquiescing in a development project which advertises itself as "creating" a handful of jobs. Rather, such projects are likely to appear, as they often in fact are, dangerously idealistic, radical, and utopian, uninformed by history and by the facts on the ground and, for local people, no substitute for the solid guarantee of secure land and water. In Thailand, in short, pragmatism and what an outsider would call "environmentalism" very often coincide. The struggle for livelihood very often *is* a struggle for the "environment."

One leader of a Muslim fishing community in south Thailand was recently entertaining some environmentalist visitors who were curious about why the villagers, after years of providing labor for a local charcoal factory which was cutting the coastal mangrove forests, decided to try to halt the logging and establish community forest zones off limits to the factory. The community leader explained that, since the mangroves served as nursery grounds for fish, the logging had resulted in declining catches by the village's fisherpeople, and that the villagers had finally decided that this had to be stopped. After a few years of efforts at limiting the charcoal factory's depredations, catches were again rising, and the community's future looked more secure. "I'm not interested in wildlife conservation," the village leader concluded, "but the sea is my rice bowl [*mau khââw*]."

RESISTING THE ANTHROPOCENTRIC-ECOCENTRIC DICHOTOMY

Rural people in Thailand, including those who have been most prominent in fighting to preserve the "environment," have typically looked at forests, streams, and wild animals largely in the light of their connection to agriculture, fishing, hunting, and gathering. Although wilderness, like community forests, has been a source of certain spiritual values (Tambiah, 1984), to some extent rural people have even shared the traditional attitude of Thai elites that the wilderness is a menace until it is, by being cleared, brought within the sphere of a polity dominated by the royal city or *muang* (Stott 1991).

Such attitudes can make visiting Western deep ecologists slightly uneasy. While they applaud Thai villagers' activism in defense of local forests and streams and are intrigued by the Buddhist tradition of respect for the rights of animals and indeed all living things (Yenchai 1989), they cannot help but look down their noses a bit at what they see as an essentially "instrumental" attitude toward nature. Thai farmers, they feel, are regrettably "anthropocentric", and their preoccupation with agriculture and ambivalence toward "wild nature" suggest a lack of appreciation of the intrinsic value of plants and animals. Even if they agree with Guha (1989) that deep ecology "is of very little use in understanding the dynamics of environmental degradation," and of equally little use in explaining the real-life motivations of the most powerful local social movements aimed at halting that degradation, they still worry that Thai activists lack sufficient reverence for untouched nature and awareness of the importance of wilderness areas. This remains so even when they are reminded of the mixed practical record of the American model of wilderness preservation in Thailand.

Thai villagers and activists are unlikely to be completely unsympathetic to the deep ecologists' concerns. At the same time, however, it would be easy for them to point out that the attitude of (say) *mŭang fǎǎi* villagers toward forests, streams, rice, and animals, when more closely examined, is not comfortably categorized as either anthropocentric or ecocentric.

That attitude is highly practical. The villagers assuredly do not leave forests, streams, animals, or rice alone, nor contemplate them from afar in the manner of middle-class backpackers pondering the peaks of the Sierra Nevada, nor devote their energies to ensuring that they survive after the end of civilization. Instead, they alter and use them for the necessities of life.

It does not follow, however, that *mŭăng făăi* villagers treat forests, streams, animals, or rice as instruments. Nor does it follow from the fact that the villagers use and alter these things that they place humans at the center of the universe (cf. Collier 1994). Rather, forests, streams, animals, and rice are valued for themselves, treated as things which have intrinsic value and in some sense even as persons who can benefit humans but who if abused will also punish them. At annual meetings of the committees responsible for maintenance of *mŭăng făăi* systems, for example, farmers offer food to the spirits of the irrigation system and the forest and to the lords of the water and ask through an incantation that water be plentiful and the harvest good during the coming year, that the water users be happy and untroubled by disease, and that the *mŭăng făăi* repairs take place without injury to anyone. Taking care to inform the spirits of what they intend to do, the villagers simultaneously beg pardon for their actions, reflecting their submission to, respect for, and friendship with nature, rather than an attempt to master it. There is even a spirit of the rice. *Mŭăng făăi* farmers, in short, do not treat nature as a means to an end which is separated from nature, any more than Westerners, when they have a conversation with their friends to try to change their minds, treat those friends as a means to their own ends. *Mŭăng făăi* thus offers a counterexample to the presuppositions of many deep ecologists (which are also presuppositions of industrialists and neoclassical economists) that all practical reasoning and action must be instrumental, and that recognizing something's intrinsic value entails leaving it alone.

Insofar as they have avoided concrete experience of the specific human-environment and self-interest–community interest dichotomies which the West has created in recent centuries, Thai villagers cannot be expected to be much moved by deep ecologists' rather strained suggestions about how to paper over these constructed gaps with abstract "feelings of kinship with everything else in the universe" or an abstract view of "nonhuman life as intrinsically valuable." Indeed, bringing *mŭăng făăi* into juxtaposition with deep ecology helps show just how much the latter—despite its pretenses of being connected to all sorts of Eastern and native American thought—is in fact a historical artefact of the middle class in industrialized societies and remains addressed to the concerns of that group.

For deep ecologists to become more self-conscious about this historical boundedness could be a positive step toward political solidarity (cf. Lohmann 1993b; Haraway 1989; Sellars 1963). It could enable them to recognize that the ambivalence they may feel toward the type of activism they find in Thailand is largely a result of mistakenly reading the pattern of Western industrial agriculture—which *is* instrumentalist—into commons regimes such as *mŭăng făăi*. Once such regimes are seen more on their own terms, and the Western obsession with dividing attitudes into anthropocentric and ecocentric is left behind, some of this ambivalence could well vanish.

CONCLUSION

In trying to describe certain Thai social movements from a Western point of view, and mainly for Western readers, this chapter has, of necessity, started from a conceptual framework which Westerners are likely to share. But because one of its motivations is to foster intercultural dialogue between movements—to ask not only What are Thai environmental movements all about? but also According to whom?—it has also tried to make this Western framework itself into a subject for scrutiny and criticism and to suggest that it be located carefully within its own history and culture. This has not been done from a Thai point of view: nor has it been done using the words that Thai activists would use. Rather, it has been done from the point of view of a Westerner looking forward to seeing closer practical engagement between Western and Thai social activists.

Chapter 7

GRASSROOTS ENVIRONMENTAL RESISTANCE IN INDIA

Vikram K. Akula

INTRODUCTION

In northeast India, peasant and tribal groups have been engaged in a long battle for the creation of a separate nation: Jharkhand or forest land. The region, encompassing parts of four states, is rich in resources and provides much of the coal, iron, and steel that fuels India's industrialization. But for many rural communities this has meant deforestation, pollution, and the loss of lands. As a result, the livelihood of peasants and forest-dwelling tribals is in jeopardy.[1] Many men have become unskilled laborers, while women have resorted to prostitution (Omvedt 1993:137).

These groups, though, have put up increasingly militant resistance to the industrial juggernaut. In one of the most recent stand-offs, tribals launched an economic blockade, bombing roads and railway lines (Anonymous 1992a). The blockade lasted only a week, but the activists sent their message: they will not tolerate the continued degradation of the environment that has resulted from India's forced march toward industrialization.

It is a message that is heard increasingly across India as the country has intensified its drive toward industrialization over the last two decades, and has consequently encroached further on the forests, rivers, and fertile lands from which subsistence communities have traditionally drawn their livelihood. Whether peasant cultivators or forest-dwelling groups or small-scale fisher people, marginalized communities are banding together and rising up against threats to the environment. The type of resistance varies—from militant blockades such as those in Jharkhand to Gandhian style nonviolent civil disobedience—but the underlying goal is the same. They are challenging a conventional development apparatus that seeks to exploit natural resources with little concern for the environment and for the people who directly draw their subsistence from the environment.

These contemporary grassroots environmental struggles are not new. They are based in resistance to the incursions on the environment that accompanied British colonialism in the eighteenth century. What follows traces the emergence of those early resistance movements and then turns to a survey of contemporary grassroots activism.

ECOLOGICAL HISTORY OF INDIA

Prior to the arrival of European traders, India consisted of a diverse range of subsistence communities that were relatively autonomous—both politically and economically—from the various princely rulers of India. Although there was some long-distance trade and taxation, basic needs were generally met locally, giving rise to regional self-sufficient economies. Geographer Brian Murton explains, "This mosaic of small territories, based upon locally available knowledge of resources characteristics and locally available energy and material for resource management, is a classic example of the principles underlying traditional resource systems. . . . Most things needed by a population were produced locally and there was virtually no specialization of the production of any important subsistence products" (Murton 1980:75).

Since communities acquired their subsistence locally, they generally understood their dependence on local resources—rivers, forests, and fertile lands. Consequently, many communities evolved a wide range of social and cultural practices that regulated access to and insured sustainable use of natural resources. In many parts of India, for instance, local village councils regulated the use of grazing lands as well as the use of forests, from which people drew fuel, fodder, and medicinal herbs (Gadgil 1992:94). Communities also moderated or removed intercaste resource competition by diversifying resource use. That is, different castes would hunt different species or would hunt in different regions (Gadgil 1992:104).

Such environmentally beneficial practices were often codified in religion—in the folklore, proverbs, hymns, rituals, and myths of Hinduism and of tribal religions. Many communities, for instance, had religious taboos against hunting certain species. Also, sacred groves and ponds often protected watersheds. In *The Unquiet Woods*, Ramachandra Guha describes traditional practices of Himalayan peasants. He writes, "Through religion, folklore and tradition the village communities had drawn a protective ring around the forest. . . . Often hilltops were dedicated to local deities and the trees around the spot regarded with great respect. . . . In fact, the planting of a grove was regarded as 'a work of great religious merit'" (1989:29–31).

Guha and Madhav Gadgil (1992:90–91) argue that these practices emerged during the fourth and ninth centuries in response to a resource crunch precipitated by a decrease in rainfall, a reduction in soil fertility, and population growth. As a result, they contend, Hinduism changed from a religion centered around fire worship to a pantheistic religion in which individual plants and animals as well as elements of the landscape began to be seen as having intrinsic worth (Gadgil and Guha 1992:103). Indeed, the idea of intrinsic worth is embodied in one of the central tenets of Hinduism, *ahimsa* or nonviolence to all living things. Whatever the reason for the emergence of such biocentricism, it is clear that there was a moral code that guided peoples' relationships with the environment.

There were of course exceptions and varying degrees of biocentricism in different parts of India. In fact, in some regions, communities had practices that were harmful to the environment. But what is clear is that the traditional mode of resource use, guided as it was by a degree of biocentricism, was far less destructive than the industrial mode of resource use introduced by the British.

The British—coming first as traders and becoming rulers by the mid-eighteenth century—sought raw materials for the industrial revolution underway in Great Britain. Either directly or through local elites, they forced cultivation of commercial crops like opium, indigo, cotton, sugar, tea, and jute for export. As a result, local elites asserted greater control over relatively autonomous subsistence communities.

After the British became direct rulers in the mid-eighteenth century, the process gradually intensified. The British collected high taxes, enforced private property rights that overturned common property regimes, and took away control of all natural resources from local communities. The intensification of resource control was epitomized by the 1878 Forest Act. The act gave the colonial government a monopoly over forest produce, obliterating centuries of customary access and threatening the livelihood of peasants and tribals. The British clear-cut these forests to build ships for the British Navy and to build railway sleepers, causing far more ecological damage than did subsistence communities (Gadgil and Guha 1992:114–16, 135).

Similar transformations took place with other natural resources. Landlords, who had previously allowed peasants to grow subsistence crops on leased lands, for instance, now reclaimed those lands, forcing peasants to cultivate more "valuable" commercial crops. This increased ecologically harmful monocultures throughout India. The cumulative impact of such changes was that peasants lost control of land, forests, and rivers—undermining their ecologically informed subsistence practices and threatening their livelihood.

EARLY RESISTANCE

There was, of course, resistance to British rule. Protest movements targeted European planters, local landlords, moneylenders, tax collectors, the military, and the police. In the Bengal peasant revolt of 1859 to 1863, for instance, peasants attacked the private armies of European planters who had forced them to grow indigo instead of subsistence crops. Throughout the early 1800s, the planters had leased lands from local landlords, or *zamindars*, and employed small private armies to coerce the peasantry. But during the revolt, peasants fought back, using spears, bows and arrows, clubs, and bats. Later the movement became a no-rent campaign against both planters and *zamindars*. By the end of the revolt, rents were reduced and planters left the area. "The revolt of 1859–63 effectively destroyed the indigo plantation system in lower Bengal," explains David Hardiman (1992:12–16).

Often resistance movements converged with the independence struggle as in the case of Bihari peasant resistance against forced indigo cultivation in the late-nineteenth and early-twentieth centuries. In 1907 and 1908, indigo factories were boycotted and factory employees intimidated. The struggle attracted the support of political activists, and in 1917 Mahatma Gandhi, the leader of the independence movement, led the Champaran *satyagraha* (civil disobedience campaign) which ended the indigo system in Bihar (Hardiman 1992:18).[2]

Resistance to forest laws was especially intertwined with the independence struggle. Defiance of forest laws was part of the country-wide Quit India campaigns led by the Indian National Congress from 1920 to 1922 and 1930 to 1932. Gandhi's visits were sometimes seen by local people as opportunities to get the forest laws abolished (Gadgil and Guha 1992:162).

After achieving independence in 1947, India was faced with a choice between the two models of development. Gandhi envisioned a revival of the organic village communities of the precolonial and preindustrial past. He rejected industrialization, writing, "God forbid that India should ever take to industrialization after the manner of the west. The economic imperialism of a single tiny island kingdom (England) is today keeping the world in chains. If an entire nation of 300 million took to similar economic exploitation, it would strip the world bare like locusts" (1928:422).

The nationalist leader Jawaharlal Nehru, however, advanced a program for accelerated industrialization. "We are not going to spend the next hundred years in arriving gradually, step by step, at that stage of development which the developed countries have reached today. Our pace and tempo of progress has to be much faster," he said in a speech to leaders of other Asian countries (Nehru 1956).

Soon after independence, Gandhi was assassinated by a Hindu fanatic who opposed Gandhi's religious tolerance. With Gandhi's death, there was no one left who could forcefully articulate a vision of sustainable development, and India adopted the industrial path. Nehru became India's first prime minister, leading the country for nearly two decades. The government not only continued the natural resources policies of the British, but it also expanded resource-intensive industrial activity and undertook major development projects like large dams, mining, and energy-intensive agriculture. The demands of the commercial-industrial sector had replaced strategic imperial needs, but the result was the same: forests were felled, rivers dammed, lands appropriated for commercial crops, and the livelihood of peasant and tribal communities was still under threat.

Not everyone embraced the industrial path, but the new leaders of India—many of whom had been educated at Oxford and Cambridge in England—had imbibed the values and ideals of the West and believed that the industrial model of development was the only path to prosperity.

Moreover, the later generation of Indian leaders also had faith in this model. Consequently, the process of industrialization has intensified in the last two decades. The intensification, coupled with population growth, has made the plight of the poor even more intense. Rural women now have to travel longer distances to fetch water and gather branches for fuelwood. Herders have to roam farther so that their cattle or sheep can get fodder from withering grass and shrinking forests. Peasants have to struggle harder to eke out a living from lands devastated by soil erosion. Some communities have even been completely displaced from their traditional lands as a result of "development" projects. As environmentalist Vandana Shiva explains, "The resource demand of development has led to the narrowing of the natural resource base for the survival of the economically poor and powerless, either by direct transfer of resources away from basic needs or by destruction of the essential ecological process that ensures the renewability of life-supporting natural resources" (1991:19).

The 450 million poor of India, the majority of whom live in rural areas, simply cannot withstand the onslaught any longer. The increasing threat to their livelihood—and a problem with the morality of the violence toward nature that often accompanies industrialization—explains in part why ecological resistance is on the rise in India today.

The resistance is diverse, and battles are waged on many fronts, addressing everything from control of rivers to the environmental impact of mining. Often a movement simultaneously addresses several environmental concerns, and frequently groups of different castes or classes come together to protect a common resource. In addition, rural women often lead or play a prominent role in many movements. This is due to the fact that women often have primary responsibility for securing subsistence, and thus they tend to feel the affects of environmental degradation most acutely and immediately.

CHIPKO AND CONTEMPORARY FOREST MOVEMENTS

Among the most volatile natural resource conflicts are those over forests, which are still a major source of livelihood for the rural poor. The best-known forest movement is the Chipko movement in the Himalayas of Uttar Pradesh, an area with a long history of resistance to forest enclosures during colonial rule (Guha 1989).

In the 1960s, the region experienced massive deforestation due to rapid growth in forest industries and expanded industrialization. This, combined with the unusually heavy monsoon of 1970, caused a devastating flood. Many people and livestock died and water washed away six metal bridges. Villagers began to see connections between deforestation and flooding. Thus, in March 1973, when the government allotted ash trees to a sporting goods company that made tennis rackets, villagers—with assistance from a local Gandhian cooperative—organized against the loggers. Local people embraced trees that loggers were about to fell. Thus, the Chipko ("to hug") movement was born (Guha 1989:152–79).[3]

The government responded by establishing a Forest Corporation, but the felling persisted. People continued to protest, and the Chipko model of resistance soon spread to nearby districts. The movement had three major strands. There was Chandri Prasad Bhatt's "appropriate technology" group that organized the initial Chipko protest and that sought a less destructive use of the forest based on local sawmill cooperatives. The second, more biocentric, group represented by Sunderlal Bahaguna sought a total ban on green felling and the preservation of the forest for traditional subsistence use such as gathering of fuel and fodder (Guha 1989:182). The third faction was led by the Marxist-oriented Uttarkhand Sangharsh Vahini. It emphasized the need for economic redistribution (Omvedt 1993:133–34). Despite their ideological differences, however, all of the strands came together to oppose felling and all organized direct action—ranging from camping in the forests to surrounding timber auction halls.

The climax of the movement came in 1981 when Bahaguna, the leader of the biocentric stream of the movement, went on an indefinite hunger fast urging a total ban on green felling above one thousand meters. Thousands of people engaged in a series of mass Chipko protests, reading from religious scriptures and singing songs with lines such as the following:

What do the forests bear? Soil, water and pure air.
Soil, water and pure air sustain the earth and all she
bears. (quoted in Shiva 1988:76–77)

The sustained grassroots struggle drew the attention of the media,
and the prime minister at the time, Indira Gandhi, met with Bahaguna and ordered a fifteen-year ban on commercial green felling in
the Himalayan forests of Uttar Pradesh (Shiva 1991:108).[4]

Soon other forest movements in India adopted the Chipko
model. In the early 1980s, for instance, the Appiko movement
emerged in the Kalase forest of the south Indian state of Karnataka
(appiko means "to hug" in the local language). The Kalase forest is
part of the tropical forests of the western ghats, which extends along
several states of the western interior of south India. As in the
Himalaya, there is a long history of forest resistance in the region.
As early as 1831, peasants engaged in a satyagraha to protest the
British policy of reserving forests.

With independence, encroachment on the forests increased. In
1950, the Karnataka government declared the forest district "backward" and took control of forests to initiate "development." Three
major industries—a pulp and paper mill, a plywood factory, and a
chain of hydroelectric dams—were started. The forest industries
over exploited the forests, decimating 70 percent of the original forest area.

In addition, the forest department clear-cut natural mixed
forests to plant commercial species such as eucalyptus and teak.
These commercial species not only deprived villagers of fuel, fodder,
and manure, they also replaced the broadleaf trees which protected
the soil from the direct onslaught of rain. Without the broadleaf
trees, rich topsoil washed away, leaving less fertile laterite soil
(Hegde 1989:29–30).

Aside from deforestation, local people also had to contend with
dams that submerged huge tracts of forest and agricultural areas.
Appiko activist Pandurang Hegde writes, "The three major p's—
paper, plywood and power—which were intended for the development of the people, have resulted in a fourth p: poverty" (1989:29).

The first Appiko movement occurred in 1983 when sixteen
men, women, and children of the Salkani village hugged trees in the
forest, forcing woodcutters to leave. Community members went on
to keep a thirty-eight-day vigil in the forest until the government
withdrew the felling orders. Within months the movement spread

to adjoining districts (Shiva 1991:117). In a nearby forest, where trees were to be cut down by a match manufacturer, Appiko participants hugged trees and performed religious ceremonies. The protests forced the minister of forests to come to the area. He subsequently stopped the operation, and the state government has since banned felling of green trees in some of the forests of the region.

Like Chipko, the goal of Appiko was not merely to protest deforestation, but also to put forth an alternate model of development—embodied in the Appiko slogan, "Ugusu, Belesu, and Balasu," meaning "to save, to grow, and to use rationally." Activists thus coupled protests with activities to raise awareness about sustainable development. For instance, they conducted foot marches, slide shows, folk dances, and street plays in villages. Local people also engaged in reconstructive work such as reforesting denuded lands and promoting fuel-efficient hearths, which save fuelwood consumption by almost 40 percent (Hegde 1989:29–30).

A final example of a grassroots forest struggle comes from the district of Bastar in the state of Madhya Pradesh. The district is the third largest in India and the last major forest frontier in India's tribal heartland. Two-thirds of the population is tribal, and forests cover over half the area, constituting the largest expanse of moist deciduous forest in India. The high biodiversity of the forests yields a variety of minor forest products for the tribal population.

Unfortunately for the tribals, the district also has rich reserves of minerals as well as vast hydroelectric potential. And the government has initiated a number of development projects since the late 1950s, which account for a third of the district's total deforestation at the time. More than 125,000 hectares of forests were destroyed for mining projects alone.

During the late 1970s, the government made plans for a World Bank–financed tree plantation project designed to convert much of the remaining forest into pine trees for a pulp mill. The pine was to replace a biodiverse forest that had fifteen native tree species, including the sal tree which is central to tribal economic and cultural life. Tribals see the sal as playing a vital role in making the land fertile because sal "catches the clouds." The tribals also place their rain god, Bhimul, under the sal tree (Bagchi 1991). Thus, the pine plantation not only threatened their source of livelihood, but transgressed their religious mores (Anderson and Huber 1988).

First, the tribals demonstrated and wrote petitions. When that failed, they became more militant, prohibiting foresters from cutting trees. In one incident in 1982, three hundred tribals—armed with traditional bows and arrows—stopped foresters from taking ten truckloads of timber out of the forest (Anderson and Huber 1988:110–12).

Despite the protests, the government initiated a pilot project, replacing 3,100 hectares of rich sal forests with monocultures of pine. Seeing the need for more drastic action, the tribals burned the trees, and the prime minister at the time, Indira Gandhi, subsequently suspended the project in 1983 (Centre for Science and Environment [CSE] 1985:89). At first glance, burning trees may not seem like an environmental strategy, but the arson played a role in saving a diverse, natural forest from becoming a monoculture of pine trees.

RESISTANCE TO DAMS

Rivers are another natural resource over which there has been tremendous conflict. The government has vastly increased the number of dam projects as it seeks to expand energy for industrial development and water for irrigation. In fact, India's ambitious plans would harness virtually every major river in the country by the year 2000 (CSE 1985:101).

These projects certainly have benefits, but often the benefits go to the few. Industries receive a disproportionate amount of electricity, and wealthy farmers typically receive the bulk of irrigation. Meanwhile, the poor bear the costs—ranging from the drowning of forests and agricultural lands to the salinization or waterlogging of surrounding lands (CSE 1985:99–120). Moreover, India has a history of failing to resettle and rehabilitate displaced people. The government often does not give evictees adequate compensation, and they are frequently moved away from traditional lands—where their communities have existed for centuries—and resettled in less fertile areas.

The most notable resistance movement to a large dam project is the struggle against the Narmada Valley Development Program in Madhya Pradesh and Maharashtra. The $450 million Narmada project was planned in the 1970s. It encompasses 30 large, 135 medium-sized, and 3,000 small dams (Morse and Berger 1992). Overall, it is estimated that 120 million hectares will be submerged and 300,000 people displaced, mostly poor tribal villagers (Omvedt 1993:267).

Activists have pointed out that the evictees have not received adequate compensation or assistance. In addition, activists have drawn attention to the inequities in distribution and to the adverse environmental impact of the project. They note, for instance, that while 90 percent of lands to be submerged and the people to be relocated are in the states of Madhya Pradesh and Maharashtra, the irrigation water for 1.8 million hectares will go to Gujarat. Moreover, much of this irrigation water is to go to wealthy farmers while nearly 70 percent of Gujarat's drought-prone areas and 90 percent of tribal areas will receive no water (Postel 1992:55–56). Also, environmentalists contend that waterlogging and salinization in the newly irrigated area could render the Narmada scheme's benefits short-lived (Shah 1993). As Baba Amte writes in *Cry, the Beloved Narmada*, the project "will draw money away from various other schemes which could provide water to those areas [in need]. . . . The government has completely lost track of what must be regarded as its basic objective: finding the best possible way of providing water to the people" (Amte 1989).

Protests in the 1980s and early 1990s—consisting of civil disobedience and many hunger fasts, including one that lasted twenty-two days—drew international attention and led to the first outside review commissioned by the World Bank. The commission, issuing its report in June 1992, confirmed many of the suspected problems. The authors reported that the project had never been properly assessed, and they described serious weaknesses in the resettlement plans and environmental protection measures. Bradford Morse, chairperson of the commission, said, "It seems clear that engineering and economic imperatives have driven the project to the exclusion of human and environmental concerns" (D'Monte 1993).

After the report was issued, the World Bank strengthened its environmental and rehabilitation standards. In March 1993, however, the Indian government—reluctant to meet those environmental and human rights standards—refused the final $170 million of the World Bank loan and is now proceeding with its own funds (D'Monte 1993; Sharma 1994).

Thus far the movement seems only to have delayed the project. But at least it has ensured that future large dam projects undergo greater scrutiny of their environmental and social impact. Many activists see this as a first step in their goal of having planners consider alternate means of providing water and electricity.

These activists hope that the country's water needs will be addressed through less damaging measures. One alternative, for instance, is developing groundwater, the water beneath the earth's surface that supplies wells and springs. Groundwater can be increased by planting trees, which retain moisture. Thus, environmentalists argue, reforestation programs are a more environmentally sound way of increasing the water supply in the long run, subsequently reducing the need for water from large dams.

In addition, environmentalists cite alternate models of water supply that build on the extensive system of storage tanks and minor irrigation schemes that existed in precolonial India. The networks effectively provided irrigation for centuries prior to colonialism, but were subsumed by more capital intensive forms of irrigation that came with mechanized agriculture.

There is an effort to revive the traditional irrigation systems. One widely touted example of such a micro-irrigation project is in Sukhomajri in Chandigarh. Three rain-fed reservoirs and several small earthen dams were constructed at the foothill of a highly eroded ravine. The water from one dam provided irrigation to eighty acres of village land, improving yields. In addition, grass yield on the hill rose from less than forty kilograms per year to more than two thousand kilograms, thus reducing pressure in grazing lands and allowing tree growth (CSE 1985:114). The Centre for Science and Environment reports that "wherever water resources have been harnessed through small reservoirs by constructing bunds or small dams, the lives and environment of the people in the area have been transformed without anyone having to pay the cost of development" (CSE 1985:112).

Environmentalists make a similar argument for electric power generation. Citing successful models in China, they argue that a considerable portion of the hydro-potential in fast-flowing hill streams, canals, and river slopes can be tapped through small dams and small hydroelectric schemes using self-contained turbine generators (CSE 1985:110).

Of course, these models are not perfect, and research is needed to assess their viability. The problem, though, has been that government planners have ignored such alternatives, giving all their attention to large dams. It is hoped that the resistance will force planners to consider alternatives.

THE BATTLE OVER THE SEAS

Another realm of water conflict is the coastal areas of India. There, small-scale fisherpeople battle commercial fishers who are threatening sustainable traditional fishing practices. Factory fishing fleets with mechanized trawlers have pushed into the coastal ranges of India's small-boat fishers. These modern fleets overtax near-shore fisheries, undermining local fishing traditions and destroying the coastal ecology and its long-term biological productivity.

Increasingly, however, fishing communities are organizing against such ecological destruction. The most notable movement is the Kerala fishworkers struggle, which involves 800,000 fishworkers and 120,000 households over the entire continental shelf of the southern state of Kerala.

The Kerala conflict began with a 1953 development project for the "transfer of technology" from Norway. Mechanized trawlers were imported with the goal of increasing fish catch and transforming a traditional artisan sector into a "modern" industry. The enormous increase in mechanized boats and indiscriminate fishing with trawlers during the spawning season destroyed young fish and damaged the aquatic ecosystem. Tom Kocherry and Thankappan Achary, organizers of the movement, explain, "The people of Kerala Province have been fishing the inshore waters for thousands of years. They have created fishing methods, craft and gear suited to their environment and to the variety of fish available at different locations. Their fishing nets have different mesh sizes to suit different species of fish; mechanized vessels, on the other hand, use a single net, which traps fish indiscriminately, including juveniles and fish eggs" (Kocherry and Achary 1989:30). As a result of these ecologically harmful fishing practices, Kerala marine fish production declined from 400,000 tons in 1973 to 268,000 tons in 1980 and 1981 (Omvedt 1993:135).

The local fisherpeople were not only affected by the decreased fish catch, they also felt that the sanctity of the sea was violated. "Kerala fishing communities had traditionally mythologized the sea as a goddess and had woven a whole set of ritual restrictions (especially regarding the chastity of women) around this notion," explains Gail Omvedt (1993:137). The mechanized trawlers were violating those ritual restrictions.

Fishworkers organized a network of cooperatives, welfare organizations, and trade unions to help cope with the commercial onslaught. Gradually, a struggle against the mechanized trawlers ensued. Local nuns and priests, members of Kerala's large indigenous Christian population, and other activists led mass rallies and direct action such as blocking road and rail traffic and sabotaging mechanized boats. Women, who were responsible for marketing fish, were especially active in the struggle. In the mid-1970s, the fishworkers organized the Kerala Swatantra Matsya Thozilali Federation and then helped form an all-India union, the National Fishworkers Federation, in 1978. The unions lobbied state and federal governments, and their efforts resulted in a law banning mechanized trawlers in the late 1970s.

RESISTANCE TO MINING

Mining, which has a devastating environmental and social impact, is another activity that has engendered resistance. For the rural poor, the major problem is the loss of agricultural and forest land—both directly and from conversion of land for transport and processing facilities. In addition, mining wastes pollute streams and toxic substances are carried by rainwater into nearby waterways, often making the water unfit for human use. Also, mineral treatment plants use enormous amounts of water for washing the ore— with untreated effluents, slimes, and tailings released into neighboring streams or lakes. Air pollution also results, from the wind sweeping mineral dust from waste heaps and from toxic fumes released during blasting (CSE 1985:22).

One of the worst affected regions is the tribal belt of central India. The region has eight super-thermal power stations, major steel plants, copper and aluminum complexes, and many cement, automobile, and other plants. Together, these industries have devastated land and forests.

In the Gandhamardan Hills of Orissa, youth and tribal groups are organizing resistance. The hills are considered sacred, providing a storehouse of invaluable plant diversity and water resources, and feeding twenty perennial streams and two waterfalls. The Bharat Aluminum Company (BALCO) came to the area in the mid 1980s in search of bauxite, but tribals engaged in direct-action campaigns such as blocking company vehicles. A series of battles followed, pitting tribals against local police, but in 1989 the tribal-led direct action forced BALCO to shut down its operation.

Another notable antimining movement occurred in the Doon Valley in the Himalayas, an area close to the site of the Chipko movement. The perennial water streams of the Doon Valley created fertile lands and secure livelihoods for inhabitants. Limestone quarrying, however, uprooted vegetation and topsoil, consequently destabilizing slopes and increasing dangers of landslides and flash floods downstream. Also, mine debris fell into river and canal beds, disrupting drinking and irrigation water supplies. Moreover, since the limestone belt is central to the flow of underground water which feeds streams, the entire ecosystem was threatened (CSE 1985:22).

In 1982, when the leases for the quarries came up for renewal, citizens' groups, including Chipko activists, lobbied the state government to prohibit mining. The government allowed mining to continue, but after a series of reports attesting to the environmental damage, the federal Supreme Court ordered the closing of fifty-three of the sixty mines in the area in 1985 (Tiwari 1986).

However, some mines continued operating, including the Nahi-Narkot mine. In 1986, activists launched a *satyagraha* campaign. For six months, protesters blockaded mining operations. Violence followed. In one incident in late 1986 two hundred men—presumably sent by mine owners and armed with sticks—attacked the *satyagraha* camp. Then, in early 1987, four truckloads of men—armed with revolvers, spears, knives, and iron rods—attacked another camp, wounding a number of people (Shiva 1991:301–2).

Despite the backlash, protests have continued into the 1990s. Unfortunately, the remaining mines are owned by the government or supply limestone to Tata Steel, a politically powerful company. Thus the struggle against them may not enjoy the success of earlier efforts.

THE JHARKHAND MOVEMENT

Perhaps the most intense form of ecological resistance in India is embodied in the Jharkhand movement, the separatist struggle with which this essay began. The movement has multiple goals, and the sustainable use of natural resources is one of them. The area of Jharkhand—encompassing parts of the four northeast states of Bihar, West Bengal, Orissa, and Madhya Pradesh—contains the country's richest coal and iron tracks and much of its steel industry. There are also several dam and plantation forestry projects. Sociologist Gail Omvedt writes, "More than almost anywhere in the country this industrialization was visibly a parasitical enclave, grabbing the land of the local population, and destroying much of the rest through deforestation and pollution, sucking the life of the native communities to turn their men into unskilled laborers and their women into prostitutes sent all over India" (1993:127).

Between 1972 and 1975, there emerged a united movement of mine workers, tribals, and low-caste peasants in the hill districts of south Bihar and adjoining districts. The alliance, formed under the banner of the Jharkhand Liberation Front, engaged in a number of protests. In 1974, for instance, the Front held "Jharkhand Day," a huge demonstration of workers and peasants. Participants viewed themselves as part of a left-wing movement as well as an environmental movement, and during the rally they carried red and green flags and shouted slogans of "Jharkhand-lalkhand" (the forest land shall become a red land). Aside from rallies, Jharkhand groups also engaged in more militant actions such as seizing land (Omvedt 1993:127–31).

But the coalition's solidarity broke down due to caste and regional differences and the defection of the leader of the movement, Shibu Soren, who was won over by Prime Minister Indira Gandhi and drawn into direct government-sponsored development programs (Omvedt 1993:127–31).

The tribals of Jharkhand, however, adopted a more militant stance. They protested against two large dams in the area during the late 1970s, both part of the Subarnarekha "multipurpose project." Tribals blockaded the Koel Karo in the Ranchi region, preventing trucks and construction machinery from reaching the site. Meanwhile, tribals in Singhbum, opposed to the Icha dam, engaged in 1978 and 1979 in near guerilla warfare in which at least twenty people died (Omvedt 1993:127–31).

Singhbum was also the area in which local people waged a militant struggle against the state Forest Corporation. In 1975, the Forest Corporation initiated a program of commercial teak forestry, at times replacing biologically diverse natural mixed forests. The mixed forests included sal trees which were important to tribal economic and ritual life. As one tribal member explained, "Sal is ours; teak belongs to the exploiters" (quoted in Omvedt 1993:130). Tribals, thus, destroyed teak nurseries and uprooted teak trees, leading to further violence (Omvedt 1993:129–30).

In the 1980s, compromises with the ruling Congress party led to the withering of this movement. But, as noted in the beginning of this essay, there has been a recent revival. The economic blockade of September 1992 lasted only a week, but it effectively shut down normal life in several parts of Bihar (Anonymous 1992b). Twenty four companies of paramilitary forces and ten battalions of national guards, in addition to local police, were required to quell the rebellion. Such resistance suggests the movement will not quickly fade away.

CONCLUSION: THE FUTURE OF THE MOVEMENTS

Just as the Jharkhand movement is sure to become stronger, so must similar movements if they are to survive the economic liberalization sweeping across India. In the last few years India has moved quickly toward a free-market economy, courting multinational corporations and embracing free-trade policies. The policies will probably be an improvement over the heavy-handed state control of industries that has characterized India, and the resulting economic competition may benefit many. But these polices are also sure to put further pressure on natural resources and to exacerbate the precarious position of the rural poor.

The extent and scope of resistance movements, however, is encouraging. Especially promising is the fact that communities are no longer acting in isolation but are increasingly forging alliances. One example of isolated struggles becoming powerful coalitions is seen in the defeat of the national forest bill of 1982. The bill would have continued the century-long process begun by the colonial state of taking over more and more forest land. This time, however, there was a national network that lobbied to defeat the bill (Omvedt 1993:140).

This is not to say that the grassroots environmental movement in India is unified. Like many other social movements, it has its share of internal rivalries and conflicting philosophies. Sometimes such divisions work against solidarity as they did with the Jharkhand movement in the late 1980s, but other times groups can set aside differences and forge coalitions, as in the Chipko movement. It remains to be seen whether the diverse elements of India's national environmental movement can transcend their differences—differences ranging from those of caste and class to those of diverse goals and conflicting ideologies.

What is clear, however, is that when these groups are unified, they are able to strengthen their movements by joining with international groups. The struggle against the Narmada dam project is among the best examples. A number of groups and many diverse communities found common cause in forming the Narmada Bachao Andolan (Save the Narmada movement). The movement in turn forged links with many other Indian and international organizations.

According to the World Bank official in charge of Narmada, the international links were crucial in forcing the Bank to drop funding for the project (Blinkhorn 1994). When local groups waged protests in India, they immediately faxed international organizations such as the Environmental Defense Fund in Washington, Survival International in London, and Friends of the Earth in Tokyo. These groups then pressured politicians in their respective countries to prohibit the Bank from funding Narmada (Blinkhorn 1994).[5]

It seems clear, then, that high levels of solidarity will be essential if the Indian environmental movement is to stand up to global capitalism. Without such solidarity the rural poor and the environment from which they draw their livelihood will remain in jeopardy. The networks that have been forged so far will have to have broader regional, national, and international bases. Such coalitions may not be successful in stopping the industrial juggernaut, but at least they will be able to put forth an alternate model of development—one rooted in the biocentric values and holistic philosophies of an earlier India.

This alternate model embodies Gandhi's vision of free India, and its philosophy is expressed well in Sunderlal Bahaguna's phrase from the Chipko movement, "Ecology is permanent economy." It may not be a model that is shared by all of India, particularly not by the urban middle class that follows in the footsteps of Jawaharlal Nehru. But for most of the rural poor—those who see and feel most directly the environmental and social impact of the industrial path—it is the model that offers the best hope for protecting the environment and for insuring a livelihood for themselves and their children.

NOTES

1. "Tribal" (also called "*adivasis*" or original people) refers to those ethnic groups that are generally outside of the major religious groups of India: Hindu, Muslim, and Christian. Tribals are distinct from these numerically dominant groups in terms of language, culture, and religion. They are engaged in a variety of subsistence activities from farming to hunting and gathering. The tribal population of India is estimated to be 60 to 80 million. In Jharkhand, tribals constitute 30 percent of the population.

2. The word *Satyagraha* means "hold fast to the Truth" and indicates a type of civil disobedience that strives to achieve what is morally right. It is a technique popularized by Gandhi and widely used during the independence struggle. See this volume's article by Rothenberg for a good description of Gandhi's philosophy of conflict.

3. Some trace the origins of Chipko to an incident in Rajasthan in 1763, when members of the Bishnoi sect laid down their lives to protect trees being felled under the orders of the king of Jodhpur. Ramachandra Guha, however, argues persuasively that there is no connection between the two struggles and that "the analogy with the incident involving the Bishnoi community obscures Chipko's origins, which are specific to the conditions of Uttarkhand" (Guha 1989:174).

4. While the Chipko movement was successful in stopping deforestation, a recent study by Haripriya Rangan (1993) suggests that the call for allowing only traditional subsistence activities has had harmful consequences for local communities. More than two thirds of the Garhwal hill region was designated as reserved forest, and Rangan reports that the federal government has held up a number of activities—ranging from building small irrigation channels to laying electricity lines—that potentially threaten part of this forestland. As a result, impoverished local communities have suffered, and many people are now demanding a separate state in order to regain local control. Rangan notes that the myth of an ecologically noble peasant is at the root of the flawed policy, and she cautions environmentalists not to let environmental measures submerge the interests of local communities.

5. Such international and domestic coalitions have had similar success in other environmental causes. Two notable examples are the Brazilian Rubber Tappers' struggle against deforestation in the Amazon (Schmink and Wood 1992) and the Filipino Lumad's fight against energy development of a mountain sacred to their people (Durning 1992:37–39).

Chapter 8

POPULAR ENVIRONMENTALISTS IN THE PHILIPPINES: PEOPLE'S CLAIMS TO NATURAL RESOURCES

Emma Porio and Bron Taylor

INTRODUCTION

Formerly a colony of the United States, the Philippines gained independence in 1946. It is composed of seven thousand islands and has a population of 62 million. The Philippines is a diverse country culturally, populated by many Christians, as well as by Muslims and a number of indigenous peoples. The Philippines has one of the fastest-growing populations (2.3 percent) in the developing world, nearly two-thirds of whom live in poverty, as defined by the National Economic and Development Authority, the government's planning agency. It is also a country with a rapidly deteriorating environment.

Three major forces have contributed to the environmental crisis gripping the Philippines: (1) the government's heavy reliance on environmental resources for export revenues, (2) its consequent encouragement of extractive industry, and (3) the majority of the country's population depend directly on the environment as their principal subsistence base.

THE POLITICAL CONTEXT

The People Power Revolution of 1986 that overthrew the martial law dictatorship of Fernando Marcos was a culmination of diverse forms of struggle, including street marches, underground publications, and noise barrages. Many people, especially those in the political and economic fringes of Philippine society, thought that dismantling the Marcos regime would bring positive changes to their impoverished lives. However, a constant struggle against poverty and malnutrition remains the grinding experience for nearly two-thirds of the Filipino people.

This chapter argues that the people's revolution strengthened marginalized people's claims to their environmental resources. Like other movements for democratization and decentralization, their methods of resisting the unjust structures preventing them from claiming resources take many different forms. Thus, acts of eco-sabotage are expressed in milder and more passive forms than those usually found in Western societies where the citizenry has easy access to the media, and where the eco-saboteurs are more motivated by the ecological survival of the planet rather than the survival of their families and children. When marginal, impoverished groups of people challenge the law, in social contexts where state and class power is very dominant, this in itself constitutes a radical move. Thus, a combination of internal forces (e.g., great inequities and the disparate strength of state/class power), and external forces (e.g., the trend toward democratization) fosters the development of popular ecological resistance which fundamentally challenges the existing political and economic institutions. This chapter presents the experiences of one coastal community and one upland forest community in their struggle to defend their environmental resources.

These movements are primarily comprised of ordinary people who have little formal education and have not read about the global environmental crisis. Nevertheless, they know deeply in their everyday experiences about the dwindling forest and coastal resources in their communities. The following cases chronicle environmental activism among two groups in the Philippines, upland forest resource users in San Fernando, Bukidnon and fisherfolks in Carigara Bay in the central Philippines. These cases represent increasingly common struggles for survival found throughout these islands.

CASE 1: POPULAR ENVIRONMENTAL RESISTANCE IN SAN FERNANDO, BUKIDNON

The San Fernando Valley is located in the southeastern part of Bukidnon in northern Mindanao, Philippines. The municipality of San Fernando, which comprises twenty-four *barangays* (communities), is mountainous with an elevation of 580 miles, and can only be reached by an unpaved road. The 1988 survey classified 76 percent of its area as forestland, 22 percent as agricultural land, and the rest as built-up or residential area.

The people of San Fernando, Bukidnon, in the southern Philippines are composed of natives (*lumad*) and migrants from the Visayas and Luzon provinces of the northern Philippines. It has a population of slightly over 35,000. Almost half (17,047) belong to the Roman Catholic church. In San Fernando, the Catholics constitute an active citizen's group. They started as members of the Gagamy'ng Kristohanong Katilingban, or Basic Christian Communities (BCCs), and later spearheaded the series of protests against loggers with other citizen's groups for the preservation of their forest resources.

Settled by agriculturalists from the north, the San Fernando Valley produces mostly rice, corn, legumes, and root crops. Thus, the families' subsistence relies heavily on their farming activities below the forests and the watershed of the valley.

Since the sixties, Mindanao—touted as the land of promise among Filipinos—has been the major source of natural resource products for export. In San Fernando, eighteen logging companies conducted operations in the 1980s, seven of which started in 1975. Armed with logging concessions which last an average of twenty-five years, the loggers are allowed to cut 1,589,949 cubic meters of timber, a figure since then reduced to 891, 430 cubic meters. These activities have systematically depleted the forest cover from about 70 percent in 1970 to about 25 percent in 1989. Thus flooding and siltation have become increasingly common in the valley, reducing its agricultural productivity.

In 1989, as a response to the environmental crisis engulfing their forest resources, the people in San Fernando began mobilizing their community to prevent further degradation of their environment. The following section is an account of their struggle to protect their forest resources from the destructive operation of big loggers.

THE HISTORY OF THE FIGHT AGAINST THE DAM CONSTRUCTION

The group began its environmental activism in 1982 when the National Power Corporation (NAPOCOR) announced plans to build a dam in the San Fernando Valley. Earmarked to be the major source of electric power for the whole of Mindanao, the dam construction meant flooding 90 percent of the municipality's land area and the displacement of over thirty thousand residents. To oppose this plan, residents organized the Pagbugtaw sa Kamatuoran (To be awakened to the truth or to witness the truth—PSK) with the help of missionary sisters. Through this organization, they sponsored public forums about the proposed dam and its consequences to the community's welfare. They also petitioned government offices to stop the dam construction. However, government authorities and military operatives harassed and threatened the PSK members with arrest and seizure orders. Members were also accused of being Communist subversives and maintaining alliances with the New People's Army of the Communist party of the Philippines. Despite these threats, they continued with their opposition activities until NAPOCOR finally decided not to construct the dam.

In 1987, consciousness had deepened about the close linkage between the environmental destruction caused by loggers and their own survival as a people. The Redemptorist Mission based in northern Mindanao at Iligan City played a critical role in bringing this issue to the fore. Invited to San Fernando to organize the BCCs, the missionaries concentrated on "providing basic Christian education, helping to set up structures around which the community becomes a worshipping, witnessing and serving community, and facilitating the rise and formation of leaders. Bible-sharing groups among clusters of neighboring families were set up. Sunday liturgical services became more creative and participative, and the people are challenged to respond to their economic needs, as well as to justice and development issues" (Gaspar 1990:53).

The emphasis on the "witnessing and serving" aspects of the liturgy propelled the BCCs to respond actively to the ecological seminars and discussions about community problems and issues. Foremost among these problems were the dwindling forest resources and their own role as stewards of God's resources. These ideas were also reinforced in the sermons delivered by the missionary priests.

COMMUNITY PROTEST ACTIONS AGAINST LOGGERS WITH PETITIONS AND HUMAN BARRICADES

In May 1987, the community started a series of demonstrations against the destruction of their forests. As happened in the protests against the dam, the residents of the San Fernando Valley wrote to the Department of Environment and Natural Resources (DENR) asking them to halt the operations of two logging companies, namely, C. C. Almendras (CCA) Enterprises, and El Labrador Company. They received no reply.

To signal their seriousness, the group mounted a human blockade to prevent the logging trucks of CCA Enterprises from transporting their logs from their concession in the Pantaron mountain range down to the town. On the morning of 20 June 1987, 30 PSK members halted the logging trucks on the main highway. Although the number constituted only a tiny fraction of PSK's 4,000 membership, it soon increased to an average of 150 people every day. For the next twelve days the blockaders took turns in keeping their vigil. However, on the twelveth day, Philippine constabulary (PC) troopers broke the human barricade by beating the people with rattan truncheons. As a result, men, women, and children suffered cuts and bruises. The PC troopers also arrested Father Kelly after he celebrated mass at the picket line. The people tried to protect him by surrounding him with locked arms. Failing in this, they accompanied him in the dump truck which carried him to the capital town of Malaybalay.

As a result of the mass actions, logging operations in the area temporarily slowed down. In October, however, CCA filed a lawsuit against the protesters and asked for compensation of P375,000 (roughly $15,000) each day or a total amount of P4,500,000 (roughly $180,000) for the delay of their operation brought about by the protest. Considering that most peasants do not earn more than P50 per day (around $1.75), this staggering amount put them in a quandary. Confronted with this new development, the PSK members, with the support of some NGOs, decided to directly contact the central office of DENR in Manila. In response, then Secretary Fulgencio Factoran sent his lawyer to Bukidnon to defend the protesters during the pretrial hearing in Malaybalay. Owing to this support, CCA decided to drop the charges on the condition that the protesters withdraw their claims of physical injuries and the destruction of their forests against the company. However, the protesters wanted the cancellation of the timber-logging agreement granted to CCA by DENR. Investigations were ordered by Secretary Factoran and on the basis of the findings, and CCA's timber license agreement was canceled (Esquillo 1992).

PSK membership has continued to grow. In order to accommodate a broader base of participation beyond the Catholic church, the group reorganized to become the Nagpakabanang Katawhan sa San Fernando (The concerned citizens of San Fernando—NKSSF). The formation of this broad-based organization came about because of the following factors. Environmental protection has gained wider recognition as one of the key apostolates of the parish. Moreover, the environmental consciousness and movement have moved beyond the confines of the original PSK members. For a while the members concentrated on keeping vigil on the logging activities in the area, but in early 1988, the group was again galvanized to action when the El Labrador Logging Company began operations in the upper San Fernando Valley. Again, the NKSSF petitioned the DENR office to stop the company's logging activities. The DENR formed a fact-finding team, but by November 1988, no action had been taken by the local DENR office. Tired of waiting for DENR's response, the NKSSF organized a picket before the Provincial Environmental and Natural Resource Office, asked for a meeting with Secretary Factoran, and demanded a halt of the logging in the San Fernando Valley. For ten days, the group also formed a human barricade in the main highway from Malaybalay to Cagayan de Oro, thus preventing the transport of logs by El Labrador Company. As a result of these mass actions, the company's TLA was suspended and later canceled by DENR. Later, when Secretary Factoran came to Bukidnon and had an audience with the protesters, he canceled *all* logging activities in the San Fernando Valley. He also directed an investigation of logging abuses in the province and encouraged the NKSSF group to continue protecting their forest resources.

COMMUNITY PROTEST THROUGH HUNGER STRIKE

The NKSSF organized several "watch" groups to monitor the felling of trees and other resources in their forests. Protecting the resources, however, was not achieved by the deputation of the people as guardians of the forests by the DENR secretary because several threats emerged to threaten NKSSF's efforts. First, the NKSSF did not have the authority to impound illegally cut logs. Second, the local DENR's support to the community watch groups was very weak. When NKSSF reported illegal logging activities, the local DENR office was very slow to respond, if they did at all. Thus, logging activities continued and the matter was further complicated by the participation of some small-scale loggers from the community. This created problems of policing and regulation, for a local market for the timber had emerged, making it a quick source of income for some members of the community who happened to be closely known to the watch groups. Policing them became harder because it caused conflicts and strained relationships.

As the problem of logging and environmental degradation continued to escalate, some NKSSF members intensified their search for solutions. They decided to band together, travel to Manila on 23 September 1989, and stage a hunger strike in front of the DENR central office. Three days later, thirteen people (farmers, mothers, students, catechists) from San Fernando set up a camp and fasted for eight days. Attracting the media's attention and the support of some social development-oriented NGOs and church groups, they held press conferences to call attention to the plight of their forests and their survival as a people. This kind of event had no precedent in Philippine history—where ordinary people with very modest education, most of whom had never even been to the capital city, were valiantly trying to draw national attention, including that of the president of the republic, to the plight of their forest.

Finally on 4 October 1989, the thirteen fasters, on behalf of the NKSSF, signed an agreement with Secretary Factoran stipulating several provisions to halt the destructive effects of logging and forest denudation. The agreement also provided for the formal participation of the people of San Fernando through the NKSSF in the rehabilitation of their forests.

The stewardship of the forests by the citizens of San Fernando continues to this date. Partly because of mass protests by citizen groups like NKSSF, a national log ban was effected by the Philippine government.

The mass actions of PSK and NKSSF in San Fernando, Bukidnon, are not isolated cases in the Philippines. They only represent some of the more celebrated cases, such as those enacted by the people of Gabaldon under the leadership of the parish priest, as well as by other people's organizations all over the Philippines.

PSK and NKSSF's activist position toward their forest resources has been fueled both by the concept of stewardship drawn from the Christian liturgy and by the principles of the theology of liberation. The majority of the priests associated with these popular movements subscribe to the key principle of the theology of liberation: that Christians should pursue social justice and overturn exploitative and unjust structures, just as Jesus Christ in the temple overturned the tables of the corrupt. Such ideas and images provide powerful inspiration to ordinary people struggling with their communities to resist the destruction of their forest resources, to fight the injustices committed by the political and economic elites. Although motivated by the narrow demand of their own survival, the efforts of participants in these movements are no less heroic or radical than those in the deep ecology movement who view themselves as "militant" or "radical" environmentalists. They also fundamentally threaten elite interests.

CASE 2: STEWARDS OF THE SEA—THE COASTAL PROTECTORS OF CARIGARA BAY

This section describes the efforts of the Mephenaij Phaton Youth Association[1] (MPYA) and other fishing groups who have spearheaded the protection and preservation of coastal resources in Capoocan, Leyte, Carigara Bay. This bay is a thirty minutes' ride from Ormoc City, the site of a tragedy in 1991 where over two thousand people died in a flash flood resulting partly from deforestation.

Located in the province of Leyte, central Philippines, Carigara Bay used to be one of the country's major fishing grounds. The fish have been depleted, however, because of intensive fishing by foreign trawlers (primarily Taiwanese and Japanese) and destructive fishing methods used by local fishermen, such as dynamiting and cynamide poisoning. The depletion has been intensified by increased levels of sedimentation from poor upland agricultural practices and the destruction of mangrove forests, tidal swamps, and coral reefs. Moreover, the high incidence of poverty among the rapidly growing coastal population further exacerbates the pressure both upon people and upon resources, leading to conflicts. The bay, covering five municipalities, is home to over twenty-five hundred subsistence fishermen and their families (roughly fifteen thousand persons).

Motivated by the impoverishment of fisherfolks in Capoocan, the MPYA's president, Perfecto Pilapil, Jr., organized the local youth for socioeconomic projects. Increasingly, however, they realized that the poverty of their people could be traced to their dwindling fish catch. MPYA youth members banded together with other concerned citizens to safeguard the bay fronting their municipality. They organized coastal resource management councils in every village and started patrolling the bay. They also pushed for stricter implementation of fishing laws to make possible the protection and rehabilitation of fish habitats in their respective villages. They have deployed artificial reefs and have themselves patrolled these areas, looking for illegal fishers. To increase the fish population, they have mobilized the community to establish a fish sanctuary. They have fined dynamiters and even suggested they might establish young, armed MPYA roving guards who would use weapons against poachers and other violators of coastal laws.

The frustration of these environmentalists results from the lack of enforcement of existing environmental laws by state authorities. For example, the cutting of mangroves for fishponds was banned; but as one circle of Carigara Bay reveals, construction of prawn/fish ponds still continues. Often these belong to wealthy concessionaires who are able to sway the law in their favor. More significantly, the government bureaucracy is ill-equipped or does not have the political will to enforce the laws. Despite these realities, in 1993 and 1994, the MPYA reduced the incidence of dynamiting by 85 percent.

The influence and impact of MPYA's environmentalism can be seen in their expansion of operations to the other municipalities of Leyte province. Their experiences are often cited and serve as a model for other fisherfolk.

Another example of popular resistance is the struggle of LAM-BAT,[2] a fishing organization based in Bataan, north of Manila.

Because of the declining fish catch, fishers in this province have organized to fight illegal fishing methods, mangrove destruction, and prawn/fish pond expansion by commercial fishermen allied with local political warlords. They have conducted education campaigns, initiated petitions to government offices, and organized marches to dramatize their cause. Consequently, LAMBAT mem bers have suffered threats, harassment, illegal arrests, and murder. This experience is typical of peasant groups in the Philippines who have dared to question the system which benefits only a privileged few.

The case of MPYA in Capoocan, Carigara Bay, and of LAMBAT in Bataan is replicated all over the archipelago—ordinary fisherfolks organizing to claim that the resources of their nearby bays or seas, which they have used sustainably for centuries, belong to them. But now these commons areas, which serve as the basic foundation of their life, are being depleted by big-time commercial anglers and trawlers. Thus, community groups or people's organizations around the country have mobilized and organized themselves to defend their aquatic commons resources.

The above peasant movements are necessitated by the poverty and environmental deterioration brought on or exacerbated by loggers and commercial fishermen, who also enjoy the strong support of politicians, the military, and the state bureaucracy. Because they seek to wrest control of land and water resources from elites, these movements are branded "radical," persecuted as communistic, and often accused by the government and military of having ties to the New People's Army. Such accusations serve to justify the harassment, intimidation, illegal arrests, incarceration, and murder of these activists, who are not attempting to overthrow the government, but rather, to democratize politics and claim a just share of their traditional environmental resources. Philippine history for the past twenty years, and especially during the Marcos era, is replete with stories such as these.

Analysis

This section analyzes the roots and conditions which nurture as well as threaten the growth of grassroots environmentalism in a third-world country like the Philippines. A combination of internal and external forces interact to foster an environmentalism that fundamentally challenges the existing political and economic institutions. The success of grassroots environmentalism in the Philippines depends on the following conditions: effective leadership, mass community mobilization, and the securing of resources both internal and external to the community.

Leadership must be effective. As we have seen, the leaders of these popular movements are often spiritual leaders perceived to be free of political and economic interests. Moreover, these leaders have assumed control because of the vacuum of political leadership in places far from the urban centers, which have long been neglected by the central government. The charisma, skill, and moral integrity of movement leadership is an important resource in these movements, and it is important to note that this leadership did emerge from the usual political and economic elites.

Movement ideology is rooted in the idea of Christian stewardship which is rooted in liberation theology. The basic ideology running through much grassroots environmentalism in the Philippines is the strong notion, rooted in liberation theology, that God takes the side of the poor in history, that they are entitled to their share of earth's bounty, and that they should be good stewards of nature. Reinforcing their claim to resources is strong community organizing and the broad democracy movement that continues to spread throughout the islands.

Composition of internal dynamics of these groups. Most of these groups are composed of farmers, fishers and their families whose livelihood depends directly on the environment. Other groups participating in ecological resistance movements in the Philippines are the indigenous natives such as the Manobos of Bukidnon and the Dumagats of Nueva Ecija.

Given such diversity, domination and conflict also occur among the grassroots environmental movements. For example, although the lowland farmers and fishers are marginalized by the dominant urban-based loggers, trawlers, and political authorities, the former dominate the indigenous communities. The migrant lowland groups, who know the state policies and programs, often take advantage of the Lumad (the native, upland, indigenous group) and their lack of education and familiarity with urban-based institutions. These divisions often reduce the effectiveness of these groups by making them more vulnerable to manipulation by commercial elites and political authorities.

Mobilization of resources. These grassroots organizations started as groups formed to address common socioeconomic or religious concerns. Soon, however, they become ecologically and politically radicalized, because they discovered that their increasing poverty is inextricably linked to both environmental degradation and their exploitation by outsiders. They realized that they must address these dynamics immediately and effectively. They also understand that this can be achieved only by mobilizing their own people, as well as by forging alliances with their urban-based contacts in the media, nongovernment organizations, government offices, and other people's organizations. Their urban-based media contacts are especially important to their struggle to bring attention to their cause and to force the government to capitulate to their demands. Such contacts also help by placing the local struggle in the broader worldwide environmental crisis.

The above patterns of environmental resistance may offer a glimpse of the future. Given what has occurred in recent years, it is likely that the struggle to reclaim resources will increasingly assume a spiritual and moral character which will empower those who would defend these resources and the traditional livelihoods dependent upon them.

CONCLUSION

This chapter only introduces ecological resistance in the Philippines. Given the great cultural diversity of cultures in the Philippines, there is great diversity to be found among the popular movements. One striking reality is how environmental deterioration has led virtually all popular movements in the Philippines to establish strong environmental agendas and rationales (Broad and Cavanagh 1993:132f). Diverse communities are finding resources, sometimes material and always ideological, *in their own traditions*, for their struggles to secure access to their ancestral lands and restore their environmental resource bases.[3]

The present case studies are representative of hundreds of peasant-based organizations who are trying to assert their rights to the dwindling resources of their forest lands, rivers, bays, mangrove swamps, tidal flats, and seas. Every day, the economically and politically marginalized are fighting elite state and class interests which deny them access to the resources they need to survive. Upland groups wage battles against loggers, while sustenance fishers struggle against commercial fishermen, trawlers, and prawn/fish pond owners. These ordinary people are fighting for their daily bread and for the future of their children. They are not fighting because they are motivated by an intellectual understanding of global environmental crisis, but usually by more pressing survival concerns. These critical needs drive them to question and challenge the existing political and economic institutions and to take actions which often are not expected of marginalized groups in third-world societies.

In the Philippines, a privileged few (roughly 15 to 20 percent) control access to environmental resources and enjoy greater access to state resources. Yet, the poor majority (roughly 60 percent or more), although confronted by great obstacles, increasingly participate in movements demanding a greater say in the management of their resources and a fair share of them. As has occurred in many regions, participants in popular ecological resistance movements have been threatened, harassed, and subjected to illegal arrests, violence, and murder. Despite these harsh realities, these movements have achieved some startling victories. They have also provided their participants another rare resource, namely, hope.

ACKNOWLEDGMENTS

Emma Porio wishes to thank community leaders in Bukidnon for access for her interviews and acknowledge her heavy reliance on the accounts by Esquillo (1992).

NOTES

1. Mephenaij Phaton according to Perfecto Pilapil, Jr., means "the unconquerable" in Hebrew. He spent some time being trained in community work in Israel.

2. The account of this movement is based largely on the account by Broad and Cavanagh (1993).

3. See Broad and Cavanagh (1993), esp. ch 2, for an example of how the conviction of an indigenous group about the sacrality of Mount Apo provides a key motivation to their resistance to its destruction.

PART III
POPULAR ECOLOGICAL RESISTANCE
IN AFRICA

Chapter 9

GRASSROOTS RESISTANCE TO DOMINANT LAND-USE PATTERNS IN SOUTHERN AFRICA

Yash Tandon

The land was a major factor in the Chimurenga War, the war of independence in Zimbabwe. It was the rallying cry. During the colonial period, most of the better arable lands (about 15.6 million hectares or about 46.9 percent of the total agricultural land) were alienated from the indigenous population and transferred (at ridiculously cheap prices) over to a minority white settler community (constituting barely 3.8 percent of the population). Land alienation was, of course, not unique to Zimbabwe. This was a general colonial pattern. But the distinguishing mark of southern Africa lay in its transparently vulgar racial dimension, the further south one went, the worse it became, until it reached proportions defying all sense of reason or humanity in the apartheid regime of South Africa. There 87 percent of the land was transferred to the whites. Where "black spots" were trapped in these lands, the blacks were forcibly removed, these removals being effected to this day. It is estimated that a total of 3.5 million people have been forcibly removed since 1960 (Surplus People Project 1983:xxiv). The physical and psychological trauma this caused was captured in the British television special, "Last Grave at Dimbaza," which shocked an incredulous world.

If we were to write about grassroots resistance to dominant land use patterns in southern Africa, we have to write about the whole history of each of the countries in this region from the beginning of colonialism to today. But history is made by historians; it is periodically reconstructed depending on the society's consciousness, and reinterpretation, of its own past. That's why we have schools of historiography. In relation to the struggle for land rights in southern Africa that school has still not emerged which would locate the present struggles in the past, which would treat history as present. It is an important debate which contemporary African historians have by and large eschewed for various reasons, but mainly because academic rigor demands that their methodology be acceptable to those conferring degrees in the citadels of knowledge in the West, the ones who license knowledge. The story of the struggles for land rights in southern Africa therefore still is largely unwritten. If what we offer in the following pages appears episodic, fragmentary, and not this worldly, that is because of the limitations of space and the language of discourse.

EARLY RESISTANCE IN ZIMBABWE

The British did not have an easy time conquering the African peasantry in (the then) Rhodesia. The peasantry knew that their conquerors would take advantage of conditions of famine to lure them into receiving famine relief, and then extract a price for this by making them provide labor to white farms. So they refused to accept famine relief. Terence Ranger writes: "In 1903 a native Commissioner could complain that even in the face of famine the men in his district would not go out to work but preferred more 'traditional' means of survival. 'If,' he noted, 'some more fortunate native guarantees to keep them in food, on promise of a sister or child as wife at some future date, well and good.' . . . More frequently labour itself was pledged in return for food, or else family cattle was sold for grain" (Ranger 1985:40). Thus, drought, even famine, did not break the Makoni peasants' resistance to colonially designed land-use programs. "Time and time again the Native Commissioner would predict that a year of dearth would result in abundant labour migration: time and time again this expectation was confounded. Time after time whites sought to offer relief maize in return for labour or for peasant acceptance of debt: time after time these offers were refused" (Ranger 1985:41). Later, during the 1930s and 1950s, when the colonial state tried to enforce removals through legislation (respectively, the Land Apportionment Act of 1930, and the Husbandry Act of 1951), peasants resisted through protest demonstrations, or by running over the borders to Zambia and Mozambique, or through legal recourse to the court. But, probably, the most striking aspect of the resistance was a reassertion of traditional religions and desertions from the mission churches into what came to be known as "independent" (meaning indigenous) churches. These were the spirit or prophetic churches (such as the Zionist and Apostolic movements) which focused on the Holy Spirit, prophecies, baptism, and faith healing, and the churches with an ideological-religious link with the state of Ethiopia (such as the African Congregational church and the African Reformed church.) These churches sprouted in the 1920s when labor migrants like Samuel Mutendi, David Masuka, and Andreas Shoko returned from South Africa. B. G. M. Sundkler wrote in 1961 that religious separatism from European parent churches represented land-protest movements.[1]

Sister Aquina wrote that among the rural Karanga, the (European) mission churches formed an upper stratum, with the Ethiopian type the middle and Zionists, Apostles, and Pagans in the lower stratum (Aquina 1969). Bishop Mutendi of the Zionist Christian church (ZCC) clashed with colonial administration and acquired the image of a rebel. Detentions and warnings did not scare him. Eventually, fifteen chiefs joined him in offering subtle resistance to the infiltration of foreign influence.

Ideologically, the Zionist church relates to Mt. Zion in Jerusalem, or to the first Apostles of Christ. The Zion camp tries to realize in an African setting something of the community as it is believed to have functioned in ancient Jerusalem. Although the spirit-type movements were opposed to many aspects of traditional religions (especially in the latters' belief in witchcraft), they retained some traditional practices, such as the fertility cults and the magical treatment of the seed whose powers were supposed to originate from *Mwari.*

Of course, the ZCC was not the only indigenous church. The Masowe church, often referred to as "VaPostori," was founded in the early 1930s (again after the 1930 Land Apportionment Act) by Johane Shoniwa who claimed to have died and risen again as a new messiah. He was brought up as a United Methodist and worked as a cobbler. His conversions (among the Shona) threatened the colonial government and the mission churches, and so in the 1940s he left for South Africa. His followers are noted for their industry, self-reliance, and resistance against modernization, such as Western medicine.

What is significant about early resistance to changes in colonially imposed land tenure was the sheer tenacity of the peasants. They had rather starve than succumb. When the state resorted to legislation and violence, they went back to their spiritual roots for sustenance. This was true of traditional religions, of course, but it was also true in the case of those that had imbibed the Christian faith. In their case, they founded their own independent churches, and drew the support of vast numbers of the peasantry, especially after legislation that transformed the character of the land tenure.

LAND AT THE CROSSROADS OF RACE, CLASS, AND GENDER STRUGGLES

Almost fifty years after the first emergence of grassroots resistance to colonially imposed land reforms, Zimbabwe won its independence. Land was at the heart of the liberation struggle. However, as part of the compromise at the independence agreement at Lancaster, the system of land tenure was frozen. Land could not be seized by the government for those who fought for it. It could only be sold on a "willing seller, willing buyer" basis, and only if the sellers were paid market-determined compensation. Ten years later (after about 250,000 people have been resettled, a quarter of the original target), the government passed a law (the Land Acquisition Act) to do away with the Lancaster limitations. The government can now designate any land it wants to for purposes of resettlement of the landless and for realigning the land-tenure system.

These ten years, however, have given breathing space to the old white settler interests to stabilize and consolidate their control over land. In the meantime, a new black Capitalist class with an interest in private ownership have emerged strong in the political arena, and the communal and landless peasants, now disarmed and effectively depoliticized, are at the mercy of a political process over which they have marginal influence. In 1993, the government set up the Land Commission in order to review the entire system of land tenure and use and to hear the evidence and arguments from interested parties. The argument is at the crossroads of race, class, and gender.

Within a racial framework, the white commercial farmers argue that the land system should be maintained more or less along the lines inherited from the colonial period. To disturb the system, they argue, would endanger both food security and overall agricultural production. A group of black farmers comprised mostly of a colonially created small Capitalist class and a section of the new political class with interest in land and land speculation want to change the inherited colonial system in terms of its ownership but not in terms of its tenure or use. They argue in favor of "indigenization" of the ownership of land, but maintaining production more or less along the same (modernist) lines as before.

The gender argument puts women at the centre of the discourse about land ownership and use. Women, by tradition (a jumble of contradictory customs evolved over centuries), by the laws of ownership (a mixture of Dutch and British colonial laws), and by a hundred other discriminatory practices (from banking practice to extension services) do not own land. They only use it. Their husbands may have been gone for decades, but the land they till in the communal areas for the families subsistence remains in the name of the husbands, and if they are widowed, the lands may be taken away from them by the husbands' brothers (indeed, by tradition, they too may be "inherited" by one of the brothers). The women want justice; they want recognition of their dignity as human beings, with the same rights of ownership and control as men.

The class argument divides the interest between large farmers (black and white) on one side and small farmers and the landless on the other. They want to return to some form of the precolonial commons system of land tenure and land use. They argue that changing ownership from white to black commercial agriculture will not help their situation.

Of the various interests involved on land, it is the male, modernizing Capitalist farmers (black and white) who have a dominant say in the system. The whites have the weight of the donor community on their side; the blacks have a voice in the government. Both have the support of global lending institutions, such as the World Bank, and of large multinational corporations who need to sell their tractors, fertilizers, and pesticides. Both have access to the media. The weakest protagonists are the landless and the land-poor (both men and women), and among them the landless women (where class and gender infirmities combine) are the weakest and the least-organized section of the society. Their daily struggle is for survival and for basic human rights.

UNITY AND STRUGGLE AMONG THE DISPOSSESSED

Although there are differences among women across classes, they are allies in the broad scheme of things. The main difference resides in what weight they give to tradition. When the landless male finally secures a piece of land, he insists it has to be in his name even if it is his wife who will work on it. But that is a domestic quarrel, one beyond the pale of state or any other kind of outside (except, perhaps, the church and kinship) intervention. At the national level, women's activist organizations (backed by considerable support from feminist international bodies) have succeeded in getting the laws changed so that women can now own land, secure bank credit, and not get dispossessed when their husbands die. But the practical effects of this come up against the bedrock of custom and tradition and against plain prejudices (including institutional ones, e.g., the biases of banks).

At the domestic level, tradition often plays a blocking role to modernization; at the national level it can, however, be a potent force for struggle against the powerful classes. The latter are modernizing forces. Both for the black and for the white commercial farmers, the modernization of agriculture is the only basis for development. They argue that to revert to the traditional system would be going backwards. For the landless and the land-poor, going back to tradition is a way of trying to preserve for their use as much of the common land as it is still possible to preserve against the encroachments of modernization; it is also a way of using parallel structures of authority and decision making in order to offer legitimacy to a different use of land from its dominant patterns; it is also a struggle against the ruling ideology of economism, which judges the value of land primarily in terms of what it can produce and how much it can add to the gross domestic product. These are not three separate battles; they are one and the same.

LAND AS THE LOCUS OF IDEOLOGICAL STRUGGLE

At the ideological level, the landless and the land-poor have a much broader perspective than the upper classes. The latter have a generally economistic perspective on land. For the poor and land-less, in addition to its use as a productive asset to generate food and cash crops, they view land in the larger cultural and spiritual context. Land is not simply the soil on which to grow crops, but it is also a place to bury ancestors and to make a spiritual home for the family. The use of land goes beyond its purely economic utility.

The culture of modernism has a unigenerational cosmology: only the present generation matters. Furthermore, in the modernist cosmology, nature is just something to exploit. You can cut down forests, make large holes in the soil to extract gold and asbestos, and divert rivers for commercial irrigation. You can hunt down wildlife for their trophy and push them into game parks, and you can chemicalize the soil for the sake of high yields. When you have thus carried out your carnage, you can quick-fix the damage by adding chemical fertilizers to the soil and growing eucalyptus trees.

Against this dominant cosmology, the landless and the land-poor apply the African (traditional) cosmology whereby the dead, the living, and the unborn are all relevant to the present. As for nature, it is not set apart from humanity; the two are one and the same. Poor crops are related to the anger of the ancestral spirits. Among the Zulu in the Natal/KwaZulu province of South Africa, they believe that "if the diviner cannot point at *umthakathi* who has put medicine into the field, then it is the shades" [ancestral spirits]. . . . That is when people say, 'This year the shades are angry.' Or sometimes they say, 'The earth is angry.'

The sacred plant of *imphepho* (*Helichrysum miconiaefolium*), the Zulu diviner warns, should never be ripped out of the earth with its roots unless one is specifically required. When the diviner himself picks the plant, he first makes sure his shadow does not fall over it. When he breaks the stem, he says: "Excuse me, thing of my people. It is the work of my fathers that I am doing." Then it breaks off easily, the plant agreeing to doing its work. But if it does not break off easily, he asks again for forgiveness; perhaps his appeal was not heard the first time. He must not look into the earth when breaking the stem. "To look there is to look at a shade. This is not done. A man must not look at his fathers."

The word *ukuthwasa* describes a coming out afresh after a temporary absence or disappearance, generally applied to the moon and the seasons of the year. It is also applied to a novice diviner who, on having completed his or her learning with a veteran, appears again in public to be accepted as diviner. The night prior to initiation the novice is expected to spend *emaphandleni* (in the fields) sleeping on the naked earth. Berglund relates the following conversation with his interlocutor:

> B. "Why is it so important that the novice sleep in the fields the night before initiation?"
> I. "It is because she must come from the earth into the home for initiation."
> B. "So when you said, 'Go to your mother!' you were not speaking of the girl's mother?"
> I. "I was speaking of the other mother."
> B. "Which mother?"
> I. "The earth."
> B. "Is the earth the mother of the child?"
> I. "A person has two mothers. The woman and the earth. A diviner cannot be born of a woman. She must come from the earth."
> B. "Is it because the shades are in the earth?"
> I. "Sometimes you can say it like that. But sometimes it is because people come from the earth."
> B. "So a diviner comes from the earth?"
> I. "That is where they come from. The earth gives birth to them." (Berglund 1989:167)

The Struggle against Encroachments on the Commons

Beyond the ideological battle is the struggle for the preservation of the commons. This battle deals not only with the resources provided by nature to which people have a common access, but also with agrarian practice and customary rights to these resources. Land use, land management, and land conservation are not simply managerial tasks embodied in a body of knowledge called "modernization" with a view to maximizing the earning of foreign exchange for the national treasury (a typically World Bank view that has become the bread and butter policy of independent African governments). Access to land and its use and management are essentially social issues, and they relate both to the rights of the people (both customary and statutory) and to the rights of mother earth and all that comes out of the earth.

The Association of Zimbabwe Traditional Ecologists (AZTREC) was founded by a spirit medium, Lydia Chabata, and others. It operates from Masvingo, some three hundred kilometers south of Harare. The main activities of the association are the protection of the sacred mountains, the preservation of *rambakutemwa (sacred forests where spirits reside)*, the growing of indigenous trees, and the protection of water resources, marshlands, and wildlife.

In the Dande Valley in the north of Zimbabwe close to the borders of Zambia and Mozambique, some people survive out of what is left of the commons. Deprived of access to wildlife, forests, and fish the people are forced to dig out past knowledge of traditional foods such as the *mupama, guruhwu,* and *mhanda* (all used as substitutes for maize); *manyanya* (used instead of onions); *musangwi* (seeds boiled for relish); *karemberembe* (baobab leaves cooked with okra); *mawuyu* (dried baobab fruits used to make porridge); *masawu* (used to make a strong alcoholic drink); and *musiga, hakwa, katunguru,* and *bwabwa* (all traditional fruits).

Zambia, in the last few years, has been targeted by investors from South Africa who are buying off fertile lands. In Chief Kabamba's area in the northwest province the Serenje District Council has already given out 4,800 hectares of land to a South African investor on the grounds that this will bring development to the district. The local population, fearful of loss of their lands, has challenged the council on its decision. In Kalomo in the same province, villagers claim that the government had ignored the plight of the local people when it allocated land to a foreign settler who was removing villagers from their land. The same situation exists in the village of Kashinakaji. Several thousands of hectares of land between Luasongwa and Kashinakaji have been appropriated by some businessmen. Here people live along the road to Kabompo. Further down the road is the Chabuwoki stream with fertile lands to which people have been moving their homesteads. In the meantime, however, an "honorable" from Lusaka with plenty of money has managed to secure 150 hectares of land along the river, and he has persuaded the chief to ask the people to move back to the road where they came from. The chief has tried to do so, on the grounds that along the road there are clinics, schools, and so on. However, the people are resisting the move. Once the honorable has established himself along the river, they say, they would be denied the use of the river as well as of the lands in between.

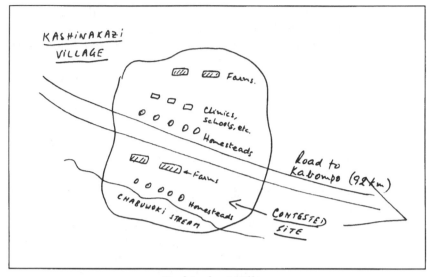

Kashinakazi Village

So the people have formed a Management committee which has approached a local NGO, the Village Development Network (VDN), to assist them to acquire titles for their ancestral land threatened by rich men masquerading as investors. The VDN director, Alex Kwandu, explains: "Although the government can preach the advantages of bringing in investors—such as employment to 'our' people, increased food production, etc.—what is the long-term impact on the people? It is true they shall get work, but only as a cheap labor force. And what cost to our natural resources?"

In the western province in the village of Mavumbe, the *litunga* (chief) gave land to a cashew company, which would have resulted in the evacuation of people (belonging to the Mbunda tribe) off the land. They protested and were even prepared to sue the Litunga (an unprecedented thing to do). The people argued that these lands were given to them long ago. Eventually, the people won and the cashew company was forced to leave.

WHO DECIDES? THE STRUGGLE FOR INSTITUTIONAL LEGITIMACY

The ideological battle to broaden the concept of "land rights," and the struggle to preserve the commons come up against still larger issues of power and authority. In the end, the state decides. It gives licenses for logging trees, building dams and roads and other "development" projects, and it sets the whole macro-economic framework of the exploitation of natural resources. Traditionally, the chiefs applied customary practice to allocate land. It was normally allocated to households for their direct use, primarily for their food for subsistence and to keep cattle and smaller animals. But the power of the chiefs was undermined during the colonial period when they were turned into civil servants to collect taxes and to enforce colonial laws.

In the Zambezi Valley in Zimbabwe, the chiefs traditionally held authority by virtue of their royal lineage. Upon death they became "royal ancestors" *(mhondoro)*, and they continued taking an interest in the welfare of the people and influenced contemporary events through the spirit mediums *(svikiro)*. The living chiefs got largely corrupted by colonial institutions of state and church, but the spirit mediums retained their purity through living rigorously abstemious lives—in their dress, relations with the opposite sex, and above all, abstention from the use of Western artifacts, Western medicine, and Western means of transport. In this the spirit mediums, as possessors of the spirit of the *mhondoro*, symbolized the resistance of the people against modernization. The most powerful spirit medium was that of Mbuya Nehanda who had fought against the British in the 1890s and was caught and executed. She was also the inspiration behind the second war of liberation in the 1970s. There are several such spirit mediums presently resident in the Zambezi Valley. They are possessed by the mhondoro whenever the latter feel that their people are being unjustly treated or something untoward has happened. These spirit mediums provide an alternative source of authority to earthly powers, including the state and the local councils. They are widely respected for their wisdom and sagacity. On occasion they have spoken against the application of fertilizers to the soil, or of spraying of medicines to kill the tsetse fly, or against government's resettlement programs.

Today, thus, two principles of democracy vie against each other in the Zambezi Valley. One is the "electoral" principle imported from the West which is mechanistic, and which says that whoever gets a majority in elections gets to be the spokesperson of the community. The second is the "sagic" principle which is organic to people's culture and says it is the *mhondoro*, speaking through their spirit mediums, who possess the sagacity to be the

genuine custodians of the welfare of the people. The earthly representatives, the people of the valley say, are always susceptible to
corruption and self-interest; the spiritual representatives are the
only ones that can be fully trusted to look after their interests.

The battle for land rights is connected ultimately with the battle for the legitimacy of those who speak for the people. This battle
is not yet over, despite the seeming triumph of the electoral system.
When development fails, as is evident everywhere in Africa, the
mhondoro will assert their presence more vigorously than now, and
then, the people say, they shall witness the emergence of new religions, just as the Zionist and the VaPostori emerged during the
1930s.

CONCLUSION: WHAT KIND OF RADICALISM?

There is need for modesty in construing popular land movements in Africa as part of the environmental movement. To do so
would fault both reality and common sense. Why? Because popular
land movements in Africa (as indeed elsewhere) are, as a general
rule, far too complex to be placed under one single social category.
In another context, feminist organizations might locate land movements within the framework of feminist liberation, and given the
fact that a great majority of peasant farmers (certainly in southern
Africa) are women, they may not be far wrong about this. But this
too would be a simplification of a complex reality.

This is a warning against reading people's struggles through an
environmentalist's eyes. There is a tendency for movements in the
Southern Hemisphere to assume, or to be given, Northern labels.
This is in part due to the fact that placing popular struggles within
the framework of environment (a fashionable agenda) opens up the
door to generous donor funds. This "naming ourselves by what the
North would like to hear" is yet another case of strategizing for survival. Of course, the reverse is also probably true. The Northern
donors too have learned ways of twisting around those areas of primary concerns (such as land, for instance) to suit their own mandates for funding.

Environmental movements have a certain "newness" about
them, new for the North, not for Africa. The contemporary newness
concerns the manner in which it is introduced into Africa. In the
West, having wantonly exploited nature to feed industrialization for
over three hundred years, the consciousness about the need to care

about the environment is new, but in Africa, the respect (even religious veneration) for land and nature is as old as the hills.

In the West it is often claimed that environmental movements in Africa are still new, or that Africa has not yet matured environmentally, or that it is still an unconquered territory as far as environmental consciousness goes, and so on. All this is palpable nonsense. It is sad, that we in Africa are forced by poverty, and by constant reminders in the media and in international fora about our developmental backwardness, to give up our cherished gods and our traditional veneration for nature. Also, consumerist ways of the West are alluring. Development is a sweet fruit, the more so when it is inaccessible. Hence we have the paradoxical situation that while the West is regaining its consciousness about the environment, and has the means and the technology to do something about it, we in Africa are in the process of losing it, and we do not have the means or the technology to save our environment.

There is no glamor in our environmental movements in Africa. Images of women clinging to trees to protect them from being logged, or of Friends of the Earth braving the rapids of the Zambezi to prevent the construction of yet another hydroelectric dam—these do not in reality exist. Maybe they will some day. Right now the struggle is one for survival, one manifestation of which is the struggle for land rights. Not enough excitement perhaps for eco-conscious observers, not glamorous for sure, but a plain reality.

If the radicalism of the popular land movements has to be given a label, it must surely be "anti-imperialism." It is only with the coming of foreign domination that land has become privatized; it has become the property of individuals who, on that basis, claim to have the right to use land as they wish. Privatization is the curse of humanity in the present era. Granted, we of this epoch have to live with the reality of private ownership; it has been forced upon us by the evolution of social history through the last barely 300 years. But private ownership of land and of natures's resources is, for the African, an unnatural phenomenon. It is profoundly antisocial and antihumanist. Land and its resources should only be held as a trust to the community and to all nature's living creatures. Its entrustment to individuals is an act against humanity and life itself.

In the meantime, the exclusive rights of all those who claim ownership of land is put to question. How did they acquire this ownership? Did they buy, borrow, or steal land? Popular belief is that the settlers in Africa stole the land of the people. It was a robbery, no less. When the concept of "private ownership" (in the western sense) was itself alien to the African in precolonial Zambia, Zimbabwe, or Azania, what did the purchase of a few thousand acres of land by a European settler mean for the African? It obviously had no meaning for him; it was completely outside his vision, his comprehension, and his cultural and customary legal system. He knew land as a common asset; it could never be privatized. Did colonial conquest legitimise privatization of land? By what law? Recognized by whom? In whose courts?

To be sure, human history, even before the dawn of capitalism, has always known wars of conquest. People have always moved, and as they have moved, they have displaced or absorbed those before them. But never before modern times has this conquest turned into privatization of land and its resources. Throughout thousands of years of waves of conquests, humanity has maintained the principle of the commons in relation to God's resources. Even the so-called King's land, where such existed in all previous civilizations, land was owned (the concept is, in fact, inapplicable), it was held as a trust on behalf of the people, and there were rules, earthly and spiritual, which regulated the use of land. Not so now. With foreign domination came the most irresponsible form of land ownership—individual ownership. One day it will have to end.

In the meantime, survival for those at the bottom of the human pyramid means resistance against the dominant culture of contemporary civilization. Of course, "resistance" does not mean rejection of modern amenities. Certainly, people want to improve their material existence. They would like better housing, access to clean water, a rural retail shop where they can buy soap, bread, and fabric, and, above all, better health and educational facilities. What it means primarily is a rejection of the system of producing these amenities which, in the end, leaves them poorer and powerless. This system has dispossessed them of land, forests, and access to water and clean air, as well as—their locally gained knowledge, their culture, and their unique way of doing things. Western economists call their system of production "adding value." Actually it reduces the moral value of society as a whole.

Against this they must assert (or re-assert) their own genius, their own inventivencss, their own knowledge. It is not as hopeless a battle as would appear to those convinced of the merits of modernization and of a value-added economy. In the remote village of Ngulula in the northern province of Zambia, for example, women get together and form a club of their own to take control of their lives. A nearby mission church from Germany preaches the Gospel of Christ mixed with that of modernization in the form of "free" packages of fertilizers. At the end of the growing season, the church takes from the peasants bags of maize to pay for the fertilizers it had (freely) loaned. The "added value" is appropriated by the church. The women are finally beginning to work out the arithmetic. Now they do not buy the fertilizers. Instead, they make their own compost. It is hard work, and the yield is less, but the Irish potatoes and soya beans they grow taste as good. Above all, what they produce they keep. The women learn as they struggle. They have dug up abandoned irrigation canals leading to a nearby river and made new ones, and these now feed water to their vegetable gardens. Now most households have fish ponds. They feed the waste from their gardens and the kitchens to the fish, and now have a diversified source and regular supply of protein for their families.

The mission church, however, continues to cause problems. Last year (1993), the Ngulula Club started a campaign against the church's attempt to cut down indigenous forest to plant eucalyptus (gum) trees, which the Church says will yield fast fuel wood. But the women want to preserve their own trees and bush. They get many medicines and wild fruits from the forest, and the ancestral spirits live there too. Furthermore, the mission church frowns upon traditional healing. The people are now asserting their culture, their values, and their sense of self-knowledge, even in defiance of the mission church and the state.

What is happening in the Ngulula village in Zambia is also happening in hundreds of villages throughout Africa. In the lower Zambezi Valley in Zimbabwe, the people are resisting "development" as preached to them by outside commercial and state interests. They have noticed that development has meant the appropriation of everything that is valuable by the state and commercial interests for their own profit or for foreign exchange. At the end they are left with nothing but semi-arid land on which to grow maize and cotton, both of which require extensive application of fertilizers. When rains fail (which is three out of five years), they not only lose the year's hard labor but incur debt with the state credit institutions, which descend on them to take away the few possessions they have for repayment of the loans. So the people are now ready for resistance. They will still grow cotton, for they have no other cash crop, and they need the cash to pay for school fees and some basic necessities. But they have begun to take in their own hands matters that affect their lives and those of their children. They hunt for wildlife in what is by law a preserve for licensed hunting with tour operators. They fish in the Zambezi River using nets and other traditional means, by law denied to them. And now they are resisting the state's resettlement program undertaken without their consent. The program brings in settlers from the rest of the country to occupy "virgin" lands. This has created overcrowding in the valley, resulting in increasing landlessness for those already there, and also increasing destruction of its natural resources. Once again, it is to the traditional systems of authority and legitimacy, namely, the spirit mediums, to which the people have turned for inspiration and guidance. These venerated spirits have access to the *mhondoro* (the ancestors) who see all and who will one day come to earth and inspire the people to revolt as they did against the white rule in Zimbabwe.

The earth, from which everything comes and to which everything returns, hears everything. The curse of the ancestors can bring madness and death. Development and structural adjustment programs are bad omens. Learn the meaning of death at the age of seven and you are doomed to walk alone the rest of your life. With the dead and dying all around, when you look at the bony remains of your cattle lying on dried river beds, is it still permissible to pontificate about the ozone layer and all that? One day, the *mhondors* will surely wake up to the plight of their people, and old religions shall lighten new tongues. It has happened in the past. It shall happen in the future.

NOTES

1. Sundkler (1961). But Daneel (1977, quoted in Bourdillon 1977) dismisses the argument that independent churches were products of land-protest movements. He says that they were an expression of interpreting Christianity according to African insights. However, can not "reinterpretation" be a form of resistance? Why is Daneel so keen to show that the independent churches were not part of the resistance against land reform?

Chapter 10

LUTA, LIVELIHOOD, AND LIFEWORLD IN CONTEMPORARY AFRICA

Ben Wisner

There are difficulties in writing about environmentalism and even more so radical or militant ecological resistance movements in contemporary Africa. This chapter will attempt to identify these difficulties and discuss their significance. Why? Why, indeed, is this book being read? Assuming a large proportion of the readership is non-African and living outside Africa, it is important to begin by discussing our standpoint.

Since their modern beginnings in the late nineteenth century, geography and anthropology have been the tools of the conquest of Africa (and other places and peoples). Geography mapped the resources that could be had and the most efficient routes of extraction. Anthropology gauged the likelihood of resistance by indigenous people and provided the basis for colonial rule. This work continues today in more subtle forms. During earlier times the colonial powers were interested in Africa as a source of cheap wage goods for the metropolitan working class: palm and cotton seed oil for soap and cooking, cotton for cloth, and the all-important class of mildly addictive stimulants and petty luxuries to dull the pain of the factory system such as coffee, tea, cocoa, and sugar. Times have changed, and the focus is now on the use of African land not only for its productive but for its absorptive capacity. The search is on for sites to accept toxic waste from the industrial megacities of the North (O'Keefe 1988). Here again, geographers using satellite images and computer models of hydrogeology are enlisted to find "suitable" sites. Anthropologists are asked to say why and how a community might resist such a facility and what it would take to make them accept it.

Readers and authors of this volume, probably approach such questions with a different perspective and purpose. The author of this chapter hopes to understand African environmentalism in order to reach out and connect with African colleagues, to find common cause in struggling against corporate power that is destroying human life and nature both in Africa and in this country (Hofrichter 1993; Bullard 1993). The assumption here is that mutual learning and support are possible between the two experiences.

WHAT IS AFRICAN ENVIRONMENTALISM?

At first glance, Northern "environmentalism" is often thought to be a middle-class attempt to protect amenities (recreational, aesthetic). In Africa, by contrast, the motive for "environmental" protest seems more connected to survival issues. However, the reality is more complex on both sides of the comparison. The rise of the movement for environmental justice in the United States calls our attention to groups of people in poor rural counties where toxic waste sites, waste incinerators, and heavily polluting industries have been located. This includes women and men in the heart of our largest cities who are asserting their rights to healthy living conditions free of lead, PCBs, and rats. Thus there are "survival" issues and motives on both side of the comparison.

The most significant events shaping the emergence of African environmentalism have been the civil and fiscal wars of the 1980s and 1990s. There are millions of land mines that make very hazardous farming, herding, and even entry to vast areas of Angola, Mozambique, and Eritrea. Displacement of millions of people into the countries surrounding those mentioned as well as Liberia, Sudan, Rwanda, Burundi, and Somalia have spread the environmental and economic burden of these wars to a further dozen or more Africa countries. Wildlife has been decimated by these wars for food and for profit in order to finance hostilities. Trading ivory and rhino horn for guns (operations acknowledged by the South African Defense Force in its collaboration with Jonas Savimbi's UNITA rebels in southern Angola and probably also carried out by some of the warring Somali groups) inverts, and complements, the infamous "guns for hostages" Iran-Contra scandal by making whole populations of endangered animals into hostages in order to pay for guns (McCullum 1991:168–71).

The fiscal wars have been no less devastating. Structural adjustment agreements with the World Bank and International Monetary Fund in dozens of African countries during the 1980s and 1990s have shifted government programs of credit and technical assistance, marketing more and more toward export commodities. Faced with low prices for these crops and little assistance in their attempts at self-provisioning, the rural smallholder farmers have turned to charcoal production and other nonfarm extractive industries (for example illegal gold and diamond mining in Zaire, Sierra Leone, and elsewhere) or given up and joined the flow of economic refugees to the cities. Cutbacks in government expenditure mandated by structural adjustment has hit hard at environmental and child health, veterinary services, and education. Schools in remote rural areas used to be nodes of innovation, of tree planting and seedling nurseries, for example. As teaching staff is fired, or not replaced at retirement, as salaries are late and buy less and less, time and motivation for these "extra curricular" activities has declined. The market-driven model of development underlying structural adjustment implies privatization of services and utilities. In a cash starved country, where the only way for many marginal rural people to make cash income is urban remittance or production of an acceptable cash crop, the privatization of health (so-called fee for service), domestic water supplies (so-called user fees), and even veterinary services such as dipping and vaccinations can be seen as the modern form of coercion that forced the great-grandparents of these Africans into the cash nexus in the first place.

The roots of an environmentalism focused on issues of access and control over land can be found in the colonial period, as Yash Tandon has demonstrated previously. The experience of displacement and exile linked to the construction of large dams by colonial authorities and newly independent modernizing elites must have been bitter. The history of resistance to massive "resettlement" (as it was and still is euphemized) has been lost. Indeed, a general problem in identifying and understanding environmental struggle in

Africa is that much resistance has been passive. The weapons of the weak have included noncooperation and abandonment of settlement schemes. Chambers' early account of the *Volta River Resettlement Experience* (1970) notes that a high proportion of the fifty thousand people affected drifted away from the planned resettlement areas. It is hard to imagine the scale of these early independence megaprojects. One-fifth of Ghana was flooded in order to generate cheap electricity for Kaiser Aluminum!

Another obstacle to understanding environmentalism in Africa is the complex mixture of motive and agency that are often lumped under this term. Take poaching for instance. In *Green Development*, Adams (1991) reviews precursors to the idea of 'sustainability' and correctly points out the significance of the charismatic macrofauna in making Africa an object of international (read: European and North American) conservationist interest. But who kills the elephants and rhinos? Poaching can be both an act of resistance against tourism-driven development that yields mostly costs and few benefits to the Kenyan and Tanzanian Maasai and an industrial-scale plunder by the economic elite (including government officials).

Even more complex are the situations where people are challenging the hegemony of tourism and elephant rights, attempting to negotiate a place for human beings in the landscape. For example, in South Africa Weiner and his colleagues have identified groups of small farmers effectively trapped between the intensive White-owned fruit orchards of the northern Transvaal and the Krugger National Park bordering Mozambique. In South Africa, where the word *negotiation* appears in every corner, there will have to be a new spatial regime and set of resource entitlements that allow for the needs of such formerly anonymous black farmers caught between the poles of export production and tourism (Weiner and Levin 1991:92–120).

Popular Movements in Africa: Defense of Livelihood I

Africa has no lack of popular movements, or, at least, there is no lack of labeling of African agency. "Democracy movement" and "women's self help movement" are the most commonly studied. Are these terms Eurocentric impositions, leading to misunderstanding? There are, to be sure, various mass movements still trying to establish a wide variety of democratic institutions. These range

from mere formal mechanisms for the periodic change over of economic elites to more aggressive, constituency-based parliaments
demanding accountability, to quite radical visions of participatory
economic democracy. The mosaic of experiences includes a series of
stalled, stalling, managed, and possibly serious attempts at democratization. Where, as in Namibia, political democratization seems
to have been achieved, there are more interesting attempts at participatory environmental management. For example, in the northern
area around the Otosha Pan and in the Kaprivi Strip villagers have
been active participants in multiple-use planning for wildlife habitat, grazing, and farming (Jones 1991:187–200; Moyo et al.
1993:158–94).

As the primary hewers of wood and carriers of water (as well as
primary stable crop farmers), women in rural Africa have a clear
interest in common property resources that provide a steady and
accessible flow of clean water and biomass for fuel. They have not
often hugged trees as in northern India, nor is it clear that groups of
women planting tree seedlings in an organized way constitutes
environmental activism. Still there are interesting and complex
relations between environmental activism and womanism (as the
assertion by African women of their material interests). Women
have resisted the imposition of various export cropping regimes in
Africa for a long time. It is not the crop *per se* they have resisted, but
the changes in land tenure, labor demands, and use of other scarce
resources such as water. Carney and others have documented the
intrahousehold negotiation over access to land and to income from
new cropping systems (Carney and Watts 1991). Groups of women
have "contracted out" their labor power on other occasions as a way
of regaining some economic control in a new situation. Women
have gone on strike against irrigation schemes in Kenya and Upper
Volta (now Burkina Faso) (Conti 1979). Is this "environmental
activism"? The women involved would probably say, "No." However, there is a strong connection between these protests and
demands and the analysis above of the impact of structural adjustment policies on rural African communities, or at least the poorer
members of them, both women and men. In some cases, as in Tanzania, women's groups have emerged that are quite clear about
these connections. For instance, Mbilinyi (1990) describes discussions among women in Tanzania at the grassroots that specifically
connect the export-driven policies of the World Bank with increased

labor demand on women and less time for food crops, child care, and maintenance of the household environment.

The last mentioned is an important and virtually invisible focus of women's environmental activism. In a similar way the Mothers of East Los Angeles and Concerned Citizens of South Central Los Angeles are campaigning for healthy air, soil, and water in their urban neighborhoods. They have identified significant health threats to their children: the lead that has accumulated in the soil after years of automobile emission from the overpasses that crisscross their communities, the many small metal plating firms that evade or fall through the net of state inspection, the attempt to locate a waste incinerator in their midst. In a similar way, many African women are protesting stalled or "rescheduled" water supply, sanitation, and drainage investments by national governments which have been crippled by debt, corruption, and the policy constraints of structural adjustment. This kind of protest and demand is more closely identifiable as "environmental militancy" than the tree planting, use of more efficient wood stoves, and acceptance of small roles in nature tourism that are often pointed to as signs of an emerging environmental awareness on the part of Africans.

Moving beyond the headlines and the more common labels— "democracy movement," "women's movement"—there are other important mass movements that have intersected with environmentalism. In other parts of the world farm workers and their protests at the use of dangerous agrochemicals are considered in the vanguard of radical environmentalism. Indeed, the International Pesticide Network, based in Malaysia, is a truly global network of plantation workers, sympathetic scientists, urban environmentalists, consumer groups, and legislators. Little has been written about the role of African plantation workers in this movement. Why have they not been more centrally involved? Although many of the export crops that require heavy use of pesticides are grown by smallholders (coffee, tea, cocoa, cotton), there are (to give only a few examples) extensive tea plantations in Malawi and Tanzania, rubber plantations in Liberia, tobacco plantations in Zimbabwe, and sugarcane and banana plantations in a number of countries including Zimbabwe, Tanzania, and Somalia. Historically, this plantation labor force has been poorly organized and remains one of the lowest paid and marginalized sections of many of the countries mentioned. Far from corresponding to the role of the "labor aristocracy" that may or may not have been played by transport workers such as stevedores and railway workers in Africa, these plantation workers are semiproletarian and are often involved in seasonal migration from peripheral locations where their wives eke out subsistence. In addition, even where there is a nominally smallholder organization of some export crops, such as cocoa in Cote d'Ivoire and Ghana, hundreds of thousands of impoverished Burkinabe and other semi-proletarians of the Sahelian zone come south every year to harvest the crop for a small wage. Under these conditions it is not surprising that there is little or no protest at the conditions of work, especially exposure to dangerous chemicals. However, the potential for this group of rural workers to develop consciousness about such issues as part of their overall levels of exploitation seems moderately high.

In a similar way, most urban squatters in Africa have not had the same role in militant struggles over the urban environment as their counterparts in, for example, the Philippines, Brazil, or Mexico. As with the so-called women's movement's tree planting, I am less interested in top-down "clean up campaigns" in such a megacity as Lagos, where urban citizens are coaxed into providing free labor to do what any legitimate urban authority should do—collect and dispose of refuse—than in the more fundamental issue of tenants' and squatters' property rights. The assassination of street children and bulldozing of squatter settlements and land invasions is as much a part of Africa's urban struggle as it is elsewhere. There is less publicity and media attention given to this struggle over urban space in Africa, and there are fewer organized groups such as the Sin Talho (homeless, literally "without a roof") movement in Sao Paulo and Rio de Janeiro. However, as in the case of agricultural workers, it is likely that the pressures of urbanization will rapidly cause more formalized groups and a clearer consciousness of how their situation fits into the overall picture of postcolonial exploitation in Africa. In Brazil there are explicit connections between the many rural groups organized for rural land invasion (the Sin Terra movement) and those organized around urban land issues. Since Northern country stereotypes of Africa include the charismatic macrofauna and the yeoman farmer (and noble savage), but no urban icon, it has been difficult for Northern environmentalists to appreciate the significance and potential for urban environmental activism in Africa.

A LUTA CONTINUA: DEFENSE OF LIVELIHOOD II

I have been arguing that one kind of environmental activism has its root in struggles over the means of subsistence, health, and the control over space. This kind of activism is evident in the struggles of marginal and oppressed groups everywhere. African independence struggles were largely fought over land, as Tandon shows concerning Zimbabwe previously in this volume. In Mozambique *a luta*, the armed struggle for independence from Portugal was fought in the northern part of the country where huge concessions had been given by the Portuguese to foreign companies. There company police or *cepai* enforced the cultivation of cotton for export. By contrast, in the south of Mozambique a smallholder peasantry was allowed to control enough land to reproduce itself and the tens of thousands of men who migrated to the mines in South Africa each year after 1913. There is a long history of struggle over access to land in Africa; however, it is simultaneously a struggle over the allocation of labor power. Land itself does one little good if able-bodied men are away in the mines or if the planting and weeding seasons for cotton and maize coincide and one is forced to give precedence to cotton.

Thus political struggle, *a luta*, is bound up with what has come to be known as sustainable livelihood security. Colonial agronomists, agricultural economists, and anthropologists such as Audrey Richards, William Allan, and Margret Haswell knew very well that rain-fed arable agriculture produced a "normal surplus" that allowed for lean as well as fat years (Richards 1939; Allan 1965; Haswell and Clark 1971). It was precisely this surplus that the colonial power set out to tax, and despite the change of political authority at flag independence, this surplus remains the object of extraction by a narrow elite. Structural adjustment and the ravages of war, the needs of refugees dependent on host communities, and years of drought have thrown these production systems into profound crisis. The land question is still alive. It is a question not merely of tenure rights but of the viability of the nexus of environmental and social relations that define these common rain fed arable systems, in dozens of countries. It is for this reason that dissident historians and renegade university students in Kenya state that Mau Mau (the Land Freedom Army that fought the British in the 1950s) is not dead. The so-called environmental crisis in Africa, far from being a simple matter of population pressure creating vicious cycles of poverty, land degradation, famine, and further spirals of compensatory female fertility, is a crisis caused by the loss of local control over land and labor.

Unfortunately, the simplistic model of population-poverty-environment (or PPE, in the shorthand of UNICEF's *State of the*

World's Children 1994) is too widely accepted by Northern environmentalists. Even radical environmentalists such as those at the
Berkeley, California, Ecology Center have reproduced this argument
in their newsletter, *Terrain*, under the title, "Why Environmentalists Should Care about Poverty and Hunger."

LIVELIHOOD AND LIFEWORLD

If political struggle, *a luta*, is inextricably bound up with the
assaults on and defense of livelihood security in Africa, these two
are also intertwined with culturally specific ways of knowing and
communicating knowledge. In the North it has only recently been
realized that environmental activism is also about knowledge and
power, in the phrase of Michel Foucault. When Lois Gibbs and her
colleagues began to generate their own data on air and water pollution, the Environmental Protection Agency dismissed their work as
"housewife data." There has been a similar lack of respect for
indigenous African technical knowledge. However, it is a mistake
to consider indigenous technical knowledge (or ITK in the fashionable shorthand) as something separate from the unitary lifeworld in
which it makes sense. Seed selection, the typology of weeds, pest
protection, and intercropping are parts of a dynamic system that is
evolving. ITK is not so much a series of propositions learned by rote
like Somali poems, Hausa genealogies, or Swahili riddles. Rather, it
is a way of communicating with others about the interdependency
of place and people—specific places, topographies, soil catenas, and
specific people or at least specific kinds of social relations. It is part
of a total lifeworld that is simultaneously natural and social. By
"lifeworld" I mean the universe of shared, often prelinguistic,
meanings that underpin and make possible practical manipulation
of the world through technology and discourse about the world.

Calestous Juma, director of the African Centre for Technology
Studies in Nairobi, has taken the interesting position that African
practice is knowledge, both in rural and in urban contexts. In one
study of communities in Busia in the west of Kenya, he describes
farmers going illegally into the Mt. Elgon rainforest to hunt out
potentially useful plants, transplanting them in their home gardens,
sharing the successful experiments with neighbors, and winning
praise and social status (Juma 1989a, 1989b). He also tells of their
returning these plants to the forest in a ritual that shows a comprehension that the forest is a reservoir of biodiversity to be maintained

in perpetuity. In his urban work, Juma has been a keen student and advocate of what is called "informal industry" throughout Africa. In Kenya these artisans and technology workers are referred to as the *jua kali* sector since they work under the open sky, a mango tree, or a rough shelter. Juma argues that they are a major underappreciated source of technological innovation and that their inventions are often stolen by the more powerful in society because they are not protected by the patent law (Juma and Ojwang 1989).

What is evident in the cases discussed by Juma in rural and urban situations alike is that knowledge, technology, practice, culture, livelihoods, social relations, and political struggles are interwoven in ways that make it impossible, or at least very risky, to try to abstract any one of these elements and treat it separately. It is also clear that the postcolonial state often works at cross purposes with those who are potentially important environmental activists.

Why should the search for useful plants in the Mt. Elgon rainforest, described by Juma, have to take place clandestinely? Why does the Kenyan state not recognize this as part of a forest-preserving ideology to be encouraged? Why are the officially gazetted boundaries of forest reserves and attitudes toward forest management inherited from colonialism so rigid? Other examples of contradictory state policies abound.

In Tanzania, the Maasai have formed their own nongovernmental organization to promote their own view of a human ecology that includes wildlife, livestock, and humans (Ole Parkipuny 1988, 1990–91). The Tanzanian state persists in viewing livestock and wildlife as incompatible, and, indeed, this seems to be a self-fulfilling prophesy. By banning hunting in such large reserves as Serengetti, the population of large animals such as wildebeest has exploded. They encroach more and more into Maasai pastures, but the Maasai are banned from "invading" the official boundaries of the park. The annual migration of the wildebeest, an extraordinary sight as the river of animals flows on and on for scores of miles, annually drives further into the remaining Maasai pasture reserves. Furthermore, the placentas of wildebeest born during the migration carry a disease fatal to Maasai cattle. These details of wildlife and livestock interaction are not the subject of government studies and policy. If there is a "win-win" solution possible in this situation, it seems that only the Maasai are looking for it, not the Tanzanian state. In this case, as well, the fusion of *luta*, or livelihood, and lifeworld issues is evident. To engage the Maasai in dialogue about a future land-use regime that provides for their needs and the needs of nature tourism, the interlocutors would have to address more than monetary compensation, alternative income earning opportunities, and tourist industry profit sharing. These are important issues, but only part of the class of livelihood issues, and they do not even begin to address the Maasai lifeworld. The Maasai consider themselves to be inheritors from God of the bioregion called the Maasai steppe. They believe they are guardians for all time of the wildlife, the cattle, and the grass, trees, water, and soil. Mutual understanding between the Tanzanian state and the Maasai would require putting on the table for discussion and negotiation the full range of material and ideological interests both sides have in the bioregion. As yet this has not happened.

It is not enough merely to acknowledge the utility of ITK, to learn it, absorb it within an outside worldview and agenda—conservationist, developmentalist, or otherwise. Beyond the existence of vernacular vocabularies for describing soil, plants, and so on, there is the entire cultural context, the understanding of what a "place" is, that may well differ drastically from what outsiders from Europe or North America normally mean by "environment" or "resource."

In the West, "environment" is often thought of as a geometrical container, a box, with "things" in it. Some of these things are useful and are called "resources." The very notion of 'carrying capacity'—at the heart of arguments about the vicious cycle of poverty, population growth, and environmental degradation in Africa mentioned above—is a derivative of such geometrical thinking. Land becomes a geometrical surface which "carries" people: the statistical expression is "persons per square kilometer " or "per square mile."

These simplified, highly pervasive mental images bear no relation to vernacular thought and action. Far from living out their lives on stages with such linear dimensions, Africans create *livelihood systems* that depend as much on other people as on the flow of energy through natural systems.[1] The shape of the lifeworld can change from season to season. There are likely to be both urban and rural lifelines.[2] Africa's poorest 40 percent of "farmers" are not farmers at all, but gain more than half their income from many such "nonfarm" activities that are seldom included in calculations of "carrying capacity" (Livingstone 1988; Wisner and Mbithi 1974). Mobility across space is common not only among the pastoral people of Africa, but also among so-called sedentary cultivators. Many diverse pockets of soil, water, wild and cultivated annual plants, perennial grasses, and trees support livelihoods.

In the flood-retreat irrigation systems of West Africa (fadama), East Africa, and also in Somalia, dozens of crops are planted as flood-waters recede into dry-season river banks and as seasonal lakes dry up. Variability in time and space is central to the livelihood systems of Africa. Local residents are aware of a wide variety of microenvi-ronments to which the outsider may be culturally blind. Chambers lists the following examples (Chambers 1990:6–7): home gardens; vegetable and horticultural patches; river banks and riverine strips; levees and natural terraces; valley bottoms; wet and dry water courses; alluvial pans; artificial terraces; silt trap fields; raised fields; water harvesting in its many forms; hedges and windbreaks; clumps, groves, or lines of trees or bushes; pockets of fertile soil (ter-mitaria, former livestock pens, etc.); sheltered corners or strips, by aspect of slope, configuration, and so on; plots protected from live-stock; flood recessional zones; small flood plains; springs and patches of high groundwater and seepage; strips and pockets of impeded drainage; lake basins; ponds, including fishponds; and ani-mal wallows.

The geometrical abstraction 'environment' is both lived and conceptualized in Africa as 'place.' Places have long, complex human histories and stories. They are associated with joy and satis-faction as well as suffering, conflict, and pain. The inability for pro-fessionals trained in the West to understand land tenure in Africa is derivative, as well, of the emptiness of the abstraction 'environ-ment.'

One must realize that no piece of territory, no island (however large), can support a person precisely because, in John Donne's words, "no man is an island." It is the human social nexus that makes production possible in the first place. Therefore carrying capacity cannot be reckoned strictly in terms of people per hectares of land. Thousands of years of exchanges among cultures were required to produce the present geography of these technologies and relations of production. Moreover, people do not stand like tenpins on geometrical surfaces, but dwell in places.

The physical properties of the place may not be immedi-ately obvious to outsiders. Thus a square kilometer of Burkina Faso in West Africa may produce (be capable of producing) a certain amount of rice, or millet, or beef. But here and there in the inter-stices the place also provides wood for cooking, reeds for making baskets, fish, wild fruits, and so on. These are the biologically diverse properties that can only be tapped with *culturally diverse* systems of livelihood.[3]

If humanized places, rather than environments are the spaces within which Africans arrange their livelihood strategies, how are we to conceptualize the physical and biological characteristics of those "many, diverse pockets" where people work? This small zone of soil has more clay, hence holds water longer in the root zone of plants; that zone of forest has trees known to resist termite attack, which are good for building houses; another zone—a swamp or stretch of river—is known for fish one can trap. The crystalline structure of the clay molecule or the chemical composition of the tree bark are not resources in themselves. They only become so when two things are added: human labor and a human project. The project may be protection of the family against the threat of drought, hence the "usefulness" of soil with good moisture-holding capacity. The project may be pride and status shown in a better, sturdier house. The project may be hospitality centered around a fish stew. Or, of course, the project may be sale of dried fish in order to pay school fees.

The human labor involved is neither brute force nor individual genius. Knowledge of an indefinite number of physical and biological characteristics of the lifeworld are socially constructed and passed along to children. In Somalia, for example, people have a highly developed body of knowledge concerning water, vegetation, soil, and animal health. These properties of the environment are not known simply technically or functionally, but as part of a shared cultural heritage whose boundaries include moral and religious teaching (*xeer*) as well.

"For the person of Siaya [Western Kenya]," Cohen and Odhiambo tell us, "'landscape' is not a reference to the physiognomy of the terrain. Rather it evokes the possibilities and limitations of space: encompassing the physical land, the people on it, and the culture through which people work out the possibilities of the land" (Cohen and Odhiambo 1989:9). Likewise the aesthetic, social, and ecological characteristics of place are fused in Somali poetry (Rirash 1988:9):

> I hate the Maaro mountain because of the early
> morning heavy rains/ I hate having camels in a windy
> place/ and I hate cattle when it comes to "jilaal,"

the dry season. . . . *Gumar* [Acacia oerfota] tree/
Can you tell me where our herds are grazing? . . .
Your beauty is reminiscent of grazing land on which
it rained recently/
and on which a bright sun shone.

Historically, outsiders have not been interested in such diverse potentials and daily practices. Africa was seen in the early days of colonization as a source of high value luxury goods: ivory, frankincense, gold, diamonds—the products (real and imagined) of King Solomon's mines. Later Africa was given the role of providing industrial countries with cheap mineral exports (copper, bauxite, cobalt, uranium, phosphates, iron)[4] and, as noted earlier, cheap raw material for the production of basic consumer goods for the industrial workers of the North, vegetable oils for cooking and soap, cotton for clothing, sugar, beef, timber, cocoa, coffee, tea, and tobacco (Dinham and Hines 1982; Ridgeway 1980).

More recently Africa has become the scene of industrial country extraction of energy sources. Kaiser aluminum still pays the lowest electricity charges in the world at the site of the Volta Dam, where it converts bauxite to alumina. There is uranium in South Africa, Namibia, Gabon, Niger, and Somalia. Petroleum or natural gas is found in Nigeria, Angola, Congo, Cote d'Ivoire, Gabon, Mozambique, Tanzania, and offshore Sudan.[5] All of these energy resources are the subject of great interest by multinational corporations.

Such a role in the international division of labor has been translated into a devaluation of peasant and pastoralist knowledge and practice. "Resource" has been defined in a very limited, euro-centric way, namely, "that which is found in nature, useful to Europeans, and importable to Europe at a profit."[6]

The environmental crisis in Africa is partly a product of economic development policies and projects based on such a narrow, euro-centric definition of what a resource is. Yet *crisis* is an ambiguous word. It can imply that the people suffering have been made passive by the enormity of their situation.[7] Certainly this is not always the case. The word also suggests a situation involving someone other than the observer, the passerby. Africa is in crisis; Northern industrial countries are not. "They" are in crisis, not "we." We are not connected, except in the role as aid givers, Samaritans, compassionate observers.

Yet many would argue that the connection is much more direct. In some parts of Africa various authorities have been declaring environmental crisis since the 1920s. This has had less to do with the ability of local populations to cope with conditions in their lifeworlds and more to do with the desire for external authorities to exert control. It has also had to do with the consequences of pushing Africans off of their most productive lands or forcing them to cultivate nonfood export crops in the highlands of Zimbabwe, Kenya, Cameroon, Angola, and Mozambique. Colonial and independent African authorities have further provoked crisis by moving large numbers of rural people by the creation of artificial lakes and irrigation schemes in Ghana, Nigeria, Mozambique, Zambia, Zimbabwe, Sudan, Niger, and Mali. State-mandated expansion of cotton, peanuts, or commercial ranching for export in much of Africa's drier lands from Botswana to Senegal and the Awash Valley of Ethiopia has also marginalized rural people, creating crisis (Molutsi 1988; Franke and Chasin 1980; Kloos 1982). Foreign concessionary companies linked historically to the old colonial powers continue to cut wood from Africa's Guinean and Zairian regions, making Cote d'Ivoire and Gabon the world's largest exporters of tropical hardwoods after Malaysia, Indonesia, and the Philippines (Gerstin 1990). In some countries such as Cameroon and Ghana the highly acclaimed UN Tropical Forestry Action Plan has been used as a thin veneer behind which commercial cutting accelerates (Colchester and Lohmann 1990:42–49, 66–72). However, blame for deforestation in Africa and a consequent crisis of disappearing wild genes in the rainforests is popularly attributed to shifting cultivators.

The threat of soil erosion was used by colonial powers as an excuse for direct control over peasant production (Cliffe 1988; Beinart 1984).[8] Likewise the threat of disease was used to control street vendors and urban squatters (Stock 1988). Today the cry "environmental crisis" continues to be used as an excuse for intrusions into the lives of common people. As noted earlier, peasants and pastoralists are often assumed to be ignorant of the value of Africa's large mammals, poachers and slaughterers who stand in the way of "rational," "nonconsumptive" use of these four-legged "resources" by the rapidly growing eco-tourism industry.

PARTICIPATORY ACTION RESEARCH: HELPING TO DEFEND LIVELIHOOD AND LIFEWORLD

If environmental activism in Africa must be understood as a fusion of *luta*, livelihood, and lifeworld, an obvious question is how the outsider—both urban-based African professionals and foreign intellectuals—can help.

In the past such outsiders have tried to act as catalysts of change and have brought their concepts, names, and labels to local situations. The point of all the foregoing is that it is often difficult and pointless to call a specific struggle a "gender" struggle, an "economic" struggle, or an "environmental" struggle. Outsiders can help by providing access to a wider universe of information—allowing understanding of a broader range of options—but control must remain local. The issue of local control is not just a matter of institutional forms, financial autonomy, or external political relations. Control is also a matter of the language used to conceptualize the situation people face and what they intend to do. It begins with the local, not external, definition of needs.

Who should define needs? There are two fundamentally opposed approaches to this question.[9] What I call the "weak" approach to the basic needs approach (BNA) imposes "expert" definitions and seeks participation in the form of acceptance of the expert's opinion and donation of community labor or individual acceptance of new technologies. By contrast, the "strong" BNA is based on the community's own analysis of its needs and obstacles to satisfying them. It tends to identify more than technical obstacles, arriving at a critique of such underlying issues as land tenure, gender power, and control over resources.

The distinction can be exemplified by the case of rural hunger. Applying a weak BNA to the problem of hunger in rural parts of the third world, so-called rural development projects have sought to do two things: draw an ever widening group of small and marginal farmers into production of a limited number of export crops and increase yields of food crops through the spread of input packages that include high-yielding varieties. The purpose of the former was to increase the purchasing power of the rural dwellers. The purpose of the latter was to provide them with more food and a larger surplus for sale. Most so-called "integrated" rural development projects in the 1970s and 1980s provided a variety of services and infrastructure (health care, education, feeder roads, rural credit, marketing, etc.) in order to maximize one or both of these two goals. A similar "package" approach was designed for pastoral people.

This weak version of the BNA encountered a series of internal contradictions that limited its effectiveness. First, access to resources—especially land and water, but also production capital to acquire hybrid seeds and other inputs—is highly skewed in these countries. In the absence of land reform, the benefits of expanded export cropping and high yielding seeds were concentrated in the hands of a limited proportion of farmers. Some poor found work for larger farmers, but their wages did not allow them to feed adequately their families. Others were driven out of rural areas to join the urban poor. Still others took advantage of land-settlement schemes in Indonesia, Malaysia, Brazil, Peru, Kenya, and elsewhere (putting further pressure on forests and wetlands).

Second, where the smallholder did begin to grow an export crop, she or he often found that the price of food and other necessities outstripped the returns from that crop (coffee, tea, cotton, cocoa, etc.) during the 1970s and especially the 1980s. The world market price of all these major agricultural export commodities fell during the 1980s. Producers of livestock for export in Somalia and elsewhere were buffered by government food-price policies and the availability of food aid; however, this pressure was still felt. The tendency under structural adjustment programs to establish fees for services such as domestic water, health care, education, and the related policy of removing government subsidies on such items as fertilizer and even such staple items as maize meal and rice added to the pressure on rural (as well as urban) household budgets.

By contrast, the strong BNA responds to such problems by recognizing the existence of a low-cost, locally available alternative to imported high-yielding seeds and their support packages. Such a "farmer first" standpoint draws on local human resources: the knowledge and skill of groups of poor farmers (Richards 1985; Chambers 1989; Conway and Barbier 1990; Moris 1991). Their seed-, soil-, forest-, and water-management techniques can be the starting point for locally controlled systems that increase yield and generate income. Many NGOs in Asia, Africa, and Latin America report successes using this approach, a particular case of the strong as opposed to the weak BNA (Harrison 1987; Wisner 1988; Adams 1990). "Farmer first" activities belong to the strong BNA because of their reliance on transformative participation and local control.

Transformative participation tends to move by its own logic and momentum outward from the specific needs and obstacles identified by a group to wider issues. Depending on the national political and economic context, this movement may involve groups in disputes with authorities or over inequities in government services or over access to land, forest, pasture, and water resources. Disputes may arise over wages or conditions of employment and safety (for instance, the use of dangerous pesticides by plantation owners). At one extreme there have been land invasions in Brazil and Honduras, confrontations over the use of forestlands in India and Mexico, and large-scale opposition to proposed dams on rivers in the Philippines, Brazil, and India. Less confrontational developments based similarly on the initiative and self-organization of the rural poor include schemes for new uses of common property resources in a number of countries (pasture, forest, groundwater) (Jodha 1991).

Such farmer first approaches tend to challenge the definition of what a natural resource is in the first place as well as challenging the distribution of access to recognized resources. Indigenous seeds and wild plants are becoming redefined as community resources (Juma 1989). The strong BNA tends toward "food first" as opposed to "production first" goals. However, it is also possible for the strong BNA to lead to marketed production, even export-oriented production, as long as control is local. This can be seen in the establishment of extractive reserves and locally controlled, sustainable production of tropical forest products for export (rubber, nuts, and pharmaceutical raw materials) in Brazil, Cameroon, Panama, and elsewhere. In Zimbabwe this idea has led to Operation Campfire through which rural communities gain income from controlled wildlife-viewing tourism in return for their pledge to conserve the habitat of the animals and limit hunting.

African struggles to reclaim control over lifeworld and livelihood can be aided by outside agents who share the strong BNA that puts farmers and food first. For example, Oxfam America engaged in a "participatory learning" exercise in Tanzania, Zambia, and Zimbabwe. University students lived in villages for several months where Oxfam projects had run. Villagers engaged in discussions of the projects and how they could have been improved. Village representatives met at the national level in each country, and later some met again in an international conference where the experiences of project villages from all three countries were analyzed (Kalyalya et al. 1988). This is one example of how many nongovernmental organizations are trying to take seriously the injunction to "put people first" (Chambers et al. 1989). When they succeed, local creativity is harnessed—the same ingenuity that has been used to dodge taxes, sabotage attempts to take over local lands, and subvert government initiatives. The results have so far included effective gully control, reforestation, wood stove improvement, local seed improvement, grain storage, and water harvesting, as well as defense of women's rights to bank accounts, day care initiatives, and legal challenges where land has been illegally occupied by the elite.

The striking thing about these examples is that they are far more than serial rural-development, land-improvement or employment-generation activities. Such old categories belong to the days when outside agencies waged "development war" on local inhabitants. Zimbabwean peasants explained what this means (Ranger 1985:288): "We, the people make the decisions. You and me, we are the decision makers. No district commissioner will tell us what fees to pay for cattle dipping. . . . We discuss among ourselves and agree. . . . We want irrigation schemes to make growing of maize possible even in winter. . . . Such things cannot run on decisions of a man in Salisbury. No! It has to be you who makes the decisions. That's what People's Power is all about."

The restoration of the lifeworld and livelihood—resulting in the satisfaction of locally defined basic needs—requires a new kind of relationship between the outside professional and the community, unlike top-down projects of the past. Rural women and men have much greater control over the process.

One more example will draw together various strands of the argument. Tete Province in Mozambique's extreme northwest corner is quite dry to the south of the Zambezi River where it borders Zimbabwe. Drought in the mid-1980s coincided with raids by terrorists supported by South Africa to drive many of the rural people into camps for displaced persons across the border in Zimbabwe. Emergency response teams entered this problem at the community level and with a view toward short-term survival of adults and children. That is what the refugees wanted at the moment. Emergency feeding, shelter, and health care were needed and provided. However, the perspective of sustainability suggested something more. The people also wanted a longer term solution. In discussing future return to their homes with the refugees UNICEF was able to design and implement an innovative plan for community rehabilitation. Families were later resettled in Tete Province with oxen loaned to them from UNICEF and seed varieties to plant from peasant fields across the border in Zimbabwe. Technological and genetic inputs were chosen to fit the longer term requirements of ecological adaptability and cultural acceptance.

This is a good example of partnership between local people and outsiders in the kind of situation that has become all too common in Africa during the 1980s and 1990s: drought and war. This is the kind of approach that is far more likely to bear fruit as Africa seeks alternatives to the World Bank's recipe for structural adjustment and begins to rebuild livelihoods in the wake of the violence and disorder in countries such as Angola, Mozambique, Rwanda, Burundi, Liberia, Somalia, Sudan.

It is also a promising approach to learning positive lessons from local struggles as well as finding new ways to work in solidarity in more promising situations, where stability and newly won political democracy provide numerous opportunities for environmental activism. In Eritrea, Namibia, and South Africa it is likely that a wide range of new needs will be defined and expressed. These may be urban—for example, involving toxic and other hazards in places like Greater Johannesburg or worker safety in the mines of Namibia and South Africa—as well as rural.

In the middle is a large group of countries—Tanzania, Zimbabwe, Zambia, Cameroon, Nigeria, Ghana, Burkina Faso, and others—with long histories of struggles by women, peasants, and workers—where the full flowering of such broadly defined environmentalism, based in local definition of needs, will have to await further democratization at the national level.

CONCLUSION

I have argued that environmental activism exists in Africa, but it can be dangerously misunderstood if categories that are derived by the recent historical experience of environmentalism in Europe and North America are applied to it. Struggle over assaults on the integrity of livelihood systems and the lifeworlds that support them is at the heart of most African popular movements—those labeled, variously, "women's movement," "democracy movement," and, indeed, "environmental movement." 'Livelihood' and 'lifeworld' are both concepts that place a high priority on local control over the natural environment, but the concept of 'environment' as such is not necessarily the key to understanding defense of livelihood and lifeworld. I have suggested that 'place' is a more common notion that does not imply the commoditization and technification of nature that Western terms such as "environment" and "resource" carry with them. Attempting to think through the integral nature of these common struggles by women, peasants, and workers in Africa from their point of view, it should be possible for outsiders to learn important lessons as well as to provide assistance.

NOTES

1. On livelihood systems see Chambers (1983) and World Commission on Environment and Development (1987). On the lifeworld, see Richards (1975).

2. The connection between rural and urban in Africa has seldom been given proper weight. See Guyer (1987) and Southall (1979).

3. On the ways that technologies interact, see Wisner (1988:245–62) and Pacey (1983). Pacey provides a very useful discussion of "interactive innovation," where cultures meet in equality (also see Brokensha et al. 1980). Unfortunately, it is more common that differences in power between nations, classes, and genders introduce relations of domination between knowledge systems (Marglin and Marglin 1990), and the weaker agents hide their understandings of the world (Scott 1985; 1990).

4. The following indicates Africa's share (excluding South Africa) in world output in 1983: iron ore, 6.4 percent; copper, 16.7 percent; bauxite, 17.6 percent; and uranium, 22.1 percent (Yachir 1988:20).

5. The Akosombo Dam in Ghana was built with the needs of foreign aluminum producers in mind. Similarly, Cabora Basa Dam in Mozambique was built by the Portuguese colonial power with international loans so it could sell electricity to South Africa. Independent Mozambique is saddled with these debts. (Uranium, petroleum, and natural gas data from World Bank 1989:122–30).

6. A conventional Western definition of "natural resource" contains two parts: (1) the existence of external, physical "neutral stuff" in the world around and (2) a socio-economic system that finds some "utility" in them.

7. Nora McKeon in discussion of the Italian Image of Africa project, 1989.

8. Soil conservation in colonial Africa was often coercively enforced, leaving a great deal of bitterness behind and the challenge of overcoming past associations for more popular authorities; see, for instance, Ranger (1985:293, 298–99).

9. This section is based on Wisner (1988).

PART IV
POPULAR ECOLOGICAL RESISTANCE
IN EUROPE

Chapter 11

HAVE A FRIEND FOR LUNCH:
NORWEGIAN RADICAL ECOLOGY
VERSUS TRADITION

David Rothenberg

Norway has been called the philosophical home of radical environmentalism. Most recently this is because it is the homeland of Arne Naess, the philosopher who invented the term *deep ecology* to refer to the growth of serious and hard-edged revolutionary ideas clustered around environmental concern. Before that, we have a country that traditionally reveres and mythologizes its mountains and rivers, such that its entire history is interwoven with the land. Norwegian national identity is nothing without nature, and its natural resources are the basis of the country's current wealth, which guarantees a pristine sense of civilization that makes the place one of the prime examples of a successful welfare state.

So are all its citizens environmentalists? Depends who you ask. All of us want to call ourselves environmentalists these days, wherever we are on the political map. Bush, Clinton, Carter, probably everyone except Reagan would like to be identified as an environmentalist by the American public. Norway's prime minister, Gro Harlem Brundtland, made an international reputation as a "Green Goddess" who many say will one day lead the United Nations. But at home, her reputation has never been so clear. Norway is *not* a country where everyone accepts the e-word. In rural areas environ-mentalists (it's even hard to say in Norwegian—*miljømennesker?*) are seen as stuck-up city types from the south who want to tell the hinterlands how to live. And the latest generation of Norse twen-tysomethings are interested in the global grit of world culture as much as they are the traditional mountain world of goat cheese and reindeer jerky.

In *Wisdom in the Open Air* (Reed and Rothenberg 1992), the history and prognosis of Norwegian ecological thought was pre-sented as a blend of the radical and the conservative, the traditional and the innovative. The present chapter examines how the country that brought the world deep ecology has fared ecosophically with time, that is, since the mid-eighties, after environmentalism has gained much political currency worldwide. First, the most salient and practical advice that the ideas of Arne Naess and his cronies have brought to worldwide environmental activism is reviewed, and then a discussion follows of a recent issue that casts a thorn in the side of this ecofriendly nation: their persistence in whaling despite previously agreeing to an international ban.

———————

Deep ecology means at least two things. As a movement, it is a name given by Arne Naess to a tendency in ecological thinking that has been around for a long time. It is a word that is meant to gather activists around a common cause. It encompasses all those who believe that environmental problems are symptoms of something deeper, some beliefs afoul at the core of our contemporary civiliza-tion. Ecological imbalances are symptoms of deeper uncertainties, and supporters of deep ecology also believe that changing ideas can change the way we live. Thought leads to action, and we will be able to make a better world upon new conceptual foundations.

The second meaning refers to specific ways of thinking and speaking encouraged by Naess—the philosophy of deep ecology—as opposed to the deep ecology movement. Here the new conception of the world is not exhaustively described, but merely hinted at. It is an incipient, or open, philosophical system in which you must fill in the blanks if you care to follow it. Its tenets include seeing the world as a net of relations, not an assembly of things. No object, ani-mal, or person has any identity without its essential connections to the world of relations around it. No ideas but in things. No things but in ideas. This is the metaphysics. In the ethics of deep ecology, there is no altruism. We do everything for self-interest, or more carefully, self-realization, with as wide a notion of the self as Gandhi understood, where he saved an entire nation so he could feel at home. The self expands to include the world, and deep ecology will extend it thus.

This philosophy has been articulated elsewhere (Naess and Rothenberg 1989; Rothenberg 1992; Bordurant 1958), and I will offer only a brief summary here. Deep ecology should appear deeper if it is understood as flowing out of empiricism, logic, possibilism, and Gandhism as they have been put to use in deliberation over one of the central issues of our time.

This terminology, introduced in a five-page article by Arne Naess in the journal *Inquiry* in 1973, came to be taken up as a banner for diverse eco-movements across the globe: "Shallow ecology" fights against pollution in the wealthy countries alone, while "deep ecology" looks for the fundamental roots of eco-problems in the structure of societies and cultures around the world. The philosophy behind the words remains suggestive, not definitive, but people who take it on don't seem to mind. Arne cautions us to distinguish between the deep ecology philosophy and the deep ecology movement. A movement can be inspired by slogans and touch millions. A philosophy is something else again. It is a path of questioning, a discipline that does not gain adherents, but a method that sets thinkers out onto their own diverse routes—ascending the same mountain perhaps, but choosing the way most appropriate for each individual climber.

Deep ecology has become an attractive phrase for many people, who tend to bend the term to their needs without bothering to learn what it was originally meant to imply. There are those who use the term to label themselves the real, bold, and serious environmentalists, opposing their chosen few to the vast majority of weak reformist thinkers, who they deem to call "shallow." And there are others who use the term *deep* simply as a substitute for *radical*, which leads their opponents to criticize them for being far "off the deep end" in respect to real problems and workable solutions.

Because the word has been twisted and turned in so many directions without agreement, I feel I need to tie some strands of the rope together here. If deep ecology is to be of any use to environmentalists, it will not be in its convenience as a name for extremism, but as a signal for us to question the foundation of our concern, asking us to articulate why we believe what we do about the singular importance of nature, and helping us to determine what basic changes in society are most worth fighting for to realize the goal of a sustainable world where humanity thinks of more than its own welfare. It should not be a pose, but a tool to gradually make the viable routes appear in our gaze.

The value of deep ecology can only be assessed by considering how it has inspired some to change the way they live. It has changed the way environmental protests are conducted: a nature with value in itself is worthy of preservation for itself, and this has led to the practice of eco-defense, in which trees may not be able to grow spikes to save themselves, but we can help them out a little. In the United States, the Earth First! movement has defended its nonviolent actions against the forest service and the lumber companies upon the principle that humans should not always be considered first. But neither can people be ignored—looking for the deep social roots of ecological problems also involves the proposal of deep solutions that are both profound and realistic. It is no longer enough to attack unnecessary gigantic freeway projects on ecological grounds alone. We need to prepare thorough well-researched recommendations for alternative transportation which will save money (satisfying economists), be locally manageable (satisfying the people most directly affected by the project), and fit into an integrated vision of a viable society for the many different communities it will serve.

Scientists, long influenced by a self-imposed taboo against involving ethics in their pursuit of abstract truth, have finally begun to come around and realize that their work is deeply entwined in a system of values, which they should use their expertise to articulate. The new field of conservation biology has been created by ecologists and naturalists who are not afraid of voicing the moral conviction behind their study of the world's life forms: preserve the diversity of life on the planet! Then they take up the scientific challenges of determining how much diversity is needed and how we may ensure it by the appropriate natural reserves and proper contact with the diverse human cultures who have lived successfully among the thousands of endangered plant and animal species. Conservation biologists have helped to plan national parks from the Amazon to the Sahara.

Any thoughtful environmentalism leads quickly to a paradox: If there is a sense in which nature is more important than human aspirations, how do we protect this aspect of nature without deprecating our situation as human beings? Human society today changes at an alarming rate. We do not want to deny it progress as much as redefine progress. A return to any self-conscious and romantic past will not work.

Deep ecology dares to hope for a way beyond this paradox. It does not pronounce that wild animals are more important than people, or that breathing in the scent of new pine needles will somehow solve the injustices of Capitalist and Socialist systems alike. No one should be so naive as to simplify it into such empty claims. If deep ecology seems too vague, it is because we have failed to catch its spark as a reassuring guide to connect a fundamental reverence for the earth with a need to act immediately and practically to save it. It is a tentative beginning, not a finished solution.

There are those who say that deep ecology is unnecessarily centered around the confining concept of the 'self.' Arne Naess tends to talk about the widening of individual concern, not dwelling on the social constraint of thought and act. Of course the intricacies of the world cannot be explained away by the experiences of individuals alone. But as a practical approach to the ecological problems of today, we need to inspire and touch individuals before we can speak of the behavior of social groups. Naess speaks of "self-realization" to explain the way in which nature is not in conflict with us. We become our fullest selves when we empathize with the world in its widest sense, when we feel compassion for the near and far reaches of the natural world; when we recognize this feeling and are not afraid of it.

Immanuel Kant revolutionized ethics by suggesting that we never use another person merely as a means to an end, but also as an end in his or her self. Deep ecology suggests that we should never use any living being or aspect of the living world as merely a means to an end. All life has intrinsic value, and this should hold beneath all our own actions and manipulations. This does not suggest that nature is something to be left alone, but only that we are entitled to change it only when we realize its value. As we empathize with more of the natural world, we improve ourselves and our lives.

Reexamining the boundaries of the natural and the human has considerable consequences for all ethical and political theories and practices. Some immediate specifics to be transformed may be the way we argue points in environmental debate, or the way laws are structured and defended. It would be a tremendous step if development projects were halted if they damaged not just a single endangered species, but whole ecosystems whose value could be determined by assessing the uniqueness of the specific interweaving of natural and human history which characterizes places important to us. A reconsideration of values that could be agreed upon by a majority of the population could result in a reallocation of a nation's resources toward different priorities than at present. The conservation of natural resources leads to the consideration of cultural resources, and we will be driven to define our own human identity more clearly in the shadow of the world's. Here the boundaries between ourselves and the environment break down, and each side makes sense only as it takes account of the other.

If you are still not sure what deep ecology means, congratulations! You are among the majority. It remains a tentative, though tantalizing, label. If it inspires you to ask more questions, you are on the right track. If one honestly upholds that a deep respect for the earth implies a need to work on behalf of our planet, then it is hard to denounce deep ecology. By putting forth the right questions, it may enable us to reconcile our human path with the rhythm of a nature with which we are inextricably bound. This is why, when people ask me "What do you think of deep ecology?" I tend to respond with a paraphrase of Gandhi's response to the question "What do you think of Western civilization?"—"I think it would be a good idea."

The relevance of Gandhi to all this will be made clear below. I want to stress how deep ecology offers specific tactical advice to environmentalists that make it the most practical kind of radicalism around, practical because it teaches us how to confront the enemy: how to speak clearly to our opponents, and how to be listened to.

It begins with respect and encompasses emotion.

NONVIOLENCE IN ECOLOGY

Nonviolent resistance is often an important part of environmental action: lying across the road to block the onslaught of bulldozers, chaining oneself to the floor of a valley as the dammed waters start to rise. These can be powerful forms of protest. The press will take notice, and the public will follow, so the world will learn of your case. If you are willing to lay your life on the line, they think, you must be quite convinced of the correctness of your position.

But does it work? Such demonstrations also seem to escalate quickly toward violence, or at least animosity. The fierceness of commitment to any cause can lead to overzealous fervor and a refusal to respect the views of the other side (whatever it takes to wake up the world to the issue). This is what motivated the militant wing of America's environmental movement, known for a while as Earth First! to support the practice of violence toward property, if not people, in the name of a free and wild nature worth more than the possessions of those people bent on paving over or stripping down nature. There is a long tradition of violence against property belonging to the ruling class in the name of a greater common good. In Norway eco-activist Sigmund Kvaløy had this to say about the application of controlled violence in environmental protest:

> People's will to defend themselves doesn't concern only their country, but also their living environment . . . One has to defend what one feels close to . . . We must get away from the idea that the dividing line between violence and nonviolence lies at the use of dynamite. *Yet no living thing should be harmed—not even a blade of grass.* If dynamite helps life to flow again where it has been stopped, this would be a truly nonviolent use of explosives, really a peace-promoting use of the name of Alfred Nobel! (Reed and Rothenberg 1992)

This is a tactic for environmentalism that does tend to incite the enemy, maybe to something less than willingness to consider alien views.

A common opinion is that mainstream environmentalists are glad that extremists exist, to make themselves appear more reasonable, but there is a flip side: opponents of the ecological cause may tend to brand all environmentalists as unreasonable provocateurs. Paul Bremer, U.S. ambassador-at-large for counterterrorism (during the Bush administration), sees little difference between eco-terrorists and other kinds:

> Like political terrorists, ecoterrorists start with a strong belief system centered on an uncompromising, utopian—even Messianic—vision. Such terrorists see their role as righting perceived wrongs, whether the "oppression of the Palestinian people" or "the rape of Mother Earth." But these worthy goals are then perverted by ideological extremism . . . They seek to

commit acts of violence which draw maximum attention to their cause with little concern for who gets hurt. (Bremer 1992)

To distinguish eco-terrorism from political terrorism, one needs to emphasize that it does uphold a moral code: only harm things, not people. And as its literary inspiration, Edward Abbey writes: Never get caught. Never seek publicity. Just get the job done. Make sure no one knows who you are. The action speaks for itself.

Does this platform of protest offer much method for solution? This is the biggest problem with violent civil disobedience. It does not encourage a cooperative spirit toward the resolution of real and difficult problems. It seems better as symbol than reality. By giving in to violence the movement may gain a visible hard edge, but it loses the opportunity to foster constructive conversation between the sides of the conflict who will still disagree.

Those who support nonviolence as political force find the strongest solace in the actions and words of Mahatma Gandhi. Although nature was not his primary cause, he offers specific insights appropriate to ecoactivism. Gandhi offers a total view of how an individual may act in an apparently selfless way, all the while pursuing a goal of self-realization in its widest sense.

It was this wide sense that most impressed Arne Naess. Before turning to ecological matters, Naess worked for many years to demonstrate that Gandhi's collection of aphorisms, life experiments, protests, and meditations constituted a coherent philosophy, not a bag of contradictory assertions and behaviors. Self-realization according to Gandhi is the root of Naess's entire philosophy of deep ecology, conceived as personal philosophy in concert with respect for the human place in nature.

The power of nonviolence is built upon belief in the essential oneness of all life. "A drop torn from the ocean perishes without doing any good. If it stays part of the ocean, it shares the glory of carrying on its bosom a fleet of mighty ships" (Gandhi quoted in Naess 1974). Realizing the full potential of the self means recognizing that one's identity as an individual is expanded by embracing the concerns of those aspects of life first near and then far from your own particular place. Act selflessly, with detachment, and above all *without regard for the fruits of one's action*, an idea taken straight from the Bhagavad Gita itself, where Arjuna calls to Krishna from the battlefield, wondering whether to give in or to fight. Choice is essential, says the god. But the action should be performed because it is right, not for any gain, public or private, personal or political.

These spiritual principles seem quite far from a strategy for any issue-based campaign. It is precisely because of this distance that they have more to do with truth than with winning a game. Nonviolence so defined becomes much more than a tactic for calling attention to environmental causes, but a strong platform from which to convince people of many different persuasions that the situation is severe. Gandhi conceived of nonviolence as a philosophical quest, a mission toward the truth, rather than a method to fight for what you already are sure of. The nonviolent action should imply searching for the answer, not representing it in advance.

And the truth which it seeks is the answer most pertinent to the situation at hand. Here is Gandhi on trial by the Hunter Committee in 1919:

> *Council:* However honestly a man may strive in his search for the truth, his notions of truth may be different from the notions of others. Who then is to determine the truth?
> *Accused:* The individual himself would determine that.
> *Council:* Different individuals would have different views as to truth? Would that not lead to confusion?
> *Accused:* I do not think so.
> *Council:* Honestly striving after truth differs in every case?
> *Accused:* That is why nonviolence is a necessary corollary. Without it there would be confusion and worse.
> (Naess 1974)

A diversity of truths, a plurality of right ways to live and fulfill the self, but each dictated by the situation—Gandhi believes nonviolence will work only in situations where parties hold *honestly* their disparate views. It will work only where opponents truly believe in their differing positions and no one is lying for political or other reasons. Opponents should not attack each other with strawman caricatures or inflamed rhetoric designed to cheaply discredit the opposite side. With action done just for its own sake, nonviolence will inspire mutual respect among all involved parties.

Does the idea of truth specific to each situation sidestep the conflicts of relativism? The answer to such disparities lies in the sincerity with which different perspectives are presented. It becomes a utilitarianism guided by respect for the principle of paying attention to the full extent of each situation. Follow the action itself, here and now. Learn as much about the different sides of the case as you can. Be prepared to give up your principles if you discover information that challenges them. Yet if you are still sure you are right, steadfastness will also hold with greater knowledge. Above all, strive to meet the enemy directly, on their own terms. If you do all this, you will be meeting the demands of radical nonviolent activism.

These principles seem calmly considered, polite, reflective, and far from the overblown pontification we have come to expect in political statement. Nonviolence may have worked wonders in India, but is it too idealistic for the arena of deception in which ideas are slyly marketed and packaged over here? I hope it can work, because unlike so many other forms of social critique, it does not begin with cynicism toward the general malaise of our time and place. It begins with the inhabitation of the other point of view. Before the divergence of your own interest comes a deep identification with the goals and aspirations appropriate to all fellow humans. There will be no hatred.

This is the aspect most often missing from nonviolent environmental protests: a real willingness and effort to communicate with the object of the protest. Demonstrations are calculated to bring media attention to an unjust situation, but they forget the importance of face-to-face, personal contact with those whom the grievance addresses. The U.S. Forest Service may be initially unwilling to listen to those who attack their clearcutting practices. They will cite the need for jobs and criticize the overemphasis on the poor little spotted owl. The resolution of any genuine struggle is never as simple as finding better images to stand for your case. Gandhi told his biographer, "I am essentially a man of compromise, because I am never sure that I am right" (Naess 1974). Here was someone who could labor tirelessly and at the same time question his whole campaign—such openness is essential to philosophy in action.

So nonviolence can be a powerful but tough moral standard to uphold. Is there any reason it is uniquely appropriate to ecological struggles? There are many who believe nature itself to be the prime arena of nonviolence, where all is a give-and-take balanced by moderation in all things. But one must be moderate in the demand for moderation as well. Nature may be calm, but there is also a backlash: a top-selling new video is entitled *The Violence of Nature*, presumably depicting all those things that Mutual of Omaha would never let us see on "Wild Kingdom." This is the age when modern conventions are to be overturned, and the romance of placid nature may well be an idea whose time has come and gone. Nature changes through history from the human vantage point. It has been alternatively inclusive and unreachable, fearsome and embracing, with all the ambiguities in between. It remains a foil to all our attempts to limit it to one value or another.

Nature will always be more than something which has inalienable rights or inherent value from our expanding perspective of care. Nature is larger than we can ever know, and limiting the purpose of this unknown is a dangerous fault of philosophy. This is why protecting our natural home with Gandhian means of nonviolence makes sense. The method can be solid and unwavering while still admitting skeptical searching.

Nonviolent eco-activism stands firm for respect for oppressed humanity *or* nature, not out of altruism, but as part of progress in self-realization, widening the grounding reaches of our identity. We learn to define truth not relatively, but absolute and precise to each specific situation. We think of responsibility to the greater whole before demanding individual rights. We try to face opposing positions without intimidation. And we will not be afraid to change our tact if new knowledge of the case appears which defies our ideology.

Nonviolence is appropriate in the defense of the environment only if it truly aims to hurt no one. For the only kind of nature that emerges as being more important than people from the human point of view is the kind which everyone will eventually admit is deserving first of respect, and then of care. That will be the largest kind of truth that is specific to the world.

SAVE THE WHALES . . . FOR DINNER

So this is the picture of a tactical attitude, a composure to hold before the storm. The ideas have been borrowed from the traditions and struggles of a nation that fought for its independence from colonialism, and now they are being tested in the waters of environmental conflict. It is a new situation, and a new time. And with newness can come clashes with the past. I would like to examine one of these now.

Norway is clearly a country that has brought forth a philosophy of radical environmentalism based on the conviction that change in the way we see the world can lead to change in the way we live. This is a country of idealists and traditionalists. The particular group of ideas called "deep ecology" leads right back to the traditions, so they are solidly ensconced.

But what happens when reverence for nature clashes with deep-seated tradition? This is its hardest test, when national identity is no longer bolstered by a new line of thinking that builds on the tradition. This most poignant challenge to radicalism was keenly felt when I last visited Norway for the World Wilderness Congress in the autumn of 1993. I found then a mysterious kind of agreement among all Norwegians, whatever their political stripe, occupation, age, or attitude. They were remarkably unanimous on one particular issue: Norway should be allowed to hunt as many whales as it wants, and it knows best for itself what is an acceptable limit of the catch within its sovereign waters. Equally unanimous was the point of view of environmentalists from throughout the rest of the world attending the conference: they all thought that whaling should be banned outright, following international consensus.

The exact facts of the matter will not be debated here. Let us assume that the statistics put forth by the Norwegians are accurate: according to their census, there is a sizable enough population of minke whales such that controlled hunting of this one species can be a sustainable enterprise.

Environmentalists from elsewhere do not dispute this fact, but they tend to hold a more emotional, spiritual attitude toward the whale. Whales sing; they may be intelligent; they are large, beautiful, peaceful, and have come to inspire deep respect. Do we really need to kill them to satisfy any vital need? Most of those who hold this view tend not to have a personal or cultural memory of eating whale meat as great tradition. The cultural relation to whales is new, based on reverence, whale watching rather than whale catching. It is easy for us to say no.

Norwegians by and large, even the radical ones, consider this an Imperialist travesty. They say these small whale species like the minke are no more intelligent than pigs. They lead better lives than chickens and calves who are bred from birth only for mechanized slaughter. The whale hunt is a noble, dangerous pursuit that pits man against ocean. The hunters are the ones who live in nature and understand the give and take. Only urban people make nature into a church or a museum. Only they can afford to.

These were the feelings expressed by well-meaning nationalists wearing T-shirts that could have been bought on any city square: "Save the Whales . . . for Dinner!" "Intelligent People Need Intelligent Food!" "Big People (showing a burly Viking in costume standing atop a beached whale carcass) Need Big Food!" The people's revenge against Greenpeace has come at last.

Norwegians were by and large feeling quite pleased with themselves during this exciting autumn. They had brought Israel and the PLO together with promises of peace. They had taken charge of their rightful and intelligent food. The economy, which was on the rise, was strong enough for them to say "Nei!" to the EEC, for mainstream political as well as bioregional reasons.

There could be no agriculture in Norway today unless the country believed enough in local subsidy to keep farmers going during the very abbreviated growing season. In the winter, one can buy vegetables from all over the world. In the summer, only local crops such as carrots, peppers, and leeks are available. Bioregionalism for Norway has meant protective nationalism or the propelling of an energy-intensive lifestyle based on that cheap and renewable local resource: hydropower. Most observers feel Norway will be won over to the European community eventually, but its traditional isolationism dies hard, supported simultaneously by radical environmentalists and staunch "Norway for the Norwegians!" conservatives.

Deep ecology encourages environmentalists to stand up for their feelings and convictions as a focal point for public debate (Naess and Rothenberg 1989). Arne Naess has implored that we not be afraid to speak up to our opponents with the words, "This river is part of myself." When you dam its waters, you also close me off and shut me in. Norway confronted this issue first in 1970, when Mardøla Falls, a spectacular cascade over a thousand meters high, was threatened by a hydropower project that would impede its flow above the cascade. Demonstrators from all over the country gathered to protest this injustice to one of Europe's highest waterfalls. Demonstrators including Arne Naess and Sigmund Kvaløy chained themselves to the earth to prevent bulldozers from marauding into the mountains. Civil disobedience brought environmentalism into national debate. A few years later a Ministry of the Environment was formed, today staffed by many of the protestors from the sixties (Reed and Rothenberg 1992).

For Norwegians, curtailing whaling also shuts off the self. If we believe in sustainable harvesting, and if there turn out to be enough of one or more whale species such that hunting can continue, why not allow a limited catch just like a hunting season on deer, moose, or bear?

The strongest argument against this is in the realm of the sacred, upholding the belief that there is something to revere in whales that should require all traditions to hold back. But traditional ways of life may die easy but change hard. As environmental concerns become increasingly multicultural, we need to find ways to continue cultural diversity within a framework of world consensus. Norwegian tradition will be a stronger thing once it can develop its own considered response to a now global problem. At present there is a tendency to defend troubled practices with a line like this: "You foreigners who don't know the first thing about whales have hunted too many, while we Norwegians represent a longstanding tradition that never killed too many or got greedy." This is a hopeless path. A tradition can remain strong even through change. Slavery was an important American tradition, and it died hard and reluctantly. Extermination of native Americans was also part of the 'Manifest Destiny' idea. These things characterized the United States for decades but they had to evolve into something more enlightened (hopefully!). Similarly, Norway ought not become nationalistic about something so transnational in scope.

Radical environmentalists in Norway have traditionally been those concerned with the mountains, not the sea. And they have urged throughout this debate that we not dwell too long on the whaling controversy: There are plenty of other reasons around to boycott Norway. It is true enough that Norway's wealth and political stability have given it the luxury to be concerned with the role of nature in establishing national identity. Often the wealth comes from the sea, in food and oil, and the nature is enjoyed up country. Greater consistency and flexibility with the ways of the past are both required upon the discovery of new information.

I once heard the following story about a top Norwegian administrator, giving a lecture on the whaling fracas. He placed on the overhead projector a copy of an official U.S. Government memo stating that President Clinton, though recognizing that the Norwegian factual data on the feasibility of a whale catch was accurate, could not condone the practice because of the overwhelming weight of American public opinion against it. The speaker was outraged that the last superpower could ignore factual information so flippantly. But my response is that public opinion matters, and it is based on faith and feeling as much as on fact. Science is just better than the rest of us at hiding its biases behind numbers. There are sound empathic reasons to feel close to whales and to argue against the killing of them unless absolutely necessary.

Whale tastes like a saltwater steak and even the most conditioned palates can learn to do without it. The country that brought us such inspiring ecoradicalism should be able to stomach the reevaluation of its own queasy past. The many uses that the body of the whale were put to in the last century have mostly been superseded by cheaper synthetics. (And all-natural as marketing moniker need not be applied to whale oil in the future!) If a tradition is to survive in an increasingly complex future, it must find ways within its own confines to adapt to a changing world. No country can act alone with regard to parts of nature that are more than resources for all of us.

———————

Environmentalism has always been both radical and conservative. It involves a critique of current society along with a longing for the bucolic idylls of the past. The traditional Norwegian interest in whaling specifically conflicts with the equally traditional love of nature. It has been said that Norwegians love their mountains as home but use the sea as resource, and this dual sense of nature to be revered and harvested has kept the country prosperous. But philosophically it is a dual standard. Progressive ecological thought does not simply come from the past. It makes use of traditional ideas and blends them with new findings to outline a path to the future.

This is why the next step for Norwegian environmental ideology is to come up with clear arguments against whaling and to integrate these with the general environmental tone of the culture. If there really are enough whales to sustain limited hunting, then there must be another reason why people are so set against the practice. It is because many people worldwide believe whales to be intelligent, sacred, and therefore worthy of a special kind of respect. This is a feeling that cannot be disputed by science. Spirituality of this kind of care does exist and it must be respected. No modern Norwegian needs to hunt whales to live. It is time for the traditions to change, if only on the basis of empathy, because of humanity's expanding sense of care for creatures we know little about.

How to get people to listen? The confrontational tactics of extremists like the Sea Shepherds are not what Gandhi would recommend. This activist organization advocates the search-and-destroy method when it comes to ships that are violating the international ban. Leader Paul Watson has defended their attacks on Norwegian whaling vessels *Senet* and *Brenna* last year in the Lofoten Islands on the grounds that the evil of whaling is great enough to allow the destruction of private property, and even human lives (*Norway Times* 1994). He has been charged on criminal counts worldwide for his no-compromise efforts. Anti-environmentalists find Watson to be the archetypal extremist eco-villain that fulfills their worst fears. Some mainstream environmentalists are either glad that a person like Watson exists, to make them look more reasonable, or worried that he gives environmentalism too much of an outlaw cast. Here's what Watson himself says:

> I do not feel like a freak. I feel normal. And sometimes I wonder if the rest of the world is normal, especially that part of it that goes around plundering nature. It is at such times that the opposing philosophies of violence and nonviolence tear at me. I know violence is morally wrong and nonviolence is morally right. But what about results? Nonviolent action alone has seldom produced beneficial change on our planet. I continue to fret over this point. I compromise by allowing myself violence against property but never against life, human or otherwise. . . .
>
> Let's get something else straight. The killing of whales in the present day is a crime. It is a violation of international law, but more importantly it is a crime against nature and a crime against future generations of humanity. Moreover, whaling is a nasty form of anti-social behavior and an atrocity which should be stamped out. So I don't want any crappy letters about tradition, livelihood, or [Norwegian] rights. (Watson 1993a)

So who knows best the definition of crime here, and who is qualified to mete out the punishment? Watson's defense of the legality of his organization is the most facile part of his argument, blurring the rules agreed upon by human society and the principles we humans have observed at work in the natural world: "The Sea Shepherd Conservation Society is a law-abiding organization. We rigidly adhere to and respect the laws of nature, or *lex natura*. We hold the position that the laws of ecology take precedence over the laws designed by nation states to protect corporate interests. If Norwegian laws were more respectful of international agreements, then there would not have been cause for Sea Shepherd intervention" (Watson 1993b).

This is not the kind of argument that will lead Norway to respect the intent of foreign environmentalists. No wonder the whole country is defending whaling as patriotically as ever! By and large, they have come to see the global environmental movement has a violent threat, and this is a sad consequence of Watson's uncompromising militancy.

In a sense, Watson would do better to let his actions speak for themselves. This kind of rhetoric only confuses things, as it is easier to argue against words than actions. Take a cue from Edward Abbey's Monkey Wrench Gang: In his novel *Hayduke Lives!* the Earth First! activists cause a lot of fracas and get media coverage, but they are unable to stop the giant Goliath earth moving machine. Only the covert Monkey Wrench Gang can get the job done. And no one ever sees them, no one knows who they are. Their actions speak for themselves, actions which were done for their own sakes, not for glory or result of any kind.

Gandhi would most likely choose a different tact than Watson. He would say, Sit down with the hunters, go with them on a hunt, learn about their way of life. Show them you respect their ways, and gradually teach them why you think they should change. To come from outside with a message of transformation is the hardest stand to take, but it is a necessary one. The change must be phrased as a positive thing, based upon genuine care for the other peoples' ways of life as much as a desire to save the whales, or any other part of nature.

Arne Naess writes that he is against whaling, "not because there is a possibility for extinction or because whales hold special status among mammals. . . . The most important argument for me is based on complete richness and diversity of life forms on Earth"

(Naess 1993). Our culture does not need to hunt whales to further its development. The nations of the world have agreed to ban whaling. This is a form of eco-cultural progress. Norway should not set global consensus back a hundred years.

By the time you read this, the political situation in Norway and in the Arctic Ocean in general may very well have changed. Perhaps a backlash against environmentalism will lead the world to consider the commercial viability of whaling once more. Or maybe respect for cetaceans may be well on the way to being a universal human belief, on par with racial and sexual equality, both ideas which have gained widespread acceptance only in the twentieth century. Or a compromise solution may be instated, whereby whaling is permitted in a very restricted manner, with the whale hunters learning to act in a responsible manner, deferential to international law and global environmental realities.

In the end, or in the beginning of the plot for a new way of life, we may all sit down to dinner, discuss our differences, and realize that we will all have to change as the world gets smaller and smaller. Environmentalism is only radical when it gets to the root of a problem, not when it is extreme for the sake of difficulty. Intelligent people are not afraid of change, in their food or their ideas. The nonviolent tradition, which has been articulated in Norway as relevant to the environmental crisis, can teach us a thing or two about how to talk to one another. Let us hope the twenty-first century will bring a revolution in conflict resolution as well as respect for the value of the earth to live and flourish with humanity within it, not above.

Chapter 12

BETWEEN MODERATION AND MARGINALIZATION: ENVIRONMENTAL RADICALISM IN BRITAIN[1]

Wolfgang Rüdig

INTRODUCTION

Environmental groups have a mass following in Britain. The largest environmental organization, the National Trust, has currently 2.2 million members (National Trust 1992); the second largest group, the Royal Society for the Protection of Birds, 850,000 members *(Birds: The Magazine of the RSPB,* vol. 14, no. 7, autumn 1993, p. 66). The total combined membership of environmental groups in Britain is put at around 5 million (cf. Grove-White 1992:128), far in excess of the membership of political parties. Few of these members of mass environmental organizations would describe themselves as "environmental radicals." Overwhelmingly, environmental groups in Britain play within the established rules of politics. They present themselves as moderate and responsible and make demands that are seen as sensible and practical. Any expression of a radical ideology, of seeking fundamental change, of direct challenges to state authority, would be seen as counterproductive.

From time to time, this dominance of "reform environmentalism" is challenged. Again and again, however, British governments have successfully managed to contain such challenges, either by integration or by marginalization. Over the years, there has been a remarkable continuity in the way such challenges have been contained. Many of today's "establishment" groups started as challengers to the system, espousing radical strategies and demands, only to be integrated into the system. Many other radical groups have disappeared without trace. It is only at the very margins of politics that radical environmentalists, or, as they would probably prefer to be called, radical "ecologists," have maintained a political base for continued activity.

To explain this peculiar shape of British environmentalism, we can draw on two types of factors: first, the British political system, and, second, the types of environmental issues prevalent in Britain. The British political system generally makes it far more difficult for any protest group or movement to make any political impact than, say, in the United States or in Germany. Decision making is extremely centralized. Britain is a unitary state. Its government has to have a majority in the lower chamber of parliament, the House of Commons, but with few exceptions, parliamentary elections give one party such a majority, and with party discipline being very strong compared with that in the United States, policy making is virtually exclusively controlled by the leader of that party, as prime minister, and his or her cabinet. If that party has a very large majority, as under much of the reign of Margaret Thatcher in the 1980s, British government is akin to an "elective dictatorship" (Hailsham 1976). Any group which is denied access to the decision-making process of that government is almost completely excluded from any influence. Unlike in the United States, there are few constitutional checks and balances. The role of the judiciary is much less important than in the United States. Environmental groups can try to influence the media, but otherwise, there are no significant other openings available to successfully challenge the authority of government. The electoral system, as in the United States, gives a dominant role to two large parties, with third parties having little chance of gaining major influence or effecting policy. One could expect that such a system has the effect both of moderating the behavior of groups that want to join the system, and of alienating and radicalizing groups that are denied access. As we shall see, British government is normally going to some length to avoid that radicalization process, and usually is successful.

Such success also depends, however, on the abilities of environmental groups to mobilize. Historically, two issues have been dominant across the world in the mobilization of radical environmentalism. Nuclear energy has been the most important radicalizing issue for modern environmentalism in most of continental Europe (Rüdig 1990). Wilderness issues have had the most radicalizing influence in North America and Australia (Hay and Haward 1988; List 1993). In Britain, as in most of continental Europe, there is practically no real wilderness left that could be protected. Even in the remotest parts of the British Isles, there is little that has not been touched by humans at some time (Huxley 1974; Hoskins 1979). In fact, the remoteness of such parts is often the result of the depopulation of such areas enforced by powerful interests, for example in Scotland. While campaigns for the protection of wildlife played an important role in Britain, this did not have the same radicalizing effect as the fight for the preservation of wilderness areas in other countries. In the case of nuclear power, Britain was in a special position with no major nuclear expansion in the 1970s and 1980s, leading to a comparatively weak antinuclear movement that could not play a radicalizing role.

Today's shape of the environmental movement can only be explained out of the specific historical context in which the movement developed. Environmental radicalism is usually understood to have two main facets: "a radicalism in environmental philosophy. . . . and a radicalism in tactics and action" (List 1993:2). In the remainder of this chapter, we will look at the development of both forms of radicalism in Britain. As we shall see, radical action by environmentalists has a very long history in Britain. However, radical environmental thinking only becomes a recognizable force in the 1970s, and the question whether radical environmentalism or ecologism should include a social or, indeed, a Socialist dimension was rather more important than any of the issues of the deep ecology debate.

HISTORICAL ROOTS: EARLY RADICALISM AND THE WAY TO RESPECTABILITY (1865-1966)

The history of the British environmental movement goes back to the nineteenth century. With increasing industrialization and urbanization, the perception of 'nature' had gone through a major transformation process (cf. Thomas 1984). Increasingly, it was town dwellers who sought to protect nature from further destruction, or gain access to nature to escape from the pollution of the industrial towns. In this context, the notion of the 'countryside' became the key cultural concept which framed the early environmental agenda. England as a green and pleasant land was, of course, a social construction, and not necessarily in tune with the realities of rural life (Newby 1980). But in the face of economic processes which more so than anywhere else in Europe separated the vast majority of the population from agriculture and forced them to live in polluted cities, the notion of 'rural idyll,' of the 'real' country, had widespread appeal.

Local groups expressing concern about aspects of their environment can be traced back to the beginning of the century, but the Commons Preservation Society founded in 1865, is usually regarded as Britain's first national environmental group. The commons was land owned by a feudal lord, the "lord of the manor," over which other persons, commoners, had certain traditional rights of use, for example to graze their herds or to cut firewood. Conflicts over the use of commons between feudal lords and commoners were carried out for many years, leading to an increasing transformation of common land into exclusive private ownership. The increasing encroachment of common land by the growing towns gave the commons a new function, however. Common land which had not been built on offered the town dweller a possibility to enjoy the benefits of nature. This was particularly true for the workers who had no means to travel to the countryside and who thus relied on areas near towns for their recreation. However, such land was the object of speculative interest for future construction as the cities expanded. It was such financial considerations that increasingly led the owners of commons to claim exclusive property rights and fence in such land to forbid its use by others. It was such activity that directly led to the formation of the Commons Preservation Society by social reformers to preserve such commons for recreational purposes.

The main tactic pursued by the Society was to seek legal protection of the rights of commoners through the courts. A large number of proceedings were entered into, and the rights of commoners were often upheld. On some occasions, however, the Society went beyond such traditional means. The most famous one concerned Epping Forest, a stretch of ancient woodland northeast of London. This area was partially fenced in by its owners to deny commoners the right of entry and use for the collection of firewood. The Commons Preservation Society challenged that action in the courts, but at first did not find success. Matters were brought to a head when three local inhabitants were arrested in 1866 after cutting firewood in the enclosed area which they claimed as their traditional right. They were sentenced to two months imprisonment, and one of them died after being put into a very damp cell. This episode attracted public attention and allowed the Commons Preservation Society to bring further court actions which delayed the clearing of the woodlands which otherwise might have taken place. An initial success was reached in 1874 when a court forbade the erection of further fences and ordered the erected fences to be removed within twenty years. With a decision about the use of the woodlands still pending, a member of the Commons Preservation Society aided by a large number of protesters, tore down the remaining fencing in 1877, an illegal act. Ultimately, the Society was successful. Epping Forest was protected and made accessible to the public as a recreational area in a ceremony attended by Queen Victoria in 1882 (Eversley 1910).

This early example of environmental direct action did not stand alone. Even earlier in the century, the illegal tearing down of fences preventing access to land used for recreational purposes had occurred on a number of occasions in the north of England, in some cases as early as the beginning of the nineteenth century (Wild 1965/66). The environmental issue at the heart of these actions was the same: access to land by people escaping the industrial towns. It was that type of demand which also led to one of the most celebrated cases of direct action in British environmental history: the Kinder Scout trespass.

Manchester and Sheffield had been two major centers of industrial development in the north of England. Industrialization and urbanization had destroyed many traditional landscapes. What was left for recreational purposes was a desolate stretch of hills between the two cities, the Peak District, and workers from these areas, often organized in ramblers clubs, extensively used the Peak District for their walking expeditions. But after having long been regarded as an economic wasteland, during the late nineteenth and early twentieth centuries, the Peak District offered a new source of income for its owners: grouse shooting. With up-and-coming British industrialists and American millionaires seeking to emulate the aristocracy, grouse shooting had become big business. Large areas of the Peak District were fenced in to protect the grouse breeding areas, and ramblers were banned from their traditional areas of recreation. A campaign to reopen rights of way for the ramblers at first had little success, and legal and political challenges failed. A group of radical ramblers thus organized a series of "mass trespasses," beginning with the Kinder Scout trespass in 1932. Several hundred ramblers forced their way through to the Kinder Scout, a high plateau and grouse moor in the Peak District, against the resistance of gamekeepers and the police. Six ramblers were arrested and given prison sentences. This caused outrage and a series of further trespasses and demonstrations with thousands of ramblers between 1932 and 1935. While these actions raised the issue of access for ramblers, the national group representing rambling interests founded in 1935, the Ramblers Association, failed to achieve a political breakthrough. It was only after World War II, in 1949, when a legal framework for the negotiation of access was created with the National Parks and Access to the Countryside Act which at least in part satisfied rambling interests (Rickwood 1973; Rothman 1982; Hill 1980; Stephenson 1989). The Ramblers Association today is a major national group with ninety thousand members (Ramblers Association 1992).

The trespasses of the 1930s and the earlier cases of direct action in the 19th century stand in a tradition of direct action which for many years was typical for working-class, industrial politics in Britain. This tradition stood, however, in major contrast to the development of mainstream environmentalism in Britain which was dominated by reformist aristocrats and the professional upper middle classes. Their actions were concentrated on influencing decision makers in parliament and in the government, or, if possible, mobilizing financial resources to purchase objects of environmental concern. The National Trust for Places of Historic Interest or Natural Beauty was formed in 1895 by Victorian social reformers and aristocrats. Its main method was to protect houses and estates by either purchasing them directly or having them bequeathed to the Trust by their owners. The Trust initially had a stronger campaigning orientation but increasingly concentrated on the management of its property (Fedden 1968; 1974). Many other establishment groups were formed in the late nineteenth century, and ensuing decades, amongst them the following:

1889   Society for the Protection of Birds
        (now Royal Society for the Protection of Birds)
        Garden Cities Association
        (now Town and Country Planning Association)
1899   Coal Smoke Abatement Society
        (now National Society for Clean Air)
1903   Society for the Protection of the Wild Fauna of the
           Empire
        (now Flora and Fauna Preservation Society)
1912   Society for the Promotion of Nature Reserves
        (now Royal Society for Nature Conservation)

Their basic political operating style was the same. They sought to gain respectability in the eyes of the authorities by mobilizing expert opinion and formulating responsible and moderate policy proposals. The groups concentrated on mobilizing the aristocracy and the professions, building up a network of contacts in governmental and parliamentary circles. British policy making then, and to a larger extent now, was largely conducted outside the public eye, but with interested parties being consulted throughout the decision-making process. For environmental groups to become part of the circle of groups consulted on new policies, they had to conform to the policy style dominating decision making in Britain (cf. O'Riordan 1979). Part of that style is a very high level of compartmentalization of policy into a series of individual issues, and, consequently, a large number of individual environmental groups emerged concentrating on specific issues or issue areas. Clearly, the environment was not seen as one all-embracing *problematic* requiring an integrated solution, but as a series of individual problems which could be resolved through specific reforms within the given economic and political system.

Despite these limitations, it is nevertheless remarkable how open the establishment in Britain proved to be toward environmental concerns. To a considerable degree, this can be seen as a reflection of the deep cultural alienation of the British upper classes with the industrialization process. As Wiener (1981) has shown, the British aristocracy sought to idealize an essentially rural lifestyle, with elite educational institutions socializing new elites, even those from an industrial family background, into a culture in which any association with modern industrial processes was despised.

Culturally, the notion of the preservation of natural beauty in the face of encroaching industrialization fell on a fruitful ground.

Such rejection of industrialization did not, however, produce any strong environmentally motivated intellectual movement which sought to challenge industrialism and present a fundamental, new alternative. The nineteenth century did see a strong romantic movement, with writers and artists celebrating "nature" in their works. Carlyle, Cobbett, Wordsworth, Ruskin, and Morris are amongst the most famous poets, writers, and artists who formulated what may be interpreted as an environmentalist view of nineteenth century developments (cf. Williams 1973; Veldman 1994). In the twentieth century, architects and planners like Ebenezer Howard or Clough Williams-Ellis expressed criticism of industrialization and urbanization processes (Howard 1965; Williams-Ellis; 1938, 1975). Such criticism of industrialization fitted the widespread cultural alienation from industrialism that spanned the party-political spectrum (Wiener 1981) but found its main political expression in the established conservation movements. For example, William Morris, who advocated an anarchist-Socialist vision of a postindustrial society in his novel News from Nowhere (1891), had formed the Society for the Protection of Ancient Buildings in 1877. Its appeal was limited to the upper and middle classes and professionals, and the Society adopted a pragmatic approach, emphasizing information and lobbying (Kennet 1972; Thompson 1976). Ebenezer Howard and other architects had a major influence on British planning. Howard formed the Garden Cities Association in 1899, later to be renamed Town and Country Planning Association (Ward 1974). For other conservationists, the National Trust, and, from 1926, the newly formed Council for the Preservation of Rural England, provided the main basis of activity (cf. Evans 1992; Allison 1975). The establishment orientation of such environmental groups contrasted vividly with the working-class roots of the more radical groups fighting for access to the countryside. While the latter were happy to engage in militant activities, the former firmly avoided any direct challenges to government and sought to achieve their aims through their elite contacts (cf. Rickwood 1973).

Traditional environmental groups survived well in the postwar political climate. The first main postwar achievement was the installation of ten national parks in England and Wales in 1949. Other early postwar legislation gave local authorities new, wide-ranging planning tasks, and many of the established environmental groups became integral parts of the new policy processes (Allison 1975).

The major new environmental issue that came to the fore in Britain in the 1950s was air pollution. While there had been legislation on air pollution since the late nineteenth century, it was only after a severe London "smog" in December 1952 was claimed to have been responsible for almost five thousand deaths that it became a major political issue. In the resulting policy-formation process, the National Smoke Abatement Society (the successor organization of the Coal Smoke Abatement Society) played a major role. In 1956, Parliament passed the Clean Air Act, allowing the designation of so-called smoke-free zones where the burning of high-sulphur coal was not permitted (Sanderson 1974). The Clean Air Act was the crowning achievement of several decades of campaigning by the National Smoke Abatement Society (later renamed National Society for Clean Air). Throughout its campaigns, it had followed the dominant pattern of a responsible pressure group (Ashby and Anderson 1981). As it happened, the implementation of the Clean Air Act coincided with a major shift in domestic heating patterns from coal to gas fires (cf. Scarrow 1972), and, as a result, air pollution ceased to be the major problem it had been previously. Nevertheless, the Clean Air Act was perceived as a success story, reinforcing the belief that environmental reform could be successfully achieved.

THE NEW ENVIRONMENTALISM: FROM INCIPIENT RADICALIZATION TO POLITICAL INTEGRATION (1966–1994)

Reformist environmentalism was not seriously challenged until the early 1970s. While British environmental policy had been ahead of most other countries, many themes of the U.S. environmental debate eventually found their way to Britain. A number of environmental disasters in Britain, such as the Torrey Canyon oil spill of 1967, also helped to make the environment a political issue (Brookes et al. 1976; Sandbach 1980; Lowe and Goyder 1983).

Starting in the mid-1960s, the rise of environmentalism manifested itself in two phenomena: first, the proliferation of local environmental groups, and, second, the foundation of a number of new national environmental groups, addressing national and international environmental issues, starting with The Conservation Society formed in 1966 to campaign on population issues. Local environmental groups proliferated in the 1960s in response to major housing and transport developments (Gregory 1971; Kimber and Richardson 1974). Some of these groups were ad-hoc protests against particular projects, following the slogan "Not in My Backyard!" (NIMBY). But often, so-called amenity societies were established to protect the environment of local community on a permanent basis (Lowe 1977). The Civic Trust had been formed in 1957 as a national umbrella organization for such amenity societies, and it expanded rapidly in the 1960s (Barker 1976; Barker and Keating 1977). On the whole, local environmental groups followed the patterns of responsible interest-group activities. In only a few instances did local environmental groups develop more radical forms of action. One such case is the fight of a working-class community in Wales against severe air pollution by a local factory. Local women and children blockaded the factory gates several times in the early 1970s to give weight to their demands (Hall 1976). Another example is the campaign against motorway constructions. Antimotorway campaigners became increasingly alienated by governmental nonresponsiveness to their demands, and consultation procedures were disrupted by antiroad lobbyists in the 1970s (Tyme 1977).

Such tactics were eschewed by the established environmental organizations. In the case of the Welsh antipollution protests, local groups appealed to national air-pollution organizations to support their cause only to be rebuffed. Some new environmental groups were, however, more prepared to go beyond the established procedures. Most visible in the early 1970s was Friends of the Earth (FOE), formed in Britain in 1970 following the foundation of its U.S. mother organization in the previous year (cf. Pearce 1991:48–50). FOE activists embarked on a high-publicity campaigns to mobilize the media in support of its demands. It organized a number of media stunts, something that had not been done previously by other organizations, and it shot to national prominence by dumping empty bottles at the Schweppes headquarters in London in support of its campaign for bottle recycling. Within a very short time, FOE succeeded in establishing itself as the major new environmental group. Invitations to consultative committees, hearings, and other signs of establishment recognition followed, and FOE toned down its direct-action campaigns so as not to endanger its newly found status of a respectable, responsible, and moderate environmental group (Bugler 1981; Lowe and Goyder 1983; Greenberg 1985).

The next major challenge to the dominance of moderate environmentalism came in the wake of the nuclear debate. It was the proposal to construct a commercial reprocessing plant at Windscale, Cumbria, that led to the emergence of a stronger antinuclear sentiment in Britain. In 1977, the proposal was examined in great detail at a public inquiry, a routine device of the British planning process involving hearings with all interested parties, and FOE was largely seen as the most influential environmental objector. But despite substantial scientific and technical evidence presented by FOE and other groups, the government gave the project the go-ahead. In the wake of governmental unresponsiveness to environmental demands, calls for a strategy of civil disobedience for the first time became louder. However, FOE firmly resisted any association with such tactics.

The first substantial acts of civil disobedience against nuclear energy were seen at Torness, the site of a planned Scottish nuclear power station near Edinburgh. The occupations of the construction site in 1978 and 1979 were rallying points for the movement. However, divisions amongst occupants over damaging construction machinery on the site and confronting police reduced the effectiveness of the action. The main Scottish antinuclear group, SCRAM, had reached an understanding with the police about its nonviolent and symbolic nature, but in view of the events decided in 1979 not to undertake any further direct action in the future (Rüdig 1990; 1994).

Direct action that was not simply symbolic became widespread in 1980 in the fight against sites selected for test drilling in the search for nuclear waste repositories. Local inhabitants in Wales were particularly militant and ejected scientists undertaking studies from the land. In 1981, civil disobedience campaigns had also sprung up in southwest England, directed against a number of sites selected for future nuclear power stations. At Luxulyan, a Cornish village, substantial parts of the local population took part in these actions and mobilized widespread support. The electricity utility had to compel the local police through legal proceedings in the high court to have the occupants evicted. The proposal for a nuclear power station at Luxulyan was eventually dropped.

Despite these individual incidences of civil disobedience, no strong national antinuclear movement emerged. No established

national group, not even FOE or Greenpeace, took up the spontaneous direct action by local people as a rallying point. Before a new,
grassroots-based, radical movement of national importance could be
organized, the test-drilling program and the controversial sites for
new nuclear power stations were withdrawn by the government. By
1981, the movement against military aspects of nuclear power had
become far more important. Most radical campaigners against civil
nuclear projects switched their emphasis to oppose the stationing of
U.S. missiles on British soil. The protest was dominated by the
Campaign for Nuclear Disarmament (CND), and major campaigns
involving civil disobedience were undertaken, most famously at
Greenham Common. But environmental considerations never
played a major role for CND's actions, and the major environmental
groups kept their distance from CND, which was seen as too left
wing and political.

One of the few groups that has traditionally combined opposition to military and civil nuclear power was Greenpeace. The
British branch of Greenpeace was formed in 1976, but it only
became a major action in the mid-1980s. Greenpeace launched a
campaign against the dumping of nuclear waste at sea in the early
1980s and later also organized some spectacular actions to demonstrate the nuclear pollution of the Irish Sea by the Windscale (now
renamed Sellafield) nuclear works. As elsewhere, Greenpeace only
relied on highly trained activists in actions organized to gain maximum media exposure.[2]

Local opposition to nuclear waste-disposal sites led to
widespread popular direct action campaigns again in 1986, at four
sites in England. Local people occupied the sites, and, after mobilizing widespread local support, the government again withdrew its
plans (Rüdig 1990, 1994).

In the late 1980s and early 1990s, calls for direct action were
heard rather more rarely. From 1988 onward, the environmental
agenda shifted to global environmental issues, and global political
initiatives eventually leading to the Earth Summit in June 1992. In
Britain, the environment for the first time became a major issue of
mainstream politics across the board. Membership of the major
environmental groups rose dramatically (McCormick 1991). However, that process was not associated with a radicalization process,
to the contrary. With the environment having become a respectable
issue, environmental groups concentrated on their participation in
national and international decision-making processes. The new

global issues, such as the greenhouse effect, did not involve protests against specific projects and thus were not ideally suited for grassroots mobilization. The enormous boom in media coverage of environmental issues was accompanied by an increasing individualization of environmental concern and fuelled by green advertising, and green consumerism became perhaps the most important manifestation of the new wave of environmentalism (Cf. Rüdig 1992; Rüdig et al. 1993; Bennie and Rüdig 1993). Environmental groups also increasingly sought to attract passive members, developing sophisticated direct mail techniques, and became more hierarchical organizations run by professional staff.

The new environmental politics of the late 1980s and early 1990s thus had little use for "civil disobedience." There are signs that the media stunts performed by Greenpeace have lost much of their novelty value. Also, Greenpeace appears to concentrate more on producing scientific reports and specific policy proposals than on preparing dare-devil actions to raise public consciousness (cf. Rose 1993). Apart from such a saturation effect, the late 1980s undoubtedly saw an increase of political opportunities for traditional environmental pressure groups in Britain. As part of the European union, Britain was under international pressure to agree to stricter environmental standards.[3] The British government also had problems in the implementation of environmental regulations agreed to earlier. Environmentalists eagerly seized on this opportunity. The late 1980s saw some major changes in the system of pollution control in Britain[4] which provided encouragement to environmental pressure groups to increase their lobbying activities.

With this respectable orientation of established groups, a revival of direct-action radicalism could only be expected from grassroots resistance against particular projects. But there have been few cases of a renewal of grass-roots environmental campaigning. In this context, the most important new issue in the early 1990s has been a major program of motorway construction. Many individual projects have attracted strong local opposition, and there have been several instances where construction work was interrupted by direct actions. Some of these actions have also reached national attention, in particular at Twyford Down in Hampshire where a motorway extension cut through an area of outstanding natural beauty. It was here that the British branch of Earth First! gained some prominence through their involvement in a civil disobedience campaign to stop the construction of the motorway (Young 1993). A number of other organizations have been formed specifically to fight motorway extensions. It remains to be seen whether the government is able to defuse the situation by a clever mix of police action and withdrawal of controversial schemes, or whether these actions will have a more profound impact stimulating a revival of radical environmentalism in Britain in the 1990s.

RADICAL ENVIRONMENTAL PHILOSOPHY AND POLITICAL ACTION

Despite the political dominance of reformist environmentalism, Britain has a long tradition of radical thinking on the environment. We already touched upon some of the influences of nineteenth-century writers. Depending on one's perception of the substance of green politics, a wide variety of historical continuities could be drawn (cf. Hardy 1979; Gould 1988; Marshall 1992; Veldman 1994; and Wall 1994). But a radical environmental philosophy questioning the very basis of the development of industrialism did not emerge until the early 1970s.

As in other countries, British environmentalism has been influenced by important U.S. authors of the 1960s, such as Rachel Carson, Paul Ehrlich, Barry Commoner, and others (cf. O'Riordan 1981). The most radical thinker in Britain in the 1970s was Edward Goldsmith, founder and editor of *The Ecologist* magazine, and principal author of the booklet *A Blueprint for Survival*, which first appeared in 1972 as a special issue of *The Ecologist* and then received even wider distribution as a Penguin paperback. It was also translated into several other European languages (Goldsmith et al. 1972). Goldsmith further developed his ideas in numerous articles published in *The Ecologist*. He essentially argued that industrial society was not sustainable and bound to break down. Society had to be reconstructed on the basis of the hunter-gatherer culture, in small, self-sustaining communities (cf. also Goldsmith 1978; 1988; and 1992). There are many other British authors who have had a major impact on environmental thinking around the world (Veldman 1994), for example E. F. Schumacher (1973) and James Lovelock (1979). Apart from *The Ecologist*, the journal *Resurgence* has been a major focus for radical environmental debate. Another major focus of debate has been the link between environmental and Marxist thinking.

The chief problem for radical environmentalism in Britain has been the political manifestation of such a new political philosophy. Individual members of environmental pressure groups and activists may hold extremely radical views, but this is not necessarily reflected by the actions of the group. Within pressure-group politics, there has always been very little scope for this. British political culture requires such groups to be non-ideological, and therefore the knowledge interests (cf. Jamison et al. 1990) of establishment environmental groups consist of "scientific" data that can be used for influencing government on specific issues, not "environmental ideology." While challenging groups may, at least initially, seek to build a new ecological worldview to justify its radical demands, these ideological elements are then usually de-emphasized once the group joins the mainstream.

Outside pressure-group politics, ideological challenges to reformist environmentalism could only find a place either within the traditions of the labor movement or within a separate ecological party. Throughout the 1970s, there was an interest within some socialist circles, manifesting itself organizationally in the Socialist Environment and Resources Association (SERA) formed in 1973, to promote environmental issues within the Labour Party and the trade union movement. At a time of continuing union militancy in the 1970s, working within the labor movement was still a major attraction. A neo-Marxist analysis of environmentalism, consisting of a critique of the "unpolitical" character of mainstream environmentalism and the need to create a new agenda responding to both green and Socialist concerns, became increasingly popular in the late 1970s and early 1980s (cf. Coates 1972; Dickson 1974; Barratt-Brown et al. 1976; Pepper 1984; 1993; Weston 1986; Ryle 1988; Atkinson 1991; and Williams n.d.). It was particularly powerful in the antinuclear and alternative-technology movements (Rüdig 1990). Eco-Socialist campaigners were quite successful in committing some unions and the Labour Party to antinuclear and other environmental policies (cf. Elliott 1988; Carter 1992), but this remained of little practical consequence as the political importance of trade unions and labor declined sharply after 1979.

Unlike in a number of continental European countries, Britain has never developed the political manifestation of the so-called new politics in the form of new social movements with a common political identity and a strong green party challenging the established order (cf. Rootes 1992). Instead, the British social-movement sector is characterized by a high degree of fragmentation and particularization in which issues and concerns are addressed by individual interest groups (cf. Rüdig et al. 1991b, and Rüdig 1994). The electoral system has made engagement with the Greens an unattractive prospect for many radicals. While the pragmatic British political culture has traditionally not placed great value on ideological justifications for political behavior, the fact that no effective realignment of radical politics on ecological lines has taken place has effectively meant that attempts to formulate a new ideological basis combining the various strands of radical thinking have remained marginal.[5]

The only political organization which has provided a continuous home for radical ecological thinking has been the Green Party. It was formed in 1973 by a very small group of people that had become alarmed about impending environmental catastrophes by an article by Paul Ehrlich. Goldsmith's survivalist thinking then became the dominant ideological force in its early development, before giving way to more pragmatic views which still considered it possible to reform the present society to avert environmental catastrophe. From about 1979, anarchist thinking became more important as a new generation of members entered the party (cf. Rüdig and Lowe 1986).

Green Party activists generally have to be classified as "dark" rather than "light" greens (cf. Porritt and Winner 1988). They believe in the necessity for fundamental social and political change. Disagreements center around the attitude to the "left," the value of nonviolent direct action, and the relative importance of fighting elections. The ideological positions of the two main camps are documented in books by leading Green Party activists of the 1980s. More pragmatic electoralist green positions are formulated by Jonathan Porritt (1984) and Sara Parkin (1991). They advocate the necessity for fundamental change, and by no means could be seen as reformist environmentalists. Both authors recognize a "spiritual dimension" of green politics, but also see the need to work for change within the given political system and reject any association with left-wing politics. The position of the "decentralists" is more strongly colored by anarchist and Socialist influences (see Wall 1992, and Kemp and Wall 1990). The building of a political organization which lives up to the green vision is considered more important than short-term electoral success.

A series of surveys of Green Party members in the early 1990s (cf. Rüdig et al. 1991a, and 1993) paints a very complex picture of the ideological composition of Green Party members. The analysis reveals three main ideologically defined dimensions: left anarchist, deep ecology, and electoralist. Left anarchists believe that greens have to commit themselves to a redistribution of wealth and support civil disobedience and are keenest on decentralized party organization. They strongly reject the "statist" traditional left-wing politics. The deep ecology dimension is primarily defined in terms of a high emphasis on biocentrism, a preference for decentralist organization, and a "survivalist" orientation with little belief in the ability to reform the present system. The electoralist dimension is chiefly defined by its high emphasis on electoral campaigning (Bennie et al. 1994).

While those who see the Green Party in more traditional party political terms may be easily frustrated by the electoral failures of the party, these results suggest that some members appear to have decoupled their evaluation of their party membership from any conventional notion of political success. Belonging to the Green Party for them is as much a lifestyle issue, of living a green life here and now, as it is a political statement about the desired future of society as a whole. The background of these green radicals is quite heterogeneous: some may have opted out of conventional economic activity, some may be involved in unconventional religions or spiritual communities (cf. Luhrmann 1993), but many others are not. Whatever the exact lifestyle of this group of people, their commitment to green politics transcends the ups and downs of the electoral fortunes of the party, and the party's existence for the foreseeable future is thus not in any immediate danger. However, with a current party membership of around five thousand, and electoral support of just 1 to 3 percent, the Green Party is a very small force in British politics.

The academic debate about deep ecology and biocentrism has been most influential in Australia and in the United States. In Britain, these issues have only recently been introduced to the broader debate about green politics (Dobson 1990; 1991; Eckersley 1992), and critical responses have slowly been emerging, too (Pepper 1993; Barry 1993). In political terms, the deep ecology debate has not played any major role so far. The basic deep ecology positions, in particular the rejection of anthropocentrism, appear to be absorbed fairly easily by the Green Party. With the relative decline of the antinuclear movement and the debate about the relationship between ecologism and Socialism, biocentrism as the litmus test of greenness (Eckersley 1992) looks like becoming a more prominent feature of green politics in Britain as well. In the absence of any serious conflict over wilderness issues, it is more doubtful whether biocentrism will have any wider appeal beyond the confines of a small group of green activists.[6]

CONCLUSIONS

In Britain, civil disobedience has been used on a number of occasions as a means of environmental political action. Civil disobedience is by no means a new feature of British political life. Riots and similar disturbances were quite common in the eighteenth and nineteenth centuries (Kiernan 1972; Poulsen 1984; Stevenson 1992). Also, there is a long tradition of direct action in working-class culture, chiefly embodied in trade-union militancy and industrial relations conflicts. In a number of cases, environmental actions have built on these traditions and have included civil disobedience tactics. In these cases, environmental direct action carried out by local people perceiving a fundamental threat to their livelihood has often been successful. Most of the British environmental movement stands in the tradition of reform politics, using establishment contacts and traditional lobbying techniques, lately supplemented by more media-oriented campaigns.

It is as an integral part of such reformist environmentalism that more recent forms of civil disobedience have been employed. Here, direct action is employed in a symbolic way to demonstrate opposition and, more recently, to create a media event to increase the coverage of a particular campaign. Influenced by the U.S. civil rights movements, this type of civil disobedience was first used systematically by the British peace movement. National antinuclear and other environmental groups have only used it sparingly, with the exception of Greenpeace who have developed it into a highly organized, deliberate way of generating political pressure through media stunts. These acts of civil disobedience have often been successful in raising issues and raising the public profile of groups organizing these actions. Unlike the first version adopted by some local populations, civil disobedience here is only designed for these purposes, with policy success being reserved to be fought for with expert opinions and traditional lobbying activity.

Environmental radical action in Britain is thus not necessarily linked to a radical environmental philosophy. Neither in the case of local populations taking direct action to preserve their environment, nor in the case of environmental groups staging direct-action events for the media can such a link be identified. A unity of environmental radicalism in theory and action is restricted to a very small group of people, located on the margins of British environmental politics.

Key developments of British environmental politics in the late 1980s and early 1990s made it very difficult for radical environmentalism to break out of its marginal position. With the general decline of other new social movements, the direct political mobilization of environmental activists for demonstrations and other actions decreased substantially. Most radical environmental groups either went through an institutionalization process, or disappeared altogether. Environmental groups increasingly became highly professional environmental organizations run by relatively small groups of activists. Ordinary members only play a passive role, restricted mainly to making financial contributions. After the success of building up a mass membership, groups concentrate their efforts on mobilizing expert opinion and traditional lobbying activities. The current focus on global environmental issues, and the opportunities for environmental groups to take part in international decision-making processes as nongovernmental organizations, has accelerated this institutionalization process. In Britain, the presence of an environmentally unresponsive national government has made it even more crucial for environmental groups to seek to challenge that unresponsiveness in the international area. The increasing environmental activism of the European Union provided one major new opportunity at the European level, the Rio Earth Summit, and subsequent United Nations initiatives provide another major policy arena.

Movements usually develop in a cyclical fashion. As we have seen, environmental groups in Britain can start as radical challengers and then become integrated into the system. But the new environmental establishment faces new challenges from new movement cycles which erupt around new environmental issues. Since 1992, there appear to be signs that a new radical environmental movement may be emerging in Britain. Following a high-profile direct action campaign against a motorway extension project at Twyford Down designed to shorten the travelling time between

Southampton and London by a few minutes, radical protest against the government's motorway construction program emerged at many points throughout the country. Apart from local people, Earth First! and other radical groups became involved. A series of spectacular acts of civil disobedience between 1992 and 1994 clearly raised the profile of radical environmental action in Britain (Vidal 1994; also see Hill et al. in this volume).

In a replication of previous episodes of the history of British environmentalism, the established groups were somewhat surprised by this sudden emergence of grass-roots protests. There appears to be a clear gap between the radicalism of the new groups and the pragmatic approach of the environmental establishment. What is less clear, however, is the extent to which the new radicalism can sustain itself. The anti-motorway campaigns got under way at the time when the political salience of environmental issues generally had dropped dramatically (Rüdig et al. 1993). The government backed down on some highly controversial plans and reduced its motorway construction program. As on many occasions before, government action has thus been used to limit the mobilizaiton potential of protest groups.

For a new radical ecological movement to develop, clearly new issues would need to emerge to maintain the current momentum. While there is no shortage of environmental and social problems which could be targets for further mobilization, the history of British environmental radicalism suggests that partial ingration, fragmentation and marginalization are still the most likely outcome of this latest development.

NOTES

1. The support of the U.K. Economic and Social Research Council is gratefully acknowledged. The work was funded by ESRC awards nos. R000 23 2404 and Y320 27 3061.

2. Cf. Rucht 1994 for a critical study of the operation of Greenpeace in Germany.

3. The West German government in particular was pushing for higher environmental standards at the European level in response to German industrial pressure to avoid any competitive disadvantages due to the strong environmental legislation adopted in Germany, partly as a result of

the high level of politicization of the environment achieved by the environmental and antinuclear movements (S. Grant et al. 1988).

4. The British system of pollution control was previously characterized by an absence of fixed standards and a high level of discretion exercised by officials (cf. Enloe 1975; Vogel 1986). This allowed a high degree of flexibility, but was generally used to allow industry to follow environmental practices which imposed low costs. For example, rather than limiting the amount of emissions of pollutants into the air, higher chimneys were built to distribute the emissions over a wider area. The prevailing western wind over the British isles carried much of that pollution to Scandinavia, contributing to the acid rain problem. Also, Britain's geography provided the opportunity to discharge wastewater directly into the sea. These practices only came under sustained political pressure in the 1980s, mainly through the European Union. A series of new European and British environmental legislation has been passed, leading to a profound change in environmental regulation in Britain; cf. Rose (1990); Weale et al. (1991); Boehmer-Christiansen and Skea (1991); Jordan (1993); and Ball and Bell (1994).

5. The reconstruction of the interrelationship between the various strands of left-wing, feminist, and ecological thinking since the 1970s is a complicated task going beyond what is possible in this article. Briefly, British left-wing politics was dominated more strongly than elsewhere by traditional industrial conflicts and class politics in the 1970s. New Left thinking developed more slowly. By the late 1970s, the linking between left and feminist politics was on the agenda (cf. Rowbotham et al. 1979). In the early 1980s, racial discrimination, gay and lesbian rights, and nuclear disarmament became the major issues for the realignment of left-wing politics, while environmental questions remained largely outside this process. Links between ecological and feminist politics materialized more strongly through common activities in the peace movement. The most important eco-feminist force in Britain was the group Women for Life on Earth formed in 1980. The main ideological inspiration appears to have come from the United States (Caldecott and Leland 1983). Women for Life on Earth fielded two candidates jointly with the Green Party in the 1983 general elections but afterward appears to have faded away. In the late 1980s, eco-feminism took its place in British academic debate, but, again, virtually all authors discussed appear to originate in the United States or in Australia (cf. McCulloch 1987 and Dobson 1990). For a thorough critique of the failure of the (British) green movement to develop a feminist perspective, see Mellor (1992a and b).

6. One such route could lie in an increasing importance of radical animal-rights issues for the green movement. The protection of animal rights has a very long history in Britain. The Royal Society for the Prevention of Cruelty to Animals (RSPCA) was formed in 1824. More recently,

there is a clear division between the established animal-welfare groups, such as the RSPCA and other lobbying organizations, and the radical animal-rights movements which have been engaged in nonviolent and violent actions aimed particularly against research institutions.

So far, animal rights and environmental groups have been quite separate. Historically, there has been some overlap as concern about animal welfare in Britain linked to the protection of wildlife and nature conservation (Lowe 1983). But animal-rights groups have not usually been seen as a part of the environmental movement, a view largely shared by both animal-rights activists and environmental groups. Only a very small minority of Green Party members has been engaged in animal-rights activities.

Chapter 13

POPULAR RESISTANCE AND THE EMERGENCE OF RADICAL ENVIRONMENTALISM IN SCOTLAND

Brendan Hill, Rachel Freeman, Steve Blamires, and Alastair McIntosh

Scotland, like the rest of Britain, is experiencing a flourishing of environmental radicalism. However, unlike the antiroadbuilding protests which have erupted across the English countryside for several years now, this revival builds both on a long-standing and distinctively Scottish concern with social inequity and on a widespread awakening to issues of environmental abuse. Furthermore, Scots are rediscovering their hidden past—particularly the recent history of colonization and clearance of the Highlands which practically eradicated a viable land-based lifestyle. Such colonization left barren overgrazed hills stripped of the forests they once had carried and a legacy of land ownership in the hands of a tiny elite, many of whom are foreign.

Environmental radicalism is a nascent phenomenon in Scotland. Within the last two years, environmental groups like Earth First! have begun to stage nonviolent direct actions against ecological destruction. To some extent, this has followed similar events to the south in England.

Among these Scottish flourishings are remnants of the 1980s antinuclear movement such as the Faslane Peace Camp, which has been leading protests against the stationing of nuclear submarines in the estuary of the River Clyde since the early 1980s. Other indigenous threads include the threat to open up so-called superquarries—among the largest holes in the world—by gouging out coastal mountains, and the rediscovery of a land-based folk culture through music and storytelling.

As in the rest of Britain, overt protest is being led by disaffected urban youth. EF! made its start in Scotland in 1993. That year, in what some warned might be interpreted as an act of colonialism in itself, a small group of activists—some traveling north from England—carried out a protest action against the building of the Skye bridge, an American-financed road scheme, which was under construction. The activists were warned that any initiative which was seen to come from "outsiders" would be derided locally, and resented by islanders.

What critics did not take into account was that there was a sizeable local opposition to the bridge based on a variety of arguments: almost forty families whose breadwinners currently operate ferries will lose their main income; there may be a significant increase in traffic and the dangers that imposes; it is rumored that the toll may be as high as six pounds (nine dollars); the bridge will be ugly and out of place, depriving Skye of its proud island status; and the construction is causing significant damage to one of the principal otter colonies in the United Kingdom, and in the process riding roughshod over European environmental protection law.

The story made the front pages and gathered favorable editorial comment. Much of the impetus for this early action came from a pool of activists in Glasgow who had researched well the adventure. The money for the bridge has come from an American bank, the profits will not be staying in the community (unlike the present ferry operators' wages), and it was being built cheaply, using a second-rate, fast construction instead of the alternatively proposed more elegant version. Bearing that in mind, the protestors did not believe that what they saw as local apathy and disempowerment should be a reason not to act in accordance with their beliefs.

Earth First! held its first action in the more genteel capital city of Edinburgh, in early 1994. Sixty activists drumming and playing penny whistles invaded a quarry industry conference, to the complete surprise of the organizers. In central Glasgow, EF! has disrupted council meetings, occupied offices, and squatted trees in the line of motorway building. The movement is burgeoning, drawing in many from existing environmental organizations and networks including Green Students and the Reclaim the Streets anticar group.

It should also be noted that virtually all mainstream environment and social reform groups exist in Scotland, many having separate entities from the English operations: Friends of the Earth, World Wide Fund for Nature, Scottish Wildlife Trust, and the Scottish Trade Union Congress. Greenpeace groups also have been successful in Scotland and have increased their independence from the London branch by setting up a special Torness Action Group designed to protest against the Torness nuclear power station. The membership numbers are impressive, with approximately seven thousand in the Edinburgh area alone, a 40 percent higher per capita membership rate than the United Kingdom average.

Direct action against other targets, in particular nuclear power plants, has a longer history. Some Scottish Earth First!ers had their first direct action experiences at the Faslane Peace Camp near Glasgow, where among the grim and often dangerous attempts to obstruct the movements of nuclear submarines throughout the 1980s, a witty tradition of breaking into the heavily guarded military base and secretly planting roses and potatoes arose. The Faslane camp itself took at least some of its original inspiration from the Greenham Common Women's Peace camp which protested throughout the 1980s against the arrival and presence of U.S. cruise missiles at an air base west of London.

These protests have not arisen in a vacuum. They stand as the latest acts in a long tradition of Scottish resistance and revolt. Beneath a surface quietude springs a strong flow of pride in that which is Scottish, a healthy nationalism that values community, self-sufficiency, and attachment to the land.

Scotland is in the process of re-asserting an authentic national identity. This arises from an identity crisis which is not so much Who are we? but more How do we portray ourselves accurately without being relegated to shortbread tins and tartan? Having felt marginalized by its more powerful and larger southern neighbor England, Scotland now wants a say of its own, in its own terms. The English, generally oblivious to the difference, maintain with easy assurance that Scotland is just part of the United Kingdom, and that any claims to independence are but comforting dreams.

The crisis is forcing the Scots to take stock of their differences and similarities which comprise the varying regions in Scotland and create a voice to describe who they are, what they stand for, and what the land means to them according to where they are in the country. The Scots, having been the latest extant indigenous tribal peoples in mainland Britain, retain traces in their folklore, customs, and social fabric that have been lost in England. In varying places, the Scots still conspicuously believe in community, social equity, and the spirit of service. For example, during the reign of Tory governments since Thatcher arose in 1979, and despite their arguably deserved reputation for financial caution, many Scottish people have quite clearly lost patience with unfeeling, accountant-led government.

The Labour and Scottish National parties are far more prominent in Scottish local government than the Tories. In the last election 75 percent of the vote went to parties that favor a Scottish parliament compared to roughly 40 percent in the referendum of the late 1970s. The feeling that governance by a party that has barely enough Scottish MPs to provide the necessary government ministers for Scotland exacerbates nationalism.

This revaluing of Scottishness is being fed by a rediscovery of the local historical and cultural background and is clearly helping cultivate the confident voice that is needed for regeneration, environmentally, politically, and culturally. Since environmental movements and issues cannot be separated from circumstance and site-specific situations, an understanding of lifestyle and tradition is helpful. The murmurs of direct eco-militancy in Scotland appear likely to increase hand-in-hand with the attempts at reasserting this indigenous voice.

An example of the concerns and proud defense of a community can be seen in the following excerpt from an article written to the *West Highland Free Press* in June 1994 by Norman MacLeod,[1] a native resident of Lingerabay, Isle of Harris, site of the proposed Redland Aggregates Superquarry:

> Ian Wilson [the man who owns the Lingerabay mineral rights] will of course profit, as will the proprietor of Rodel Estate, but they will be about the only Scots to profit. Redland Aggregates in their magnanimity promised about 20 jobs to Harris men in Lingerabay quarry, but, judging from their record on promises to date, half that number would be a far safer estimate. They will have little interest in the unemployed, women or anyone approaching the age of 50. With some luck, some of the daily tonnage of explosives will be manufactured in southern Scot-

land. That about sums up all the advantages from such drastic surgery as superquarrying for the ills of unemployment, not only for Harris but for the Scottish nation in total.

Harris will have a scar on its landscape visible from the moon, the largest man-made hole in the world—big enough eventually to hold 80 of the Great Pyramids of Egypt. A veritable hell-hole of dust, disease and din to work in. Our island will be overhung by a huge pall of death-grey dust that will find its way into every corner of our homes and into our lungs, shortening our lives, stunting the health of our children from the day they are born or even before. (MacLeod 1994)

A look at historical events affecting both the cultural and the environmental landscapes in Scotland (with a focus on the north west) will show that many events, in particular the traumatic Highland clearances, still define the realities of life for Highland Scottish natives. There has been a rise in indigenous awareness, and groups like the popular Adult Learning Project help feed and fuel curiosities by offering courses in aspects of Scottish life, ranging from song, dance, and fiddle, to land issues and principles of democracy in Scotland.

The northwest of Scotland, known as the Highlands and Islands, has a distinct cultural history which differs from that of other parts of Scotland because of its strong Viking and Celtic influences and native Gaelic language. In the wake of Roman and Norman invasions of southern mainland Britain, the Celtic cultures of Old Europe were pushed to this western edge. Here an ancient spirituality, music, literature, and art found sanctuary—a repository at the periphery, now becoming central as the spiritual coherence of the "center" comes to recognize the paucity of its values. As President Jacques Delors of the European Commission put it in 1993, "If in the next ten years Europe doesn't discover a soul, a sense of meaning and direction, the game will be up" (Hulbert 1993).

As the Highlands are farthest north in Scotland, they were not and still are not readily accessible, so traditions and beliefs were not as strongly affected by invading cultures as those of neighboring regions. Although Gaelic was spoken throughout Scotland at one time (in the tenth and eleventh centuries), it was short lived and did not reflect the underlying culture of many of the other non-Highland regions. Areas in the south (Borders, Dumfries, and Galloway) and east (Fife and Grampian) experienced other influences through trade and settlement and primarily spoke Scots, which is a blend of Anglo-Danish, Norn, French, Anglo-Norman, and Gaelic (although a strain of Gaelic survived in Galloway until the seventeenth century) (Robinson 1987; ix).

In terms of landscape, the Highlands and Islands are commonly thought to be barren, bereft of trees, and having a particularly acidic soil. Grampian, the Borders, Dumfries, and Galloway are considerably more fertile, greener, and more conducive to large scale farming and dairying.

Scotland has seen many settlers and invaders throughout the centuries, including the Norse, the Picts, the Anglo-Saxons, and, of course, the Celts. Playing host to these groups has enriched the fabric of the nation and contributed to traditions in tales, motifs, designs, language, place names, and material culture (e.g., household and farming implements). But in the mid to late 18th century the history of northern Scotland reveals not an increase in cultural exchange but a distinct attempt to curtail, if not destroy, many cultural and environmental developments.

This was a result of the "Highland clearances" which forced the Highland and Island people (often known as the Gaels) off their land, as late as the twentieth century. This was an event of cultural genocide which paralleled and in many respects pioneered patterns of colonial conquest elsewhere in the British Empire. The effects persist in the national psyche to this day; in an aching sense of loss, concealed beneath a veneer of relative material affluence and a growing sense of the importance of reclaiming the commons.

Under the Highland clan system land was held by the chief effectively in common for the clan, the extended family. People understood themselves as being a part of a place to such an extent that a farmer would often be referred to by the name of the farm rather than the family name. Here we see implicit recognition that the land is more permanent than those who live on it. In losing the land, the psychospiritual effect was a loss of self. As a lyric by Scotland's top folk-rock band, Runrig, has it when discussing the twenty years the songwriters had had to wait before learning their true social history:

> Twenty years for the truth
> I had to wait
> I had to search

Twenty years of deceit
They denied me knowledge of myself. (Morton 1991:66)

The clearances, in which some half a million (Thompson 1984; 2) Highlanders were directly or through economic pressure forced off their land, must be understood in relation to the process of enclosure that originated in fourteenth- and fifteenth-century Britain, and especially England. In defining land as "property," enclosure (sometimes pejoratively termed the "theft of the commons") accorded tradable status to land and water rights.

Such "improvement," as it was termed by apologists, was associated with profit in the same way that "development" has become associated with "economic growth." Dispossessed peoples had little choice but to become wage-laborers, and labor too became a tradable commodity. Enclosure therefore represents not only the removal of land from subsistence communities, but a profound step toward viewing the land and its people as tradable, exploitable commodities. Thus begins the loss of a sense of place and identity. *Inner colonialism* has been used to describe this state.

Unlike their Roman predecessors, who never made it farther north than lowland Scotland, the "great improvers" who had enclosed England and lowland Scotland did reach the Highlands and Islands, albeit rather late. This bioregion was an area at the remote periphery, inhospitable to intruders, and mostly mountainous. Human settlement had been based on hunter-gatherer and subsistence arable and cattle agriculture. Today it supports a population of approximately 350,000.

Very little of Scotland remains undisturbed by humans. It is difficult to assess the state of the natural environment over time since the process of change has been long, slow, and complex. However, the loss of forest cover is undisputed. Only 1 percent of Scotland is now covered in the ragged remnants of native forest which once blanketed as much as 75 percent of the land area called the "Great Forest of Caledon" by the Romans (Roberts 1992). Even the little that is left continues to degenerate, with a 75 percent reduction since 1600 (Smout 1991). Land productivity in general is widely believed to have suffered. The destruction of the forest has taken many centuries, but it has become critical in the last 200 years.

In 1707 the parliaments of Scotland and England combined for a mixture of reasons to do with secession, religion, security, and access to mutual markets. This led to much popular resentment in Scotland. The great Scots nationalist poet Robert Burns termed the Scottish leaders that surrendered sovereignty "a parcel of rogues." Reaction to this consolidation of parliaments and events surrounding the earlier 1603 Union of the Crowns meant that by 1745 Scotland was effectively in a state of civil war over the Treaty of Union.

Intent upon preventing further rebellion, pacification of the clans became the immediate priority of the British state, comprising the English, lowland Scots, and Royalist clan chiefs. A process known as "proscription" was set in place to take the heart out of traditional Highland culture by banning the wearing of Highland dress (namely kilts), meetings of Highlanders, and playing of the bagpipes and other forms of traditional entertainment, while leaving many outward structures intact for administrative purposes.

Under other names—*civilization, education, Christianization* —this was to become a cornerstone of colonialism around the world as it had earlier been in Ireland. Speaking from Latin America, Paulo Freire was later to describe the phenomenon as "cultural invasion." Freire's analysis is having a significant influence in a contemporary Scotland trying to remember its past in order to revision and reclaim its future (Kirkwood 1989). Freire says:

> In this phenomenon, the invaders penetrate the cultural context of another group, and ignoring the potential of the latter, they impose their own view of the world upon those they invade and inhibit the creativity of the invaded by curbing their expression. . . . Cultural invasion is thus always an act of violence against the persons of the invaded culture, who lose their originality. . . . [It] leads to the cultural inauthenticity of those who are invaded; they begin to respond to the values, the standards, and the goals of the invaders. . . . It is essential that those who are invaded come to see their reality with the outlook of the invaders rather than their own; for the more they mimic the invaders, the more stable the position of the latter becomes . . . it is essential that those invaded become convinced of their intrinsic inferiority (Freire 1971:121–22).

The Act of Proscription took effect in August 1747 and was not repealed until 1782, by which time its effects had been internalized into a Freirian "culture of silence."

The first wave of clearance forced a previously self-reliant peasant people onto marginal land. This was done to clear the interior lands for sheep while also creating a waged labor force for the fishing and kelping (seaweed-based alkali production) industries. The introduction of cheviot and blackface sheep in the 1760s was the driving force behind agricultural improvement, enabling substantial profit to be made from terrain previously suitable only for peasant subsistence.

The final stage of consolidating present patterns of enclosed land tenure came after the military demand for wool collapsed with the ending of the Napoleonic Wars. Remaining unenclosed lands had been consolidated with former sheep farms to make the great "sporting" estates. By 1912, 3,599,744 acres, or one-fifth of the entire Scottish land mass (Jarvie 1991:64), had been converted so that landed gentry could stalk stag, fish for salmon, and shoot grouse and the thrush-sized snipe. Older folk in the early twentieth century could recall firsthand the human tragedy in the wake of village clearances. The following account is by Catriona McPhee of South Uist in the Outer Hebrides:

> Many a thing I have seen in my own day and generation. Many a thing, O Mary Mother of the black sorrow. I have seen the townships swept, and the big holdings being made of them, the people being driven out of the countryside to the streets of Glasgow and to the wilds of Canada, such as them that did not die of hunger and plague and smallpox while going across the ocean. I have seen the women putting the children in the carts which were being sent from Benbecula and the Iochdar to Loch Boisdale, while their husbands lay bound in the pen and were weeping beside them, without power to give them a helping hand, though the women themselves were crying aloud and their little children wailing like to break their hearts. I have seen the big strong men, the champions of the countryside, the stalwarts of the world, being bound on Loch Boisdale quay and cast into the ships as would be alone to a batch of horses or cattle in the boat. The bailiffs and the constable and the policemen gathered behind them in pursuit of them. The God of life and He only knows all the loathsome work of men on that day. (Hunter 1976:81)

Conditions on marginalized land for those remaining at home were often miserable because of limited space and denial of access to many local resources such as fish and seaweed for personal consumption. Replacement of the former, largely subsistence, cattle-based economy by sheep, deer, grouse, and other game birds has been associated with diminution of the several indigenous forms of nutrient recycling (Dodgshon and Olsson 1988) as well as intensification of grazing and burning pressures. Density of predators such as hawks and polecats would appear to have dramatically declined since the sporting estates were first established (Smout 1991: 244).

The spaces allotted for those remaining in the Highlands and Islands were called "crofts," otherwise known as "smallholdings." As less land was available to the people, and many of the landlords raised rents and made further demands, dissatisfaction was apparent but unfocussed.

John Murdoch, founder of *The Highlander*, an early newspaper based on campaigning for Scottish cultural and land reform, is known to have said; "Our Highland friends must depend on themselves and they should remember that union is strength. We do not advocate that they should fight or use violent means, for there is a better way than that. Why do they not form societies for self improvement and self-defense?" (*The Highlander* 27 June 1879).

With written encouragement and work of other vocal activists, protests were staged and testimony gradually emerged. In the aftermath of a particularly strong protest on the Isle of Skye, the Highland Land League was formed in 1883 in London to apply political pressure in Westminster and organize mass rent strikes, demonstrations, and support for reform by constitutional means by friends at home and abroad.[1]

After much protest, the 1886 Crofters Act was passed which gave heritable security of tenure with controlled rents on those smallholdings, or crofts. Because many areas of land remained without crofting tenure, the 1886 act fell far short of returning to the people land which had been taken from them. However, the act did secure the survival of crofting life into the present era, albeit effectively through having designated native reservations since most of the land, including the best land, remains outside of crofter control. Today it is increasingly recognized that the convivial landscapes of crofting areas are cultural landscapes. To preserve them, crofting as a way of life—including agriculture, fishing, and weaving—must be upheld. This has been justified on grounds of tourism, but a new justification is emerging within the rubric of sustainability.

In the crofting communities we retain one of the few bases of indigenous land-based knowledge in western Europe. Sustainability was implicit to much crofting practice. As a Hebridean doctor of crofter stock, Dr. Donald Murray, has put it: "In the old days people were ecological without knowing that they were or why. [Today's challenge is] to understand the why and not just follow the how" (McIntosh 1994:62).

A distinctive crofting identity has been bred in the Highlands through adverse clearance history, land practices (which developed out of necessity to try to make the land more productive), community activities, and stories, songs, and anecdotes—most of which were passed down in Scottish Gaelic. A unique form of music produced by the mouth known as *puirt a beul*, a Gaelic expression meaning "music of the mouth" came as a direct result of the Act of Proscription. To avoid getting caught with banned instruments, the people simply played music by mouth.

In trying to make the land more productive, crofters grew potatoes (which were the staple food until early this century) on *feannagan* or "lazybeds" in English—an unfortunate misnomer since it was hard work to create them. These lazybeds were designed to improve drainage by piling what little earth there was onto strips of land in order to gain soil depth and avoid rocks. They were laborious to set up, but working together and sharing tools the whole community put seaweed, shell sand, and old thatched roofs on the lazybed strips as fertilizer. In this way local resources and innovation allowed potatoes to be grown in an otherwise unsuitable environment. Such understanding may be valuable as the limitations of much current land management by technologically minded "experts" become more evident.

When the Act of Proscription was lifted, community spirit could again be rekindled in a more informal way during *ceilidh* evenings when people would gather and tell stories, sing songs, play music, and talk of the day's occurrences. Aspects of the landscape would be remembered by exchanging stories, riddles, and rhymes to test one's local knowledge.

Many of these traditions have died out. However, in recent times there have been attempts to remember the past and add a new dimension to it. The contemporary works of writers and poets such as Liz Lochhead and Angus Peter Campbell are becoming increasingly popular as they address issues of Scottish history, identity, and disenfranchisement in the greater United Kingdom. An example is Iain Crichton Smith's book *Consider the Lilies* (1987), which is a poignant account of a old woman who is cleared from her cottage in Sutherland. Such works seem to be another way of healing the wounds and coming to terms with past events.

Another route is through music festivals. Young people are listening to recording groups and stars such as Capercaillie, Runrig, and Dougie MacLean. Groups and singers performing both traditional tunes and songs and composing original material in the traditional idiom are becoming more popular. Festivals are becoming busier, and therefore the opportunities for dialogue between like-minded people are becoming increasingly frequent. With powerful songs such as Capercaillie's "Waiting for the Wheel to Turn" and "Servant to the Slave" and Dougie Maclean's "Real Estate," along with the tremendously popular Runrig's classics such as "Dance Called America," *"Tir an Airm"* ("Land of Weapons"—a reference to the heavy military presence in the Western Isles) and "Recovery," the audience is not only hearing top-quality music but is also being exposed to its history. As well as the "stars" singing what used to be called "protest songs," lesser known groups and local musicians, poets, and storytellers are commenting on what they see happening around them.

In its own time and of its own accord, this cultural rediscovery is taking place in the hotel lobbies and bars, in the restaurants and cafes, on camp sites, and in buses and trains. Old passions are being revived and new ideas exchanged—in the traditional oral manner.

Integration of old and new ideas may be the best way to plan for the future while still nurturing an attachment and understanding of place. Many crofters today have full-time or part-time jobs of varying descriptions. Current modes of crofting have the potential to maintain growing and informed communities. Improved communications (via fax machines and computer modems) with the mainland are enabling people to work from home instead of migrating to the cities.

According to Frank Rennie, in his article "The Electronic Crofter": "Through an investment of over 16 million pounds, 43 key exchanges are to be converted to digital operation accompanied by new ISDN (Integrated Services Digital Network) lines . . . this initiative is an attempt to overcome the unalterable physical barriers of the Highlands and Islands" (Rennie 1993:44).

New schemes for land use are also in place, including forestry projects, fish farming, and land management for public access and leisure. Pilot studies for renewable energy resources may also be funded (*West Highland Free Press* 1993b). New alliances are emerging, one of the most seminal being the 1992 collaborative report between the radical Scottish Crofters Union and the relatively conservative Royal Society for the Protection of Birds. Entitled "Crofting and the Environment: A New Approach," the report signaled that future conservation measures to protect rare birds such as the Corncrake must be carried out in ways which involve and benefit the land-using community. This has resulted in Corncrake subsidies, whereby crofters are paid not to cut their hay too early so that the nesting cycle can reach its full conclusion.

There are still pockets of overt oppression caused by unsympathetic, feudalistic landlords. In a region with eight hundred applicants on a housing waiting list, a landlord, Sheik Mohammed bin Rashid al Maktoumm of Dubai, one of the richest men in the world, bulldozed twelve houses in his "glen of sorrow" in Wester Ross. The local press considered this to be due to his suppositions about "the night-time poaching activities of the local population" (*West Highland Free Press* 1993a). Increasingly, such landlordism is being resisted by various forms of direct action. Two young men are currently serving prison terms for sinking Sheik Maktoumm's half-million-pound yacht.

On the island of Eigg, a trust was established to challenge the "lairdship" of former Olympic bobsleigher and car salesman, Keith Schellenberg. Conflict came to a head early in 1994 when a mysterious fire destroyed Schellenberg's vintage Rolls Royce, which had been a symbol of his presumption of imperialism on the island. (McIntosh 1992:159). Through a strategy of market spoiling, the Isle of Eigg Trust has effectively knocked the bottom out of the island's saleability in the marketplace. Schellenberg is holding out against community ownership, but even without direct control over their land, in challenging their landlord's legitimacy the community members have found a voice and have begun to speak out for their rights.

Another sign of changing times whose significance can hardly be overstated is the case of the Assynt crofters. Assynt, a large twenty-one thousand acre sporting estate in the far northwest formerly owned by English aristocracy and managed, according to local residents, with many of the insensitive and paternalistic attitudes of the past, was successfully bought by approximately one hundred resident crofting families in 1993. Their success may come to be regarded as the turning point of the whole exercise of colonization of Scotland. The jubilant inhabitants are now communally governed through their own land trust, which is planning to encourage repopulation, increase economic self-reliance, and carry out ecological restoration through reforestation programs. At the smaller site of Borve on the Isle of Skye a similar exercise has taken place.

There is also a strong tide of rising consciousness over the parlous state of Scotland's natural heritage. Perhaps the best example of this is the organization Reforesting Scotland. Set up in 1990 initially as a magazine (*The Tree Planters' Guide to the Galaxy*, now simply *Reforesting Scotland*) by ecologically educated incomers working in conservation and restoration ecology in the far north, it has quickly become perhaps the most prominent radical voice linking the almost total deforestation of Scotland with its colonial history and the associated dispossession of the land from the people.

It was observed as far back as the 1940s by early conservationist Sir Frank Fraser Darling that much of Scotland was a "wet desert." One of the founders of Reforesting Scotland, Bernard Planterose, recalls how the vision of a newly reforested Scottish landscape came to him in the late 1980s during repeated vacations to Norway. There, a controlled land market and a vastly higher number of smallholders living close to the land has allowed a mixed coniferous wooded landscape to endure. Planterose is now attempting a model reforestation project on the tiny Isle Martin, and he and many others have set up native tree nurseries.

Almost every environmental group is now promoting the same idea of reforestation. Official bodies are quickly changing policies, organizing tree-planting schemes. Preserving and rehabilitating existing woodlands, until recently ignored by the media, for instance, has also become increasingly fashionable. The main barrier to regrowth of forest is now seen as overgrazing by sheep and deer, predators having long ago been hunted to extinction. Numerous reports are suggesting a major reduction in the numbers of grazing animals, and the state forestry agency is now attempting to protect areas for five hundred meters around old growth remnants in an effort to encourage natural regeneration.

In the city of Glasgow, Earth First! protestors allied to strong local working-class support have set up Pollok Free State in local parkland that was left to the people of Glasgow in perpetuity, but through which the regional council is now threatening to build a motorway. The camp, complete with totem poles at its entrance, celtic motifs carved in stone, tree houses, and a floating population of several dozen, represents a popular grassroots revolt against the powers that be.

In the formal education sector the response has been mixed. In schools, the curriculum is framed by the London government, albeit through a separate and much-praised Scottish Education Department. Nevertheless, the curriculum does not emphasize past injustices or degradation. Teaching Highland clearance history is an option—not a requirement. However, in the northwest, Gaelic is again being taught in many schools. This is following the lead of other Celtic countries such as Ireland and Wales, who have already installed the facilities (in media and education) to accommodate their native tongues.

Increasingly pan-Celtic links are being made. Alan Stivell, a Breton musician, contributed much with his groundbreaking album of the early seventies, *The Renaissance of the Celtic Harp*, which mingled Breton and Hebridean melodies. Now, overcoming at last the Catholic-Protestant divide, groups of crofters are starting to go to Eire (southern Ireland) to study integrated rural development in a country which has its political independence. Other bridgings are also being made. When the Assynt crofters' buyout news was at its peak, a visiting campaigner of Reforesting Scotland found the Sammi of Lapland to be greatly excited by the news. The pan-Atlantic flavor grows too as, for example, BBC Radio Scotland's folk music presenter, Danny Kyle, came back from North America having discovered that Hebridean cloth making songs are indistinguishable from many native American songs also used when making cloth. Comparisons and commonality can be found across cultures, from pleas for land to forms of expression and language which are used to assert identity.

Scotland contains some of the most ancient universities in the world and has always been recognized for its "generalist" tradition in education, focusing on all-round development of the individual in community. However, like universities everywhere, the typical academic's distancing from nature has retarded the speed with which new environmental and social challenges have been drawn to the leading edge of scholarship. But there are some exciting exceptions. For example, since 1972 Edinburgh University has tolerated and sometimes even encouraged its radical green think-tank—the Center for Human Ecology. Increasingly, the Center teaches deep ecology and eco-feminist theology alongside cost-benefit analysis and econometric modeling, hard on the heels of depth psychology. Other centers outside the universities but part of the great "university of life," include the Iona Community, Findhorn, and Samye Ling, the largest Tibetan Buddhist monastery outside the Indian subcontinent.

Although crofting communities comprise only a small part of the Scottish population, Francis Thompson closes his short crofting history by emphasizing that the contribution of crofting is genuinely national. He writes: "These communities [are] instrumental in producing folk who are still proving to be the 'bank' of social value and ideas for the nation as a whole. And it is from those reserves of character that the will to survive against multinational and national government interest is drawn. That indeed is a song worth the singing" (Thompson 1984:135).

There is much to be learned from such examples. An understanding of the political and ecological landscape as well as the history and wealth of culture Scotland has to offer instills an identity and fortifies determination and confidence to speak out and use a collective voice against those forces which have for so long suppressed. This is not a narrow ethnocentrism. It is an inclusive understanding of what it means to be part of an ecological and human community—a vision as valid for the Scots as it is for the French, the Americans, or the English.

NOTES

1. This may be considered a foreshadowing of more recent events to bring about reform, such as the poll tax riots. Scotland is often a testing ground for U.K. legislation, and in 1989 the Conservative government tested a flat-rate community-charge (local taxation) system in Scotland one full year before it was to be implemented in England and Wales. There was deep resentment at such inequity, a widespread refusal to pay, and street riots. The tax was amended.

PART V
CONCLUDING REFLECTIONS ON THE GLOBAL EMERGENCE OF POPULAR ECOLOGICAL RESISTANCE

Chapter 14

Postmodern Environmentalism: A Critique of Deep Ecology

Jerry A. Stark

Introduction

Critics have pointed out the eclectic and contradictory character of deep ecology and question its intelligibility. The premise of this chapter is that deep ecology is completely intelligible—not as a distinct philosophical position but rather as a variant of postmodern social thought. This argument is developed by means of (1) a reconstruction of the basic tenets of deep ecology, (2) a review of the philosophical distinctions between modernism and postmodernism, (3) a discussion of the affinity between deep ecological approaches and postmodernism, and (4) a summary examination and assessment of a postmodernist, deep-ecological perspective approach to science, ethics, and politics.

A point of terminology is in order. When I use the terms *deep ecology* and *deep ecologists*, I refer to philosophical expositions and philosophical expositors, respectively, and not to political practices or organizations. Nonetheless, I pursue my analysis of deep ecology precisely because of its practical implications. I often encounter environmental activists (and many students) who, when asked to explain *why* they engage in or advocate eco-politics or *how* they justify their action or advocacy, use the terms *biocentric philosophy* or *deep ecology* to explain or justify their views. Their reasoning intrigues me.

In other words, I take philosophical discussions of deep ecology seriously precisely because nonphilosophers regard it as a noteworthy perspective. Philosophical reasoning flows from and is grounded in practical experience. Even the most abstract philosophical deliberations have practical implications; even the most mundane experiences are rich with philosophical implication. Furthermore, philosophical orientations, whether they are systematically worked out or not, provide a framework by means of which we guide, explain, and justify our actions. In this sense, an analysis of deep ecological philosophy is necessarily practical, and it is for this reason I pursue the topic here.

What Is Deep Ecology?

The phrase *deep ecology* was coined by Arne Naess in 1973 to (1) distinguish between two forms of environmentalism, "shallow ecology" and "deep ecology,"[1] and to (2) provide a philosophical framework for social transformation. Naess (1973, 1989, 1993) refers to shallow and deep ecology as *social movements* linked to philosophical-scientific perspectives:

1. *The Shallow Ecology Movement:*
Fight against pollution and resource depletion. Central objective: the health and affluence of people in developed countries.
. . .
2. *The Deep Ecology Movement:*
a. Rejection of the man-in-environment image in favor of the *relational total-field image.* . . . The total field model dissolves not only the man-in-environment concept, but every compact thing-in-milieu concept—except when talking at a superficial or preliminary level of communication.
b. *Biospherical egalitarianism—in principle.* . . . To the ecological field worker, *the equal right to live and blossom* is an intuitively clear and obvious value axiom. Its restriction to humans is an anthropocentrism with detrimental effects upon the quality of life of humans themselves. This quality depends in part upon the deep pleasure and satisfaction we receive from close partnership with other forms of life. The attempt to

ignore our dependence and to establish a master-slave role has contributed to the alienation of man from himself.

Naess (1989:29) established these "ecosophical" premises as a platform for deep ecological theory and practice:

1. The flourishing of human and nonhuman life on earth has intrinsic value. The value of nonhuman life forms is independent of the usefulness these may have for narrow human purposes.
2. Richness and diversity of life forms are values in themselves and contribute to the flourishing of human and nonhuman life on earth.
3. Humans have no right to reduce this richness of diversity except to satisfy vital needs.
4. Present human interference with the nonhuman world is excessive, and the situation is rapidly worsening.
5. The flourishing of human life and culture is compatible with a substantial decrease of human population. The flourishing of nonhuman life requires such a decrease.
6. Significant change of life conditions for the better requires change in policies. These affect basic economic, technological, and ideological structures.
7. The ideological change is mainly that of appreciating *life quality* (dwelling in situations of intrinsic value) rather than adhering to a high standard of living. There will be a profound awareness of the difference between big and great.
8. Those who subscribe to the foregoing points have an obligation directly or indirectly to participate in the attempt to implement the necessary changes.

Others have explored the implications of this platform. Devall and Sessions present deep ecology as a new social philosophy in *Deep Ecology* (1985); Devall portrays it as both personal and political ideology in *Simple in Means, Rich in Ends* (1988); Fox develops a comprehensive theory of 'transpersonal' consciousness in *Toward a Transpersonal Ecology* (1990); and Zimmerman assembles key philosophical discussions of deep ecology in *Environmental Philosophy* (1993). All attribute central importance to the works of Naess (Dobson 1989).

Deep ecology reflects the following assumptions: (1) the interrelatedness of all life (biotic community), (2) the essential equality of all organisms as part of an overall system of biotic relationships (biodemocracy), (3) the rejection of human-centered arguments (antianthropocentrism), (4) the conception of the "intrinsic value" of nature (ecocentrism), and (5) the goal of humanity as a fundamental identification nature (self-realization, reimmersion) (Dobson 1990; Eckersley 1992; Fox 1989; 1990; O'Riordan 1977; 1981; Rifkin 1991; Rolston 1988; Taylor 1986). In other words, deep ecology is an *ecocentric philosophy*, or *ecosophy* (Naess 1989), advocates of which claim to offer a new definition of science, ethics, and politics (see Devall 1988; Devall and Sessions 1985; Fox 1989; 1990; and Naess 1989).[2]

MODERNISM, POSTMODERNISM AND DEEP ECOLOGY

Several authors have noted a connection between deep ecological thinking and postmodernism (Bookchin 1990b; Cheney 1989a; 1989b; Frodeman 1992; Lewis 1992; Manes 1992; Zimmerman 1983). Oelschlaeger (1993) even advocates 'postmodern environmentalism' as the key to an environmentally sustainable society. Even a cursory reading of this literature makes it clear that deep ecology explicitly rejects Enlightenment ideas,[3] an approach it shares with postmodernism.[4]

The Modern Categories of Subjectivity/Objectivity

In the Enlightenment tradition, subjectivity occupies a pivotal position. The individual (the "subject") is viewed as a reference point for action, reflection, and moral responsibility. Subjects are conceived as distinct from objects and from other subjects, as well. The concepts of 'freedom,' 'rationality,' 'reason,' 'individuality,' 'science,' 'epistemology,' 'ethics,' 'ideology,' and 'nature' are all bound together in their presumptive dependence upon the notions of human subjectivity and correlated notions of objectivity.

According to Enlightenment philosophy, modern subjects are unique in that they are free to know and free to act in ways distinct from their historical and evolutionary predecessors. A number of distinctions follow from the assumption that humanity is separate from nature by virtue of reason, language, and labor: reason is divided from religion; knowledge is set apart from myth; action becomes distinct from habit; subjectivity is opposed to objectivity;

history becomes distinct from the present; and the notions of 'Progress' and the 'Future' become part of that history.

These notions are so essential to the Enlightenment-based reference points of the modern age that they are often presumed to be inherent in human nature, per se.[5] It is the attack on these presuppositions which defines and distinguishes what we now refer to as the "postmodern style," a style clearly evident in deep ecology.

The Postmodern Rejection of Subjectivity and Objectivity

Postmodernism rejects the notion of 'subjectivity' at the heart of Enlightenment thinking. Rather than accepting the categorical oppositions between mind and body, self and other, subject and object, individuality and university, knowledge and belief, science and mythology, and humanity and nature, postmodernists have generally argued that, far from being universal, these categories represent truncated aspects of human experience in the modern age.[6]

For postmodernists, categories of "subjectivity" and "objectivity" are *not* fundamental aspects of human experience. They are merely artificial appearances which conceal the underlying mythological core of every human experience—a mythological core of experientially based awareness that is antecedent to reflection and action, to subjectivity and objectivity, and to the distinction between humanity and nature.[7] The postmodern approach is not only critical of the notion of an abstract human subjectivity, it also refutes all categories and epistemological positions built upon the notion of a rational individual referring to these as "metanarratives" (Lyotard 1984). Cheney (1989:117-118) makes this point clearly:

> In the light of postmodernist deconstruction of modernist totalizing and foundationalist discourse, can we any longer make sense of the idea of privileged discourse, discourse which can lay claim to having access to the way things are? The dominant postmodern view is that this is not possible, that language can be understood only as either a set of tools created for various human purposes or as the free creation of conscious persons or communities. . . . To the extent that the notion of objectivity enters into postmodern discourse at all it tends to take the form that "truth" is simply the result of social *negotiation*, agreement achieved by the participants in particular conversations.

This rejection of modern philosophical justifications of human knowledge (epistemology) is an essential quality of postmodernism which deep ecology shares—what Ricoeur (1974) calls the "anti-foundational" strategy.

Deep Ecology as Postmodern Environmentalism

Deep ecology also rejects the dualisms between subject and object, self and other, ideology and science, and humanity and nature. In Sessions words,

> As the search for causes of the environmental crisis has tended to move to the deeper level of examining Western society's most basic assumptions and attitudes towards non-human nature, an increasing number of scholars have concluded that the anthropocentric orientations of our Western religious and philosophical traditions have played a major role in the formation of ideologies which have resulted in the crisis. (1974:71)

Underlying the Enlightenment tradition, according to deep ecologists is an *anthropocentrism* which places humanity[8] at the center of all knowledge, belief, judgment, or conduct. In deep ecology, humans as a subjects disappear and are replaced by Naess's conception of humans in terms of a "relational total field image which . . . dissolves the man-in-environment concept"(1989:28).

According to Fox (1989), Naess's (1989) formulation of deep ecology is unique because it proposes a philosophy of "self-realization,"[9] that is, of identification with nature, which results from an inward examination of one's intuitions. Reflecting the postmodern strategy of antifoundationalism, deep ecology presumes that all knowledge is intuitional and that rational distinctions between subject and object, humanity and nature conceal rather than reveal the inner experience of human nature. It is this approach which gives deep ecology its mystical and spiritual qualities.

METATHEORIES OF MODERNISM, POSTMODERNISM AND ENVIRONMENTALISM

Postmodernism characterizes itself as the criticism and rejection ("deconstruction") of systematic, "theoretical," or "totalizing" elements of all thought.[10] As Lyotard (1984:xxiv) has so succinctly stated, "Postmodernism is an incredulity toward metanarratives," that is, *any* philosophy of human nature, human thought, science, religion, art, and so on. From the standpoint of the postmodernist, epistemologically oriented theories of human nature and knowing are *metanarratives*, therefore to be rejected out of hand.[11] The implications of rejecting theories of knowledge warrant examination.

Rejection of Empirical Analytical

Empirical-analytical science presumes the existence of a system of relationships open to observation by means of an objective methodology. From the postmodern perspective, both the concepts of a systematized social world *and* the categories of methodology are expressions of the "totalizing discourse" and "universalistic language game" of science itself. Rather than viewing concepts and categories of empirical science as "tools" of research, postmodernists contend that these represent the distortion and domination of human existence in the technological milieu we call "modern society."[12]

Rejection of Interpretive Science

The postmodern perspective disallows a conception of tradition which informs the work of interpretive social scientists like Weber and Mannheim, for example. Further disallowed would be a more recently developed interpretive (hermeneutic) restoration of tradition proposed by Gadamer. The concepts of 'culture' and 'tradition' are simply too broad for the postmodern vision. In their place one finds "regional narratives," "language games," and "heterogenous discourses" no one of which can (1) be legitimately reducible to a larger historical tradition or (2) take precedence over any other localized narrative. All knowledge is an expression of regionalized discourse in the postmodern view, and all discourses are, therefore, of equal "value."

Rejection of Critical Social Science

The notion that social science can lead to emancipation is regarded as a hoax by postmodernists. Science, they say, is a totalizing system which can only lead to social repression, "truth is terror," "truth is torture." The historical materialism of Marxism is rejected because the argument that human beings can or should be anything other than what they are is rendered impossible in postmodern exegesis. Since no single form of discourse can assume precedence over another, the distinctions between ideology and truth, and between reality (*wirchlichkeit*) and possibility (*actualität*) disappear—the very call for social critique is rendered moot at the outset. According to postmodernism, the ideas of critical social science are so uncritically bound up with bureaucratic domination and the technical rationality that accompanies it that they must be dismissed out of hand (Smart 1983).[13]

In sum, *all* of the knowledge claims and related conceptualizations of modern science and philosophy are rejected by postmodern philosophers. I review this point to emphasize the distinctions between modernist and postmodernist forms of environmentalism.

MODERN AND POSTMODERN ENVIRONMENTALISM

The central idea of empirical-analytical environmentalism is that the natural environment is a *system;* for interpretive environmentalism, nature is a *cultural tradition;* and for critical theory nature reflects *historical modes of production.* The societal and theoretical orientations which accompany these ideas are *progress and scientism, rationalization and reinterpretation,* and *crisis and critique,* respectively.

Humanity and Nature as System

Attached to the idea of natural and social systems are the logically related ideas of 'evolution' and 'adaptation.' Nature is the largest system which encloses all human (and nonhuman) systems. Implied by the very idea of a 'system' is the notion that modern society is an adaptively more fit type of social organization than the various forms of traditional society to which it is successor.

Modernity, or modernization, becomes the ideally equilibrated end-point of the development of all societies. Scientific-technical progress, market economies, and democratic-bureaucratic states become the ideal reference points for human social evolution. As social progress (history) proceeds, scientific knowledge of natural and social systems, and of human-nature interactions, develops to the point of an increased ability to predict, manage, and control more and more aspects of the natural world, the social environment, and the systematic relationships between the two.

The essence of this scientism is a management approach to all problems. In environmentalism this appears as *applied ecology*, which promotes improved knowledge and increased management of environmental problems. This approach to ecology as applied science is the conventional definition of ecology (Bowler 1992).

Humanity and Nature as Tradition

From the standpoint of interpretive sociology, particularly in the general context of the *geisteswissenschaften*, modern civilization represents the rationalized, secularized, and often hidden traditions of previous cultural formations. In the context of an interpretive sociology, one often encounters a distinction between formal and substantive rationality. This reflects a historical situation in which modern understandings have displaced the original meaning of value-oriented ideas, especially in the frameworks of religious and ethical and legal traditions.

Modernism in this context brings forth imagery of lost tradition, lost community, and, ultimately, a tragic sense of a modern existence devoid of meaning. The environmentally relevant intention is to recover submerged conceptions of nature from within our own religious and ethical traditions by means of systematic reinterpretaion (hermeneutics), an approach evident in recent works by Nash (1989), Oelschlaeger (1991), and Passmore (1974).

Humanity and Nature as Mode of Production

The concept of a 'historical mode of production' has been central to critical social theory from Marx to Habermas. From this perspective, the historical differentiation of spheres of activity and knowledge lays the basis for the contradictory institutions of late-Capitalist society *and* for the possible transformation of those institutions in the direction of a more enlightened, egalitarian, and democratic future.

Modernism in this context is a crisis-laden institutional framework which embodies transformational contradictions. Modernity is the embodiment of social and cultural *crisis* (Habermas 1973) which are revealed through theoretical and practical critique. Bookchin's (1993; 1991; 1990a; 1990b; 1990c; 1986a; 1986b) approach to social ecology is based upon a dialectical naturalism explicitly grounded in this tradition of thought. Others have also explored dialectical philosophy as a foundation for ecology (Biehl

1993; Bradford 1989; 1993; Clark 1993; Jung 1983; Kheel 1985; Kovel 1993; Lee 1980a; 1980b; 1982). The essence of this approach is political praxis in pursuit of a new social order made possible by institutional contradictions and social crises.

In sum, the general themes of modernity within the metatheoretical domains (epistemic contexts) of sociological theory are centered upon the paired concepts of system and progress, tradition and rationalization, and mode of production and crisis. Deep ecology rejects the foundations of each of these sets of ideas, to which I refer hereafter as science, ethics, and politics, respectively.

ANTINOMIES OF POSTMODERN ENVIRONMENTALISM

Deep ecology is postmodern environmentalism. It therefore reflects the assumptions, analytical forms, and styles of postmodern discourse. This has decisive implications for any claims made by deep ecologists about the development of new approaches to science, ethics, and politics.

Deep Ecology as Science

The deep ecological approach to science would best be presented in a review of how ecosophers have tried to incorporate metaphors from physics, ecology, and anthropology into their philosophy. This exercise, however, exceeds the scope of this essay. Suffice it to say that a fundamental flaw in deep ecology is its rejection of the very principles and possibilities of scientific inquiry.[14]

Naess's notion that all knowledge is based on intuitions means that there is no distinction possible between science and non-science, between what is true and what is false. This is an important point: Deep ecology is not a form of science—it is a form of anti-science. Formulated another way, both postmodernism and deep ecology reject the empirical-analytical foundations upon which scientific notions of 'nature' and 'system', of 'objectivity' and 'methodology' are based. It is paradoxical, then, that much of the information deep ecologists use to point out the crisis of the ecosystem is based upon scientific inquiry.

If we are to take the intuitional approach offered by Naess and Fox, there can be no reason to accept the findings of any of the natural or social sciences. There can be no reason to argue that improved scientific knowledge will improve the manner in which human beings live on this earth. This rejection of scientific principles serves to highlight the spiritual character of deep ecology. In the place of scientific knowledge, it offers a conception of spiritual purification whereby we explore our intuitions and experiences of the natural world in pursuit of ever-deeper identification with nature.

Deep Ecology as Ethics

The deep ecology platform presented above is, essentially, a series of claims about what is right and what is wrong, from the first proposition about the intrinsic value of nature to the last statement about the obligations of those who accept this platform. However, a painfully obvious problem emerges. Having rejected the rational foundations of philosophical reasoning, how is it possible that advocates of deep ecology presume to formulate an ethic for environmentally acceptable conduct? If all knowledge is based upon intuitions derived from a "reimmersion of humans in nature" (Hallman 1991), who is to say that two or more people will share the same intuitions? Who can argue reasonably that "the equal right to live and blossom is an intuitively obvious value axiom"(Naess 1989) when someone else simply disagrees?

Rather than reviewing the troublesome notion that nature has 'intrinsic value', I will simply ask the question: *How would we know?* Intuitionism cannot reasonably address this question. It can only reformulate it as a *condition of belief*—either we believe in the platform of deep ecology, or we do not. Naess (1989:20) makes this point in characteristic style: "I'm not interested in ethics or morals. I'm interested in how we experience the world. . . . If deep ecology is deep it must relate to our fundamental beliefs, not just to ethics. Ethics follow from how we experience the world. If you articulate your experience then it can be a philosophy or religion." Fox's commentary on this issue reveals the quandary in which this places the deep ecologist:

> deep ecologists—or transpersonal ecologists—sometimes reject approaches that issue moral "oughts" [sic] without offering any explanation. . . . However, my analysis of the kind of self that is emphasized by approaches that issue moral "oughts" suggests that the most fundamental reason for the fact that transpersonal ecologists reject these approaches is

that these thinkers explicitly emphasize a wide, expansive, field-like conception of the self whereas advocates of approaches which issue moral "oughts" necessarily emphasize a narrow atomistic or particle-like conception of the self— whether they intend to or not. If this view is correct then transpersonal ecologists consider these approaches to be superficial, repressive, or ineffectual precisely *because* they emphasize a limited and limiting conception of the self. (1989:243)

To establish any ethical claim, it is essential that one assign to a moral agent (the Subject) sufficient moral reflection and individual identity to make reflection upon and judgment about conduct possible and meaningful in the first place (Bookchin 1986; Paden 1992; Strong 1992).[15] It is precisely this which deep ecology rejects (Callicott 1986; 1987; 1993; Potter 1988). How can one judge the acceptable or unacceptable character of conduct once one has already rejected the idea that judgment has rational foundations?[16] This approach rejects not only the Enlightenment ethical tradition of personal responsibility, morality, and rights, it also rejects *the possibility of ethical reasoning itself.*

In place of ethical reasoning, deep ecology offers quaint spiritualistic assertions about nature. It can offer no clear ethical arguments (Harlow 1992), if for no other reason than that it rejects the legitimacy of rational discourse about individual conduct *a priori.* As Thompson (1990) observes, bioethics is not really ethics at all. It is simply a rejection of the tradition of ethical reasoning. It is nature mysticism (Wood 1985). One is led to inquire, "If deep ecology and related ethical positions lack a grounding or rationale, we might wonder if their value recommendations can be saved" (Berman 1988:7).

Deep Ecology as Politics

It is commonplace for deep ecologists to assert the essential egalitarianism and bioregionalism of the new environmentalism (Daly 1980; Devall and Sessions 1985; Devall 1989; Eckersley 1992; Fox 1989, Naess 1989; Porritt 1985), but it should be pointed out that the fundamental egalitarianism of deep ecology is not an equality between *persons* but rather an equality in moral and political standing between human and nonhuman *species.* This leaves the question of equality between human beings entirely open to question.

Further, the notions of 'bioregion' and 'community' attached to this notion are equally problematic.

Equality. O'Riordan (1981) has persuasively argued that an environmentally sound society is conceivable in a variety of political structures ranging from centralized and hierarchical authoritarian states to decentralized and anarchistic communities. What I wish to address at this point is the contention that deep ecological philosophy provides a philosophical basis for democratic and egalitarian community. I argue that it does not and cannot (see Bookchin 1990a; 1990c; 1991; Bradford 1989; and Watson 1983).

An assertion of "biospherical egalitarianism" does not translate into a sociopolitical egalitarianism. Simply asserting that all species are equal does not specify the character or condition of this equality for any individual, group, or community within a species. If anything, an identification with nature would lead humans in the direction of status hierarchies which are species-typical of animals living in packs or groups.[17] The political notion of 'equality' is intimately connected to the notion of the 'free individual,' a conception which postmodern environmentalism strives to dissolve and for which there is no counterpart in nonhuman species.

Bioregion. The additional question of what constitutes a bioregion in the first place is not so simple as advocates of bioregionalism assume (Bahro 1986; Spretnak and Fritjof 1986; Sale 1985).[18] The *ecological* notion of a 'bioregion' is based in scientific examination of the distribution and interrelation of species in definable habitats. Even in this context, the specific differentiation of one bioregion from another is open to continuing question at increasingly broad levels of analysis. However, deep ecology chooses to rest its *ecosophical* reflections upon aesthetic and spiritual intuitions rather than upon rational and empirical scientific discourse, the very foundations of which it already rejects.

This renders questionable the assumption of deep ecologists that ideal communities are necessarily smaller in scale. There is no reason to assume that bioregions *must*, of necessity, be smaller in scale than existing political entities—especially in light of the deep ecological proclivity toward speaking of nature as if it were an undifferentiated whole or a spiritual entity in its own right.[19] The scale of a bioregion would be far from obvious, even if there were no other human groups defining their own bioregions at the same time, which would complicate matters considerably.

Equally problematic are the standards for determining whether a specific group of people reside in a natural harmony or balance with nature, either in whole or in part. Not only is the definition of a bioregion arbitrary, so is the determination of which particular form of community operates in the most 'natural' manner. Again the questions: How would we know? How would we decide?

Community. Nonhuman communities are defined in terms of patterned species-interrelated activities in a localized habitat; human communities are defined largely in terms of traditionalized conventions and locally institutionalized forms of conduct. In other words, human communities are linguistically not genetically mediated. For all of the discussion of eco-communities, deep ecological philosophy ignores this aspect of human communities, in effect (though probably not in intention), by advocating a philosophy of spiritual isolation from humans and identification with nature.

For all postmodern thought, and therefore for postmodern environmentalism, the essential connection to existence is manifest in the authentic[20] individual who resists participation in all repressive and externally imposed contexts, including social interaction operating under taken-for-granted norms of daily life. This includes a rejection of all conventional restrictions or obligations, whether or not the individual agrees with them.[21] In this framework, community *is* repression, community *is* inauthentic. At best, what postmodernism implies is communities without unity in which all persons are (Rorty 1989; Clarke and Simpson 1989) united in their alienation and isolation and can do little more than pursue private virtues (Norris 1993).

Aside from deep ecological assertions to the contrary, there is no reason whatsoever in deep ecosophy that two or more people should share the same intuitions of nature. Yet this is necessary to the formation of a community based upon common spiritual vision. Even if a group of people did share a common spiritual vision, there is little in the history of politics or religion to assure one that a community united around a spiritual vision would necessarily be a community based upon egalitarianism. Far from it, utopian spiritual communities tend to be based upon a clear spiritual hierarchy between a dominant charismatic leader and a group of adherents who subordinate their thoughts and conduct to that leader. duBois (1991) argues that a postmodern philosophy based in "deep ethical concern" and an ontological identification with nature lends itself very nicely to the purposes of a status-based, caste-like social formation in which there is a rigid distinction between those who *know* truth as a matter of spiritual reflection [self-realization] and the rest of the community who can only *act out* revealed truths. Romantic appeals to native American tribalism (Booth and Jacobs 1990; Devall 1980; Devall and Sessions 1985) exacerbate this problem.

The only guarantee that individual interests will be honored in this type of community lies in an unquestioned acceptance of one person's definition of everyone's interests, which implies a rather extensive control over the process of socialization and interaction (Dryzek 1987; Norris 1993). This type of community cannot be based on any conceptions of rights or responsibilities, for both require a framework of law and institutions in which those rights can be defined, delineated, and defended both against the encroachment of others and against unintended effects of community practices and policies (Lenk and Maring 1992).[22] As one author correctly observes, "Moral persuasion *per se* lacks any spontaneous, decentralized coordinating device. If elements of other decentralized social choice mechanisms cannot be trusted to perform the coordinating function, then the burden falls ineluctably upon centralized devices. Such devices may be imposed from above or, developed 'spontaneously' from below" (Dryzek 1987:158). This institutional arrangement is what we call "government," and it is precisely what postmodern environmentalists reject, at the level of philosophical reasoning, as an illegitimate and unsustainable form of political structure.

Deep ecologists prefer natural, spiritual communities (Devall and Sessions 1985; Fox 1989; Naess 1989) which are as decentralized and autonomous as possible (Sale 1985). However, a spiritual community, apart from any legal or constitutional guarantees, is as unlikely to protect the so-called rights (Nash 1989) or values (Rolston 1988) of nature as it is to protect the rights of individuals. As Bookchin (1987; 1990a; 1990b; 1991) and Bradford (1989; 1993) make clear, deep ecologists tend to assume that human rights have already been fully established and that the only rights remaining are those of nature itself. Thus it is easier to disregard the human impact of community organization in their philosophy.

The scale and structure of communities in deep ecology are entirely problematic. On a smaller scale, a community based on nature worship might reflect our historical experience with isolated and local communities bound by parochial traditions. On a larger scale, it might reflect our experience with modern states which have emphasized the connection between nation and nature, such as Nazi Germany (Bowler 1992). To suggest that such a community, by virtue of its spiritual insights into nature, would be an "ecotopia" (Callenbach 1975) is logically and historically absurd (Bookchin 1986; 1990c; 1991; Bradford 1989; Lewis 1992; Norris 1993; O'Riordan 1977; 1981). If anything, appeals to a new democratic community must derive from the very Enlightenment traditions that postmodern environmentalism rejects in the first place, because the very notions of 'democracy' and 'community' are antithetical to postmodern thought.

Finally, there remains the question of political practices derivable from deep ecology.[23] Dobson (1989, 1990) is essentially correct that one problem of deep ecology is that it is so vague and spiritually oriented that it offers no guidance to political practice. Another way of saying this is that there is no political strategy that deep ecology excludes. This accounts for the confusing array of political recommendations from Naess's (1989) insistence upon a Gandhian nonviolent strategy, to calls for ecotage (Foreman 1990; Scarce 1990), to quests for personal empowerment through "right action . . . words, acts and feelings true to our intuitions and principles" (Devall 1988:122).

A philosophy that includes all political strategies excludes nothing and necessarily provides no guidance to activists engaged in the development of alternative communities and political action. Rather than public political strategy, what deep ecology actually offers is a theory of personal spiritual identification with nature and spiritual purification of the unnatural influences of the industrial world. This theme of a pursuit of "oneness, wholeness, and Self-realization" is evident in this representative passage:

> In the obscure regions of human unconsciousness, where the primordial archetypical symbols function as ultimate controlling factors in human thought, emotion, and practical decision making, a profound reorientation toward this integral human-earth relationship is gradually taking place. This archetypical journey must be experienced as the journey of each individual, since the entire universe has been involved in shaping our psyche as well as our physical being from that first awesome moment when the universe began. In the creation of the viable human, the universe reflects on and celebrates itself in con-

scious self-awareness, and finds a unique fulfillment. (Berry 1993)

Ultimately, such thinking (implicitly if not explicitly) reflects and justifies isolation from the political structures and standards of the larger public sphere. For this reason, Bradford (1989; 1993) criticizes deep ecologists not only for their political naiveté but for their cynicism about participating in modern public life, as well.

CONCLUSION

Sylvan (1984) argues that deep ecology's philosophical and ethical foundations are promising and important, though confused and unclear. Frodeman (1992) argues that postmodernism and deep ecology, though clearly linked, disagree on fundamentals. I disagree with both. The philosophical foundations of deep ecology are abundantly clear, wholly unpromising, and logically indefensible. Deep ecology is a postmodern ecosophy based on an antifoundational approach to science, ethics, and politics. Even though it holds out a platform of scientific, ethical, and political imperatives with one hand, like other forms of postmodernism it rips away the foundation of rational argumentation with the other hand. It can build foundations for no science of humanity in natural context, no eco-democratic, bioregional model of society, no possible conception of rights (either individual or natural), no philosophical justification for the existence of political community and no meaningful framework for practical politics.

In its rejection of reason itself (Sikorski 1993), postmodern environmentalism renders questions of knowledge, ethics, and politics utterly unresolvable except through the exercise of spiritual consensus, differential power, or both (Callinicos 1990; Habermas 1987; Norris 1990). As Norris (1993:292–93) astutely observes, "The effect of these ultra-relativist arguments is to throw thinking back to a stage or pre-critical tutelage where the only thing that counts is the trick of commanding assent through a rhetoric adapted to the purposes and interests of those with *de facto* power to decide such matters." As fashionable and compelling as it may seem, such an appeal to nature "generally originates in a common tendency for humans to want to find in 'nature' a source or grounding for whatever ethical system they take as authoritative in their lives" (Gardiner 1990).

In substituting a spiritual identification with nature for a rational examination of complex social, historical, and ecological situations, deep ecologists confuse their own aesthetic feelings with anthropological facts (See Bodley 1985). They assume it is both possible and desirable for humans to live in a manner which is "natural," that is to say, not in contradiction with nature. However, human beings are creatures *of* nature, *in* nature, and *at* nature— always and all at the same time. This is the irreducible, contradictory fact of human existence that cannot be dissolved with any meditatively or aesthetically derived feeling or attitude of oneness with nature. As others have said of antifoundational approaches to philosophy, one does not practically resolve a problem by abstractly dissolving it (Bakhtin 1993; Bradford 1993; Merleau Ponty 1962; 1964a; 1964b; Ricoeur 1974; Habermas 1987a). Human experience is always *our* experience; it is always *an* experience. It is never experience as such and in general. The complexities of human experience find no place in the simplistic formulations of postmodern environmentalism.

Postmodern environmentalist philosophers claim to do away with real problems by philosophically ignoring them and by appealing to intuitive, spiritual claims. They offer us metaphors (Gardiner 1990) like "ecocentrism," "non-anthropocentrism," "bioregional diversity," "biospherical egalitarianism," devoid of content, rich in emotional appeal to tacit knowledge (Botwinick 1993), and fraught with retrograde political implications. In other words, deep ecologists not only make an appeal for an intuitive, nonrational approach, their appeal is itself intuitive and nonrational. Ultimately, what impresses one is the profoundly uncritical character of postmodern environmentalism.

Deep ecology's appeals to romantic and spiritual naturalism have not arisen in a cultural vacuum. There have been many successful appeals to spiritualism, nationalism, and fundamentalism (Habermas 1989a). As Bowler (1992) has demonstrated in his comprehensive survey of the history of ecology, spiritual appeals to nature are nothing new, and, as Albanese (1990) has also shown, the roots of nature-spirit religions are deeply embedded in our culture.

My point is this. The issue posed by postmodern environmentalism is not the fate of the planet. What is at issue in this discussion is the fate of reason in radical environmentalism. A truly radical environmentalism can ill afford to reject reason itself and leave no standpoint for social critique. It must proceed in another direction to develop a critical theory with a practical intent.

Habermas's (1987; 1988; 1992b) discussion of the pragmatic foundations of normative standards in speech itself offers an approach to the pragmatic foundations of rational discourse (Apel 1977; Chaloupka 1987; Fuller 1992; Honneth 1991; Paehlke 1989; Weston 1985). This requires an elaboration of concepts of 'communication', 'system', and 'lifeworld' as a basis for a humanely developed, nature-considering and nature-considerate philosophy (Dryzek 1990; Honneth 1991; Vogel 1991; Whitebrook 1979). This poses a complex critical task, to be sure, but it is preferable to the misguided mysticism of postmodern environmentalism.

NOTES

1. Naess's followers attribute originality to Naess's terminology, even though the distinction between reform/radical and materialistic/holistic approaches to environmentalism is quite similar to a number of earlier formulations (Bowler 1992; Pepper 1984, 1985).

2. Critics respond to such claims with one or more of the following arguments: (1) deep ecology is "conceptually murky," an eclectic, superficial, and contradictory perspective that cannot constitute a philosophical system (Bradford 1989; Brennan 1988; Sylvan 1984; Tokar 1988a, 1988b); (2) deep ecology is an impractical philosophical perspective which does not and, perhaps, cannot lend itself to concrete political strategy (Dobson 1989; Pepper 1985); (3) deep ecology is a modern form of mysticism (Bookchin 1990a; 1990b; Bradford 1989; Dobson 1990; Lewis 1992).

3. Banuri and Marglin (1993); Callicott (1986); Cheney (1989); Fox (1984, 1989, 1990); Harrison (1992); Leiss (1972, 1976); Manes (1990); McWhorter (1992); Naess (1989); Oates (1989); Oelschlaeger (1991); Passmore (1974); Pepper (1984, 1985); Rolston (1988); Sale (1985); Sessions (1974); Simon (1990); Spretnak and Fritjof (1986); Warren (1987); White (1967, 1990); Zimmerman (1983, 1993).

4. Arac (1986, 1988); Berman (1982); Bernstein (1985a, 1991); Best and Kellner (1991); Callinicos (1990); Carroll (1987); Connor (1989); Dreyfus and Rabinow (1982); Featherstone (1985, 1988); Habermas (1987); Kaplan (1988); Nielsen (1991); Turner (1990).

5 On this general point Berman's (1982, 1970), Lukács' (1981), and Wellmer's (1985, 1990) discussions of reason and rationality, modernity and postmodernity are instructive.

6. See Bernstein (1985b) and Habermas' (1987, 1989a) discussions of Nietzsche and Heidegger; Dallmayr and McCarthy's (1977) discussion of Heideggerian critiques of certain categories assumed to be essential to Marxian thought is also pertinent here. Also see Arac (1986, 1988), Bernstein (1985b), Ferry and Renaut (1990), McWhorter (1992), and Zimmerman (1983).

7. Merleau-Ponty (1962, 1964a, 1964b) deals with this issue at length in the form of an "existential phenomenology," as opposed to an "essential phenomenology" (Husserl), which examines the precategorical embodiment of all experience.

8. Use of the term *humanity* rather than *man* at this point allows me to sidestep a discussion of the relationship between deep ecology and eco-feminism. This is a matter worthy of the extensive discussion it has received elsewhere (Biehl 1987, 1993; Cheney 1987; Dobson 1990; Fox 1989; Eckersley 1992; Kuletz 1992; Marietta 1984; Merchant 1982, 1989; Murphy 1988; Sallach 1992; Warren 1987, 1990; Zimmerman 1987).

9. Rothenberg's "Introduction" to Naess (1989:11) offers a further discussion of the concept of 'self-realization'. "This becomes the root of the most powerful application of ecophilosophical thinking to specifically environmental conflicts. We must see the vital needs of ecosystems and other species as our own needs: there is thus no conflict of interests. It is a tool for furthering one's own realization and fullness of life. . . . So, if we progress far enough, the very notion of 'environment' becomes unnecessary. Identification in this sense is the widest interpretation of love. In love one loses part of one's identity by gaining a greater identity, something that in the truest sense cannot be spoken of."

10. The following premises allow us to pursue this epistemologically oriented analysis of deep ecology:

1. All philosophy is social philosophy. All social philosophy makes assumptions about epistemology and the interests of knowledge, especially scientific knowledge.
2. Social philosophies may be understood as constructions upon epistemologically conceived metatheories. The latter reflect domain assumptions about subject-object relationships in theory, method, and practice. This approach is central to efforts by contemporary critical theorists (Apel 1973; Habermas 1971, 1979, 1988) to lay out the intellectual foundations of modern social thought (also see Ashley and Orenstein 1992; and Radnitzky 1988).

In this context, various formulations of the binary relation between subject and object, self and other, are at the foundation of different epistemological positions, for example, empiricism, naturalism, materialism, and idealism, among others. Many of these positions find direct and indirect expression in philosophy and social sciences. They are also reflected in philosophical efforts to overcome these dualistic categorizations. Following Apel and Habermas, I refer to the three epistemological traditions according to the following terminology:

1. Empirical-analytical approaches
2. Hermeneutic-phenomenological approaches
3. Critical-emancipatory approaches

Empirical-analytical approaches: Empiricist epistemologists view knowledge as a natural process of cognition and the world as a set of natural relationships. This is sometimes referred to as a "naturalistic" or "objectivistic" view of knowledge and of the world. In this context, that knowledge which is most true and most reliable is the type of knowledge which is conceived as a direct objective relation to the world: "perceptions" and "sensations" are the basis for real knowledge of "relations between objects" and of "functions of events."

Hermeneutic-phenomenological approaches: Phenomenologists reject the notion that empirical-analytical science provides an exclusive entry to knowledge of the world. In the context of a hermeneutic-phenomenological framework, human consciousness is viewed as the primary focus of knowledge of the world of experience and interpretation of that experience. Here empirical description is not a means to the development of functional concepts but rather of meaningful interpretations of human experience and judgment. Knowledge is based upon a reflective examination of our awareness of actions, and not upon descriptions and empirical generalizations about behaviors themselves.

Critical-emancipatory approaches: Critical theory developed out of a critique of the epistemological and philosophical positions of both empirical-analytical and hermeneutic-phenomenological points of view. According to this perspective, human consciousness is an aspect of historical human praxis which reveals simultaneously what is institutionally possible and what is historically possible in human experience. Historically specific analyses of forms of labor, interaction, and authority are central to this type of metascience. The basic view of critical-emancipatory social philosophy is that thought is a reflective moment of human experience—neither a function of natural relationships nor a transcendental consciousness of such relationships. Human history is regarded as a contingent process of producing and reproducing human nature and of transforming nature.

11. It will become obvious to thoughtful readers of postmodern literature that postmodernism is itself a metanarrative and that it fails to escape the categories of thought it claims to overthrow. This, however, is matter

for another essay, and I refer the reader in the meantime to Habermas (1987a) and Norris (1990, 1993).

12. See Wuthnow et al. (1984) for related discussions.

13. Marcuse's concept of 'one-dimensional man' and Adorno and Horkheimer's related discussion of the 'dialectic of enlightenment' also suggest the impossibility of transcending the institutions of modern society.

14 Brennan's *Thinking about Nature* (1988) is offered as a corrective to this type of nonscientific reference to science.

15. I urge the reader to review the debate among Eckersley (1989), Fox (1989), and Bookchin (1990).

16. See, for example, a number of articles in Plant and Plant, *Turtle Talk* (1990) for illustrations of this point.

17. It is almost incomprehensible that Sale (1985:101) can make the following statement in light of existing research on animal ethology: "The lessons of the law of complementarity from the animal world to traditional societies seems obvious enough as applied to a bioregional polity. Hierarchy and political domination would have no place." Hierarchy and domination are commonplace in animal groups, though these are not necessarily the basis of *political* insitutions in human social life.

18. "Biological communities and ecosystems seem to have a status that is not quite as clear as that of experimental entities. . . . A forest, pond, or grassy field can be easily enough identified, treated as separable from its surroundings and considered as a unit for community studies. The problem is not so much one of reality as of usefulness. If community ecology is to say anything of interest about such systems of populations, then there has to be some way in which one system can be segregated from others and described as having properties of biological substance. . . . The problem of the theoretical status of communities and ecosystems is therefore a real one, even if there is no problem with reality" (Brennan 1988:119–20).

19. I refer here to the Gaia hypothesis first developed by Lovelock (1979).

20. The connection to the existential notion of authenticity is intended here. See Berman (1970).

21. What postmodernism serves to promote, according to Norris (1993:23), "is a skeptical ethos which simply takes for granted the collapse of all realist or representational paradigms, the advent of a postmodern 'hyperreality' devoid of ontological grounding or experiential content, and the need henceforth to abandon any thought of criticizing social injustice

from the standpoint of . . . solidarity based on communal perceptions and interests."

22. White (1987, 1988) offers an extensive and insightful discussion of the inherent problems of attempting to ground rules, laws, or conceptions of justice in postmodernist reasoning.

23. Bahro (1986) and Spretnak and Fritjof (1986) offer ample evidence of the complexities of eco-political strategies in an international context.

Chapter 15

IN SEARCH OF GAIAN POLITICS: EARTH RELIGION'S CHALLENGE TO MODERN WESTERN CIVILIZATION

Daniel Deudney

RADICAL EARTH RELIGION AND WESTERN CIVILIZATION

Earth religion and its associated political activism is relent-lessly, deeply, and loudly radical (Manes 1988; Taylor 1991). It challenges the status quo in very fundamental and far-reaching ways. Its radical challenge is unlike any previously raised in the West. It differs from the radicalism of the Marxist left because it seeks to overthrow rather than to perfect industrial modernism. Unlike the radicalism of post-modern deconstructionists who hold that reality is socially constructed, earth religion asserts the existence of a natural basis for human values and aims to recover this lost ground.

Today earth religion is a phenomenon at the margins and is far from realizing its vision of a transformed world. Nevertheless, it deserves close and serious scrutiny, because religion has always been such a powerful force in human life and because the issues of ecological destruction promise to loom larger and larger in human affairs. Already environmentalists have rethought technology, economics, politics, and culture. But with the emergence of strong religious claims, it begins to pose as an alternative civilization. Like Christianity when it was a small sect with big ambitions, earth religion is not simply another interest group; rather, it seeks to remake the world. The ecological wisdom that one "cannot change just one thing" applies to the cultural and political sphere as well as to the natural. Earth religion and politics based upon deep ecology radically force us to rethink the entire political and cultural value system.

Radical earth religion sharply and directly confronts the dominant civilization on the planet—Western modernity—and its purest and strongest polity, the United States of America. Because it is aimed at the "overdeveloped world" of Western industrial modernity so implicated in ecological destruction, it attacks the most basic and accustomed Western ways of life and thought with particular force.

What would a civilization based upon the radical claims of earth religion and deep ecological politics look like? How would it differ from modern Western civilization? Because we are dealing with a religiously infused movement, we should begin our investigation of the cluster of issues traditionally known as the "theological political question." What are the implications of earth religion for state power, political legitimacy, group conflict? Examining the radical claims of the nascent earth religion with lenses and concerns of the theological-political problem sheds new light on its appeals and implications.

Earth religion and deep ecological political activism are in many ways inchoate and evolving. They exhibit varied, even contradictory, tendencies that point in different directions. Like other religious doctrines and movements that we see in history, it is likely to evolve in complex and unpredictable ways. Religious traditions persist in part because of the elasticity of their doctrines and their ability to adapt to new circumstances and compromise where necessary. Therefore, this investigation must necessarily be both tentative in its conclusions and mixed in its assessments.

The Western civilization challenged by earth religion originated in the early modern era when particular—and very novel—answers to the political-theological question became dominant in northern and western Europe. Among the core elements in the modern Western civilization are a relationship between religion and politics based upon separation, a new view of a de-animated natural world derived from the new cosmology of seventeenth-century astronomy and physics, and a new economic system of capitalism that emphasized the individual over the group. The emergent modern Western civilization was so radically distinct from what came before it that it represents a fundamentally new type rather than a variation within the same genus. This civilization has been explosively successful on its own terms. With the collapse of communism as a credible systemic challenger, it is now more hegemonic on earth than any other civilization has ever been.

EARTH RELIGION AND THE SEPARATION OF "CHURCH" AND STATE

Earth religion makes claims upon all aspects of life and asserts the need to subordinate the secular to the sacred. Secular civilization has violated the earth, and saving the earth requires recovering its sacredness. As such it calls into question the modern Western tradition of the separation of church and state. In ancient and Medieval Europe, as in all other regions of the world, the religious and the political were closely and intimately linked (Coulanges 1970). The land, the God, and the people were part of one sacred community. In the modern West the theological-political question has been answered in a new way: the secular and sacred, the state and church, are separate. As John Locke put it "the church . . . is a thing absolutely *separate* and distinct from the commonwealth. The *boundaries* . . . are fixed and immovable" (Locke 1970:27). This new approach arose in the wake of the religious wars in the sixteenth and seventeenth centuries that culminated in the generation of unrestrained bloodshed in central Europe known as the Thirty Years War. Fueled by the schism between the Roman Catholic church (the center of European public order during the preceding millennium) and new the Protestant sects and heresies, these wars and their massive disruption of life drove the Europeans to experiment with a new relationship between religion and politics.

The first remedy that was tried to deal with the conflicts arising from Catholic-Protestant strife was the Peace of Augsberg (1555) based on the principle of *cuius regio, eius religio* (whose region, his religion) that linked separate territories (*regio*) to separate religions (*religio*). But this only worsened the strife because it meant that Protestant and Catholic princes had new mandates to oppress minorities in their territories. After decades of warfare, the novel principle of religious separation was tried as much out of exhaustion as commitment. The Westphalia settlement of 1648 codified the principle that no one religion would be officially established as a state religion and hence that state powers would not be employed for the realization of religious agendas (Krasner 1993). Within bounds, the private exercise of many religions would be tolerated. Once separation is achieved, it is but a short step to religious toleration and religious freedom.

Separation of church and state greatly expanding the freedom of individuals, reinforced social pluralism and increased civil peace. Of course, these principles of separation, toleration, and peace have not been perfectly realized, and their actual application involves the resolution of a host of second-order interpretive questions. But, they have been the dominant pattern for political-religious relations in the West ever since.

Most Westerners now take these principles for granted. But in the broader record of world civilization this answer to the theological-political question is exceptional and inherently precarious. This approach is not compatible with all or even most forms of religious belief and tradition. The Westphalian solution is not really religiously neutral because it requires religious communities to renounce or at least suspend the desire to exercise state power in order to further religious agendas and to share political community with members of other religions who may have beliefs and practices at variance with their own. It also undermines religions based upon reverence for the land and landscape by foreclosing state protection.

Thus nascent earth religion challenges one of the most fundamental pillars of Western modernity. Can this reinsertion of the sacred into the secular be accomplished without undermining freedom, toleration, and civil peace? An earth based religion backed by state power could be particularly inhospitable to individual freedom. Because ecology and the environment are so comprehensive, a political order infused with a religious mandate might also be all-encompassing in its tendencies. A persistent theme in radical environmental thinking is that modernity is too fragmented and needs more holistic integration. But this yearning for integration and wholeness could undermine the important separations and compartmentalizations upon which rest the peace and freedom of Western modernity.

EARTH RELIGIOUS FUNDAMENTALISM AND DISPASSIONATE POLITICS

Earth religions and radical ecologism are passionate political agendas. Unlike more mainstream or reformist environmentalism, they evoke emotion, passion, and intense personal commitment (Manes 1988; Scarce 1990). As such they challenge the modern Western practices of civil politics of reasoned discourse, compromise, and a spirit of moderation. The secularization of politics entailed in the church-state separation was defended as a great boon to peace and public order because it meant that men would pursue mundane and potentially reconcilable interests rather than uncompromising ideological passions (Hirschman 1977).

Earth religion is part of a more general resurgence of religious fundamentalism. Contrary to the modernist assumption that concern for religion would decline with the spread of education and industrialism, religion has demonstrated renewed vitality, perhaps in part because of the exhaustion of communism as a source of messianic salvation for the world's woes. There seems to be a worldwide resurgence of radical political activities and agendas by intensively committed religious believers, ranging from Protestant Evangelicals in the United States, to Islamic fundamentalists in the Middle East and North Africa, to radical Hindu revivalists in India (Marty and Appleby 1991; Juergensmeyer 1993).

Although they arise from very different religious traditions and promote very different political agendas, these resurgent religious fundamentalisms are alike in being reactionary responses to modernity and Western secular civilization. In many parts of the world, religious fundamentalism has emerged in societies suffering from extremes of dislocation, marginalization, inequality, and political oppression. These movements aim to accomplish in the spiritual and the cultural realm what the revolt against Western imperialism accomplished in the political sphere during the mid-twentieth century. As such they often pose a violent challenge to the established order and inspire their followers with the belief that even seemingly random or theatrical acts of violence are both legitimate and necessary.

These fundamentalist appeals are not found solely outside the West, but within it as well. Christian critics of secular humanism have sought to recover, revive, and apply religious forms displaced or marginalized by Enlightenment reason. In all these instances, religious fundamentalism is in part a reaction to the miseries resulting from the failure of nation and state building, and a rejection of the project of building nation-states in favor of a return to more "authentic," "original," or "fundamental" indigenous traditions.

Earth religion and deep ecological activism are similar to other forms of antimodern religious radicalism in the West. Many of the key figures of the conservation and preservationist movements, ranging from John Muir to Gary Snyder, advance views of nature that had a significant spiritual content but were marginalized by the rise of an urban-based environmental movement eager to seem compatible with science and reason. However with the religious activism of networks such as Earth First! these spiritual dimensions have returned in a much more vigorous form (Taylor 1991, 1993a, 1993b), not simply raising religious issues, but evoking a primordial primacy of the natural, strong claims to community through ritual, sacrament, and ceremony, and a strongly activist political agenda. Like fundamentalist Christianity, earth religions challenge secular humanism and Enlightenment reason. Like Islamic and Hindu fundamentalism, earth religion attacks the modern project of state-building and economic modernization in the name of traditional values and ways of life being destroyed by them.

If religious conflict continues to grow and serves to define the era of postmodernity, as many have predicted, then the postmodern era will look much like the premodern era.

THE NATURAL AND THE NATIONAL

Another central feature of Western modernity called into question by the claims of earth religion and radical deep ecological politics is the *nation* as a primary unit of political identity and community. In the wake of the decline of political religion and as a response to the disintegrative tendencies of industrialization, the nation took on a central role first in Europe in the nineteenth century and then globally in the twentieth (Anderson 1988; Gellner 1975).

Conventional accounts of the nation as a political group and of nationalism as an ideology emphasize ethnic identities and community (language, religion, or shared traditions) or loyalty to particular political regimes and principles. American nationalism in particular is more connected to political principles—individual liberty and democracy—rather than ethnic or racial factors (Kohn 1957). Whether constituted by ethnic or political factors, nations appear to have little to do with nature or ecology.

In fact, however, nations contain and exploit a powerful sense of identification to place that has a strong natural dimension.

National identities are constituted by a "here feeling" as well as by a "we feeling" of group solidarity and ethnic attributes (Deudney 1993, 1995). The here feeling component of nationalism has been much less studied and appreciated than the we feeling. This identity and loyalty based upon the experience and feeling of connectedness to a particular place is based upon a sentiment labeled "geopiety" by John Kirtland Wright and "topophilia" by Yi-Fu Tuan (Tuan 1976, 1990). Nationalist rhetoric makes claims about the natural or primordial character of national identity, and claims about specific places figure prominently in these constructs. Existing national identities rely upon claims about the character of the relationship between the human and the biological natural, both of "race and blood" and of "soil and land." Evidence for the importance of topophilia in modern national identity can be found by examining the symbolic content of various mottos, anthems, monuments, and literary works. "National" songs, literatures, and symbols often heavily evoke the particular places. For example, the patriotic song "America the Beautiful" evokes a domain extending "from sea to shining sea," that contained "alabaster cities," "waves of grain," and "mountain majesty." Thus, nationalism is actually composed of the conflation or uneasy and at times unnatural union of three very different claims to loyalty: to a place, to a group of people with shared characteristics, and to political principles. A better understanding of this element of the national will shed light on the political ramifications of earth religion.

Because a loyalty to a physical place is so important in the formation of identities and loyalties, states and political ideologues have sought to harness it for their own purposes. Edmund Burke, the great nationalist thinker, spoke of "love of his country" as "an instinct" "which extends even to the brute creation." All creatures "have a fondness for the place where they have been bred, for the habitations they have dwelt in, for the stalls in which they have been fed, the pastures they have browsed in, and the wilds in which they have been roamed." Such an instinct "binds all creatures to their country" (Burke 1901, 11:422–23) What is striking in Burke's argument is the central role he assigns to topophilia in "love of country." From this core insight Burke and other theorists of the national typically leap to an identity claim for a country that carries over into ethno-national and regime patriotic dimensions. Yet an important difference between identities based upon place and those based upon ethno-national identities is that place-centered identities do not depend upon an "other" against which to define itself. Topophilia is not threatened by peoples who are different coming in, but by the experience of the loss or displacement from the native place.

Defense of the land from despoliation is thus an act of "national defense." The power of this loyalty to place and land in nationalism was vividly demonstrated during the collapse of the Soviet Union and the Soviet Empire during the late 1980s and early 1990s. In many cases the first issues that were politicized outside the Communist party's monopoly of political activity were over ecological destruction. The Communist party was not initially challenged on the basis of its oppression of ethnic group identities, but of its despoliation of the land and place. This was a national uprising by "defenders of the nation" who were challenging the industrial destruction wrought by the Communist ideology of progress through industrialization (Jancar-Webster 1993).

Because the nascent earth national identity and community claims have many similarities with religion and state nationalism, we are led to ask how this new cultural formation will relate to the existing nationalisms that are largely connected to states. Logically there are three possibilities: (1) earth identity and community will replace state nationalism, providing a substantive cosmopolitan community for the first time; (2) environmental awareness will color state nationalism, (the "greening" of nations), making existing nationalist groupings less truculent and more amenable to international cooperation; or (3) environmental awareness will be captured by existing statist nationalism, giving it additional virulence and thus reinforcing the conflictual tendencies of the international system.

Earth-centered identity and community claims are not likely to enhance and intensify existing national identities, but rather to displace or color them. The crucial reason is the strength of *science* in deep ecology. All previous nationalisms contain pre-ecological or anti-ecological understandings of place and human links to place, but the emergent earth nationalism integrates scientific ecology into its claims about place. Environmental awareness contains a major strain of ecological and earth-systems natural science, and these scientific constructs are fundamentally incompatible with the parochial orientations of all existing national identities. Localist bioregional ideologies and political practices exist within the radical environmental community, but the unmistakable message of ecological science is that the earth is the only integral bioregion, and that the "homeland" of all humans is the planet rather than some piece of it.

Environmental science reveals the interconnected and interdependent character of the earth's diverse inhabitants. Although environmental mobilization almost always begins with some specific local environmental grievance, the increased awareness of ecological principles that accompanies such mobilizations leads toward a globalist rather than a statist or ethnic sensibility. Anthropologist Luther Gerlach (1993) has documented that people first come to environmental issues with a NIMBY (Not in My Back Yard) mentality, but as they learn more about the actual issues involved, soon develop a NOPE (Not on Planet Earth) mentality.

EARTH RELIGION AS PLANETARY CIVIC RELIGION

Earth religion may also serve as the civic religion of the planetary civilization. Because of the great influence that religious ideals have upon people, many political philosophers have imagined designing a religion whose dictates and values would be maximally congruent with the needs of the polity. In Plato's *Republic*, Socrates spins an elaborate cosmological myth that supports morality and justice by holding that the wicked are punished after death for their transgressions. In the early modern era both Hobbes and Rousseau, who disagreed about far more than they agreed about, advocated a religion tailored to reinforce the needs of the polity. What all these visions have in common is that they are based not upon a love or reverence for God, but rather upon a use of religion as an instrument for creating and maintaining a particular social order.

In a similar vein, earth religion may be a force capable of underpinning the social norms and behaviors necessary to achieve a sustainable society but that are very difficult to support on their own right. The effects of many environmental problems are most likely to be felt in the future, or in distant places, while the tasks necessary to achieve a sustainable society involve real immediate sacrifice and must be done routinely by vast numbers of people. Reason and appeals to higher self-interest or long-run self-interest may be insufficient to motivate sufficient action. The appeal of earth religion is that it helps motivate behavior respectful of the earth that otherwise would be difficult to achieve. So at first glance, earth religion appears to be very anti-utilitarian and antirationalistic in character. There may, however, be a more subtle rationality and utility behind earth religious ideas.

If earth religion can motivate where the appeals of reason and immediate self-interest fail, it may have the effect of reducing the need for coercive regulation by state authorities. In his path-breaking work, *Ecology and the Politics of Scarcity*, William Ophuls (Ophuls 1976) argued that voluntary and decentralized action to protect the environment would not be forthcoming in sufficient quantities to achieve sustainability. To avert disaster, society would have to accept coercion by an all-powerful sovereign such as proposed by Hobbes. This bleak picture of the necessity of an authoritarian solution seems all the more compelling when difficult sacrifices like the foregoing of economic growth and the regulation of human reproduction are involved.

Earth religion offers a possible escape from this bleak choice between ecological destruction and authoritarian government. If large numbers of people were believers in earth religion and their belief translated into more ecologically responsive behavior, the necessity of coercive state regulation would be reduced. Religiously inspired self-discipline would obviate the need for externally imposed discipline.

BIOREGIONALISM AND THE STATE

Thus far, we have focused mainly upon elements of political culture, community and identity and their political implications. But earth religion also has direct implications for the most political of all political institutions—the state. Radical earth religion touches upon the state in a very primary way through its claims about the bioregion. Territory is at the core of what makes a state, and strong forms of bioregionalism pose a direct challenge to the dominant Western relationship between the state and territory.

A recurring theme in radical environmental thinking is that political units should be reorganized to more closely match different bioregions. Although radical in its implications, this way of thinking about how to define the borders of political units has a long, complex history. The idea of 'bioregion' is central to ecological science and is the most recent version of the ancient idea that political units should and will tend to have "natural frontiers" with one another. Montesquieu in *The Spirit of the Laws* (1989), the greatest work of eighteenth-century Enlightenment political science, emphasizes the importance of natural forces and natural regional differences in shaping all aspects of human social life, from culture to military security. In the United States during the Progressive Era and the New Deal reformers sought to develop regional interstate governments matched to the river basins. The most substantial and successful of the bioregional development authorities, the Tennessee Valley Authority became a model exported to many third-world countries (where it proved to be much less successful).

Radical environmental resistance movements and earth religiosity have emphasized bioregions, particularly watersheds. In Ernst Callenbach's (1975, 1981) widely read series of fictions about Ecotopia, this vision is fleshed out as a seemingly practical path to sustainability after the northern part of California and much of Oregon and Washington secede from the United States and set up an inward-looking, isolated ecological utopia. Lewis Mumford and Kirkpatrick Sale also have advanced the idea of a reorganization of political units along bioregional lines (Sale 1985). In radical environmental thinking, peoples living in different bioregions should develop reverences and identities based upon the specific watershed and bioregion, and the denial of the bioregionality is implicated in environmental decay for "uprooting" people from a sensitivity to place and nature.

The ideal of a bioregionally organized political system runs against the geopolitical approach of the United States Constitution. Keenly aware that different bioregions tended to produce different cultures, economies, and societies, the designers of the American federal Constitution intentionally sought to draw juridical borders so as to counteract such bioregional tendencies. They sought to create juridical borders in such a way that natural variations were as much as possible not reflected or were averaged out among the units. They did so not out of environmental insensitivity, but rather because they wanted to prevent separate states from generating political communities and identities. Left to evolve on their own, the borders of political units would come to correspond to these differences in human institutions rooted in nature. The units would tend to be different in size and type, and the antagonisms between them would be deeply rooted. They feared that if this naturally based diversification were allowed to run its course unchecked, the union would be hard to maintain and much more conflict would occur between the states. They looked to Europe and saw the distinctive nation-states with "natural frontiers" to be a model to be avoided rather than emulated.

In the minds of many observers at the time of the American founding and after, the real alternative to the Union was not the persistence of the thirteen original states as fully independent sovereignties, but rather their consolidation into two or three large states with sufficient size and internal homogeneity to be nation-states. The logic of sectionalism as the basis for a nation-state system in North America grew as the Union expanded across the continent. The default order for North America is not dozens of fully independent states, but rather a handful of nation-states based upon *sections* defined and divided by natural obstacles such as mountain ranges and rivers. As Frederick Jackson Turner famously argued, "The significance of the section in American history is that it is the faint image of a European nation" and that the United States is "like what a United States of Europe would be" (Turner 1932:50, 316).

The designers of the American Constitution were keenly aware of the European pattern and its possibilities in North America, and they were determined to avoid and counteract it. The key to their geopolitical strategy was to rely upon unnatural borders. In *The Federalist* John Jay argued that the redrawing of state borders and the consolidation of regional states in New England, the middle Atlantic region, and the South would inevitably lead to disunion and war. Similar concepts and designs also lay behind the Northwest Ordinance of 1787 which settled the western land disputes between the original thirteen states and established the procedures by which additional states could form and join the Union. For the American union, the ideal constitutive state was one with borders shaped by geometry, rather than natural morphology, and one with a range of topographies, economic activities, and political orientations. By insuring that the constitutive states lacked the size to be viable autonomous states, and the homogeneity to be distinct nations, the founders hoped to prevent the emergence of a European-style warlike state-system in North America.

Given all this, the reorganization of political units along bioregional lines might have several undesirable consequences. First, such a reorganization would change the current map of the world virtually beyond recognition, and it is difficult to imagine such change occurring without widespread violence and dislocation. Second, the sizes of the bioregionally based states would vary greatly because bioregions vary greatly. This would mean that some states would be much more powerful than others. While such inequality also characterizes the contemporary interstate system, it is not inevitable that balances of power would emerge to constrain the possible imperial pretensions of the larger and stronger states. Third, states in a world organized along bioregional lines would be more prone to conflicts rooted in differences in identity and traditions.

ANTHROPOCENTRICISM AND THE HUMANE SOCIETY

A central tenet of earth-religious thinking is that anthropocentrism should be replaced with an eco-centric world view (Naess 1989). This indictment of "humanism" challenges one of the most central features of modern Western civilization. The dominant Western ideologies emphasize the specialness of human beings, and from this emphasis stems the humane society in which individuals are treated as equals with regard to fundamental rights and are accorded freedom from enslavement and murder. Is it possible to preserve the "rights of men" while denying the "rights of man"?

This humane society is quite different from the ancient pagan society based upon more naturalistic religious views. The gods were perceived to be arbitrary and capricious with regard to humans. Slavery was endemic, and various harshly hierarchical social pyramids were legitimated by this religion. Today's radical environmentalists do not advocate slavery, but the extent of their antihumanism opens the door for a wide range of antihumane practices. Echoing late-nineteenth-century social Darwinists, Christopher Manes, writing as Miss Ann Thropy (i.e., misanthropy) praised AIDS as a solution to the overpopulation of third-world countries.

One factor that may help moderate the antihumane potential of deep ecology antihumanism is feminism. Ancient Greek and Roman cultures were strongly patriarchal and phallocentric. Their hypermasculinity was intensely agonistic, emphasizing military prowess, athletic competition, and the pursuit of glory. In contrast, modern revivalist earth religion is heavily slanted toward the maternal and the matriarchal. The quintessential earth religious form is Gaia, the Greek goddess of the earth. In contrast, patriarchy and the remote judgmental sky gods of desert monotheisms are rejected as contributing to the violation of the earth. If this maternal nurturing and healing is strong enough, it may reduce the antihumanity of deep ecological antihumanism.

GAIAN RELIGION AND NATURAL EARTH SCIENCE

Another way in which the new earth religion and deep ecological politics differ from modern Western civilization is in the relationship between their cosmological narratives and modern natural science. Religions bind their adherents with narrative accounts of origins that situate their members in an intelligible cosmos. Earth religion, particularly the metaphors of Gaia, pioneers a new relationship between religion and science.

Ever since its inception in fourth-century B.C. Greece, natural science has been in sharp tension with the claims of almost all forms of religion. Nature philosophers developed a materialist and mechanistic view of the cosmos as an alternative to the traditional view that nature was divine and animate. Science was a rare and precarious enterprise because the prevailing religious sentiments were far more powerful than the skeptical and rational impulse behind science. Perhaps the most famous of Greek philosophers, Socrates of Athens, was indicted, convicted, and executed for teaching, among other things, that the "moon is an earth" rather than a goddess and "the sun is a stone" rather than a god (Plato 1971:60). At the dawn of Western modernity, Latin Christendom, like the other great religions and civilizations, viewed the cosmos as a giant hierarchy, a "great chain of being" (Lovejoy 1936) in which everything had its proper place. In this view of the cosmos rooted in the Bible and Aristotle, humanity held an exalted position, and the earth was seen as the center of the universe.

In the modern era, the immense progress and prestige of natural science have been powerful forces undermining religion, particularly the universal claims of the Roman Catholic church, by discrediting its cosmological narratives. The new science of Galileo and Copernicus called into question the notion that the earth was the center of the universe. A corollary of this Copernican displacement was Giordano Bruno's theory that there existed "other worlds"—planets around other stars (Dick 1982). The idea that the earth was not the center of the universe and that there were other worlds (and thus presumably other life forms) undermined the dominant cosmological narratives of established Christian theology. Not surprisingly, the reaction of the Roman church to the new astronomical discoveries was strongly hostile. Galileo was forced to recant his views, and Giordano Bruno was burned at the stake.

In the mid-nineteenth century, biology joined astronomy to dethrone the exalted self-perception of humans and to undercut the dominant cosmological narrative. Charles Darwin's theory of natural selection and his argument that humans had descended from monkeys dealt another powerful blow to the cosmological narrative of human primacy. This period saw vigorous clashes between the spiritual humanism of Evangelical Christianity and the secular humanism of modern science. In the Scopes "Monkey Trial" in Tennessee over prohibitions of the teaching of evolution in public schools, the Evangelicals won a pyrrhic victory that signaled their retreat from the mainstream of American culture.

The net effect of modern science was to create a dominant cosmological narrative that deflated the uniqueness of the earth and humanity. One of the ironies of the modern era has been that as human power over nature has increased because of science, the status and importance accorded humanity in nature by science has steadily declined. In recent decades, this trend has been taken to its logical extreme, as many in the space movement envision leaving the earth behind and setting up totally artificial worlds in space. This devaluation of the earth reaches its most extreme in the radical Evangelical Christian dispensationalist theology, which holds that the Second Coming is immanent, thus making unnecessary the preservation of the earth's ecosystems and resources. The practical consequences of this religious view were revealed when Secretary of the Interior James Watt, appointed by President Ronald Reagan in response to the Sagebrush Rebellion backlash against environmental regulation, declared that there was no point in conserving resources because the Second Coming of Christ is imminent. Given such history, many radical environmentalists and deep ecologists are deeply hostile both to Western science and to otherworldly religion.

But an entirely new relationship between natural science and religious cosmological narratives has also emerged at the intersection of Gaian earth religion and the earth-system science. Earth religion has many rich currents that defy simple summary or generalization, but Gaia (the earth as goddess or superorganism) is one of the most prevalent and evocative of its theological formulations. As the Greek goddess of the earth, Gaia can be traced back to Homeric Greece. However, the route to the Gaian revival has not been through classical scholarship. It is the product of the most advanced science.

The turn to Gaia in natural science was inaugurated by James Lovelock, a British scientist of cybernetics and planetary development. His "Gaia hypothesis" holds that the earth is currently habitable for life because life has manipulated the geophysical parameters of the planet for its own benefit, and that the combined system of the earth's organisms and geophysical aspects constitutes a living organism (Lovelock 1979, 1988, 1991).[1] As a proposition of earth-system science, Lovelock's hypothesis has been extensively discussed and debated by scientists. Some vigorously reject the need for a holistic approach to earth systems, what Lovelock calls "geophysiology," and insist that teleology has no place in natural science (Schneider and Boston 1991). Despite this resistance, several of its important hypotheses have been verified (Lovelock 1991) and the Gaian perspective has spawned much new research.

In the Gaia hypothesis, astronomy and biology again join to subvert the dominant cosmological narrative, but this time in ways that restore earth to its previously central and special role. The Gaia hypothesis originated in space science and the comparative study of other planets, most notably Earth's near neighbors, Mars and Venus. As part of a team of scientists seeking to design experiments to be carried on the *Viking Mars Lander*, Lovelock began to think about how he would test for the existence of life on earth by looking only at its geophysical systems. His key insight was that earth's geophysical environment has been stabilized within parameters hospitable to life.

Lovelock stops short of saying that Gaia is a goddess as conceived by the ancients, a sentient being, but does hold that the earth as a whole is a living organism and suggests that religious sentiments are appropriately devoted to this entity. Others go further and interpret these powerful new scientific theories as vindication for earth animism and Gaian religion. In one of his most evocative passages, Lovelock suggests that the relationship between God as a distant creator of the universe and Gaia is similar to that between Jahweh of the Old Testament and the Cult of Mary in Catholic Christianity. He suggests that much of the energy devoted to the Cult of Mary is really directed at Gaia, and he implies that the Catholic church should reorient its doctrines in order that this cloaked Gaian devotion can contribute to a renewed respect for nature necessary to heal Gaia's wounds (Lovelock 1988:206, 223).

An early hint at the types of political struggles that this new religious orientation can generate are vividly illustrated in the conflict over Mt. Graham in Arizona (Taylor 1995). Astronomers have long favored the mountain tops in Arizona because of their clean desert air. In the mid-1980s the University of Arizona moved to establish a cluster of large new telescopes on the top of Mt. Graham. Mt. Graham is also the site of an endangered variety of red squirrel, but the university was able to convince the U.S. Congress to exempt the telescope project from normal environmental reviews and laws protecting endangered species. In response, Earth First! in alliance with Apache Indians who also consider the mountain to be sacred, engaged in a lengthy campaign in the courts, the press, and with direct-action demonstrations, to prevent the construction of the telescopes. The religious dimensions of this conflict were particularly revealing because the Jesuit order of the Roman Catholic church was part of the consortium and was planning to build a scope designed to look for planets around other stars, in order to help locate other life in the universe.

Gaia imagery has been employed in two very different ways in earth-religious thought. One tendency, feminist in character, sees the Gaian as the "earth mother" a nurturing spirit, which is evoked to combat the patriarchal and to recover the importance of nurturing the earth. Here the tendency is to see Gaia as a corrective within religious traditions that speak directly to humans by drawing moral lessons and reinterpreting scriptural traditions. Another appropriation of the Gaian image is radically antihumanistic in character. In Gaian science little importance is placed upon human life as part of Gaia. The most important organisms for Gaia are the bacteria, protozoans, plankton, and fungi who process important atmospheric gases and alter the chemical composition of the oceans. This is reminiscent of ancient pagan religions in that it posited divine indifference to human concerns.

CONCLUSIONS

Today the human world is run with great indifference to the requirements of the natural world. Environmentalists, taking the longer view and considering the interests of the myriad of other life forms threatened by humanity, insist that the priorities must be dramatically changed. A healthy earth life-support system may well be the most important human priority, but it is not the only thing of value. Earth religion and deep ecologic political activism are so radical and comprehensive in their claims that the survival of other valued institutions of Western civilization is called into question.

Radical earth religion is full both of promise and of peril. By redirecting human devotion to the earth and its life, earth religion could perhaps play a decisive role in saving the earth. As a form of civic religion, earth religion could achieve self-discipline without an all-powerful state. As an earth nationalism, earth religion may redirect topophilia away from the national state, laying the basis for much greater community between the different peoples of the planet. Likewise, Gaian earth religion holds forth the promise of ending the long and painful split between science and religion.

But earth religion holds great peril as well. Deep ecologists emphasize the importance of holism, of bridging gaps and uniting what has been sundered. But the civil peace and religious tolerance of the West rest in no small measure upon separations that have been institutionalized. The passionate commitment of religious devotion threatens the dispassionate politics of interest and toleration and thus perhaps civic peace. And bioregionalism can undermine the mismatch between natural and political regions and borders that moderates political distinctions and differences. And perhaps most important, there is a risk that the "baby" of the humane society will be thrown out with the "bathwater" of humanism.

Whether it is promise or peril that is realized depends in large measure on whether the core impulse of earth religion can be successfully blended and melded with other values, some old and some new. The strength of feminist currents will be important in determining whether or not earth religion is a return to the hard natural religion and social structures characteristic of the premodern era, or whether a distinctive postmodern synthesis of the best of modernity and earth religion can be forged. More generally, it is the unalloyed, purest forms of earth religion that hold the greatest threat to civil traditions and the territorial state system. The great question thus is whether earth religion can achieve its transformative potential without complete upheaval. Like natural biological systems, cultures are most sustainable and resiliant when they are mixed and balanced.

NOTES

1. The name *Gaia* was suggested to Lovelock by the novelist William Golding, well-known author of *The Lord of the Flies.*

Chapter 16

IN DEFENSE OF BANNER HANGERS:
THE DARK GREEN POLITICS
OF GREENPEACE

Paul Wapner

Greenpeace occupies an uncomfortable position within the environmental community. It is the target of two sets of criticisms emanating from different sides of the political spectrum. On the one hand, many environmentalists see Greenpeace as too radical. Its direct actions, which include positioning activists between harpooners and whales, parachuting from the tops of smokestacks, and floating a hot-air balloon into a nuclear test site, are too confrontational. They shock people and generate more resentment toward rather than sympathy for Greenpeace's efforts. As a consequence, many believe that Greenpeace is so out of touch with mainstream ideas of politics and environmentalism that its actions undermine efforts to protect the environment.

On the other hand, militant environmentalists see Greenpeace as not radical enough. Greenpeace's direct actions, according to these people, consist of glorified banner hanging. Sailing between harpooners and whales on the high seas or parachuting from smokestacks is like holding up a sign. It advertises certain environmental threats but does not *do* anything about them. Advertisement does not affect or change the structures of power which create and support environmental destruction. Greenpeace's efforts, according to this line of thinking, work against genuine environmental protection because they make people believe that simply knowing about environmental abuse will go a long way toward stopping it.

While each of these critiques is significant for understanding contemporary environmental activism, it is the second which is most relevant for this volume. Militant environmentalists are skeptical about the political efficacy of Greenpeace's work and therefore do not embrace, and at times explicitly denounce, Greenpeace's efforts. In this chapter, I argue that this criticism is misplaced. It misunderstands the nature of Greenpeace's actions and underestimates the political consequences of Greenpeace's work. Greenpeace's direct actions are, to be sure, a type of banner hanging. But banner hanging is not simply a reformist, so-called light green type of activity unconnected with large-scale structures of power. Rather, it involves directly engaging structures of power of a particular kind. It works at the ideational level of political life and tries to alter widespread understandings of the natural world and the place of human beings in it. Greenpeace aims to change structures which govern the way people think about the world and counts on the efficacy of this, in itself, to change the way vast numbers of people act with reference to the environment.

THE MILITANT ENVIRONMENTALIST CRITIQUE

If there is a single, defining characteristic of militant environmentalism, it is the radical quality of its practice. Militant environmentalists present sweeping critiques of contemporary society, live lives which fundamentally challenge widespread assumptions about meaningful experience, and undertake actions which concretely enfeeble forces which harm the earth. Such practice is "radical" because it attempts to get to the root of contemporary environmental abuse. As Marx relates, "To be radical is to grasp things by the root" (Tucker 1978:60). Militant environmentalists attempt to identify the foundational dynamics of environmental problems and work to change them.

Engaging in such politics is no easy matter. It requires that one first gain a purchase point on contemporary events such that one can clearly diagnose social ills. This calls for some degree of independence from ruling social, economic, cultural, and political conditions. Additionally, it requires an ability to devise actions which will be genuinely interventionary and ultimately transformative. This means actions which conflict with, and can act as levers to shift, contemporary situations. Both demands, as the history of political thought and action make clear, are impossible to achieve in any purist form and difficult to achieve in lesser degrees. There is no archimedean point from which to evaluate political life and no set of actions which are free from co-optability or disciplinary effects (see, for example, Foucault 1980; Nagel 1986; and Walzer 1987). The best one can hope for is to guess at those agents which appear more primary than others (in particular contexts) and experiment with actions which use these to overturn dependent conditions.

The best language for such considerations still seems to be the Marxist distinction between base and superstructure. The base consists of that realm of collective life which decisively influences all other aspects of social affairs. For Marx this was the economic realm, although other thinkers have suggested alternative understandings of what is primary. The central idea behind the notion of 'base' is that whatever happens within its sphere of action conditions all else. Put differently, changes in the base of society shape the superstructure, which refers to the complex cultural, religious, and philosophical ideas and customs that accompany the base. Thus, to return to Marx, changes in the ownership of production will affect the nature of cultural, social, and political life.

For environmentalists, the base/superstructure distinction directs one toward particular strategies of change. If the character of society is, in fact, primarily determined by one arena rather than another, then strategies of change should target the most significant arena. Militant environmentalists differ from mainstream ones in their interpretation of which dimension is most decisive and of how to orient oneself and undertake action which will eventuate in meaningful structural change. Such interpretation distinguishes dark from light green, or radical from reformist orientations.

Militant environmentalists such as Earth First! and the Sea Shepherd Conservation Society negotiate their way through questions of base and superstructure by, on the one hand, demanding of themselves that any means taken to reach a goal not compromise the end that is ultimately desired. On the other hand, militant environmentalists commit themselves to undertaking only those actions which actually engage the visible forces of ecological abuse. In the first case, they organize themselves in ways which prefigure future social relations. They attempt to be nonhierarchical, nonbureaucratic, and refuse to use methods which utilize practices that contradict ecological wisdom (for example, sending out reams of paper in the form of junk mail, of which 90 percent or more will probably be discarded [Scarce 1990:53]). The insight here is that hierarchy, bureaucracy, and compromised strategies support anti-ecological practices and therefore must be eschewed. At another level of understanding, it means that one can never extricate oneself completely from the forces which constitute the structure of contemporary life and therefore must rely upon the process of personal commitment to defang and transform the structure within which one finds oneself. In the second case, militant environmentalists direct their efforts to stop concrete instances of ecological abuse. This includes pouring sand in bulldozer gas tanks, confiscating forty-mile-long driftnets, occupying a crane used to construct an animal experimentation laboratory, and a host of other, so-called ecotage tactics. According to militant environmentalists, these actions resist ecological destruction in its capillary forms and thus provide the only effective method of reversing environmental degradation. In such instances, militant environmentalists claim to stop agents of environmental destruction in their tracks and shift, in the most fundamental and concrete way, the basic dynamics of environmental harm (see Foreman and Haywood 1987:21–22, and Earth First! 1989).

It is from such a perspective that Greenpeace appears too soft or not radical enough. Greenpeace is a multi-million-dollar corporation with thousands of employees. Critics point out that it is organized in a hierarchical and bureaucratic manner and uses methods of gaining support which compromise future goals (for example, direct-mail campaigns). Additionally, critics assert that Greenpeace misunderstands the nature of widespread environmental abuse and therefore misdirects its actions. They argue that the foundational dynamic of ecological destruction can be accessed only at those sites of actual environmental destruction. All other realms, according to these critics, are enmeshed in conditions of power in which fundamental questions about environmental abuse cannot be raised. For instance, they argue that legal processes are more often than not charades in which significant decisions are made behind closed doors or in which the scope of debate is preordained by the legal process itself. Likewise, critics maintain that lobbying efforts are superficial arenas for fundamental reflection and change insofar as they entail compromising principles in an effort to gain political legitimacy and to be pragmatic within a context of plausible policy options. Finally and most relevant, critics contend that winning access to media is a feeble form of political work because this only alerts people to environmental destruction without forcing them to alter their lifestyles, which directly or indirectly influence the issue at hand. Thus, according to militant environmentalists, while Greenpeace's direct actions may, at times, take place in potentially promising sites for confronting instances of environmental harm, the group's attempt to capture news coverage quickly and its overall tendency to stay within the bounds of the law override the aim of genuine political engagement and turn actions into mere media stunts. The criticism is that these are aesthetically intriguing but politically insipid. Taken together, these critiques implicitly argue that Greenpeace has never quite figured out a proper interpretation of the issue of base and superstructure. Its practice of employing impure means and its tendencies to choose superficial sites for its actions reveal the reformist character of Greenpeace. Militant environmentalists argue that Greenpeace undertakes actions which are, at best, incremental. They will not fundamentally transform the engines of environmental abuse but will only contribute to ameliorating actions which will, at best, temporarily stave off environmental catastrophes. More radical insight and action are necessary for genuine environmental protection.[1]

This critique, while theoretically insightful, lacks a sensitivity to the complexity of social change. It assumes that, while there may not be a decisive answer to the issue of base and superstructure, one can negotiate one's way through it merely by taking a number of principled stands. Unfortunately, this does not quite do the trick. It ignores the interdependence of social forces and how actions in one realm will influence events in another. In a different context John Muir is famous for saying, "When we try to pick out anything by itself, we find it hitched to everything else in the universe" (1911:157). The same could be said regarding social affairs. There is no single base which determines a given superstructure, nor can principles in themselves create a mode of change invulnerable to perversion, co-optation, and defeat. Greenpeace's efforts aim at spheres of collective life which may not be capable of abruptly stopping environmental abuse in its tracks, but which connect and influence the myriad of social relations which perpetuate environmental degradation in the first place.

GREENPEACE AND THE POLITICS OF BEARING WITNESS

Greenpeace started in a Unitarian church in Vancouver in 1971. A group of people were sitting around trying to figure out how to stop the United States from testing nuclear weapons on Amchitka in the Aleutian Islands. The United States had already detonated one bomb and planned a number of future tests. The group had been meeting informally for over a year and saw itself as the only organization willing to object to the testing. At one point, Marie Bohlen said, "Why the hell doesn't somebody just sail a boat up there and park right next to the bomb? That's something everybody can understand" (Hunter 1979:7). The idea caught on. Over the next few months, the group sent two ships toward the test site. The first was forced to retreat after the test was postponed. The second ship, although better stocked and funded, was far from Amchitka at the time of the test. Notwithstanding the failure of both ships to stop the detonations, what had appeared as failure actually proved to be success, especially the sort Greenpeace has enjoyed through the years and that which it works hardest to achieve. Both voyages enjoyed extensive media coverage in Canada and the United States, and by the time the second ship arrived home thousands of people had joined Greenpeace in opposition. Each ship, according to Robert Hunter, an early Greenpeace member, was seen as a "mind bomb sailing across an electronic sea into the minds of the masses" (Hunter 1979:61). When the ships arrived back in Vancouver, the bombs had gone off both literally and figuratively. Thousands of people had joined Greenpeace's opposition. (It is worth noting that shortly after the Greenpeace protests, the United States decided to halt its plans to test nuclear weapons in Amchitka. It originally intended to detonate seven bombs but, after exploding only three, returned the area to a bird and game sanctuary [Turner 1972:A29]).

Greenpeace started out as an antinuclear group. Its mission was to "give the apocalypse form," in the sense of publicizing and criticizing the dangers associated with nuclear testing. Over time, it expanded its concerns and has come to focus upon environmental issues in general. Nuclear threats are seen as just another facet of a broader set of assaults on the planet's environment, including species extinction, toxic wastes, water pollution, ozone depletion, oil slicks, and so forth. The name, perhaps more than anything else, represents this expansion. According to one account, in the early days, after one of the group's notoriously long meetings, Irving

Stowe held up two fingers in the sign of a "V" and said "peace." Another member added, referring to the environmental dimensions of nuclear testing, "Make it a *green* peace" (Hunter 1979:7).[2]

From its beginnings in 1972 to the early 1990s, Greenpeace grew from having a single office in Vancouver to staffing offices in over thirty countries, plus a base in Antarctica. Greenpeace established offices in the developed as well as the developing world, including Russia and eastern Europe. Its "eco-force" has grown over the years, and in the early 1990s consisted of eight ships, one helicopter, and a hot-air balloon. By the early 1990s it employed over one thousand full-time staff members, plus hundreds of part timers and thousands of volunteers. With a worldwide membership in excess of over 6 million members by 1994 and an estimated annual income of 149 million dollars, Greenpeace began to coordinate efforts throughout its network of offices by focusing on four so-called campaigns: toxic substances, energy and atmosphere, nuclear weapons, and ocean ecology.

While Greenpeace works for environmental protection in many ways—including lobbying government officials, undertaking research, influencing environmental diplomacy between nation-states, and organizing protests to pressure governments to support environmental legislation—it is most famous for its direct actions. In fact, few images capture the environmental age as dramatically as the picture of Greenpeace activists maneuvering inflatable rafts between harpooners and whales or protecting seal pups by shielding them with their bodies. These actions are not meant simply to make the group famous, although this is certainly part of it, but there is also a strategy behind them based on an understanding of the dynamics of social change. This understanding rests on the view that people do not damage the environment as a matter of course but rather operate in an ideational context which motivates them to do so. People are moved by, to use the language of social science, "predispositions which pattern behavior" (Eckstein 1988:790). These predispositions are not simply reflections of materialist conditions but have their own integrity based partly on patterns of social reproduction which consist of prevailing values, norms, and modes of discourse. Put differently, human behavior is a matter of oriented action by which people process experience into action through general conceptions of the world. At the most general level then, the first step toward protecting the earth is to change the way vast numbers of people understand it.

Greenpeace's so-called direct actions are based on the notion of 'bearing witness'. This is a type of political action, originating with the Quakers, which links moral sensitivities with political responsibility. Having observed a morally objectionable act, one cannot turn away in avoidance. One must either take action to prevent further injustice or stand by and attest to its occurrence. When Greenpeace confronts whalers on the high seas or blocks railway cars carrying toxic substances or plugs up industrial discharge pipes, it is attesting to what it believes is ecological injustice. Greenpeace is trying to create an image of ecological abuse which can be broadcast through the media to the widest possible audience. The idea is to invite the public to bear witness, to enable people throughout the world to know about ecological dangers and try to pique their sense of outrage.

A number of years ago it was difficult to use bearing witness as a strategy of political action in a global context. In the 1970s, for example, Greenpeace ships used morse code to communicate with their offices on land to report their actions and, after weeks at sea, returned with only still photographs to catalog instances of environmental abuse. In contrast, Greenpeace ships now use telephones, fax machines, and satellite up-links to communicate with home offices, and video cameras to record environmentally harmful, and sometimes criminal, behavior. Together this allows Greenpeace to send footage almost immediately to media sources throughout the world. In fact, within hours Greenpeace can distribute edited, scripted, and narrated video news spots to television stations in eighty-eight countries.

When Greenpeace sends footage through the media to enable the world to bear witness, it is engaged in political action, though not necessarily the kind we are used to seeing. It is not trying simply to educate people about environmental abuse with the intention that people will, in turn, pressure their respective governments. Rather, Greenpeace is trying literally to change the way people think about the natural world and the effects of human action upon it.

THE STRATEGY OF DIRECT ACTION

In 1989, Greenpeace activists infiltrated a DuPont manufacturing plant in Deepwater, New Jersey. Activists climbed the plant's 180-foot water tower and hung a huge, blue-ribbon banner awarding DuPont a prize for being the world's number-one ozone destroyer. (At the time, DuPont produced half of the chloroflouro-carbons [CFCs] used in the United States and 25 percent of world annual production.) The following day, Greenpeace bolted a steel box—with two people inside—onto the plant's railroad tracks and blocked the export of CFCs from the plant. Greenpeace draped the box with a banner which read, "Stop Ozone Destruction Now" and used it to stage an eight-hour blockade holding up rail cars carrying forty-four thousand gallons of CFCs.

What is curious is that, *according to Greenpeace*, within min-utes of removing the blockade, business proceeded as usual. The plant continued to function, producing and sending out substances which are proven to erode the stratospheric ozone layer. Nonethe-less, something had happened in those brief eight hours; something had changed. While DuPont workers continued to manufacture CFCs, they now did so knowing that others knew about and were concerned with the ecological effects. Moreover, because Green-peace captured its actions on film and distributed video news spots to television stations throughout the world, vast numbers of people were now able to understand the connection between the produc-tion of CFCs and ozone depletion. In short, the utility of Green-peace's activity in this case had less to do with the blocking *action* and more to do with the *message* that was conveyed. Greenpeace gave the ozone issue form and used the image of disrupting DuPont's operations to send out a message of concern.

Greenpeace constructs its messages along two lines. First, it undertakes actions which will bring instances of ecological abuse to the attention of people throughout the world. CFC production takes place in the guarded corridors of the world's laboratories and facto-ries; harpooners kill whales on the high seas; species extinction takes place in the depths of the world's rainforests; and nuclear weapons are tested in the most deserted areas on earth. Through television, radio, newspaper, and magazine stories, Greenpeace brings these "hidden" spots of the globe into people's everyday lives. Perhaps the best example of this is Greenpeace's efforts to publicize environmental abuse of Antarctica. Far from the observer's eye, researchers, often inadvertently, damage the fragile ecosystem of Antarctica. By, at first, stationing a base on the conti-nent and later simply monitoring research activities, Greenpeace alerts much of the world to environmentally destructive practices. Greenpeace, in other words, acts to extend the eyes and ears of the world into remote areas which have ecological significance.

Greenpeace also constructs its messages to translate complex scientific information into more accessible languages. Few people read the trade journals in which environmental issues are studied or keep up with current scientific understandings, even though many people have environmental concerns. Not only has environmental science become too arcane for ordinary citizens, it has also become a sprawling industry which produces more information than the average person can assimilate. Greenpeace has become expert at penetrating, synthesizing, and publicizing contemporary environmental science and uses its actions as a condensed form of public education. When reports of Greenpeace's action against DuPont came out, for example, the media carried explanations of ozone depletion and of DuPont's role in it. For a problem which is almost impossible to witness in its physical form and in which the science involved is fairly complex, Greenpeace's action served as a quick lesson in environmental science. Ozone depletion became a matter of public discourse; Greenpeace removed the issue from the strict domain of policy wonks and policy-oriented scientists and made it a part of public concern and involvement.

Bringing the hidden spots of the earth into view and informing people about scientific understandings aim to change the way the world is seen. Greenpeace seeks to dislodge traditional understandings of environmental abuse and substitute new interpretive frames. This was put particularly well by Robert Hunter, a Greenpeace activist who participated in the group's early antiwhaling expeditions. For Hunter, the purpose of Greenpeace's efforts was to change fundamental images about whaling. The predominant view was that whaling was a matter of brave men battling vicious and numerous monsters of the deep. Greenpeace documented a different image. As Hunter put it, "Soon, images would be going out into hundreds of millions of minds around the world, a completely new set of basic images about whaling. Instead of small boats and giant whales, giant boats and small whales; instead of courage killing whales, courage saving whales; David had become Goliath, Goliath was now David; if the mythology of Moby Dick and Captain Ahab had dominated human consciousness about Leviathan for over a century, a whole new age was in the making" (1979:229).

BANNER HANGING AND SOCIAL CHANGE

The new age envisioned by Hunter is not something that will harbor itself in any set of institutions. To be sure, Hunter expects that governments, corporations, and other collectivities will act more "green," as it were, as Greenpeace's messages make their way onto airwaves, wire services, and so forth. But this is not the whole story. Rather, what is at stake is much broader. It is, to put it vaguely for the moment, a matter of extensive changes taking place throughout all levels of society. It is a qualitative shift in collective understandings and a consequent alteration in the standards of good conduct. What is at stake, in other words, is the success of a social movement.

It is curious that many militant environmentalists, whom David Brower called the "generators" of "*motion* within the [environmental] movement" (1990:ix), have an impoverished understanding of the notion of 'social movement' itself. Because many militants are so wrapped up in their own understanding of the politics of environmentalism, they assume that certain sites and activities of confrontation are more genuinely political than others. They assume, for example, that pulling up stakes for proposed logging roads is a more authentically political act than, say, parachuting from the top of a smokestack. Or, they presume that cutting down a billboard which advertises an ecologically unsound product is more political than hanging a banner from DuPont's water tower. Behind these assumptions is the notion that social movements achieve success only when actors involved target material instances of ecological abuse and not the accompanying ideational component. Many militant environmentalists, to put it another way, assume that material conditions harbor the most fundamental dynamics of ecological harm almost independent of the mind-set that goes along with them. In this context, yes, only monkeywrenching will make a difference because only ecotage can literally change the conditions "on the ground," as it were. Anything else is mere spitting in the wind. From this perspective, a new age can only come about by resisting environmental destruction in its most corporeal form. There is no other way to turn the wheels of society.

Greenpeace obviously subscribes to a different understanding of social change. There is no a priori privileging of material conditions over ideational dimensions. Rather, as Muir suggests, everything is hitched to everything else. Intervening into society is a multifaceted exercise in which changes in one sphere influence conditions in another. When Greenpeace works to provide alternative understandings, it assumes that material circumstances are as much a reflection of collective values, mores, and sensibilities as they are a determining factor. Ideas shape material reality, and material reality, in turn, sets limits on what can be thought, experienced, and so forth. Thus, undertaking actions in which publics bear witness targets the ideational realm with the belief that it will influence the way people behave.

This has to do with the concept of social movement because an appreciation for what a social movement is sensitizes one to the impact of ideational forces. A social movement is not simply made up of efforts to change government policies and directives, as is often thought to be the case. Rather, a social movement consists of efforts to change the whole host of public and private expression involved in the issue at hand. The peace movement, for example, aims not only to convince governments to cease going to war but also tries to create more peaceful societies. This entails propagating expressions of nonviolence, processes of conflict resolution, and, according to some, practices which are more cooperative than competitive (Joseph 1989:377–82). Likewise, the feminist movement aims not simply at enacting legislation to protect women against gender discrimination. Additionally, it works to change patriarchal practices and degrading representation of women throughout society. Thus, as Joseph Gusfield notes, the successes of the feminist movement can be seen "where the housewife finds a new label for discontents; secretaries decide not to serve coffee and husbands are warier about using past habits of dominance" (1981:326). The same is true of the environmental movement. The movement is not simply about passing environmental protection legislation but rather involves changing the prevailing economic, political, moral, cultural, and social dispositions of society which support environmental degradation. The environmental movement, like other movements, attempts to create, to use Herbert Blumer's language, a particular "cultural drift," "societal mood," or "public orientation" (1969). Such drifts, moods, and orientations pervade society and, although they do not gain authority through governmental support per se, they still act as forms of governance which shape the way vast numbers of people live their lives.

By extension, environmental action, as part of a movement, cannot be restricted to any single set of targets or assume any absolute character. If the intent is to shift widespread dispositions, then multiple tactics, taking place in diverse arenas, are legitimate and, in fact, necessary. Thus, when Greenpeace works at the ideational level of collective life and tries to change the way people understand the world, it is not relinquishing its political project but directing its efforts to a specific slice of social dynamics.

In 1970, one in ten Canadians said that the environment was worthy of being on the national agenda; twenty years later, one in three felt not only that it should be on the agenda but that it was the most pressing issue facing Canada (Starke 1990:2, 105). In 1981 in the United States, 45 percent of those polled said that protecting the environment was so important that "requirements and standards cannot be too high and continuing environmental improvements must be made regardless of cost"; in 1990, 74 percent supported the statement (Wald 1990:A1). This general trend is supported around the world. In a recent Gallup poll, majorities in twenty countries gave priority to safeguarding the environment even if it entailed slowing economic growth; additionally, 71 percent of the people in sixteen countries, including India, Mexico, South Korea, and Brazil, said they were willing to pay higher prices for products if it helps protect the environment (Dunlap, Gallup, and Gallup 1993).

These figures suggest that over the past two decades there has been a significant shift in awareness and concern about the environment. It is worth noting that people have also translated this sentiment into changes in behavior. In the 1960s, the U.S. Navy and Air Force used whales for target practice. Twenty-five years later an international effort costing 5 million dollars was mounted to save three whales trapped in ice in Alaska (Day 1987:157).[3] Two decades ago corporations produced products with little regard for their environmental impact. Today, it is incumbent upon corporations to reduce environmental impact at the production, packaging, and distribution phases of industry (see Council on Economic Priorities [1988] and Shea [1989]).[4] When multilateral development banks and other aid institutions were formed after World War II, environmental impact assessments were unheard of. Today, they are commonplace (Warford and Partow 1989). Finally, in the 1960s, few people gave thought to the idea of linking environment and development and pursuing what is now called "sustainable development." Today, it is almost a household phrase with small but significant proven instances of success (Commission on Environment and Development 1987; Ramphal 1992).

Two observations can be made about these shifts in widespread understanding and behavior. First, the actions cited are not the result of government policies. Changing sentiments about whales, corporate environmentalism, multilateral bank reforms, and the notion of 'sustainable development' involve widespread voluntary shifts in collective understanding. Second, these shifts cannot be easily correlated with a single or even a set of material transformations. The types of changes noted have been taking place in diverse societies in multiple arenas. One cannot simply say that they are reflective of more fundamental, materialist changes

When Greenpeace undertakes its direct actions, these are the types of changes it aims to provoke. It seeks to shape the way vast numbers of people think about and act within the world. When Greenpeace undertakes this kind of work, it is not leaving the realm of politics and entering the strictly social or cultural dimension of collective life. It is not foregoing issues of power and governance and simply becoming politically uninvolved. Rather, Greenpeace recognizes that widespread understandings themselves structure human activity, and thus it works within and across societies to change such understandings.

CONCLUSION

Environmental activism aims at changing the world. Specifically, it seeks to transform the way societies interact with nature. Many militant environmentalists believe that the best way to do this is to focus on actual instances of environmental abuse and act in ways which directly frustrate them. The idea is that the structural dimension of environmental abuse is material in character and manifests in specific instances of deforestation, damming of rivers, cruel treatment of animals, killing of whales, and so forth. Genuinely transforming society entails intervening at the material level and trying to stop the physical enactment of these types of activities. Militant environmentalists with this orientation believe that such efforts address environmental harm at its most fundamental level and therefore represent an effective, radical approach.

Greenpeace takes a difference stance. The foundational causes of environmental abuse are not simply embedded in material forces nor exclusively present in actual instances of environmental destruction. Environmental abuse is governed, in part, by ruling public ideas and moral sentiments. Widespread understandings, values, and mores have a power of their own to condition behavior. The tricky thing is that these are much more difficult to engage. They are intangible, insofar as they consist of sentiments rather than behavior and do not respond easily to hands-on types of actions.

Greenpeace's efforts to bear witness aim to shape this dimension of collective life. They work at the ideational and affective level of human experience and activity.

While many observers may consider such effort "light green," or reformist, Greenpeace's activities are, indeed, radical. They aim to change the root causes of environmental harm. Ruling public ideas set the conceptual context within which people decide how to treat the natural world. Targeting this realm may be less dramatic, less confrontational, and unable to produce short-term, verifiable results but represents a necessary, although not sufficient, form of environmental protection. It is, then, a significant site for political activity. It is the point where banner hanging turns into dark green, transformative politics.

NOTES

1. It should be noted that the criticisms presented here are not necessarily held by all members of groups such as Earth First! and the Sea Shepherds Conservation Society. There is much debate between so-called hard cores and less dogmatic members. The arguments expressed are ideal-typical of hard-core members' views. See, for example, Watson (1992:3) and Ryberg (1993:3). Many of these criticisms are summarized by Scarce (1990:51–56).

2. On the origins of Greenpeace, see Brown and May (1989); Greenpeace (1988); Dykstra (1986); The *Sunday Times* Insight Team (1986:112ff) and Greenpeace (1986).

3. For a critical view of Operation Breakout, see Rose (1989).

4. According to a 1991 Gallup poll, 28 percent of the U.S. public claimed to have "boycotted a company's products because of its record on the environment," and, according to Cambridge reports, in 1990, 50 percent of respondents said that they were "avoiding the purchase of products by a company that pollutes the environment"—an increase of 28 percent since 1987 (quoted in Dunlap 1991:36). See, more generally, Smart (1992).

Chapter 17

THE EFFECTIVENESS OF
RADICAL ENVIRONMENTALISTS

*Sheldon Kamieniecki, S. Dulaine Coleman,
and Robert O. Vos*

INTRODUCTION

Activities of radical environmentalists have been both praised and criticized by scholars and commentators. When environmental actions are considered "acceptable" behavior, they tend to draw less fire. In these instances, environmental problems are brought to the forefront of political discourse, obtain credibility, and increase public awareness. Deep ecologists and oppressed social groups, however, often employ unconventional techniques to accomplish their goals. In response, prevailing social, economic, and political forces attempt to discredit their actions. In such cases environmentalists are frequently classified as eco-terrorists or radical utopian extremists (see the Rothenberg chapter). Criticism of the activities of deep ecologists may vary not only because of the unconventional action employed by environmentalists, but also because of the social, cultural, and political context of their action. Understanding the milieu is essential because it gives meaning to the characterization of the environmental movement in a specific part of the world.

This chapter examines how the success of radical environmental movements is influenced by group structure, membership, and public awareness. No one specific activity will necessarily yield the desired results, but rather a combination of different actions carried out by several groups may garner the required public support to accomplish short-term and long-term goals. However, efforts by environmentalists may be adversely affected, when actions are viewed as publicity stunts designed to interfere with progress, economic growth, and government stability. Environmentalists in different nations must design protest strategies to fit preexisting social, cultural, and political contexts if they are to have an impact. Consequently, radical action in any region may exhibit different discrete objectives on the surface, while simultaneously serving the greater good of the global environmental movement.

This chapter is divided into several sections. The first discusses exactly what is meant by the effectiveness of a radical environmental group. The next two sections review the mobilization and impact of radical environmentalists. These are followed by a discussion of how deep ecologists can be successful. The pitfalls of rearguard mobilization are examined in the last part of the chapter.

DEFINING EFFECTIVENESS

The level of effectiveness of radical environmental groups, which in this chapter encompasses both mainstream splinter organizations (e.g., Earth First!) and popular grassroots activists (e.g., the Chipkos in India), is determined by the extent to which they achieve their stated goals. The success of these groups is influenced by membership and organizational characteristics as well as the political, economic, and geographical contexts in which they operate. The goals of these groups can range from fairly modest to extremely bold and ambitious. Only a very few groups, such as Greenpeace (discussed in the Wapner chapter), possess funds and technical expertise, while most other groups lack money and professional help. These factors must be taken into account when making judgements about the comparative effectiveness of radical environmentalists.

Ecological radicals can differ in their intentions to alter the prevailing power structure as well as over how natural resources should be used. Radical environmental groups also possess both short-term and long-term goals, and definitions of effectiveness must take both into account. The ability of a group to secure incremental and short-term gains in public support and public policy should be included in assessments of effectiveness. Such gains can

be measured in terms of discrete victories for radical environmentalists, which can include increasing public concern over a polluted
stream, blocking tractors attempting to cut down trees in a rainforest, and preventing the construction of a dam.

As the previous chapters in this book indicate, a common goal
of radical environmental groups is sustainability. This is evident,
for example, in Hadsell's research on the *ribeirinhos* in the Amazon,
Lorentzen's discussion of women's participation in Central America, and Akula's analysis of the Chipko and Appiko movements in
India. However, it is important to note, that the meaning of sustainability differs from one location to the next and especially between
poor, agricultural countries and affluent, industrialized nations.
Thus, while sustainable development for Norwegians encompasses
both the preservation of whales and the traditions of whalers (in
Rothenberg's chapter), the people of Thailand work for the continued life of their forests (in Lohmann's chapter).

In addition to being located in various parts of the world, radical environmentalists also operate in vastly different political
spheres. Clearly, it would be unfair to compare the effectiveness of
extremists in an authoritarian nation with the success of radicals in
a democratic society. Democratic countries, by guaranteeing many
civil liberties, generally provide more leeway for extremists to act.
Although radicals in the United States have faced some government
repression, substantial freedom to protest is apparent in Rüdig's
chapter on Britain and Rothenberg's chapter on Norway.[1] Radical
environmentalists operating in authoritarian countries not only
risk arrest, but have faced physical harm and even death for their
actions in the past.

How well radicals are organized can influence their level of
success. Short-term victories require the skillful exercise of interest-group tactics, a task for which the loose, grassroots structure of
radical environmentalism is poorly suited. An oligarchic structure,
for example, is more efficient than rule by consensus when it comes
time for the hallmark of the interest-group process, negotiation. A
small group of people must be authorized to state positions and bar-
gain for the group, and there must be an implicit guarantee that the
whole group will accept the outcome. Participants in the radical
movement often tend to reject an oligarchic structure in favor of a
more free-floating model consistent with movement goals and
important solidary benefits. Many radicals attempt to "practice
what they preach" and forgo the short-term victories achieved in

the traditional political process. In this sense, "Effectiveness is not what it is all about. Effectiveness is a concept relevant for companies not movements" (Gundelach 1989:427).

But effectiveness also should be viewed as a long-term assessment that captures the potential of protest to operate as an agent of change at the level of "symbolic" codes, creating new opportunities for interest intermediation (Diani 1992). These new opportunities arise because movements force open the agenda to include a new range of policy options that were not present before. Does the movement set into motion a process that eventually alters societal values, changes the political socialization of the individual, and establishes new policies and institutions? This consideration should be included in efforts to measure the impact of a movement that seeks to transform the present "materialist" system into one that is "postmaterialist" in character (Inglehart 1981).

With these considerations in mind, a number of effective environmental movements are identified and discussed in this book. Gedicks, in his chapter on native ecological resistance, reports on how the Cree and Inuit Indians were successful in forestalling the expansion of a hydroelectric project in Quebec, Canada. Similarly, Hill and his colleagues describe in detail the achievements of environmental activists in Scotland. While Taylor and Wapner discuss the positive contributions of Earth First! and Greenpeace, respectively, Lorentzen and Hadsell provide evidence of successful popular ecological resistance movements in developing countries. Although the future effectiveness of individual environmental resistance movements may be difficult to predict, the examples presented in this volume on the whole point to an expanding effort to curtail environmental degradation in many parts of the world.

THE MOBILIZATION OF RADICAL PROTEST

In assessing the effectiveness of radical protest, the factors that mobilize groups to action are important, since a threshold of mobilization must be achieved to create an impact. Social movement theory identifies three primary ingredients for mobilization. A leading theory is called "resource mobilization" and speaks to the importance of resources, a term broadly conceived to mean financing, expertise, and even social networks (Zald 1992; Hadsell this volume). Another factor is the development of a political consciousness that defines the issue as a problem that can be solved through political means. McAdam (1982) calls this change in consciousness a "cognitive transformation" and postulates the importance of government outputs in causing the transformation. A third ingredient, identified by Chong (1992), is charismatic leadership, the "highly dedicated, morally committed activists" that are necessary to convince others to act in the face of possible repression.

LOCATING STREAMS OF PROTEST

As this volume has shown, the global radical environmental movement is characterized by great diversity. For this study, the term *radical environmentalism* links together not particular groups but rather the broad range of popular ecological resistance and civil disobedience that takes place outside the laws and institutional procedures of the state. Based on the evidence presented in this book, two major streams of radical environmentalism can be seen to be mobilizing from perceptions of worsening ecological conditions. On the one hand, there are "mainstream splinter activists" who care passionately about wilderness and view it as a finite entity that can only be protected through a fundamental restructuring of society. On the other hand, there are "new grassroots activists" who have been forced to bear the brunt of worsening environmental conditions and are organizing for the survival of their communities.[2] Generally speaking, the manner and style of protest and the reasoning and justification for action are different for the two groups of environmentalists.

The typology presented in table 17.1 simplifies a highly diverse movement by identifying broad differences across five factors in mobilization. As with any typology, the types identified here represent maximum differences at opposite ends of a continuum, and very few activists are actually located at either extreme. Grasping differences within the global movement, however, is important for assessing the possibilities of coalition formation—itself an important factor in effectiveness.

Mainstream splinter activists include many groups such as Earth First!, Sea Shepherds, Greenpeace, Friends of the Earth, and the Rain Forest Action Network. The activists in these groups were originally drawn to radical protest by frustration with the mainstream groups. Many of the leaders of these groups were originally associated with mainstream conservation interest groups (Scarce 1990; Zakin 1993). Activists in these groups are generally discouraged by the bureaucratic routine of the conventional groups, and they eschew the compromises mainstream groups feel compelled to make.

TABLE 17.1
Two Main Categories of Environmentalists

Mobilization Factor	Mainstream Splinter Activists	New Grassroots Activists
Economic Orientation	Post-Materialist	Survival Issues
Demographic Tendency	White, Middle-Class Educated	People of Color, Poor Communities, Female Leadership
Cultural Orientation	Nature Above Culture/ Biocentric	Cultural Continuation
Identity Formation	Identification with Nature	Identity Rooted in Oppression
Issue Concern	Global and Long-Range Concerns	Local and Immediate Concerns

The economic orientation of activists in these groups is post-materialist insofar as splinter activists are confident enough about their economic security to have given up material gain (such as a large house) for quality-of-life considerations (e.g., clean air). The self-deprivation they have accepted in pursuing a life of activism is a matter of pride within the movement (Zakin 1993). Additionally, the splinter stream of the movement appears to be white, middle-class, and generally well educated. The economic orientation of these activists helps provide the resources for their activism.

The cultural orientation of splinter activists is deeply biocentric, and a faction within this stream holds misanthropic attitudes. Taylor (1995) notes the religious orientation that radicals feel toward the sacred places of nature and gives their cultural orientation a religious expression, "pagan environmentalism." Following the insight of Thoreau and Muir, these activists view wilderness as a temple, a place to go when epiphany is sought.

This cultural orientation allows for important solidary benefits in activism. Participation itself can grant an enlargement of personal identity and an increase in self-fulfillment. Some activists who have engaged in tree sitting report an almost mystical experience and often emerge more committed to the movement than when they began (Scarce 1990). Indeed, the activism of many radicals stems from having enjoyed transcendental experiences in the wilderness.

The fourth category explains the role identity formation plays in mobilization. Identity formation is crucial in building group solidarity and political consciousness (Morris 1992). However, identity is intrinsically problematic in explaining splinter mobilization because not all activists are arrayed in opposition to the oppression of specific human groups. Perhaps identity exists vicariously for radical environmentalists. Identification with nature is a strong element of the deep ecology outlook, thus splinter groups may be reacting to a mutual identification with the oppression of nature. Splinter activists also draw identity resources from long struggles against militarism and perceived U.S. imperialism.

A final factor in mobilization is the scope and range of issue concern. Mainstream splinter activists are concerned primarily with issues that are long range and global in scope. Species extinction, for example, is an issue whose implications are primarily long range ("extinction is forever"). Splinter activists are also deeply concerned about emerging global ecological changes such as global warming and the thinning of the ozone layer. Because a sense of history making through movement participation is an important solidary benefit of activism, splinter activists' beliefs in the large implications of their movement function as a factor in mobilization.

A second broad wave of radical mobilization can be identified both in the United States and globally.[3] These activists also are distinct from what they refer to as the "gang of ten," the major environmental interest groups that capture most attention as environmental advocates. In the United States, Taylor (1992) has coined the term *new grassroots* to describe these movements which utilize broad-based and local support to bring environmental issues, especially toxic pollution, to the forefront in poor and minority communities. Globally, new grassroots activists have also been identified in less-affluent countries where they confront the ecological problems associated with development (Taylor et al. 1993). These groups are distinct from mainstream environmentalists not only because they eschew the compromises mainstream groups make, but also because they charge that the mainstream has ignored their issues.

New grassroots activists are certainly less affluent and in many cases are living at the margins of subsistence. Radical tactics emerge partly because the activists lack the financial resources and expertise necessary to compete in the conventional political arena (Snow 1992). Conventional compromises are rejected because policy decisions are directly related to health and survival. These activists depend directly on the resource that is being exploited, and the exploitation of the resource is the near equivalent of the exploitation of the people. This is seen, for example, in the destruction of the fishery resources of the *ribeirinhos* in Brazil as described by Hadsell in this book. Issue concerns among the new grassroots, therefore, are immediate and related to economic conditions. Pressing ecological problems, like particular toxic pollutants and land degradation, are typical issues that set these groups apart from the mainstream and the splinter groups.

New grassroots activists are oriented toward cultural preservation—the survival of their community. While factions in the splinter groups have misanthropic tendencies, new grassroots groups do not hold such beliefs. Indeed, some dogmatic deep ecologists might apply the pejorative "anthropocentric" to the human concerns of the new grassroots movements. The very cultures grassroots groups seek to preserve sometimes facilitate the development of ecological consciousness. In this volume, Akula notes the importance of Hindu religion in mobilizing and legitimizing radical struggles in India. These groups may also conceive of particular wilderness places as sacred, but the struggle over wilderness intertwines with the struggle over cultural preservation. Tandon's chapter shows how this is the case in southern Africa. The destruction of the area would mean an end to religious practices often central to the culture (Taylor 1995).

The demographic characteristics of new grassroots activism are also distinct. They tend to be poor and minority groups, often with female leadership. Lorentzen's chapter, for example, highlights the important role that women have played in environmental activism in Central America. The important role of women in this activism can be explained by noting that ecological issues confronted by new grassroots activists typically revolve around family and consumption activities, roles that women have been socialized to fill in many cultures.

Mobilization of new grassroots activists is also highly dependent upon identity formation. These groups view themselves in opposition to the directives of an outside, centralized authority, and identity formation is often aided by overt racial or ethnic dimensions. In this volume, Akula reports that marginalized groups in India have a long history of resistance rooted in colonial oppression, and Tandon describes land movements in Africa as "anti-imperialism." The common historic struggle over civil rights shared by activists in the U.S. environmental justice movement operates as an important factor in mobilization (Novotny 1994). Common histories serve as resources for developing political consciousness. The importance of identification with a historic struggle is underscored by Hadsell when she reports the difficulty of mobilizing the *ribeirinhos* given that long authoritarian rule in Brazil has convinced the peasants that they have no rights. The intervention of the Catholic church was crucial here in defining the problem as one that could be solved through protest.

This analysis of mobilization reveals two broad streams of radical environmental protest across the world, speaking to the difficulties of coalition formation and the potential for a larger mobilization. Although this dual mobilization indicates important differences in issues and goals, it does not directly address differences in tactics. Mainstream splinter activists strategically place demonstrations to attract media coverage and thus have received more attention. But new grassroots groups are also likely to use the media when the opportunity becomes available. Neither stream of activists seems particularly prone to violent tactics. Rather, instances of violent protest are found in small factions of the movement after all other remedies for securing goals have been exhausted.

THE IMPACT OF RADICAL ENVIRONMENTALISM

There is considerable disagreement over whether radical environmental groups have an overall positive or negative impact on the environmental movement (Dalton 1993). Some argue that radical environmentalists play into the hands of development and economic-growth advocates by alienating average citizens as a result of their extreme appeals and actions (e.g., Lewis 1992). As a consequence, people tend to view all environmentalists as radicals and ignore their calls for increased pollution control and conservation of natural resources, regardless of how sensible such demands might be.

Several recent books have condemned environmental groups for their "scare tactics" and have questioned the scientific foundation on which their arguments and recommended solutions are based (e.g., Bailey 1993, and Wildavsky 1991). For the authors of these books, global warming, the thinning of the ozone layer, and toxic waste threats are simply "hoaxes" perpetrated by researchers eager for funding and radical environmentalists who promote egalitarian values and are anxious for political power. Therefore, policies designed to address current environmental problems are the result of politics rather than good science.

Following a similar vein, both President Reagan and President Bush, as well as their appointees, tried to minimize the influence of all environmental groups by attempting to categorize them as "nuts," "wackos," and "political extremists." During the 1992 presidential election, Vice President Quayle tried to label Senator Al Gore, "the ozone man." These labels failed to affect public opinion. In Japan, however, environmentalists have long been accused by government officials and industrial leaders of fighting against the country's national interests and being unpatriotic (McKean 1981). Unlike in the United States and most other advanced industrialized countries, these efforts have been quite effective at limiting the political influence of environmentalists and marginalizing the movement.

Others, however, believe that radical environmentalists help to counteract the strong influence of business and industry over government policy (e.g., Caldwell 1990). While mainstream environmental groups are content to work through the system to bring about change, radicals help to raise public consciousness about pollution threats. In countries where the media operate openly and freely, radicals have been able to expand the scope of conflict of local environmental problems and to force national government officials to become involved. The Love Canal incident in New York state in the late 1970s, for example, was elevated to national prominence largely through the efforts of a well-organized group of homeowners led by Lois Gibbs (O'Brien, Clarke, and Kamieniecki 1984).

The efforts of radical environmentalists often can have a bearing on the success of mainstream environmental groups. The extreme positions of radical environmentalists, for example, may make government and business leaders more likely to negotiate with "moderate," mainstream environmental groups. In addition, radical actions sometimes lead to lengthy delays in development activities that are costly and give mainstream groups time to utilize legal or political processes. This provides leverage to traditional environmental groups which they otherwise would not have. However, due to the perceived positive and negative contributions of extremists, mainstream environmental groups have long held ambivalent feelings about the role and activities of their radical counterparts in the movement.

WHEN RADICALS CAN MOVE MOUNTAINS

Several researchers have theorized about the mechanisms required to bring about social, economic, and political change (e.g., Castells 1983; Chong 1992; Piven and Cloward 1992). Radical environmentalists believe that such large-scale change may be necessary to protect natural resources and therefore make it a primary objective of their efforts. Some social movement scholars emphasize the importance of coalitions in particular. In a major empirical work comparing a number of urban social movements, Castells (1983) reports that broad coalitions, reflecting a web of interrelated issues, were large enough to sustain protest over time and were successful movements. In the case of civil rights, Chong (1992) notes the importance of a brief but large coalition during the historic march on Washington, D.C., in 1963. This coalition stayed together and was instrumental in the eventual passage of major civil rights acts in 1964 and 1965. In this volume, Akula shows how environmental groups successfully banded together to form the Narmada Bachao Andolan in opposition to the Narmada dam project. In addition, Lohmann mentions how the defeat of the Nam Choan dam project in Thailand established new political alliances among varied groups.

Social-movement theories strongly point to the importance of coalitions between mainstream splinter and new grassroots activists within the radical environmental movement (again, see table 17.1). Radical environmentalists, for instance, sometimes differ in their concern over the plight of employees in polluting industries. The jobs-versus-the-environment rhetoric that dominates contemporary political discourse places environmentalists at odds with one another. If a coalition between the major streams of radical environmentalists were developed, an ideology that balanced concerns for full employment and the environment might result.

This portrayal of environmentalists may even have validity when directed toward the misanthropic factions within the movement. Christopher Manes, for example, wrote an *Earth First!* column under the pseudonym Miss Anthropy, suggesting that, among other things, AIDS might be Mother Nature's population control. Other radicals are so misanthropic as to exclude any role for humans within the ecosystem.[4] A coalition forged with new grassroots groups might temper this misanthropy, resulting in an ideology that specifies the ecological niche humans should occupy in a sustainable system.

There is evidence that splinter groups have begun to recognize the need to encompass grassroots concerns. Earth First! activists in Los Angeles, for example, join in the struggles of inner-city groups like the Mothers of East Los Angeles (MELA) and the Concerned Citizens of South Central Los Angeles (CCSCLA). Greenpeace also organizes local toxics programs around the country (Scarce 1990).[5] Akula's chapter shows how new ways of producing hydroelectric power that both protect ecosystems and provide economic development may be discovered if activists push as a coalition.

While splinter groups can find deeper insight into human concerns from the new grassroots groups, a coalition can also teach the grassroots groups to see their problems as part of a larger picture. The nature of new grassroots groups is that they tend to fixate on single issues (e.g., "stop the dam," "clean up the river," or "remove the dump") and miss the broader implications for social change. Such implications involve socioeconomic changes of great scope. Environmentalists cannot contain their action to single issues and hope to solve each new environmental problem. Coalitions help to develop an ideology which goes beyond the single-issue approach, presenting the opportunity for long-range solutions.

In addition to ideological coherence and specification, a coalition would guide protest strategies and improve the reaction of the public to protest actions. The progress made by Earth First! activists Judi Bari and Darryl Cherney in forging an alliance with workers employed by the timber industry in the Pacific Northwest is instructive. Bari and Cherney worked for two years to convince timber workers that their safety and future job security were threatened by accelerated clear-cutting and the export of timber to other nations for processing. As a concession to the timber workers, Earth

First! dramatically renounced tree spiking. Unfortunately, Bari and Cherney were nearly killed in a suspicious car bombing just as a coalition between environmentalists and timber workers was coming together (Scarce 1990). Although their efforts have continued with some notable defections from the timber workers to Earth First! such a coalition has yet to emerge with any significant political force.

Finally, coalitions between mainstream splinter groups and new grassroots groups tend to engender much greater public support than if either group protests on its own. Snow (1992) reports that many of the greatest victories for the environmental movement have come about because of strong local support in opposition to natural resource industries. The 1982 Earth First! protest at Little Granite Creek, Wyoming, for example, benefitted from local support. This action involved resistance to the plans of the Getty Corporation to drill for oil and natural gas on public lands, and eventually escalated to include monkey-wrenching. Local support was instrumental in creating a successful protest action. The local district attorney refused to prosecute the environmentalists since he believed "that no jury in the county would convict the culprits" (Scarce 1990:65).

Such examples are not confined to the United States. After a major monkey-wrenching protest by two members of the Sea Shepherds on whale-processing facilities in Iceland, public support was enhanced by the claim from an Icelandic citizen that he had helped the Sea Shepherds with the logistics of their raid. Although the Sea Shepherds denied that any Icelanders had participated in the action, the claim was a significant factor in generating public support for the incident. This was so much the case that when the responsible parties returned to Iceland, the government declined to prosecute them for their "crime" (Manes 1990).

SKILLFUL USE OF THE MEDIA

Media coverage of protest actions by radical environmentalists can help to capture public attention. Because protest actions often involve shocking stunts, the public may be especially enticed to follow television or radio stories about protest actions until some explanation or resolution is provided. Many viewers may think that something must be very wrong if a few people are willing to risk their lives to dramatize a point. Media dependency theory indicates that such enticement is an extremely effective way to produce attentive publics (Ball-Rockeach and Cantor 1986). In this book, Wapner discusses how Greenpeace has effectively used the media to attract international attention to its cause.

Although major studies of media coverage and its impacts on public values are missing from the social movement literature, some research suggests that changes in prevailing attitudes are possible. In one study, Ball-Rockeach and Cantor (1986) established that a media event as simple as a single thirty-minute television exposure could alter sympathies individuals express for a variety of movements, including the environmental movement. Media coverage can also have an impact upon movement mobilization. Media reports communicate information useful to potential activists in deciding whether or not to join, such as the movement's chances for success and the costs and benefits individual activists experience (Ball-Rockeach and Cantor 1986).

The capacity of media coverage to alter public attitudes will likely rest on the interpretations given to protest actions. Actions that involve breaking the law may either be interpreted as socially deviant criminal activity or as legitimate social protest. If the movement can communicate that it has used restraint in the past and that nonviolent protest predominates in its activities, it will tend toward greater legitimacy (Turner 1969). Actions that demonstrate a love for nature—and the willingness to risk personal injury to preserve it—may be most effective. Tree sitting, for example, communicates the movement's message both in symbolic and in "gut level" terms.

If the movement is successful in utilizing the media, important changes in public discourse may result. Traditionally, discourse about environmental protection has revolved around the jobs-versus-the-environment dichotomy identified in the Lohmann chapter. On the one hand, the biocentric focus of the splinter activists may increase public appreciation for biodiversity and thus support for policies that rest upon noneconomic values inherent in the natural world (e.g., species protection or river restoration). On the other hand, as Lohmann's analysis shows, the new grassroots activists may be able to communicate the shallowness of the predominantly perceived dichotomy by showing how the economy and environmental protection are closely interrelated and can improve simultaneously.

The capacity for the radical movement to create a shift in public discourse, however, rests upon its ability to win a media contest with large economic interests. In the advertising war fought over the Big Green and Forests Forever ballot initiatives in California's 1990 election (propositions 128 and 131), for instance, environmentalists proposed two costly propositions that would have tightened a wide range of environmental policies from pesticide regulation to greenhouse gas emissions. Despite the backing of a number of celebrities and an extensive advertising campaign, the environmentalists were out-spent by business and industry.[6] Big Green lost by a large margin (36 percent to 64 percent) and Forests Forever was narrowly defeated (47 percent to 53 percent).

In the advertising campaign, the proposition backers used a number of very frightening television spots that angered a usually supportive scientific community and broad public. The initiatives may also have been harmed by a high-profile monkey-wrenching incident when powerlines associated with nuclear power were downed in an "Earth Night" action, near Palo Alto, California, in April 1990. As the loss of the initiatives shows, the media are a difficult tool to use to achieve movement objectives.

AVOIDING REARGUARD MOBILIZATION

One final factor that must be balanced in understanding the political effectiveness of radical environmentalism is the extent to which protests generate a rearguard movement. Although some backlash or rearguard movement seems inevitable, it is possible that certain forms of protest (e.g., monkey-wrenching) could cause particular segments of the population to mobilize in a rearguard stance. Clearly, this would be disastrous for the broader environmental movement. If the environmental movement is to create significant social change, it can only do so if it avoids a rearguard mobilization.

Using an eloquent euphemism, the rearguard groups have assumed the moniker "wise use" to describe their position toward the natural world. In reality, their positions are even less environmentally oriented than the Pinchot-conservation ethic that their name implies. The movement has taken root mostly in the western United States, perhaps as an extension of the "sagebrush" rebellion of the Reagan years. A rearguard leader from the Center for the Defense of Free Enterprise in Washington state reports that the countermovement's objective is "to destroy the environmental movement" (Dolan 1992:A1).

It is difficult to know exactly how large the wise-use movement is since accurate figures on membership or allegiance are unavailable. In 1992, the Center for the Defense of Free Enterprise estimated that the wise-use movement numbers in the tens of thousands in the western United States. Recognizing the tendency of movements to inflate reports of their own numbers, this estimate seems somewhat high. But in 1990 one of the most extreme wise-use groups, the Sahara Club, reported a membership of four thousand (Warren 1990).

Wise-use groups use a broad brush to paint all environmentalists as dangerous fanatics. This could be a particularly troubling phenomenon if the public begins to blur the distinction between radical and mainstream groups. Representatives from the Sahara Club, for example, were recently quoted applying the phrase *eco-terrorist* to the mainstream Sierra Club. Lewis (1992) fears the linking of environmental issues to radical activists will dampen public support that would otherwise be widespread.

The rearguard appears to result from a strict adherence to the dominant social paradigm (Milbrath 1984, 1989). Those who support this paradigm favor economic growth and development at almost any cost. At the same time, they promote the perception that environmentalists are out to stop economic growth, lower the present standard of living, and limit personal freedoms. Therefore, some rearguard mobilization may be inevitable as the conventional movement secures distributive gains. Skillful tactics and strategies will be required on the part of traditional environmental groups to prevent such characterizations from sticking.

CONCLUSION

As this analysis has shown, environmental groups differ in their level of effectiveness because of the resources available for mobilizing protest. The level of funding, expertise, commitment of leadership, and power status of activists are all-important components that ensure the success of short-term and long-term goals. Often, the immediate visibility of short-term goals overshadows long-term effects. Temporarily stopping a forest from destruction may be readily observed; meanwhile, as a result of this form of direct action, a shift in public discourse may follow. Ultimately, it is the masses, through public consciousness raising, that will ensure long-term solutions to environmental destruction by demanding changes in economic practices.

Despite the diversity within the global movement, coalition building may occur even when activists appear to espouse different ideologies. Radicals are likely to form coalitions if the issue is broad enough to encompass the concerns of diverse group membership. Strength of moral conviction may cross over social, cultural, and political boundaries. When environmental issues are considered sacred and held close to the heart, a wide range of supporters may align themselves with the cause. In an international context, coalitions can encourage the media to play a major role in presenting otherwise little-known struggles to a global audience, drawing strands of the movement together.

Movement leaders in developing countries may adopt the language of deep ecology and form coalitions to muster international financial resources. As Lohmann states, the term *deep ecology* is a western postmaterialist philosophy which cannot be understood in the same context in many less-developed countries. But as Tandon and Akula argue, some elements of deep ecological thinking have been present in southern Africa and India prior to colonization. The preservation of nature may be part of an effort to sustain a traditional way of life for present and future generations. Given some flexibility in definitions of preservation, this concept is similar to the philosophy of western deep ecologists.[7] Although recently ascribed, the term *deep ecology* may be part of the historical pursuit of indigenous populations to ward off the environmental degradation experienced by Western industrialized societies.

As this chapter shows, the milieu of the activism is an essential factor in explaining effectiveness. The political freedom provided in democratic nations usually avails more opportunities for people to protest and join radical environmental movements. Radical environmentalists in these contexts benefit from extensive interest groups and even partisan support (e.g., Rüdig's chapter) in achieving their goals. Environmental activism in countries under authoritarian rule requires complete dedication to achieve objectives. Often, activists must seek the assistance of global organizations, such as Greenpeace or the United Nations, to put pressure on the World Bank and international economic interests. In this milieu, a substantial victory is achieved when environmental issues are established as legitimate and concerns about natural resources become part of the political process.

Finally, some analysts conceive of politics in terms of "who gets what, when, and how" (Lasswell 1958). In these terms, the use of natural resources is an inherently political and distributive question. The likelihood that sustainability will be achieved by the radical movement may depend on the extent to which it is able to foster redistribution within the global system. Technology, expertise, and fiscal resources will be essential for activists in developing nations as they strive to balance the tricky equation that includes population growth, concomitant desires for economic expansion, and the maintenance of traditional ways of life.

Movements chronicled in this book articulate the common moral message that people should be content to live in harmony with nature without attempting to conquer it. This rejection of domination by radicals is posited not for the sake of creating hardships for humankind, but rather because activists hold a deep commitment to mother earth and the sanctity of her creatures. Their reasoning stems from the awareness that natural resources are limited and that nature will cease to provide the spiritual and physical resources necessary to sustain humanity once it has been vanquished. Ultimately, as this view of the natural world is borne out by scientific understanding and conveyed to the public by activists, it will fuel the moral commitment essential to make the movement effective.

NOTES

1. The United States Federal Bureau of Investigation has closely followed (activists say "infiltrated") the group Earth First! The group's leader, Dave Foreman, has apparently also been targeted, with one undercover agent recorded on tape saying that Foreman was not "the guy we need to pop, I mean in terms of an actual perpetrator. This is the guy we need to pop to send a message" (quoted in Zakin 1993:335).

2. At its most macroscopic level, this typology may be viewed as distinguishing radical activists in developed and developing countries. As a global model, the typology neglects a third comparison that may eventually be possible with activists in eastern Europe and the former Soviet Union. As Jancar-Webster (1993) demonstrates, these activists were instrumental in the democratic revolutions in these states. The environment provided an important symbolic focus for populist discontent at key moments, undermining the legitimacy of the authoritarian regimes. Activism in these

countries has declined since the revolution as ecological concerns have given way to pragmatism in encouraging the economic development necessary to support the building of free markets.

3. The analysis here blurs a distinction that could be made between the "environmental justice movement" and "environmental livelihood movements." The former term generally refers to movements in poor and minority communities in the United States, while the latter term has been applied to less affluent nations. But it is important to note that U.S. environmental justice activists have sought to include a global perspective in their movement. For example, these activists and their supporters in Congress have called for an end to the export of toxic and hazardous waste to less affluent countries. President Clinton has announced his support for legislation designed to ban the export of toxic and hazardous wastes to developing nations. The legislation was introduced following a United Nations' Conference Committee's decision on 25 March 1994 to forbid international trade in toxic waste. The United States has not yet ratified the U.N. decision.

4. Some Earth First! activists have been known to celebrate natural calamities (e.g., earthquakes) that cause human death. The notion of a "voluntary extinction movement" is prevalent among some radicals who see overpopulation as the root of the environmental crisis.

5. These examples are not isolated incidents, and other instances of coalition formation could be drawn from case studies; see Taylor (1995) and his introductory chapter in this volume. The increasing prevalence of coalitions reflects a shift in thinking of groups like Earth First! which seeks to embrace a larger concept of tribe, including indigenous people throughout the world who are believed to hold a reservoir of ecological wisdom.

6. A major problem faced by activists was the charge that the initiatives would be costly both to the state treasury and to the economy. Big Green was labeled the proposition that "tries to do too much." Consequently, the initiatives suffered in a poor economic climate that fostered fiscal austerity in the electorate. A total of $4.7 million was spent by supporters of Big Green compared to $17 million by its opponents. Supporters of Forests Forever spent $7 million compared to the $11 million spent by opponents.

7. As Guha (1989) warns, the concept of 'wilderness preservation' as setting aside "pristine" areas comes from a peculiarly American context and may not be tenable in the context of developing countries. The underlying goal of ecosystem preservation may, of course, be achieved without entirely forbidding human intervention.

Chapter 18

POPULAR ECOLOGICAL RESISTANCE
AND RADICAL ENVIRONMENTALISM

Bron Taylor

The diversity of popular ecological resistance movements serves as a caution against hasty generalization. Nevertheless, thoughtful critique of these movements does reveal certain trends and tendencies among many of these movements and the contexts from which they emerge. Such analysis allows consideration of the international foundations of popular ecological resistance and also makes it possible to speak of the emergence and potential of a global radical environmentalism.

After a review of the trends and tendencies that can be discerned among these movements, this chapter will briefly return to questions posed at the outset of this inquiry, namely: What are the international impacts of these movements thus far? What are their likely future prospects? And finally, what are the problems posed by the emergence of popular ecological resistance that deserve greater in-depth scrutiny?

TRENDS AND TENDENCIES IN THE GLOBAL EMERGENCE OF POPULAR ECOLOGICAL RESISTANCE

Fueling the Flames of Resistance: Understanding Causes and Motivations

This volume (especially the chapters by Akula, Wisner, Tandon, Lorentzen, Lohmann, Porio, and Hadsell) demonstrates that popular ecological resistance often originates in a desperate quest for survival as industrial processes threaten habitual modes of existence and as people recognize that their well-being is threatened by environmental degradation. Most ecological resistance is indeed *In Defense of Livelihood*, as suggested by Friedman and Rangan (1993).[1] Discussing popular environmental movements in India, Ramachandra Guha concluded similarly that, among their many causes, "undeniably [the most important is] the deterioration of the ecosystem" and the social stresses which follow (1993:82). In less economically marginal contexts, resistance may be grounded more in concerns about health than subsistence, as Edwards's analysis shows. Nonetheless, threats to human livelihood and health provide the most important reasons for the global emergence and proliferation of popular ecological resistance.

Obviously, such motives are far from misanthropic. Indeed, a central justification for popular ecological resistance is the protection of the world for the sake of children (see especially Edwards, Porio, and Lorentzen; see also Broad and Cavanagh [1993:18]; Gottlieb [1993]; and Tovey [1993:427]). That such human-centered motives provide the most common basis for ecological resistance might surprise those radical environmentalists who believe that a *transformation of consciousness*, from anthropocentrism to biocentrism, is a prerequisite of ecological resistance and the eventual reconciliation of humans and nature. Our examination of the factors animating ecological resistance, however, demonstrates the inadequacy of blaming anthropocentrism as the primary cause of human indifference to environmental deterioration—because many on the front lines of such resistance movements are fundamentally anthropocentric in orientation.

Believing that consciousness is the most important ecological battleground leads some radical environmental activists to give top (but not exclusive) priority to promoting spiritual transformation through various forms of nature-based ritualizing (Seed 1994). These studies suggest that such strategies are unlikely to be more effective than ecological education combined with appeals to enlightened self-interest and concern for children, families, and communities.[2] Through such appeals the defense of sustainable land uses can be promoted and justified as self-defense—a practical version of the notion of inseparability pursued by the more spiritually oriented members of these movements.

To emphasize self-interest as the central underpinning of these movements is not to deny that newly invented ritual processes are powerful means of evoking and deepening affective and spiritual connections to nature, including among those drawn to the deep ecology movement. Such ritualizing is prompting increasing numbers to reconsider their perceptions about the value of nature, their place in the natural world, and their lifestyles (Taylor 1993; see also Grumbine 1992:233). And within the deep ecology movement, creating new ritual forms is often viewed as part of a broad effort to create new "tribes" and an ecologically sustainable culture. Desires for intentional community among those who perceive industrial cultures to be unfeeling, impersonal, and bureaucratic play a significant role in fostering radical environmental countercultures and activism, especially in more affluent countries (Taylor 1993, 1994).

Similarly, to acknowledge that *basic human needs provide the most decisive impetus to ecological resistance* (especially in less affluent countries) is not incompatible with recognizing that moral and religious idea motivations are deeply intertwined with the material motivations or that *popular ecological resistance cannot be accounted for if moral and religious variables are overlooked*, or reduced to after-the-fact justifications. Wapner, Hadsell, Lohmann, Lorentzen, and Gedicks all made specific arguments along these lines, and Porio, Tandon, Akula, and Hill et al., buttress our conclusion that human motivations are embedded both in material interests and in ideal factors.

These chapters demonstrate a diversity of ways that moral and religious motivations help shape and contribute to the increasing "environmental" character of many popular movements. Sometimes moral claims to "self-determination" or "human rights" or "democracy" are advanced in quests for land and sustainable agrarian practices. Sometimes such claims are buttressed with religious legitimations (see especially Hadsell for how liberation theology promotes such "secular" ideas). Sometimes religious ideas—for example, natural resources are God's gift to humans who should prudently use and distribute them equitably—play important roles in these movements (see Hadsell, Lorentzen, Hill et al., and Porio). Sometimes the perceptions that the natural world is animate or that it embodies spiritual intelligences of one sort or another (see Gedicks, Akula, Lohmann, and Tandon), or newer forms of nature mysticism (see Taylor, Hill et al., Deudney, and Stark) convey a sense of duty toward nature that helps inspire the defense or restoration of ancestral lands or traditional lifeways. Whatever the tradition, religions are malleable. In the face of environmental deterioration, they have been mutating into forms capable of inspiring (or reinforcing) ecological activism, both by articulating ideals that participants find compelling (and thus legitimations for resistance) and by providing concrete institutional resources for ecological struggles.

As we have seen, ecological deterioration directly fuels popular resistance by threatening human well-being. Another reason ecological deterioration provides the decisive breeding grounds for ecological resistance is that it places additional burdens on women who were already disproportionately responsible for child rearing and the agrarian economy. Consequently, women tend to be more acutely aware of the direct threats posed by ecological deterioration. They also tend to know more than men about traditional, yet ecologically sustainable, agrarian alternatives. The contributions by Lorentzen, Akula, Edwards, and Wisner underscore these dynamics, which have also been noted by many other observers (Banuri and Marglin 1993:11; Shiva 1988; Guha 1993:82; Tandon 1993).

Another important reason for the prominence of women in many popular ecological resistance movements is the displacement of men, who in another survival strategy often migrate to cities (e.g., see Akula and Wisner), or whose interests conflict with women's objectives, even within broader popular movements (see Lorentzen). Gedicks also noted that another reason women are often important in indigenous environmental movements is their important roles in spiritual matters. Taken together, ecological decline, the place of women in local subsistence production, the absence of men, and spiritual responsibilities, all contribute to the widespread mobilization of women in popular ecological resistance movements. Consequently, women are decisively shaping many of these movements.

Popular Analysis Fans the Flames of Resistance

Examining how ecological deterioration threatens families, communities, and traditional livelihoods certainly helps account for the emergence of popular ecological resistance. By examining in more detail the way people in these diverse movements *explain* ecological decline—who and what they blame for their precarious situations—we can begin to comprehend why these *are* kindred movements and why and how they are *radical*.

The most common explanation for ecological deterioration and livelihood threats cited by those in popular ecological resistance movements is that the land has been stolen and abused by outsiders—either multinational commercial interests or, more commonly, commercial elites within the nation in question—interested in quick profits rather than ecologically sustainable land uses (see Edwards, Lohmann, Akula, Hadsell, Gedicks). Popular analysis often traces these realities to the arrival of colonial armies and the commercial enterprises that follow (see Wisner and Tandon). Popular analysis thereby links immiseration to the ecological and cultural impoverishment that began with the direct theft of mineral resources and continued with the replacement of traditional agriculture with cash-crop monocultures. The resulting historic shift to international agribusiness targeted for export, such analysis explains, reduced the availability of subsistence crops for local populations and enriched merchants and elite landholders, and eventually bankers and corporations, while displacing or marginalizing the original inhabitants.[3] Such dynamics also produced cultural erosion and declining knowledge of the ecologically sustainable practices that had previously sustained local populations. Thus do rural "peripheries" come to be exploited by two "centers": financial and military powers in the industrialized world, and the metropolitan elites in less affluent countries who mimic in ideology and practice their mentors in the corporate, industrialized world.

Such criticism emerges from long-standing leftist analysis of economic imperialism. As this volume and related research demonstrates, popular ecological resistance in less affluent countries often emerges from existing social movements already influenced by such analyses. Popular ecological resistance movements in Western industrial countries have also been strongly influenced by such social criticism, emerging substantially as they do from the left-wing, peace and social-justice movements (see Rüdig and Edwards in this volume, and Gottlieb 1993). But there is something significantly new in the analysis employed by what we are calling "popular ecological resistance movements"—even those emerging from subcultures influenced by leftist theories of imperialism. It is the recognition of how resource scarcity exacerbates all the dynamics which accompany the global extension of market capitalism. Interestingly, in the late 1960s and early 1970s, an emphasis on resource scarcity (Erlich 1968; Meadows et al. 1972), was sometimes derided by leftists as a means whereby the affluent could deny equity to those heretofore denied the fruits of industrialization.

Of course, progressive analysis has long argued that global market capitalism and industrial growth rarely benefit peasants, workers, or tribals, but rather guarantees their dispossession from ancestral lands. More recently, many leftists have begun to acknowledge that long-term industrial growth is not sustainable ecologically. This has forced a rethinking of many assumptions. If industrial growth is unsustainable, then it *cannot* benefit ordinary people. Like Gandhi, social activists increasingly recognize that only grief will follow if all marginalized people seek to follow the West's path of natural resource imperialism to development.[4] It is obvious to these actors that large-scale hydroelectric dams benefit elites while exacerbating inequalities and destroying communities and livelihoods, and that commercial forestry is likewise a disaster, uprooting people, eroding soil, polluting water supplies and destroying fisheries (Guha 1993:82, 98; Broad and Cavanagh 1993:56–63).

The obvious consequences of unrestrained "development" reinforce perceptions that the land has been expropriated by outsiders who are using it up for their exclusive benefit, and that the further extension of international commerce works against local needs and interests.[5] (The destructive impact of modern commercial enterprise is also fostering a renewed appreciation of and experiments with traditional livelihoods, medicines, and agricultural practices, as shown by Wisner, Hill et al., and especially Tandon and Lorentzen). It is the realization of the connections between commercial development, ecological deterioration, and declining life prospects that leads to the "ecologization" of many popular social movements.[6]

At this point we discern central common denominators emerging among popular ecological resistance movements. Increasingly, they trace the theft and abuse of their lands, that now threatens their physical and cultural survival, to the enclosure of the commons (see especially Hill et al., Lohmann, Lorentzen, Akula, Tandon, and Gedicks).[7] The appropriation of the commons by those who fenced it in, claiming it as their "private property," is seen as the necessary precursor to mineral theft, monocultural cash cropping or animal husbandry, road building, mining, commercial forestry, dam construction, and other "development" projects that, taken together, degrade ecosystems, imperiling those they purport to benefit, while simultaneously making possible capital accumulation on a scale otherwise impossible. In 1992 *The Ecologist* (which had already played a pivotal role in advancing emerging green critiques of industrial societies that take growth as a central objective, and of the multilateral lending and development agencies who promote the extension of such destructive societies) published yet another influential critique. This time it attributed much environmental deterioration to the forces unleashed by the global enclosure process, while noting that resistance always accompanies assaults on commons regimes.[8] This analysis has struck a responsive chord and has been rapidly and widely republished.[9]

Another common denominator to popular ecological resistance movements, and related to the critique of enclosure, is the rejection of economic growth and industrialization as desirable social goals.[10] Dieter Rücht (1989), for example, finds that anti-industrial attitudes are increasingly widespread among environmentalists from many cultures, dividing them into radical and reformist camps. In this volume, Lorentzen, Tandon, and Akula well illustrate Hadsell's observation that the very idea of sustainability, originally borrowed from international sectors, is an increasingly important organizing principle for these movements. Indeed, Hadsell's point that sustainability serves as an important "ideological resource" for popular environmental movements can be generalized widely. Thus, within popular environmental movement analysis, an important trend is to view growth and industrialization as illusions offered by elites to keep ordinary people from defending and promoting appropriate and sustainable alternatives.

Finally, another critique common among popular ecological resistance movements in both affluent and less affluent countries is of the *scale* of governance. Popular ecological resistance movements seek to gain greater local autonomy (or preserve it) against the encroachment of national and international centers of power (see especially Hill et al., and Tandon). Thus a common denominator related to commons defense and restoration, and the rejection of industrial lifeways, is the fundamentally democratic impulse to bring decision making back to local populations.[11] Observing such commonalities, Guha (1993) suggests that there is a remarkable congruence between the anti-industrialism and anti-imperialism of Gandhi and his followers, and the bioregional social ecology of ecotopian visionaries such as Murray Bookchin who promote decentralized economics, participatory democracy, and "appropriate" technology.[12]

Despite the common critique of the scale of governance in the modern world, popular ecological resistance movements are seldom revolutionary.[13] Most of these movements envision neither the overthrow nor the withering away of nation-states. They seek, rather, to wrest concessions from them, to protect or reclaim access to and control over land, and then to secure government compliance with such concessions.[14] Those involved in popular ecological resistance movements are rarely utopian; they cannot afford to be. Even in contexts characterized by greater affluence, most activists recognize that, at least presently, their victories depend on federal legislation or legal rulings. Involvement in ground-level campaigns often tempers ideology with pragmatism. While radical environmentalists nearly always have anarchistic leanings and desire comprehensive decentralization, many know that the most important environmental victories have usually resulted from federal legislation or legal rulings which contravene the desires of local communities. This has been especially true in the United States, as well as in Australia, where large tracts of Tasmanian forest were saved by federal power, not public sentiment (Hay 1992:95). A need for pragmatism is likewise evident to activists who seek to prevent or reverse oceanic and atmospheric degradation—tasks which can be accomplished only through comprehensive international agreements, regulations, and enforcement. The unlikelihood that such agreements will emerge through "politics as usual" is one key reason for the militancy of those radical environmental groups who attend to these issues.

Those involved on the front lines of ecological resistance generally recognize that concessions gained depend on the enforcement powers of the nations or states from which they were won; otherwise the elites whose privileges have been restricted may use their superior wealth and power to thwart popular victories. Moreover, even the most radical within popular ecological resistance movements recognize that the law enforcement agents they despise are often in a position to protect them from the illegal attacks of those whose interests they oppose.[15]

POPULAR ECOLOGICAL RESISTANCE AS RADICAL ENVIRONMENTALISM

By examining how those engaged in popular ecological resistance perceive the causes and consequences of environmental deterioration we can better comprehend how they justify their militant and sometimes illegal tactics. Given their distrust of existing political processes and their relative lack of power, they experiment with a wide variety of oppositional tactics. But whatever the means chosen, the attempt to restore or defend commons regimes fundamentally challenges landowners' ability to control and exploit the land for their own benefit.

In practical terms, the broad priority of popular ecological resistance movements is to protect land from corporate expropriation.[16] As popular environmental movements seek to defend or restore the integrity of ecosystems (sometimes believing they have intrinsic value, but more often to preserve their own livelihoods and health) they also seek to restore commons regimes, even when they do not conceptualize their struggle using such terms. Only when the land is reclaimed or secured, movement activists are convinced, can ecosystem health be restored and sustainable lifeways recovered. Only when they control the land and its uses, these activists believe, is there hope for both it and themselves. To summarize, *renewing sustainable lifeways is the overall objective of popular ecological resistance movements, and this depends on the restoration of the commons.*[17]

This priority is related to a second objective—not to seize the government, but rather to capture its authority over specific places and to prevent the wider extension of its power. Such ambitions derive from the perception that governments *are* or *represent* the very elites monopolizing scarce resources.

There is an additional trend that buttresses our argument that popular ecological resistance movements presage the global emergence of radical environmentalism. Increasingly, participants in these movements are expressing the literally radical idea that, to resolve our ecological predicament, we must "return to our roots"— specifically, our traditional agricultural roots. By supplanting non native plant species (that were imported by imperial powers for cash-crop agribusiness) with native species and more traditional agricultural practices, it is hoped healthy ecosystems can be restored (see Tandon, Lorentzen, Gedicks, Lohmann, and Wisner in this volume, and Shiva 1988). In a similar way, other groups are resisting modern forestry and fishing practices, hoping to supplant them with more traditional ways of taking trees, fish, or game (see Hill et al., and Hadsell). Such efforts challenge current social, economic, and environmental realities as fundamentally as do direct assaults on elite domination of land.[18] Of course, such radical efforts to recover traditional lifeways usually depend on equally radical campaigns to recover and secure the land.

The preceding analysis suggests that despite great diversity, popular ecological resistance movements generally share *a common perception of their predicament* (environmental deterioration is threatening survival), *a common understanding of the causes* (outsiders have stolen the land and are abusing it for short-term profits; they are fencing out those who know best how to live sustainably; and nation-states are deeply complicit in this process),[19] and *a common prescription* (the land must be taken from the abusers and managed according to traditional wisdom, supplemented judiciously by modern knowledge, while vigilance is maintained against those who would usurp the commons for private gain).[20] Such shared perceptions unify and make clear the radical agenda of popular ecological resistance movements around the globe.

ECOLOGICAL RESISTANCE MEETS REACTIONARY RESPONSE

Although specific situations give rise to particular political objectives, all ecological resistance movements call for a fundamental reordering of land uses, and thus of many political and economic relationships. In this sense, these movements are radical in orientation. This is not lost on those whose interests they threaten. Consequently, activists in ecological resistance movements have faced widespread reactionary violence, especially where elites fear such movements might succeed. Several case studies in the present volume provide examples of such violent reaction (see especially Gedicks, Akula, and Porio). However, these cases do not convey a sense of the extent of such violence.

In Brazil, where popular movements of rural workers and tribals have been particularly strong—where there have been repeated land invasions (or "recoveries") by peasants, and rubber tappers have confronted loggers, sometimes with hundreds of families, occasionally even tearing down their camps (Melone 1993)—the Pastoral Land Commission reports over 1,684 rural workers killed between 1964 and 1992 (Monbiot 1993). In the Philippines several of the most prominent popular environmental leaders have been murdered (Broad and Cavanagh 1993). In 1985, agents of the French government killed a Greenpeace photographer when they bombed a ship being equipped to disrupt a French nuclear test (Dalton 1993).

In 1990, two Earth First! forest activists were the targets of a car bombing while they campaigned to save the California redwoods. Immediately afterward they were arrested and accused of carrying the bomb that had injured them. They have a case pending against federal and state law enforcement agencies for false arrest and believe that law enforcement may even be complicit in the bombing itself (Bari 1994).[21] We could detail other examples. As reactionary violence has escalated, so has the number of instances where members of popular ecological resistance movements threaten to "fight to the death" in defense of their lands and livelihoods. Some have already used violence. Others have turned to arson or forms of sabotage that place human lives at risk.[22] The apparent escalation of a violent dimension to these conflicts is likely to continue because the conditions leading to ecological radicalism and reactionary violence show no signs of abating.

THE IMPACTS OF POPULAR ECOLOGICAL RESISTANCE

Many impacts of popular ecological resistance movements have already been discussed in this volume. A few of the major points are emphasized here. First, these movements have had an impact on public awareness of environmental issues and problems. They and their sympathizers (including anthropologists, filmmakers, human rights groups, and rock stars)[23] have contributed significantly to global awareness of the contemporary extinction crisis and other environmental calamities. As Litfin (1993:102) points out, and Wapner and Kamieniecki et al. contend in this volume, in the absence of grassroots ecological resistance, it is unlikely that an urbanized humanity's understanding of such issues would have developed to the extent that it has (1993:102).

Second, these movements have had clear political impacts. By challenging the legitimacy of the state to determine who owns, controls, and benefits from the land, by challenging its plans, intentions, and bureaucratic-scientific expertise, by haranguing states for failing to address the threats posed by environmental deterioration, these movements are significantly reducing the range of autonomous state action—reducing the spheres where states can pursue their own objectives without consulting with and granting concessions to popular movements.[24] Consequently, popular ecological resistance is already significantly contributing to the contemporary erosion of state power and promises to do so further in the coming decades.[25] As concessions are won, so is confidence that sometimes the weak can thwart the strong, popular pressure can bring victories, and with vigilance, compliance with concessions can sometimes be secured. As Edwards explains, crude and rude protest often works, and as Lohmann adds, government environmental action generally *follows* popular action. Moreover, as both

Edwards and Kamieniecki et al. argue, the presence of radical environmental ideas and tactics makes moderate environmentalists seem reasonable by comparison, and more concretely, their obstructionist tactics sometimes provide time for moderates to gain concessions or victories by less militant means.

Third, these movements *have* altered the "constitutive rules" (Lipschutz and Mayer 1993) governing a variety of land-use practices. Radical environmental groups have been effective in shifting environmental debate around the world from issues of aesthetics and wildlife conservation to more comprehensive and fundamentally challenging issues of biological and cultural diversity. An important part of this process occurred when grassroots environmental activists rejected the leadership of the mainstream environmental groups,[26] embarrassing them by accusing them of being members of an elite leisure class, concerned only with their own enjoyment of visually spectacular places and "charismatic megafauna." Radical environmental groups argued instead that a priority should be placed on the conservation of biologically important ecosystem types.[27]

Such challenges have contributed to some change in the public rhetoric and actual priorities of the mainstream groups as well to shifting rhetoric among many nations and international agencies. Of course some within these organizations were also arguing for such changes in priorities, but it is difficult to imagine that such changes would have occurred as they did without the militant challenges posed by radical environmental groups. Mainstream environmental groups in the United States are increasingly making the conservation of biological diversity a high priority. Even though substantive political commitment to biological diversity and the preservation of the global commons have not followed the rhetoric—the rules are changing—governments and international agencies must now present at least a facade of concern about biological and cultural diversity. Even extractive enterprises such as the timber industry must now claim that their practices are sustainable and compatible with biological diversity. Moreover, they increasingly recognize that false claims could lead to legal challenges, fiscal problems, and public relations disasters. (The chapters by Hadsell, Gedicks, Wapner, and Lohmann demonstrate especially well how "development" is increasingly threatened by popular resistance, international attention, and changing values that are often expressed in demands for environmental impact assessments and sustainable land uses.) These are relatively new political realities for which radical environmental movements can claim significant credit. As increasing numbers of social actors are forced to justify their practices as sustainable, popular environmental groups gain significant new leverage in their political struggles.[28]

It should also be noted that many of the groups studied in this volume have won significant outright victories (Gedicks, Akula, Porio, Lohmann, Tandon). Nevertheless, as Gedicks points out, most such victories could be overturned in the future.

THE FUTURE OF RADICAL ENVIRONMENTAL RESISTANCE

Despite the repression radical environmental movements often face, it may be that they will continue to transform international politics in important ways. Moreover, all the available evidence suggests that the social conditions giving rise to these movements are worsening. Thus it seems likely that the coming decades will witness further proliferation of popular ecological resistance. As Broad and Cavanagh explain, "The ranks of the opposition grow [with] the degradation of resources and peoples" (1993:156). Yet there are obstacles to the proliferation and growth of these movements.

For example, it is likely that the conflicts they engender will be increasingly violent. One reason for this is that the conflicts fostered by radical environmental resistance seem destined to become intertwined with competing religious perspectives. This is partly because conservative Christians often believe that ecological resistance movements are animated either by forms of Christianity they consider false or misguided (such as Liberation Theology) or by pagan spiritualities they consider demonic.[29] Moreover, many supporters of ecological resistance movements agree that these conflicts are grounded in fundamentally different religious worldviews—or as Banuri and Marglin (1993) put it, differing "systems of knowledge."[30] It is not surprising to find religion deeply involved in conflicts such as these, since historically, economic interests nearly always become linked to religious worldviews and legitimations.

Also critical to the future of these movements is the role of international solidarity actors. As the contributions by Hadsell, Gedicks, and Lohmann demonstrate, international actors make violent repression more difficult by making such violence visible. They also can provide important ideological, technical, and financial resources, help navigate legal processes, and counter government and corporate reassurances about "development" schemes. Yet the extent to which such international actors will contribute to the proliferation of popular ecological resistance remains unclear.

Equally important to the future of these movements will be the success of international alliances among these groups themselves. This will depend at least in part on how successful people's alliances will be in gathering resources from international sectors and making visible their local struggles for self-determination, local land control, and sustainable lifeways. Many of the movements in this volume are clearly building the types of broad coalitions, addressing diverse but related issues, that are likely to be sustainable over time (see Kamieniecki et al.).

PROBLEMS POSED BY THE GLOBAL EMERGENCE OF POPULAR ECOLOGICAL RESISTANCE

Radical environmentalism, in its many forms, poses fundamental questions about meaning and values. In dispute, as Dan Deudney has explained elsewhere in this volume, are answers about which if any religions are intellectually plausible in the modern era, an era informed by astronomy and evolutionary biology. A related question has to do with what knowledge systems, what worldviews, are *adaptive*, that is to say congruent with the long-term flourishing of life on this planet. This leads us back to our initial reflections on narratives—do any of the stories we have been confronted by in this volume move us? Do any of these stories of ecological resistance, international solidarity, spiritual and cultural renewal and revisioning, make sense?

Must the religious mysticisms of deep ecology and primal peoples be jettisoned, as Stark contends, and replaced by human knowledge about how to live sustainably and peacefully gained through the natural and social sciences? Or should we instead—as is argued by deep ecologists such as Max Oelschlaeger (1991), Gary Snyder (1990), David Abram (1995) and Lone Wolf Circles (1991)—return to the lifeways and spiritualities of small-scale societies, with their perception of nature as full of spiritual intelligences and sacred places? Should we await new religions or return to traditional spiritualities, as Tandon suggests, allowing ourselves to be guided by "the ancestors" or spirit mediums? Or should we rather—as Deudney in this volume (and 1993), and Theodore Roszak (1992), propose—synthesize such primal spiritualities with more scientifically respectable notions like the Gaia hypothesis, and the "new physics," to create new religious stories capable of promoting the kind of trans-border (and trans-species) loyalty to the earth and its creatures that seems so desperately needed?

This volume illustrates that popular ecological resistance is fueled most decisively by the conflicts that arise from the extension of industrial processes globally and from the consequences of these processes where they have already been established. Yet this volume also shows that the success and impacts of social movements depends not only on how desperate are the material conditions giving rise to them. Nor do the impacts of these movements depend solely on the material resources they can muster. The success and impacts of these movements also hinges on how compelling are the ideas and stories that undergird these struggles. Among the unresolved questions emerging from our study of the global emergence of radical environmentalism are whether the ideas that are emerging from it, as amorphous and nascent as they may be, can provide the kind of inspiration able to sustain movements that face very long odds indeed. Another line of inquiry posed but unanswered by this volume is why movements of popular ecological resistance have not emerged elsewhere where environmental conditions, motivations, ideas, cultures, and so on, are comparable.[31]

Although often originating in the quest to meet basic human needs, these movements nevertheless pose fundamental and enduring questions. They also offer as answers a host of new narrative amalgamations, based both on old and on new perceptions and stories. It may well be that contemporary environmental disputes, as with many previous historical conflicts, will continue to be deeply embroiled in the differing ways people conceive of the sacred: Is the Divine located above or beyond the world? Is the Sacred located, instead, right under our feet, or in "our" place rather than "your" place? Ought we revere the earth as Gaia, the one responsible for our own existence? Or rather, is the Divine in some sense the universe itself, with all the entities sacred, because in a mysterious way they all participate in the life of God?

Complicating matters further, how in the world do stories based in astronomy and evolutionary biology fit in? Some suggest that the narrative of the unfolding of the universe provides a compelling story into which humans can locate themselves, discovering their proper place (Swimme and Berry 1992). Others discuss how evolutionary narratives themselves and ecological understandings of interdependence confer a proper perception of the human place in nature, helping people to see that they are but one part of the natural world, and not even the most important one at that, but nevertheless a part with unusual responsibilities to the whole (Milbrath 1993). How are we to weave such narratives into the host of other stories spun throughout our cultures?—such as enlightenment stories of people learning to act rationally, universalizing moral principles, and promoting democratic polity?—or stories of the historical unfolding of the idea of human rights?—or stories depicting the kinship of all creatures?

Such questions lead to a perplexing ending for this volume exploring the global emergence of radical environmentalism and popular ecological resistance. Whatever the impacts, prospects, and diverse forms these movements take—however we evaluate these diverse stories or the propositions embedded in them—whatever we conclude about who we are, where we fit, to whom we belong, and how we should live in the immense universe that surrounds us— these movements pose fundamental, radical questions. The answers can only be discerned through a life lived passionately and intelligently in their pursuit.

NOTES

1. This book most closely parallels the focus of the present volume. Two other edited volumes provide especially helpful comparative reference points and provocative reflection relevant to this volume's themes: Colchester and Lohmann (1993) and Lipschutz and Conca (1993). Broad and Cavanagh (1993) recently published an excellent in-depth case study of popular ecological resistance in the Philippines.

2. See Gottlieb (1993) who argues that in the United States the most effective way to galvanize a community for environmental action has been to describe the environmental threats to it.

3. For an excellent example of this kind of analysis see Broad and Cavanagh (1993).

4. See Guha (1993:98) for representative quotes expressing Gandhi's views that industrial societies are unsustainable and depend on imperialism.

5. For a good example of such analysis, see Rangan's analysis of how such a view animated some of the earliest Chipko actions (in Friedmann and Rangan 1993a:172–73).

6. A more cynical view is that popular movements adopt ecological dimensions and rhetoric to secure resources from international environmental organizations. One can find some examples where environmentalists from affluent countries were manipulated by those in popular movements for their own ends—see e.g., Pezzoli's (1993) description of a Mexican squatters' movement that abandoned its sponsor's eco-utopian vision once title to land was secured. Certainly popular environmental movements need resources, and thus it is no surprise that they learn to use the rhetoric of potential benefactors. Nevertheless, the evidence is overwhelming that the ecologization of existing movements and the spontaneous emergence of new activist groups in areas with little or no history of popular resistance are sincere responses to threats posed by ecological deterioration. Broad and Cavanagh state that virtually all popular movements in the Philippines have become ecologically radicalized as a direct result of the dire environmental situation there, perhaps even the New People's Army (1993:146). It should be remembered that most popular ecological resistance has emerged from preexisting social movements promoting community development, literacy, and political empowerment, not from ecological movements per se.

7. A "commons" is community-owned or controlled land that is managed for the well-being of all. For a good discussion of the enclosure process in tropical rainforests, see Hurst (1990: esp. 247–48). He explains that even though rainforests are incredibly productive, upon colonization, they were not privately owned, and therefore could not produce wealth in European terms. Wealth creation required that the Europeans privatize and enclose land, prohibit traditional lifeways, and replace them with practices from which they could extract profit.

8. *The Ecologist* 22(4). Here "regime" refers to not to a government in power but to "a set of norms, rules, or decision-making procedures" that govern practices and expectations in "a particular issue area" (Porter and Brown, cited in Kamieniecki 1993:8), and a "commons" refers to any place—land, ocean, and even atmosphere—controlled by popular decision making.

9. E.g., this special issue was republished in 1993 by Earth Scan in England and in 1994 by New Society Publishers in the United States. Also in 1994, the *Earth Island Journal* 9(2):20–40 published excerpts as part of a long section on "defending the commons," including numerous brief articles about various ecological resistance movements around the world. Jeremy Rifkin (1991) similarly blames the destruction of the commons for ecological decline and envisions its restoration. See Peluso (1993) for an excellent discussion of how colonialism leads to enclosure of the commons

and diverse forms of peasant resistance attempting to reclaim access to ancestral domains, and Farlie (1994) for another article in *The Ecologist* that links contemporary antiroad resistance in England to earlier commons defense movements.

10. Dalton (1993) traces such critiques to E. F. Schumacher's *Small as Beautiful* (1976) which he believes significantly contributed to the new ecologist orientation of the 1970s, which viewed environmental deterioration as a direct consequence of growth-manic industrial societies and their highly centralized government forms.

11. Colchester and Lohmann (1993) demonstrate that a fundamental factor animating popular rainforest defense movements is the quest to replace corrupt patronage systems with democratic processes. This animating motive is often ignored by observers of popular ecological resistance movements, particularly by those who disapprove of their occasionally militant tactics.

12. The present analysis also reveals significant parallels between Bookchin's ideas and the most prevalent forms of ecological resistance emerging globally.

13. Writing of peasant resistance in Indonesia, Peluso (1992) states that, generally speaking, peasant movements do not envision abstract goals such as overthrowing the state, but rather are trying to resist the criminalization of their traditional agrarian practices.

14. Friedman (in Friedman and Rangan 1993:19) insightfully observes the irony that enhancing local autonomy requires the support of the state. He concludes that this is why peasants want not an eco-anarchistic utopia, which they cannot envision, but a more responsive state. He also observes that while revolutions sometimes overthrow states, they do not do away with such institutions. Such a recognition vitiates romantic anarchistic hopes for the withering away of the state.

15. It is interesting to observe that Earth First!ers often appeal to governments for protection from their opponents, even when they do not trust them to provide it.

16. In the United States and other countries with large tracts of publically owned lands used by private extractive industries, it may not always be private *property* interests from whom the land must be re-claimed. However, the struggle over who uses and benefits from the land remains essentially the same, whether or not the public holds legal title to the disputed land.

17. Here I speak of "sustainable lifeways" not "sustainable development" because the latter term is viewed as an oxymoron by many within ecological resistance movements. Although not all popular ecological resis-

tance movements have fully adopted sustainability as their overarching organizing principle (for example, the antitoxics movement apparently does not usually conceive of its struggle in such terms) the logic of these movements does propel them toward such conceptualizations. Activists involved in the environmental justice movement, for example, will eventually have to address questions such as whether it is possible to create a safe and sustainable industrial society, and if so, how?

18. It is interesting, that with colonial enclosures, traditional agrarian practices have often been criminalized (see Peluso 1992 for examples in Indonesia). Thus poaching and timber theft have become forms of popular resistance—in some places self-consciously as part of popular efforts to restore sustainable lifeways. Tandon (1993:222) asserts that with socialism and capitalism both discredited, people are forced to look toward their own resources, however meager.

19. One of the most radical aspects of these movements is how they often deny the very territorial assumptions upon which nation-states are based, thereby rejecting their legitimacy, at least implicitly. See, e.g., Litfin (1993) and Tandon (1993).

20. This summary likely applies to the deep ecologists, including Earth First!ers, although they would insist that the survival of nonhuman life forms ought to be fully considered, and most would also want to see large tracts of the commons left completely undisturbed by humans, a goal shared by few of those in popular ecological resistance movements globally.

21. Other Earth First!ers in the United States have had their homes burned down, two activists died under circumstances considered suspicious by their comrades, others have been shot at or threatened, and many have been battered. Attacks on environmentalists have become common enough that *Time* magazine ran an in-depth article about such attacks. Helvarg (1994) details the violence and other repressive tactics used against environmental activists in the United States.

22. I once heard Earth First! activists defending arson as a nonviolent tactic—if precautions are taken to insure the burned structure is vacant. When I pointed out that such tactics imperil responding firefighters, they admitted that they had not considered this possibility. This illustrates an important problem with militant tactics—often their practicioners are unable, or disinclined, to calculate the full range of likely (or possible) consequences.

23. Human rights groups such as Cultural Survival and Survival International, sometimes led by anthropologists, have been among the most important international solidarity activists. By documenting human rights abuses against those in popular movements they have reduced vio-

lence and forced governments to provide greater protection than they would have otherwise. See Melone (1993) for more discussion about the role of international solidarity actors.

24. See Edwards in this volume, and Litfin (1993), Gottlieb (1992), and Gerlach (1993), for discussion of how state power erodes in the face of legitimacy crises resulting from an erosion of confidence in government abilities to mitigate environmental threats.

25. As Deudney puts it, the nation-state, although remaining a crucial player, is being displaced "from the center of world political life" (1993:281).

26. See Gottlieb (1992) for numerous examples of grassroots refusal to accept the leadership, diagnoses, or tactics of mainstream environmentalists.

27. This critique of the mainstream has come from popular ecological resistance movements both in less affluent and in more affluent countries. In the United States, such criticisms have been made forcefully by members of Earth First!. This illustrates that Guha's claim that "radical environmentalists" promote nature preservation for their own leisure (1993:109 n. 49) is misplaced. His criticism would more accurately be applied to groups like the Sierra Club (before it increased its attention to biological diversity issues in the mid to late 1980s). Guha also accuses radical environmentalists of not resisting consumerism and militarism. That this is untrue of most of them is clear to anyone well acquainted with radical environmentalism in the United States. Gottlieb (1993) is correct that environmental resistance in the United States originated primarily in antinuclear, peace, social justice, back-to-the-land, and voluntary simplicity subcultures. Resentment of Northern environmentalists who recommend simple living for others fuels criticisms like Guha's. However, what Schubert concludes about Asia could provide a basis for a rapprochement between environmentalists everywhere: "Asia can afford no luxuries, but ecosystem viability is no extravagance" (Schubert 1993:240). This insight can be generalized to many contexts.

28. Lipschutz and Mayer (1993: esp. 265) point out that even loggers have to justify their practices in terms of their impact on biological diversity and global issues, a fundamental change in the rules governing forest practices. They also claim that "the types of actions [taken by radical environmental groups in the United States] challenge property relations as fundamentally as did the 1917 Russian revolution." Their views here buttress my own conclusion that globally, popular ecological resistance movements are all fundamentally radical in this way (among others).

29. See Monbiot (1993) for a discussion of conservative versus liberationist Christianity in Brazil, and McDonald 1993 for a description of an innovative Catholic (liberationist) ritual where survey stakes for a planned dam were gathered and ceremonially burned. For a detailed case study and discussion of the religious dimensions to environmental conflicts in the United States, see Taylor (1995). This study describes the resistance of Earth First! activists and traditionally religious Apache to a telescope project on Mt. Graham, a site in Arizona considered sacred by both groups. The conflict assumed a religious character as representatives of the Vatican defended the project, one calling the opposition "a Jewish conspiracy," another suggesting that their paganism "must be suppressed."

30. For views typical of those sympathetic to ecological resistance movements, that non-Western spirituality is superior to Western monotheism at supporting sustainable lifeways, see Guha with regard to India (1993) and Witte with regard to Africa (1993:183). Guha well describes how peasant protest gets wrapped up in the surrounding religious milieu as protesters seek religious sanction for their resistance, noting that "symbols from the Hindu epics [have been used to characterize governments] as evil and demonic" (Guha 1983:89). Peluso (1992:219) describes how telling stories about cursed sites "is a form of local resistance to outsiders treading uninvited on village territory." Such tales can function like sacred groves, which Guha explains function to preserve forests by restricting peasant access to them (1993:88).

31. When reviewing this chapter, Bob Edwards raised this important question. He suspects that the more desperate the circumstances, the less likely are resistance *movements*, since poverty weakens and repression usually works. Consequently, he properly cautions against viewing desperation as the *cause* of movements of ecological resistance. Although such circumstances are surely not a *sufficient cause* for these movements, this volume does show that environmental decline does play a role. Certainly more research is needed into the problematics Edwards raises.

REFERENCES

Abbey, Edward. 1989. *Hayduke Lives!* New York: Viking.

Abram, David. 1994. *The Eclipse of the Earth: Animism, Language, and the Ecology of Sensory Experience.* New York: Pantheon.

Acosta, Rosario. 1993. *Interview by author.* Executive Committee Member of National Union of Salvadoran Workers; San Salvador, El Salvador, June 22.

Adams, W. 1990. *Green Development.* London: Routledge.

Albanese, Catherine. 1990. *Nature Religion in America: From the Algonkian Indians to the New Age.* Chicago: University of Chicago Press.

Allan, W. 1965. *The African Husbandman.* Edinburgh: Oliver and Boyd.

Allison, L. 1975. *Environmental Planning: A Political and Philosophical Analysis.* London: George Allen & Unwin.

Alvarado, Elvia. 1987. *Don't be Afraid Gringo: A Honduran Woman Speaks from the Heart: The Story of Elvia Alvarado.* Trans. Medea Benjamin. New York: Harper and Row.

Amte, Baba. 1989. *Cry, The Beloved Narmada* (Quoted in Postel, 1992, Page 56). Chandrapur, Maharashtra, India: Maharogi Sewa Samiti.

Anderson, Robert S., and Walter Huber. 1988. *The Hour of the Fox, Tropical Forest, the World Bank, and Indigenous People in Central India.* Seattle: University of Washington Press.

Angelsey, Zoe, ed. 1987. *Ixok Aman Go: Central American Women's Poetry for Peace.* Penobscott, ME: Granite Press.

Anonymous. 1992. *Crofting and the Environment: A New Approach.* Inverness: Royal Society for the Protection of Birds and the Scottish Crofters Union.

———. 1992a. "Fourth-World Statehood." *The Economist* (September 26).

———. 1992b. "Jharkand Bandh Hits Normal Life in Bihar." *Indian Express* (September 16).

Apel, Karl-Otto. 1977. "The a Priori of Communication and the Foundation of the Humanities." In *Understanding and Social Inquiry,* ed. F. Dallmayr and T. McCarthy, 292–315. Notre Dame, IN: University of Notre Dame Press.

Apffel-Marglin, Frederique, and Stephen A. Marglin. 1994. *Decolonizing Knowledge.* Oxford: Oxford University Press.

Apffel-Marglin, Frederique, and Stephen A. Marglin, eds. 1990. *Dominating Knowledge.* Oxford: Oxford University Press.

Aquina, M. 1969. "Zionists in Rhodesia." *Africa* 39 (April 2).

Arac, Jonathan. 1986. *Postmodernism and Politics.* Minneapolis: University of Minnesota Press.

———. *After Foucault: Humanistic Knowledge, Postmodern Challenges.* New Brunswick, NJ: Rutgers University Press.

ARC (Anthropology Resource Center). 1981. "Transnational Corporations and Indigenous Peoples." *ARC Newsletter* 5 (3).

Ashby, E., and M. Anderson. 1981. *The Politics of Clean Air.* Oxford: Clarendon Press.

Associated Press. June 20, 1992. "Ecuador Indians Regain Title to Amazon Forest." *Milwaukee Sentinel.*

Associated Press. 1994. "Great Whale Project on Cree Land Collapses." Citing *News From Indian Country* (23) (Mid December.).

Atkinson, A. 1991. *Principles of Political Ecology.* London: Belhaven Press.

Bagchi, Saugata. 1991. "Harming Trees, Hurting Tribals." *Inter Press Service* (March 18).

Bahro, Rudolf. 1986. *Building the Green Movement.* Baltimore: New Society Publishers.

Bailey, Ronald. 1993. *Eco-Scam: The False Prophets of Ecological Apocalypse.* New York: St. Martin's Press.

Bakhtin, M. M. 1993. *Toward a Philosophy of the Act.* Trans. Vadim Liapunov. Austin, TX: University of Texas Press.

Ball, S., and S. Bell. 1994. *Environmental Law.* 2nd ed. London: Blackstone Press.

Ball-Rokeach, Sandra J., and Muriel G. Cantor. 1986. *Media, Audience, and Social Structure.* Beverly Hills: Sage.

Banuri, Tariq, and Frédérique Apffel Marglin. 1993. *Who Will Save the Forests?: Knowledge, Power, and Environmental Destruction.* London and New Jersey: Zed.

Bari, Judi. 1994. "The Bombing Story." *Earth First!* 14 (4,5,6).

Barker, A. 1976. *The Local Amenity Movement.* London: Civic Trust.

Barker, A., and M. Keating. 1977. "Public Spirits: Amenity Societies and Others." In *Participation in Politics,* ed. C. Crouch, 202–21. British Political Sociology Yearbook, vol. 3. London: Croom Helm.

Barratt-Brown, M., and T. Emerson, eds. 1976. *Resources and the Environment: A Socialist Perspective.* Nottingham: Spokesman.

Barry, J. 1993. "Deep Ecology and the Undermining of Green Politics." In *Perspectives on the Environment,* ed. J. Holder, P. Lane, S. Eden, R. Reeve, U. Collier, and K. Anderson, 43–57. Aldershot: Avebury.

Beinart, W. 1984. "Soil Erosion, Conservationism, and Ideas about Development." *Journal of Southern African Studies* 11 (1).

Belcher, Martha, and Angela Gennino, eds. 1993. *Southeast Asia Rainforests: A Resource Guide and Director.* San Francisco: Rainforest Action Network.

Bennie, L. G., M. N. Franklin, and W. Rüdig. 1994. "Green Dimensions: The Ideology of the British Greens." In *Green Politics Three,* ed. W. Rudig. Edinburgh: Edinburgh University Press.

Bennie, L. G., and W. Rüdig. 1993. "Youth and the Environment: Attitudes and Actions in the 1990's." *Youth & Policy* 42 (Autumn): 6–21.

Berglund, Axel-Ivar. 1989. *Zulu Thought-Patterns and Symbolism.* London: Hurst & Co.

Berman, Marshall. 1970. *The Politics of Authenticity.* New York: Atheneum.

———. 1982. *All That Is Solid Melts into Air.* New York: Simon and Schuster.

Bernstein, Richard J. 1985. *Habermas and Modernity*. Cambridge, MA: MIT Press.

———. 1985. "Heidegger on Humanism." *Praxis International* 5:95–114.

———. 1991. *The New Constellation*. Cambridge, MA: MIT Press.

Berreman, Gerald D. 1989. "Chipko: A Movement to Save the Himalayan Environment and People." In *Contemporary Indian Tradition: Voices on Nature and the Challenge of Change*, ed. Carla Borden, 239–66. Washington and London: Smithsonian Intsitution Press.

Berry, Thomas. 1993. "The Viable Human." In *Environmental Philosophy*, ed. Michael E. Zimmerman, Baird Callicott, Karen Warren, John Clark, and George Sessions, 171–81. Englewood Cliffs, NJ: Prentice Hall.

Best, Steven, and Douglas Kellner. 1991. *Postmodern Theory*. New York: Guilford Press.

Betsworth, Roger G. 1990. *Social Ethics: An Examination of American Moral Traditions*. Louisville, KY: Westminster/John Knox.

Biehl, Janet. 1987. "It's Deep, But Is It Broad? An Eco-Feminist Looks at Deep Ecology." *Kick It Over* (Winter):2.

———. 1993. "Dialectics in the Ethics of Social Ecology." In *Environmental Philosophy*, ed. Michael Zimmerman, et al., 374–89. Englewood Cliffs, NJ: Prentice Hall.

Bingman, Mary Beth. 1993. "Stopping the Bulldozers: What Difference Did It Make?" In *Fighting Back in Appalachia: Traditions of Resistance and Change*, ed. Stephen L. Fisher, 17–30. Philadelphia: Temple University Press.

Blauner, Robert. 1969. "Internal Colonialism and Ghetto Revolt." *Social Problems* 16 (4):393–408.

Blinkhorn, Thomas. 1994. *Environment versus Development: Where Does the World Bank Stand?* Presentation at Yale University, New Haven, CT., March 24.

Blumer, Herbert. 1969. "Social Movements." In *Studies in Social Movements: A Social Psychological Perspective*, ed. Barry McLaughlin. New York: The Free Press.

Bodley, John H. 1985. *Anthropology and Contemporary Human Problems*. Mountain View, CA: Mayfield.

Boehmer-Christiansen, S., and J. Skea. 1991. *Acid Politics: Environmental and Energy Policies in Britain and Germany*. London: Belhaven Press.

Bondurant, Joan. 1958. *Conquest of Violence*. Berkeley: University of California Press.

Bookchin, Murray. 1986. "Freedom and Necessity in Nature: A Problem in Ecological Ethics." *Alternatives* 13:29–38.

———. 1986. *Modern Crisis*. Philadelphia, PA: New Society Publishers.

———. 1987. "Social Ecology versus Deep Ecology." *Green Perspectives* 45:1–23.

———. 1987. "Thinking Ecologically: A Dialectical Approach." *Our Generation* 18:3–40.

———. 1990. *The Philosophy of Social Ecology*. Montreal: Black Rose Press.

———. 1990. "Recovering Evolution: A Reply to Eckersley and Fox." *Environmental Ethics* 12:253–74.

———. 1990. *Remaking Society: Pathways to a Green Future*. Boston, MA: South End Press.

———. 1991. *The Ecology of Freedom*. Montreal: Black Rose Press.

———. 1993. "What Is Social Ecology?" In *Environmental Philosophy*, eds. Michael Zimmerman, et al., 354–73. Englewood Cliffs, NJ: Prentice Hall.

Bookchin, Murray, and Dave Foreman. 1990. *Defending the Earth: A Dialogue between Murray Bookchin and Dave Foreman*, ed. David Levine. Boston: South End Press.

Booth, Annie L., and Harvey M. Jacobs. 1990. "Ties That Bind: Native American Beliefs As a Foundation for Environmental Consciousness." *Environmental Ethics* 12:27–44.

Botwinick, Aryeh. 1993. *Postmodernism and Democratic Theory*. Philadelphia: Temple University Press.

Bourassa, Robert. 1985. *Power from the North*. Canada: Prentice Hall.

Bowler, Peter J. 1992. *The Environmental Sciences*. New York: Norton.

Bradford, George. 1989. *How Deep Is Deep Ecology? A Challenge to Radical Environmentalism*. Novato, CA: Times Change Press.

————. 1993. "Toward a Deep Social Ecology." In *Environmental Philosophy*, ed. Michael Zimmerman, et al., 418–37. Englewood Cliffs, NJ: Prentice Hall.

Bremer, Paul. 1992. "Eco-Terrorism: The Rise of the Green Revolutionaries." *CEO/International Strategies* 5 (3).

Brennan, Andrew. 1988. *Thinking about Nature*. Athens, GA: University of Georgia Press.

Broad, Robin, and John Cavanagh. 1993. *Plundering Paradise: The Struggle for the Environment in the Philippines*. Berkeley: University of California Press.

Brokensha, D., D. M. Warren and Oswald Werner, eds. 1980. *Indigenous Knowledge Systems and Development*. Washington, D.C.: University Press of America.

Brookes, S. K., A. G. Jordan, R. H. Kimber, and J. J. Richardson. 1976. "The Growth of the Environment as a Political Issue in Britain." *British Journal of Political Science* 6:245–55.

Brower, David. 1990. Foreward. In *Eco-Warriors: Understanding the Radical Environmental Movement*, ed. Rik Scarce. Chicago: The Noble Press.

Brown, Michael, and John May. 1989. *The Greenpeace Story*. Ontario: Prentice-Hall Canada.

Brown, Phil, and Edwin J. Mikkelsen. 1990. *No Safe Place: Toxic Waste, Leukemia, and Community Action*. Berkeley: University of California Press.

Bryant, Bunyan, and Paul Mohai. 1990. *Race and the Incidence of Environmental Hazards:A Time for Disclosure*. Boulder, CO: Westview Press.

Bugler, J. 1981. "Friends of the Earth Is Ten Years Old." *New Scientist* 90 (30 April): 294–97.

Bullard, Robert D. 1990. *Dumping in Dixie: Race, Class, and Environmental Quality*. Boulder, CO: Westview Press.

————. 1992. "The Quest for Environmental Equity: Mobilizing the African-American Community for Social Change." In *American Environmentalism: The U.S. Environmental Movement, 1970–1990*, ed. Riley E. Dunlap and Angela G. Mertig, 39–50. Washington, D.C.: Taylor & Francis.

Bullard, Robert D., ed. 1993. *Confronting Environmental Racism: Voices from the Grassroots*. Boston: South End Press.

Bullard, Robert D., and Beverly H. Wright. 1987. "Environmentalism and the Politics of Equity: Emergent Trends in the Black Community." *Mid-America Review of Sociology* 12:21–37.

Burbridge, Jake, and Jason Torrance. 1993. "Road War Victory." *Earth First!* 13 (7): 1,12.

Burger, Julian. 1987. *Report from the Frontier: The State of the World's Indigenous Peoples*. London and Cambridge, MA: Zed Books and Cultural Survival.

———. 1990. *The Gaia Atlas of First Peoples*. New York: Anchor.

Burke, Edmund. 1901. *The Writings and Speeches of the Right Honourable Edmund Burke*. Boston: Little, Brown.

Caldecott, L., and S. Leland, eds. 1983. *Reclaim the Earth: Women Speak Out for Life on Earth*. London: The Women's Press.

Caldwell, Lynton K. 1990. *International Environmental Policy: Emergence and Dimensions*. 2nd ed. Durham: Duke University Press.

Callenbach, Ernest. 1975. *Ecotopia*. New York: Bantam.

———. 1981. *Ecotopia Emerging*. Berkeley: Banyan Tree.

Callicott, J. Baird. 1986. "The Metaphysical Implications of Ecology." *Environmental Ethics* 8: 301–316.

———. 1987. *Companion to "A Sand County Almanac."* Madison, WI: University of Wisconsin Press.

———. 1993. "The Conceptual Foundations of the Land Ethic." In *Environmental Philosophy*, ed. Michael Zimmerman, et al., 110–34. Englewood Cliffs, NJ: Prentice Hall.

Callinicos, Alex. 1985. "Postmodernism, Post-Structuralism, Post-Marxism?" *Theory, Culture & Society* 2:85–101.

———. 1990. *Against Postmodernism*. New York: St. Martin's Press.

Canas, Mercedes. 1991. "En Nosotros Crece La Vida: Un Punto De Vista Ecofeminista." *Palabra De Mujer* 3 (2):6–10.

Capek, Stella M. 1993. "The Environmental Justice Frame: A Conceptual Discussion and an Application." *Social Problems* 40 (1):5–24.

Carballo, Alma. 1993. Interview by author. San Salvador, El Salvador, June 23.

Carney, J., and M. Watts. 1991. "Disciplining Women? Rice, Mechanization and the Evolution of Mandinka Gender Relations in Senegambia." *Signs* 16 (4): 651–81.

Carter, N. 1992. "The 'Greening' of Labour." In *The Changing Labour Party*, ed. M. Smith, and J. Spear, 118–32. London: Routledge.

Caruso, Andrea, and Kevin Russell. 1992. "Journey to Borneo and the Resistance of the Penan." *Earth First!* 12 (7):14.

Castells, Manuel. 1983. *The City and the Grassroots: A Cross-Cultural Theory of Urban Social Movements*. Berkeley: University of California Press.

Centre for Science and Environment. 1985. *The State of India's Environment 1984–85: The Second Citizen's Report*. New Delhi: Centre for Science and Environment.

CESR (Center for Economic and Social Rights). 1994. *Rights Violations in the Ecuadorian Amazon: The Human Consequences of Oil Development*. New York: CESR.

CESTA (Centro Salvadoreno de Tecnologia Apropiada). 1993. *Information Brochure*. San Salvador, El Salvador.

Chaloupka, William. 1987. "John Dewey's Social Aesthetic as a Precedent for Environmental Thought." *Environmental Ethics* 9: 243–60.

Chambers, R. 1970. *Volta Resettlement Experience*. London: Pall-Mall Press.

———. 1983. *Rural Development: Putting the Last First*. London: Longman.

———. 1990. "Microenvironments Unobserved." In *Gatekeeper Series*, no. 22, 6–7. London: International Institute for Environment and Development.

Chambers, R., Arnold Pacey and Lori Ann Thrupp, eds. 1989. *Farmer First*. London: Intermediate Technology Publications.

Charmaz, Kathy. 1983. "The Grounded Theory Method: An Explication and Interpretation." In *Contemporary Field Research*, ed. Robert M. Emerson. Boston: Little Brown.

Chartier, Clem. 1987. "Malaysia: Logging Greatest Threat to Indigenous Peoples of Sarawak." Statment to the UN Working on Indigenous Populations. *IWGIA Newsletter* 51–52 (October/November).

Chatchawan, Tongdeelert, and Larry Lohmann. 1991. "The Traditional Muang Faai Irrigation System of Northern Thailand." *The Ecologist* 21 (2): 101–6.

Chavis, Jr., Benjamin F. 1993. Forward. In *Confronting Environmental Racism: Voices from the Grassroots*, ed. Robert D. Bullard, 3–5. Boston: South End Press.

Cheney, Jim. 1987. "Eco-Feminism and Deep Ecology." *Environmental Ethics* 9: 115-145.

———. 1989. "The Neo-Stoicism of Radical Environmentalism." *Environmental Ethics* 11:293–325.

———. 1989. "Postmodern Environmental Ethics: Ethics as Bioregional Narative." *Environmental Ethics* 11:117–34.

Chong, Dennis. 1991. *Collective Action and the Civil Rights Movement.* Chicago: University of Chicago Press.

Circles, Lone Wolf. 1991. *Full Circle: A Song of Ecology and Earthen Spirituality.* St. Paul, MN: Lllewellyn New Times.

Citizens Clearinghouse for Hazardous Wastes. 1993. *Ten Years of Triumph.* Falls Church, VA: Citizens Clearinghouse for Harardous Wastes.

Clark, John. 1993. "Marx's Inorganic Body." In *Environmental Philosophy*, ed. Michael Zimmerman, et al., 390–405. Englewood Cliffs, NJ: Prentice Hall.

Clarke, Stanley, and Evan Simpson. 1989. *Anti-Theory in Ethics and Moral Conservatism.* Albany, NY: State University of New York Press.

Cliffe, L. 1988. "The Conservation Issue in Zimbabwe." *Review of African Political Economy* 42:48–58.

Coates, D., ed. 1972. *Socialism and the Environment.* Nottingham: Spokesman.

Cohen, D., and E. S. Atieno Odhiambo. 1989. *Siaya: The Historical Anthropology of an African Landscape.* London: John Currey.

Cohen, Gary, and John O'Connor. 1990. *Fighting Toxics: A Manual for Protecting Your Family, Community and Workplace.* Washington, D.C.: Island Press.

Cohen, Michael P. 1988. *The History of the Sierra Club: 1892–1970.* San Francisco: Sierra Club Books.

Colchester, Marcus, and Larry Lohmann. 1990. *The Tropical Forestry Action Plan: What Progress?* Penang/Sturminster Newton: World Rainforest Movement/The Ecologist.

———. 1993. *The Struggle for Land and the Fate of the Forests,* ed. Marcus Colchester and Larry Lohman. Penang, Malaysia: World Rainforest Movement.

Collier, Andrew. 1994. "Value, Rationality and the Environment." *Radical Philosophy* 66: 3–9.

Community Environmental Health Program. 1992. *Environment and Development in the USA: A Grassroots Report for UNCED.* New Market, TN: Highlander Research and Education Center.

Conner, Steve. 1989. *Postmodernist Culture.* London: Basil Blackwell.

Conti, A. 1979. "Capitalist Organization of Production through Non-Capitalist Relations: Women's Role in Pilot Resettlement in Upper Volta." *Review of African Political Economy* 15/16:75–92.

Conway, G. R., and E. B. Barbier. 1990. *After the Green Revolution: Sustainable Agriculture for Development.* London: Earthscan.

Corbin, David Alan. 1981. *Life, Work, and Rebellion in the Coal Fields: The Southern West Virginia Miners, 1880–1922.* Urbana: University of Illinios Press.

Corlett, William. 1989. *Community without Unity: A Politics of Derridian Extravagance.* Durham, NC: Duke University Press.

Coulanges, Fustel de. 1864. *The Ancient City.* Garden City, New Jersey: Doubleday/Anchor.

Council on Economic Priorities. 1988. *Shopping for a Better World.* New York: Council on Economic Priorities.

Curtin, Deane. 1993. *Women's Knowledge as Expert Knowledge: Environment and Community Development in India.* Paper presented at International Development Ethics Association annual meeting, June 24. Tegucigalpa, Honduras.

D'Monte, Darryl. 1993. "A Dam Too Far." *Far Eastern Economic Review* (October 18).

Da Matta, Roberto. 1983. *Carnavals, Bandits Et Heros.* Paris: Editions du Seuil.

Dallmayr, Fred, and Thomas McCarthy. 1977. *Understanding and Social Inquiry.* Notre Dame, IN: University of Notre Dame Press.

Dalton, Russell J. 1993. "The Environmental Movement in Western Europe." In *Environmental Politics in the International Arena,* ed. Sheldon Kamieniecki, 41–68. Albany: State University of New York Press.

———. 1993. "The Environmental Movement in Western Europe." In *Environmental Politics in the International Arena,* ed. Sheldon Kamieniecki, 41-68. Albany: State University of New York Press.

Daly, Herman E. 1980. *Economics, Ecology, Ethics: Essays toward a Steady State Economy.* San Francisco: W. H. Freeman.

Daneel, M. L. 1977. "The Growth and Significance of Shona Independent Churches. In *Christianity South of the Zambezi,* ed. M. F. C. Bourdillon, vol. 2.

Davis, Henry Vance. 1990. "The Environmental Voting Record of the Congressional Black Caucus." In *Race and the Incidence of Environmental Hazards,* ed. Bunyan Bryant and Paul Mohai, 55–63. Boulder, CO: Westview Press.

Davis, Wade. 1993. "Death of a People: Logging in the Penan Homeland." In *State of the Peoples: A Global Human Rights Report on Societies in Danger,* ed. Marc S. Miller. Boston: Beacon.

Day, David. 1987. *The Whale War.* San Francisco: Sierra Club Books.

Deudney, Daniel. 1993. "Global Environmental Rescue and the Emergence of World Domestic Politics." In *The State and Social Power in Global Environmental Politics,* ed. Ronnie D Lipschutz and Ken Conca, 280–305. New York: Cornell University Press.

———. 1994. "Ground Identity: Nature, Place and Space in American and Earth Nationalism." In *Nationalism and Identity,* ed. Fredrich Kratochwil and Yosef Lapid. New York: HarperCollins.

Devall, Bill. 1980. "The Deep Ecology Movement." *Natural Resources Journal* 20:299–322.

———. 1980. "Shifting Paradigms: From the Technocratic to the Person-Planetary." *Environmental Ethics* 3:221–40.

———. 1988. *Simple in Means, Rich in Ends: Practicing Deep Ecology.* Salt Lake City, UT: Gibbs-Smith.

Devall, Bill, ed. 1993. *Clearcut: The Tragedy of Industrial Forestry.* Sierra Club Books: San Francisco.

Devall, Bill, and George Sessions. 1985. *Deep Ecology: Living as if Nature Mattered.* Salt Lake City, UT: Peregrine Smith.

Diani, Mario. 1992. "The Concept of Social Movement." *The Sociological Review* 40 (February):1–24.

Dick, Stephen J. 1982. *The Plurality of Worlds: The Origins of Extraterrestrial Life Debate from Democritus to Kant.* Cambridge, MA: Cambridge University Press.

Dickson, D. 1974. *Alternative Technology and the Politics of Technical Change.* London: Fontana.

DIGNAS (Mujeres por la Dignidad y la Vida). 1993. *Information Brochure.* San Salvador, El Salvador: DIGNAS.

Dinham, B., and C. Hines. 1982. *Agribusiness in Africa.* London: Earth Resources.

Dobson, Andrew. 1989. "Deep Ecology." *Cogito* (Spring): 41–46.

———. 1990. *Green Political Thought.* London: Unwin Hyman.

Dobson, Andrew, ed. 1991. *The Green Reader.* London: Andre Deutsch.

Dolan, Maura. 1992. "Bush Woo's West by Trying to Ease Land Restrictions." *Los Angeles Times* (August 4).

Downs, Anthony. 1972. "Up and Down with Ecology: 'The Issue Attention Cycle.'" *Public Interest* 28:38–50.

Dreyfus, Hubert L., and Paul Rabinow. 1982. *Michel Foucault: Beyond Structuralism and Hermeneutics.* Chicago: University of Chicago Press.

Dryzek, John S. 1987. *Rational Ecology: Environment and Political Economy.* London: Basil Blackwell.

———. 1990. "Green Reason: Communicative Ethics for the Biosphere." *Environmental Ethics* 12:195–210.

La Duke, Winona. 1993. "Hydro Quebec Fears Cree Activists." *Earth First!* 13 (7).

Dunlap, Riley. 1991. "Public Opinion in the 1980's: Clear Consensus: Ambiguous Commitment." *Environment* 33 (8 October).

Dunlap, Riley, George Gallup, Jr., and Alec Gallup. 1993. "Of Global Concern: Results of the Health of the Planet Survey." *Environment* 35 (9) November).

Durning, Alan. 1993. *Guardians of the Land: Indigenous Peoples and the Health of the Earth*. Washington, D.C.: Worldwatch.

———. 1994. "Redesigning the Forest Economy." In *State of the World 1994*, ed. Lester R. Brown. New York: W.W. Norton.

Dykstra, Peter. 1986. "Greenpeace." *Environment* 28 (6) (July/August).

Earth First! 1989. *Introductory Guide to Earth First!* (Pamphlet).

———. 1993. "Malaysian Army Attacks Penan." *Earth First!* 14 (2).

Eckersley, Robyn. 1989. "Divining Evolution: The Ecological Ethics of Murray Bookchin." *Environmental Ethics* 11:99–116.

———. 1992. *Environmentalism and Political Theory: Toward an Ecocentric Approach*. Albany, NY: State University of New York Press.

Eckstein, Harry. 1988. "A Cultural Theory of Social Change." *American Political Science Review* 82 (3 September).

The Ecologist. 1992. "Whose Common Future?" 22 (4).

———. 1993. *Whose Common Future?* London: Earthscan, 1993. Reprint. Philadelphia, PA: New Society.

———. 1994. "Campaigns: Keeping Hydro-Quebec at Bay." 24 (2).

Edelman, Murray. 1977. *Political Language: Words That Succeed and Policies That Fail*. New York: Academic Press.

Edelstein, Michael. 1988. *Contaminated Communities: The Social and Psychological Impacts of Residential Toxic Exposure*. Boulder, CO: Westview Press.

Edwards, Bob, and Sam Marullo. 1995 forthcoming. "Organizational Morality in a Declining Movement: The Demise of Peace Movement Organizations in the End of the Cold War Era." *American Sociological Review*.

ELF (Earth Liberation Front). 1993. "Earth Liberation Front Ignites Britain." *Earth First!* 13 (8): 34.

Elliott, D. 1988. *Nuclear Power and the UK Trade Union and Labour Movements: The Erosion of Opposition?* Milton Keynes: Technology Policy Unit, Open University.

Ellison, Katherine. 1992. "Environment Takes Back Seat to Petro-Politics." *Saint Paul Pioneer Press* (October 11).

Ellul, Jacques. 1964. *The Technological Society*, trans. John Wilkenson. New York: Alfred Knopf.

Emerson, Robert, ed. 1983. *Contemporary Field Research*. Boston: Little Brown.

Enloe, C. K. 1975. *The Politics of Pollution in Comparative Perspective: Ecology and Power in Four Nations*. New York: Longman.

Esquillo, Ruth. 1992. "Community Action on Forest Preservation: The Case of San Fernando, Bukidnon." Thesis presented to the Department of Sociology-Anthropology, Ateneo De Manilla University.

Evans, D. 1992. *A History of Nature Conservation in Britain*. London: Routledge.

Evans, Sara. 1980. *Personal Politics*. New York: Vintage Books.

Eversley, Lord. 1910. *Commons, Forests and Footpaths: The Story of the Battle during the Last Forty-Five Years for Public Rights over the Commons, Forests and Footpaths in England and Wales*. London: Cassell and Company.

Exxon. 1983. *Forecast of Future Conditions: Socioeconomic Assessment, Crandon Project*. Prepared for Exxon Minerals by Research and Planning Consultants, Inc. (October).

———. 1994. Proxy statement.

Faber, Daniel. 1993. *Environment under Fire: Imperialism and the Ecological Crisis in Central America*. New York: Monthly Review Press.

Farlie, Simon. 1994. "Them That Trespass against Us." *The Ecologist* 24 (1): 5–7 .

Faulstich, Paul. 1990. "Hawaiians Fight for the Rainforest." *Earth First!* 10 (5): 1, 7.

Fay, Chip, and Jim Barnes. 1989. "Mt. Apo Natives in Hot Water." *Earth First!* 10 (1): 9–10.

Featherstone, Michael. 1985. "The Fate of Modernity: An Introduction." *Theory, Culture & Society* 2:1–6.

———. 1988. "In the Pursuit of the Postmodern: An Introduction." *Theory, Culture & Society* 5:195–215.

———. 1988. Special issue on postmodernism. *Theory, Culture & Society* 5:2–3.

Fedden, R. 1968. *The Continuing Purpose: A History of the National Trust.* London: Longman.

———. 1974. *The National Trust: Past and Present.* London: Jonathan Cape.

Ferguson, James. 1990. *The Anti-Politics Machine: "Development," Depoliticization and Bureaucratic Power in Lesotho.* Cambridge: Cambridge University Press.

Ferraro, Paul. 1988. "Noted Environmentalist Lectures in Area." *The Forest City News* (June 2).

Ferree, Myra Marx, and Beth Hess. 1985. *Controversy and Coalition: The New Feminist Movement.* Boston: Twayne.

Ferry, Luc, and Renaut Alain. 1990. *Heidegger and Modernity,* trans. Franklin Philip. Chicago: University of Chicago Press.

Figueira, Ricardo Rezende. 1986. *A Justica Do Lobo, Posseiros E Padres Do Araguaia.* Petropolis, Brazil: Editora Vozes.

Fisher, Stephen L., ed. 1993. *Fighting Back in Appalachia: Traditions of Resistance and Change.* Philadelphia: Temple University Press.

Foreman, Dave. 1990. "Becoming the Forest in Defense of Itself." In *Turtle Talk,* ed. Christopher and Judith Plant. Santa Cruz, CA: New Society.

Foreman, Dave, and John Davis, eds. 1992. *The Wildlands Project (Wild Earth, special issue).* Published by the Cenozoic Society.

Foreman, Dave, and Bill Haywood, eds. 1987. *Ecodefense: A Field Guide to Monkeywrenching.* 2d ed. Tucson, AZ: Ned Ludd Books.

Foreman, Dave. 1990. *Confessions of an Eco-Warrior.* New York: Harmony Books.

Foucault, Michael. 1980. *Power/Knowledge: Selected Interviews and Other Writings.* New York: Pantheon Books.

Fox, Christopher. 1988. *The Coming of the Cosmic Christ.* New York: HarperCollins.

Fox, Warwick. 1984. "Deep Ecology: A New Philosophy of Our Time?" *The Ecologist* 14:194–200.

———. 1989. "The Deep Ecology-Ecofeminism Debate and Its Parallels." *Environmental Ethics* 11:5–25.

———. 1990. *Toward a Transpersonal Ecology: Developing New Foundations for Environmentalism.* Boston: Shambala.

Franke, R., and B. Chasin. 1980. *Seeds of Famine*. Montclair: Allenheld.

Freire, Paulo. 1971. *Pedagogy of the Opressed*. UK: Penguin.

Freudenberg, Nicholas. 1984. "Citizen Action for Environmental Health: Report on a Survey of Community Organizations." *American Journal of Public Health* 74 (5): 444–48.

Freudenberg, Nicholas, and Carol Steinsapir. 1992. "Not in Our Backyards: The Grassroots Environmental Movement." In *American Environmentalism: The U.S. Environmental Movement, 1970–1990*, ed. Riley E. Dunlap and Angela G. Mertig, 27–38. Washington, D.C.: Taylor & Francis.

Friedmann, John, and Haripriya Rangan. 1993. *In Defense of Livelihood: Comparative Studies in Environmental Action*, ed. John Friedmann and Haripriya Rangan. West Hartford, CT: Kumarian Press.

Frodeman, Robert. 1992. "Radical Environmentalism and the Political Roots of Postmodernism: Differences That Make a Difference." *Environmental Ethics* 14:307–19.

Fuller, Robert C. 1992. "American Pragmatism Reconsidered: William James' Ecological Ethic." *Environmental Ethics* 14:159–76.

Gadgil, Madhav, and Ramachandra Guha. 1992. *This Fissured Land: An Ecological History of India*. Berkeley: University of California Press.

Gale, Richard. 1986. "Social Movements and the State: The Environmental Movement, Countermovement, and Government Agencies." *Sociological Perspectives* 29:202–40.

Galtung, Johan. 1989. "The Peace Movement: An Exercise in Micro-Macro Linkages." *International Social Science Journal* 40 (117) (August): 377–82.

Gamson, William. 1992. *Talking Politics*. New York: Cambridge University Press.

Gandhi, Mohandas K. 1928. *Young India* (December 20).

Gardiner, Robert W. 1990. "Between Two Worlds: Humans in Nature and Culture." *Environmental Ethics* 12:339–52.

Gaspar, Karl. 1990. *A Peoples' Option to Struggle for Creation*. Quasan City: Claretian.

Gaventa, John. 1980. *Power and Powerlessness: Quiescence and Rebellion in an Appalachian Valley*. Urbana, IL: University of Illinois Press.

Gaventa, John, and Bill Horton. 1984. "Land Ownership and Land Reform in Appalachia." In *Land Reform, American Style*, ed. Charles C. Geisler and Frank J. Popper, 233–44. Totowa, NJ: Rowman & Allanheld.

Gaventa, John, Barbara E. Smith, and Alex Willingham, eds. 1992. *Communities in Economic Crisis: Appalachia and the Deep South*. Philadelphia: Temple University Press.

Gedicks, Al. 1993. *The New Resource Wars: Native and Environmental Struggles against Multinational Corporations*. Boston: South End.

Gellner, Ernst. 1975. *Nations and Nationalism*. Ithaca: Cornell University.

Gerlach, Luther P. 1993. "Negotiating Ecological Interdependence through Social Debate: The Minnesota Drought." In *The State and Social Power in Global Environmental Politics*, ed. Ronnie D. Lipschutz and Ken Conca, 185–220. New York: Cornell University Press.

Gerstin, J. 1990. "No Permanent Condition: The Rainforests of Africa." In *Lessons of the Rainforest*, ed. S. Head and R. Heinzman, 88. San Francisco: Sierra Club.

Gibbs, Lois Marie. 1982. *Love Canal: My Story*. Albany, NY: State University of New York Press.

Gilligan, Carol. 1982. *In a Different Voice*. Cambridge, MA: Harvard University Press.

Glazer, Barney G., and Anselm L Strauss. 1967. *The Discovery of Grounded Theory: Strategies for Qualitative Research*. Chicago: Aldine.

Goldsmith, E. 1978. *The Stable Society*. Wadebridge, Cornwall: The Wadebridge Press.

———. 1988. *The Great U-Turn: De-Industrializing Society*. Bideford, Devon: Green Books.

———. 1992. *The Way: An Ecological World View*. London: Rider.

Goldsmith, E., R. Allen, M. Allaby, J. Davoll, and S. Lawrence. 1972. *A Blueprint for Survival*. Harmondsworth: Penguin.

Goldsmith, Edward, and Nicholas Hildyard. 1984. *The Social and Environmental Effects of Large Dams*. San Francisco: Sierra Club.

Gordon, Greg. 1991. "Huanorani Fight Oil Companies." *Earth First!* 7 (1): 8.

Gottlieb, Robert. 1993. *Forcing the Spring: The Transformation of the American Environmental Movement*. Washington, D.C.: Island Press.

Gough, Robert P. W. 1980. "A Cultural-Historical Assessment of the Wild Rice Resources of the Sokaogon Chippewa. In *An Analysis of the Socio-Economic and Environmental Impacts of Mining and Mineral Resource Development on the Sokaogon Chippewa Community*. Madison, WI: COACT Research, Inc.

Gould, P. C. 1988. *Early Green Politics: Back to Nature, Back to the Land, and Socialism in Great Britain, 1880–1900*. Brighton: Harvester.

Graber, Linda H. 1976. *Wilderness as Sacred Space*. Washington, D.C.: Association of American Geographers.

Grant, W., W. Paterson, and C. Whitston. 1988. *Government and the Chemical Industry: A Comparative Study of Britain and West Germany*. Oxford: Clarendon Press.

Greenberg, D. W. 1985. "Staging Media Events to Achieve Legitimacy: A Case Study of Britain's Friends of the Earth." *Political Communication and Persuasion* 2:347–62.

Greenpeace. 1986. "Fifteen Years at the Front Line." *Greenpeace Examiner* 11 (3) (October/December).

———. 1988. *Overview of Greenpeace Origins* (Pamphlet). Vancouver: Greenpeace.

Gregory, R. 1971. *The Price of Amenity: Five Studies in Conservation and Government*. London: Macmillan.

Greider, William. 1992. *Who Will Tell the People: The Betrayal of American Democracy*. New York: Simon & Schuster.

Griffin, David Ray, ed. 1988. *Spirituality and Society: Postmodern Visions*. Albany: State University of New York Press.

Grove-White, R. 1992. "Grossbritannien." In *Umweltverbande Und EG*, ed. C. Hey, U. Brendle, and C. Weinber, 115–44. Freiburg: EURES—Institut fur regionale Studien.

Grumbine, R. Edward. 1992. *Ghost Bears: Exploring the Biodiversity Crisis*. Washington, D.C.: Island Press.

Guha, Ramachandra. 1989. "Radical American Environmentalism and Wilderness Preservation: A Third World Critique." *Environmental Ethics* 11 (Spring):71–83.

———. 1989. *The Unquiet Woods: Ecological Change and Peasant Resistance in the Himalaya.* Berkeley: University of California Press.

Gundelach, Peter. 1989. "Effectiveness and the Structure of New Social Movements." In *International Social Movement Research,* ed. Bert Klandermas, 427–42. London: JAI Press, Inc.

Gusfield, Joseph. 1981. "Social Movements and Social Change: Perspectives on Linearity and Fluidity." In *Research in Social Movements, Conflicts and Change,* ed. Louis Kriesberg, vol. 4. Connecticut: JAI Press.

Gutpa, et al., Ashok. 1993. "Letter from NRDC staff." *The Amicus Journal* 14 (4).

Guyer, J., ed. 1987. *Feeding African Cities.* Manchester: Manchester University Press.

Habermas, Jurgen. 1971. *Knowledge and Human Interest.* Boston: Beacon.

———. 1979. *Communication and the Evolution of Society.* Boston: Beacon.

———. 1981. "Modernity Versus Postmodernity." *New German Critique* 22:3–14.

———. 1983. *Legitimation Crisis.* Boston: Beacon.

———. 1984. *The Theory of Communicative Action, Vol. 1: Reason and the Rationalization of Society.* Boston: Beacon.

———. 1987. *The Philosophical Discourse of Modernity: Twelve Lectures,* trans. Frederick Lawrence. Cambridge, MA: MIT Press.

———. 1987. *The Theory of Communicative Action, Vol. 2: Lifeworld and System—A Critique of Functionalist Reason.* Boston: Beacon.

———. 1988. *On the Logic of the Social Sciences,* trans. Shierry Nicholsen and Jerry Stark. Cambridge, MA: MIT Press.

———. 1989. *The New Conservatism: Cultural Criticism and the Historian's Debate.* Cambridge, MA: MIT Press.

———. 1989. *The Structural Transformation of the Public Sphere.* Cambridge, MA: MIT Press.

———. 1990. *Philosophical-Political Profiles,* trans. Frederick Lawrence. Cambridge, MA: MIT Press.

———. 1991. *Moral Consciousness and Communicative Action,* trans. Christian Lenhardt. Cambridge, MA: MIT Press.

———. 1992. *Autonomy and Solidarity: Interviews with Jurgen Habermas*. London: Verso.

———. 1992. *Postmetaphysical Thinking: Philosophical Essays*, trans. Mark Hohengarten. Cambridge, MA: MIT Press.

Hadjor, K. B. 1990. *Africa in an Era of Crisis*. Trenton: African World Press.

Hadsell, Heidi, and Robert Evans. 1991. "Is President Collar Green?" *Christian Century* (November 6).

Hailsham, Lord. 1976. "Elective Dictatorship." *The Listener* (October 21).

Haines, Herbert H. 1984. "Black Radicalization and the Funding of Civil Rights, 1957–1970." *Social Problems* 32 (1): 31–43.

Hall, I. M. 1976. *Community Action versus Pollution: A Study of a Residents' Group in a Welsh Urban Area*. Cardiff: University of Wales Press.

Hallman, Max O. 1991. "Nietzsche's Environmental Ethics." *Environmental Ethics* 13:99–125.

Hanbury-Tension, Robin. 1990. "No Surrender in Sarawak." *New Scientist* (December 1).

Haraway, Donna. 1989. *Primate Visions: Gender, Race and Nature in the World of Modern Science*. London: Routledge.

Hardiman, David. 1992. *Peasant Resistance in India: 1858–1914*. Oxford: Oxford University Press.

Hardy, D. 1979. *Alternative Communities in Nineteenth Century England*. London: Longman.

Harlow, Elizabeth M. 1992. "The Human Face of Nature: Environmental Values and the Limits of Anthropocentrism." *Environmental Ethics* 14:27–42.

Harrison, P. 1987. *The Greening of Africa*. London: Penguin.

Harrison, Robert Pogue. 1992. *Forests: The Shadow of Civilization*. Chicago: University of Chicago Press.

Hassan, Ihab. 1985. "The Culture of Postmodernism. *Theory, Culture & Society* 2:119–31.

Haswell, Margaret, and Colin Clark. 1971. *The Economics of Subsistence Cultivation*. 1964. Reprint. MacMillian: New York.

Hay, P.R. 1992. "Vandals at the Gate: The Tasmanian Greens and the Perils of Sharing Power." In *Green Politics Two*, ed. Wolfgang Rüdig, 86–110. Endinburgh: Edinburgh University Press.

Hay, P. R., and M. G. Haward. 1988. "Comparative Green Politics: Beyond the European Context?" *Political Studies* 36:433–48.

Hayter, Teresa, and Catharine Watson. 1985. *Aid: Rhetoric and Reality*. London: Pluto Press.

Hecht, Susanna B., and Alexander Cockburn. 1989. *Fate of the Forest: Developers, Destroyers and Defenders of the Amazon*. London: Verso.

Hedge, Pandurang. 1989. "The Appiko Movement: Forest Conversation in Southern India." *Cultural Survival Quarterly* 13 (2):29–30.

Helvarg, David. 1994. *The War Against the Greens: the "Wise-Use" Movement, the New Right, and Anti-Environmental Violence*. San Francisco: Sierra Club.

Hirsch, Philip, and Larry Lohmann. 1989. "The Contemporary Politics of Environment in Thailand." *Asian Survey* 29 (4): 439–51.

Hirschman, Albert O. 1977. *The Passions and the Interests: Political Arguments for Capitalism before Its Triumph*. Princeton: Princeton University Press.

Hofrichter, R., ed. 1993. *Toxic Struggles: The Theory and Practice of Environmental Justice*. Philadelphia: New Society Publishers.

Hohendahl, Peter. 1986. "Habermas' Philosophical Discourse of Modernity." *Telos* 69:51–64.

Homer-Dixon, Thomas. 1991. "On the Threshold: Environmental Changes as Causes of Acute Conflict." *International Security* 16 (2):76–116.

Homer-Dixon, Thomas, Jeffrey H. Boutwell, and George W. Rathjens. 1993. "Environmental Change and Violent Conflict." *Scientific American* 268 (2):38–45.

Honneth, Axel. 1985. "An Aversion against the Universal: A Commentary on Lyotard's Postmodern Condition." *Theory, Culture & Society* 2:147–56.

Honneth, Axel, Thomas McCarthy, Claus Offe, and Albrecht Wellmer. 1992. *Cultural-Political Interventions in the Unfinished Project of Enlightenment*, trans. Barbara Fultner. Cambridge, MA: MIT Press.

Horowitz, M., and F. Jowkar. 1992. *Pastoral Women and Change in Africa, the Middle East and Central Asia.* Binghamton: Institute for Development Anthropology.

Hoskins, W. G. 1979. *The Making of the English Landscape.* Harmondsworth: Penguin.

Howard, E. 1965. *Garden Cities of To-Morrow.* London: Faber & Faber.

Hulbert, A. 1993. "Quo Vadis Europa?" *Journal of the South-North Network* 13/14 (5): 13–14. *Cultures and Development.*

Human Rights Commission of El Salvador. 1993. "And Speaking of Rights, Let's Talk about Women's Rights." *La Voz* 12 (November-December): 6–7.

Hunter, James. 1976. *The Making of a Crofting Community.* Edinburgh: John Donald.

Hunter, James Davison. 1991. *Culture Wars: The Struggle to Define America.* New York: Basic Books.

Hunter, Robert. 1979. *Warriors of the Rainbow: A Chronicle of the Greenpeace Movement.* New York: Holt, Rhinehart, and Winston.

Hurst, Philip. 1990. *Rainforest Politics: Ecological Destruction in South-East Asia.* London & New Jersey: Zed.

Huxley, T. 1974. "Wilderness." In *Conservation in Practice,* ed. A. Warren and F. B. Goldsmith, 361–74. London: John Wiley & Sons.

Ingemar, Hedstrom. 1990. "Latin America and the Need for a Life Liberating Theology." In *Liberating Life: Contemporary Approaches to Ecology and Theology,* ed. C. Birch, W. Eakin, and J. McDaniel. Maryknoll, NY: Orbis.

Inglehart, Ronald E. 1981. "Postmaterialism in an Environment of Insecurity." *American Political Science Review* 75 (December): 880–900.

Ingram, David. 1986. "Foucault and the Frankfurt School: A Discourse on Nietzsche, Power, and Knowledge." *Praxis International* 6:311–27.

International Treaty Council. 1977. "International NGO Conference on Discrimination against Indigenous Populations in the Americas." *Treaty Council News* 1 (7).

Jaakko Poyry Oy. 1993. *Thai Forestry Sector Master Plan, Final Draft.* 6 Vols. Helsinki: FINNIDA.

Jagoff, Jake. 1992. "Earth First! Takes on Tropical Imports." *Earth First!* 13 (1):1, 6.

———. 1992. "U.S. Tropical Rainforest Activist Responds." *Earth First!* 13 (1):18.

Jamison, A., R. Eyerman, and J. Cramer. 1990. *The Making of the New Environmental Consciousness*. Edinburgh: Edinburgh University Press.

Jancar-Webster, Barbara, ed. 1993. *Environmental Action in Eastern Europe*. New York: M. E. Sharpe.

Jarvie, G. 1991. *Highland Games: the Making of a Myth*. Edinburg: Edinburg Univ. Press.

Jodha, N. 1991. "Rural Common Property Resources: A Growing Crisis." In *Gatekeeper Series*, no. 24. London: International Institute for Environment and Development.

Jones, B. 1991. "A Fragile Land." In *Restoring the Land: Environment and Change in Post-Apartheid South Africa*, ed. Mamphela Ramphele, 187–200. London: Panos Institute.

Jordan, A. 1993. "Integrated Pollution Control and the Evolving Style and Structure of Environmental Regulation in the UK." *Environmental Politics* 2:405–27.

Joseph, Paul. 1993. *Peace Politics*. Philadelphia: Temple University Press.

Juergensmeyer, Mark. 1993. *The New Cold War? Religious Nationalism Confronts the Secular State*. Berkeley: University of California Press.

Juma, C. 1989. *Biological Diversity and Innovation: Conserving and Utilizing Genetic Recources in Kenya*. Nairobi: African Centre for Technology Studies.

———. 1989. *The Gene Hunters*. London/Princeton: Zed Press/Princeton University Press.

Juma, C., and J. B. Ojwang, eds. 1989. *Innovation and Sovereignty: The Patent Debate in African Development*. Nairobi: African Centre for Technology Studies.

Jung, Hwa Yol. 1983. "Marxism, Ecology, and Technology." *Environmental Ethics* 5:169–71.

Kalyalya, D., K. Mhlanga, J. Semboja, and A. Seidman. 1988. *Aid and Development in Southern Africa: A Participatory Learning Process*. Trenton: Africa World Press.

Kamieniecki, Sheldon. 1993. "Emerging Forces in Global Environmental Politics." In *Environmental Politics in the International Arena*, 1–18. Albany: State University of New York Press.

Kaplan, E. Ann. 1988. *Postmodernism and Its Discontents*. London: Verso.

Kaplan, Robert D. 1994. "The Coming Anarchy: How Scarcity, Crime, Overpopulation, Tribalism, and Disease Are Rapidly Destroying the Social Fabric of Our Planet." *Atlantic Monthly*, 44–76.

Kellner, Douglas. 1988. "Postmodernism as Social Theory: Some Challenges and Problems." *Theory, Culture & Society* 5:239–69.

Kemp, P., and D. Wall. 1990. *A Green Manifesto for the 1990s*. London: Penguin.

Kennet, W. 1972. *Preservation*. London: Temple Smith.

Kerr, Mary, and Charles Lee. 1993. "From Conquistadors to Coalitions." *Southern Exposure: A Journal of Politics and Culture* 21 (4): 8–19.

Kheel, Marti. 1985. "The Liberation of Nature: A Circular Affair." *Environmental Ethics* 7:135–49.

Kiernan, V. G. 1972. "Patterns of Protest in English History." In *Direct Action and Democratic Politics*, ed. R. Benewick and T. Smieth, 25–48. London: George Allen & Unwin.

Kimber, R., and J. J. Richardson, eds. 1974. *Campaigning for the Environment*. London: Routledge and Keegan Paul.

Kimerling, Judith. 1991. *Amazon Crude*. New York: Natural Resources Defense Council.

Kirkwood, G. & C. 1989. *Living Adult Education: Freire in Scotland*. UK: Open University Press.

Kloos, H. 1982. "Development, Drought, and Famine in the Awash Valley of Ethiopia." *African Studies Review* 25 (4): 21–48.

Kocherry, Thomas, and Thankappan Achary. 1989. "Fishing for Resources: Indian Fisheries in Danger." *Cultural Survival Quarterly* 13 (2):31–33.

Kohn, Hans. 1957. *American Nationalism*. New York: Macmillian.

Kolenka, Tomas. 1993. "Resistance in Slovakia: Earth First! Defends Danube." *Earth First!* 8 (5): 1, 13.

Kovel, Joel. 1993. "The Marriage of Radical Ecologies." In *Environmental Philosophy*, ed. Michael Zimmerman, et al., 406–17. Englewood Cliffs, NJ: Prentice Hall.

Krasner, Stephen. 1993. "Westphalia." In *Ideas and Foreign Policy*, ed. Judith Goldstein and Robert O. Keohane. Ithaca: Cornell University Press.

Krause, Celene. 1993. "Women and Toxic Waste Protests: Race, Class and Gender as Resources of Resistance." *Qualitative Sociology* 16 (3): 247–62.

Kuletz, Valerie. 1992. "Eco-Feminist Philosophy. Interview with Barbara Holland-Cunz." *Capitalism Nature Socialism* 3:63–78.

Lasswell, Harold, 1958. *Politics: Who Gets What, When, How.* New York: Meridian Books.

Lee, Donald. 1980. "On the Marxian View of the Relationship between Man and Nature." *Environmental Ethics* 2:3–46.

———. 1982. "Toward a Marxian Ecological Ethics: A Response to Two Critics." *Environmental Ethics* 4:339–42.

Leiss, William. 1972. *The Domination of Nature.* New York: George Braziller.

———. 1976. *The Limits to Satisfaction: An Essay on the Problem of Needs and Commodities.* Toronto: University of Toronto Press.

Lemus, Oscar. 1993. Interview by author. Staff of COPAZ, Comision Para La Consolidacion Para La Paz; San Salvador, El Salvador, June 24.

Lenk, Hans, and Matthias Maring. 1992. "Ecology and Ethics: Notes about Technology and Economic Consequences." *Research in Philosophy and Technology* 12:157–76.

Leopold, Aldo. 1948. *A Sand County Almanac.* Oxford: Oxford University Press.

Levine, Adeline. 1982. *Love Canal: Science, Politics and People.* Boston, MA: Lexington Books.

Lewis, Helen Matthews, Linda Johnson, and Donald Askins, eds. 1978. *Colonialism in Modern America: The Appalachian Case.* Boone, NC: The Appalachian Consortium Press.

Lewis, Martin W. 1992. *Green Delusions: An Environmentalist Critique of Radical Environmentalism.* Durham, NC: Duke University Press.

Light, Andrew F. 1992. "The Role of Technology in Environmental Questions: Martin Buber and Deep Ecology as Answers to Technological Consciousness." *Research in Philosophy and Technology* 12:83–104.

Lipka, Mitch. 1994. "Rally at Texaco Ends in 9 Arrests." *Reporter-Dispatch* (April 5).

Lipschutz, Ronnie D., and Ken Conca. 1993. *The State and Social Power in Global Environmental Politics*, eds. Lipschutz, and Conca. New York: Cornell University Press.

Lipschutz, Ronnie D., and Judith Mayer. 1993. "Not Seeing the Forests for the Trees: Rights, Rules, and the Renegotiation of Resource Management Regimes." In *The State and Social Power in Global Environmental Politics*, ed. Ronnie D. Lipschutz and Ken Conca, 246–73. New York: Cornell University Press.

List, Peter. 1993. *Radical Environmentalism: Philosophy and Tactics*. Belmont, CA: Wadsworth.

Litfin, Karen. 1993. "Ecoregimes: Playing Tug of War with the Nation-State." In *The State and Social Power in Global Environmental Movements*, eds. Ronnie D. Lipschutz and Ken Conca, 94–117. New York: Cornell University Press.

Livingstone, I. 1988. *Poverty in Africa*. New York: Oxford University Press.

Livingstone, Louise Hamilton. 1974. "Sheiling Transhumance and Changes in Land Use in the Scottish Highlands." University of Edinburgh: Faculty of Science. M. Phill thesis (unpublished).

Locke, John. 1693. *A Letter Concerning Toleration*. Indianapolis: Bobbs-Merrill.

Lockhead, James. 1992. "The Sarawak Campaign: Perspectives for Discussion." *Earth First!* 13 (1):18.

Lohmann, Larry. n.d. "No Rules of Engagement: Interest Groups, Centralization and the Creative Politics of 'Environment' in Thailand." In *Counting the Costs: Environmental Growth and Economic Change in Thailand*, ed. Jonathan Rigg. Singapore: Institute of Southeast Asian Studies.

———. 1991. "Peasants, Plantations and Pulp: The Politics of Eucalyptus in Thailand." *Bulletin of Concerned Asian Scholars* 23 (4):3–17.

———. 1991. "Who Defends Biological Diversity? Conservation Strategies and the Case of Thailand." In *Biodiversity: Social and Ecological Perspectives*, ed. Vandana Shiva. Penang, London, and New Jersey: World Rainforest Movement and Zed Books.

————. 1993. "Green Orientalism." *The Ecologist* 23 (6): 202–4.

————. 1993. "Land, Power and Forest Colonization in Thailand." In *The Struggle for Land and the Fate of the Forests*, ed. Marcus Colchester and Larry Lohmann. London and New Jersey: Zed Books.

————. 1993. "Resisting Green Globalism." In *Global Ecology: A New Arena of Political Conflict*, ed. Wolfgang Sachs. London and New Jersey: Zed Books.

————. 1993. "No Rules of Engagement: Interest Groups, Centralization and the Creative Politics of 'Environment' in Thailand." Paper presented to the Fifth Annual Thai Studies Conference, July.

Lopez, Maria Mirtala. 1994. Class presentation at University of San Francisco, March 3. San Francisco, California.

Lovejoy, Arthur. 1936. *The Great Chain of Being*. Cambridge, MA: Harvard University Press.

Lovelock, James. 1979. *Gaia: A New Look at Life on Earth*. New York: Oxford University Press.

————. 1988. *The Ages of Gaia: A Biography of Our Living Planet*. New York: Norton.

————. 1991. *Healing Gaia: Practical Medicine for Healing the Planet*. New York: Harmony.

Lovelock, James E. 1979. *Gaia: A New Look at Life on Earth*. Oxford: Oxford University Press.

Lowe, P. 1977. "Amenity and Equity: A Review of Local Environmental Pressure Groups in Britain." *Environment and Planning* 9:39–58.

Lowe, P., and J. Goyder. 1983. *Environmental Groups in Politics*. London: George Allen & Unwin.

Lowe, P. D. 1983. "Values and Institutions in the History of British Nature Conservation." In *Conservation in Perspective*, ed. A. Warren, and F. B. Goldsmith, 329–52. Chichester: John Wiley & Sons.

Luangaramsri, Pinkaew, and Noel Rajesh, eds. 1992. *The Future of People and Forests in Thailand after the Logging Ban*. Bangkok: Project for Ecological Recovery.

Luhmann, Niklas. 1989. *Ecological Communication*, trans. John Bednarz, Jr. Chicago: University of Chicago Press.

Luhrmann, T. M. 1993. "The Resurgence of Romanticism: Contemporary Neopaganism, Feminist Spirituality and the Divinity of Nature." In

Environmentalism: The View from Anthropology, ed. K. Milton, 219–32. London: Routledge.

Lukacs, Georg. 1981. *The Destruction of Reason.* Atlantic Highlands, NJ: Humanities Press.

Lyotard, Jean-Francois. 1984. *The Postmodern Condition: A Report on Knowledge.* Minneapolis: University of Minnesota Press.

———. 1988. *Peregrinations: Law, Form, Event.* New York: Columbia University Press.

MacIntyre, Alasdair. 1988. *Whose Justice? Which Rationality?* London: Duckworth.

MacLeod, Norman. 1994. "What Profit for Harris in the Wake of the Lingerabay Superquarry?" *West Highland Free Press* (June 24).

Maguire, Daniel C. 1978. *The Moral Choice.* Garden City, NJ: Doubleday.

Mainwaring, Scott. 1986. *The Catholic Church and Politics in Brazil, 1916–1985.* Stanford: Stanford University Press.

Maller, Peter. 1994. "Mole Lake Expect Allies in Mine Fight." *Milwaukee Sentinel* (June 16).

Manes, Christopher. 1990. *Green Rage: Radical Environmentalism and the Unmaking of Civilization.* Boston: Little, Brown, and Company.

———. 1992. "Nature and Silence." *Environmental Ethics* 14: 339–50.

Marglin, F., and S. Marglin, eds. 1990. *Dominating Knowledge.* Oxford: Clarendon Press.

Marietta, Donald E. 1984. "Environmentalism, Feminism, and the Future of American Society." *The Humanist* 44:15–25.

Marshall, P. 1992. *Nature's Web: An Exploration of Ecological Thinking.* London: Simon and Schuster.

Marty, Martin E., and E. Scott Appleby, eds. 1991. *Fundamentalisms Observed.* Chicago: University of Chicago Press.

Marx, Karl. 1978. "Contribution to the Critique of Hegel's *Philosophy of Right*: Introduction." In *The Marx-Engels Reader,* ed. Robert Tucker. New York: W. W. Norton.

Massey, Douglas, and Nancy A. Denton. 1993. *American Apartheid: Segreation and the Making of the Underclass.* Cambridge, MA: Harvard University Press.

Masty, Sr., David. 1991. "Traditional Use of Fish and Other Resources of the Great Whale River Region." *Northeast Indian Quarterly* 8 (4).

Maull, Samuel. 1993. "Ecuadorian Tribes Sue Texaco, Inc." *News from Indian Country* 7 (22).

Mbilinyi, M. 1990. "'Structural Adjustment,' Agri-Business, and Rural Women in Tanzania." In *The Food Question: Profits Versus People?*, ed. H. Bernstein, B. Crow, M. Mackintosh, C. Martin, 111–24. London: Earthscan.

McAdam, Doug. 1982. *Political Process and the Development of Black Insurgency, 1890–1970*. Chicago: University of Chicago Press.

McAdam, Doug, John McCarthy, and Mayer Zald. 1988. "Social Movements." In *Handbook of Sociology*, ed. Niel J. Smelser, 695–738. Newbury Park, CA: Sage.

McBride, Stewart. 1983. "The Real Monkeywrench Gang." *Outside* 7 (8):34–38, 69–73.

McClosky, Michael. 1992. "Twenty Years of Change in the Environmental Movement: An Insider's View." In *American Environmentalism: The U.S. Environmental Movement, 1970–1990*, ed. Riley E. Dunlap and Angela G. Mertig, 77–88. Washington, D.C.: Taylor & Francis.

McCormick, J. 1991. *British Politics and the Environment*. London: Earthscan.

McCulloch, G. 1987. "Eco-Feminism: An Understanding of the Relationship between Feminism and Green Thought." Paper presented to the annual conference of the UK Political Studies Association, Aberdeen, April.

McCullum, H. 1991. "From Destruction to Recovery." In *Restoring the Land: Environment and Change in Post-Apartheid South Africa*, ed. Mamphela Ramphele, 168–71. London: Panos Institute.

McCutcheon, Sean. 1991. *Electric Rivers: The Story of the James Bay Project*. Montreal: Black Rose.

McDaniel, Jay B. 1994. "Emerging Options in Ecological Christianity." In *Ecological Prospects: Scientific, Religious, and Aesthetic Perspectives*, ed. Christopher Key Chapple. New York: State University of New York Press.

McDonald, Mark D. 1993. "Dams, Displacement, and Development." In *In Defense of Livelihood: Comparative Studies in Environmental*

Action, ed. John Friedmann and Haripriya Rangan. West Hartford, CT: Kumarian Press.

McIntosh, Alstair. 1992. "A Collector's Item or Community Ownership The Isle of Eigg Debate." *Edinburgh Review* 88 (Summer): 158–62.

McIntosh, Alastair. 1994. "Journey to the Hebrides." *Scottish Affairs* 6 (Winter): 52–67.

McIntosh, Alastair, Andy Wightman, and Daniel Morgan. 1994. "Reclaiming the Scottish Highlands: Clearance, Conflict, and Crofting." *The Ecologist* 24 (2):64–70.

McKean, Margaret A. 1981. *Environmental Protest and Citizen Politics in Japan*. Berkeley: University of California Press.

McKibben, Bill. 1989. *The End of Nature*. New York: Random House.

McLaughlin, Andrew. 1993. *Regarding Nature: Industrialism and Deep Ecology*. Albany: State University of New York Press.

McRae, Peggy Sue. 1994. "The Tree Huggers." *Earth First!* 14 (3):25.

McWhorter, Ladelle. 1992. *Heidegger and the Earth*. Kirksville, MO: Thomas Jefferson University Press.

Meadows, Donella H., Dennis C. Meadows, Jorgen Randers, and William Behrens III. 1972. *Limits to Growth*. New York: Universe.

Meese, Mike. 1992. "Earth First! Occupies Liverpool Docks and Halts Unloading of Sarawak Timber Ship." *Earth First!* 12 (5).

Mellor, M. 1992. *Breaking the Boundaries: Towards a Feminist Green Socialism*. London: Virago.

———. 1992. "Green Politics: Ecofeminist, Ecofeminine or Ecomasculine?" *Environmental Politics* 1:229–51.

Melone, Michelle A. 1993. "The Struggle of the Seringueiros: Environmental Action in the Amazon." In *In Defense of Livelihood*, 106–26. West Hartford, CT: Kumarian.

Melucci, Alberto. 1980. "New Social Movements: A Theoretical Approach." *Social Science Information* 19:97–136.

———. 1981. "Ten Hypotheses for the Analysis of New Social Movements." In *Contemporary Italian Sociology*, ed. D. Pinto. Cambridge: Cambridge University Press.

———. 1989. *Nomads of the Present*. Philadelphia: Temple University Press.

Merchant, Carolyn. 1982. *The Death of Nature: Women, Ecology and the Scientific Revolution.* London: Wildwood House.

———. 1989. *Ecological Revolutions: Nature, Gender, and Science in New England.* Chapel Hill: University of North Carolina Press.

Merleau-Ponty, Maurice. 1962. *Phenomenology of Perception.* London: Routledge and Kegan Paul.

———. 1964. *The Primacy of Perception.* Evanston, IL: Northwestern University Press.

———. 1964. *Sense and Non-Sense.* Evanston, IL: Northwestern University Press.

MIDAS Agronomics Co., Ltd., and Centre de Cooperation Internationale en Recherche Agronomique pour le Developpement. 1993. *Conservation Forest Area Protection, Management and Development Project. Pre-Investment Study Draft Final Report.* Washington: Global Environment Facility.

Milbrath, Lester W. 1984. *Environmentalists: Vanguard for a New Society.* Albany: State University of New York Press.

———. 1989. *Envisioning a Sustainable Society: Learning Our Way Out.* Albany: State University of New York Press.

Miss Ann Thropy (pseud. for Christopher Manes). 1987. "Population and Aids." *Earth First!* 32 (May 1).

Mitchell, Robert Cameron. 1989. "From Conservation to Environmental Movement: The Development of the Modern Environmental Lobbies." In *Government and Environmental Politics: Essays on Historical Developments since World War Two,* ed. M. J. Lacey, 81–113. Washington, D.C.: Wilson Center Press.

Mohai, Paul, and Bunyan Bryant. 1992. "Environmental Racism: Reviewing the Evidence." In *Race and the Incidence of Environmental Hazards: A Time for Discourse,* ed. Bunyan Bryant and Paul Mohai, 163–76. Boulder, CO: Westview Press.

Mokhiber, Russell. 1993. "The 1993 Corporate Hall of Shame." *Multinational Monitor* 14 (December):12.

Molutsi, P. 1988. "Environment and Peasant Consciousness in Botswana." *Review of African Political Economy* 42:40–47.

Monbiot, George. 1993. *Brazil: Land Ownership and the Flight to Amazonia,* ed. Marcus Colchester, and Larry Lohmann. Penang, Malaysia: World Rainforest Movement.

Montesquieu. 1989. *The Spirit of the Laws*. Cambridge, MA: Cambridge University Press.

Moris, J. 1991. *Extension Alternatives for Africa*. Agricultural Administration Unit Occasional Paper No. 7. Overseas Development Institute.

Morris, Aldon D. 1992. "Political Consciousness and Collective Action." In *Frontiers in Social Movement Theory*, ed. Aldon D. Morris and Carol McClurg Mueller, 351–75. New Haven: Yale University Press.

Morris, Aldon D., and Carol M. Mueller. 1992. *Frontiers in Social Movement Theory*, ed. Aldon D. Morris and Carol M. Mueller. New Haven: Yale University Press.

Morris, W. 1891. *News from Nowhere*. London: Reeves and Turner.

Morrison, Denton, and Riley Dunlap. 1986. "How and Why Environmental Consciousness Has Trickled Down." In *Distributional Conflict in Environmental Resource Policy*, ed. Alan Schnaiberg, N. Watts, and K. Zimmerman, 187–220. New York: St. Martin's Press.

Morse, Bradford, and Thomas R. Berger. 1992. *Sardar Sarovar: Report of the Independent Review*. Ottawa, Ontario: Resources Future International, Inc.

Morton, T. 1991. *Going Home: The Runrig Story*. Edinburgh: Mainstream.

Moyo, S., P. O'Keefe, and M. Sill. 1993. *The Southern African Environment: Profiles of the SADC Countries*. London: Earthscan, pp. 158–94.

Muir, John. 1911. *My First Summer in the Sierra*. Boston: Houghton Mifflin.

Mujeres '94. 1993. *Plataforma De Las Mujeres Salvadorenas* (August 31). San Salvador.

Murphy, Patrick D. 1988. "Sex-Typing the Planet: Gaia Imagery and the Problem of Subverting Patriarchy." *Environmental Ethics* 10:155–68.

Murton, Brian. 1980. "South Asia." In *World Systems of Traditional Resource Management*, ed. Gary A. Klee. New York: Halsted Press Books.

Myers, Norman. 1988. "Threatened Biotas: 'Hotspots' in Tropical Forests." *The Environmentalist* 8 (3).

Myrdal, Gunnar. 1968. *Asian Drama: An Inquiry into the Poverty of Nations*. 1898, New York: Pantheon.

Nachowitz, Todd. 1989. "Opposition to Tehri Dam Grows." *Earth First!* 9 (8):11.

NACLA (North American Congress on Latin America). 1975. "Ecuador: Oil Up for Grabs." *NACLA's Latin America and Empire Report* 9 (8).

Nader, Ralph. 1982. "Approaching Strategy for Confronting the Corporate Threat." *Akwesasne Notes* 14 (6).

Naess, Arne. 1974. *Gandhi and Group Conflict.* Oslo: Universitetsforlaget.

———. 1984. "Intuition, Intrinsic Value, and Deep Ecology." *The Ecologist* 14:201–4.

———. 1989. *Ecology, Community, and Lifestyle: Outline of an Ecosophy,* trans. David Rothenberg. Cambridge: Cambridge University Press.

———. 1993. "The Deep Ecological Movement: Some Philosophical Aspects." In *Environmental Philosophy,* ed. Michael Zimmerman, et al., 193–212. Englewood Cliffs, NJ: Prentice Hall.

———. 1993. "Simple in Means, Rich in Ends." In *Environmental Philosophy,* ed. Michael Zimmerman, et al., 182–92. Englewood Cliffs, NJ: Prentice Hall.

Naess, Arne, and David Rothenberg. 1993. "Hvem Er Hvalsakens Tapere?" [Who loses in the whaling debate?]. Center for Environment and Development.

Nagel, Thomas. 1986. *View from Nowhere.* New York: Oxford University Press.

Nash, Roderick Frazier. 1989. *The Rights of Nature: A History of Environmental Ethics.* Madison, WI: University of Wisconsin Press.

National Trust. 1992. *Accounts 1992.* London: The National Trust for Places of Historic Interest or Natural Beauty.

Navarro, Ricardo A. 1990. "Urge Desarrollar Una Teologia Ecologica and La Iglesia Se Vuelve Ecologista." In *El Pensamiento Ecologista,* ed. R. Navarro, G. Pons, and G. Amaya. San Salvador: El Centro Salvadoreno de Tecnologia Apropiada.

Nehru, Jawaharlal. 1956. *Address at Opening of 1956 Session of the Economic Commission for Asia and the Far East, Bangalore* (Quoted in Myrdal, 1968, p. 716).

Newby, H. 1980. *Green and Pleasant Land? Social Change in Rural England.* Harmondsworth: Penguin.

Nielsen, Kai. 1991. *After the Demise of the Tradition: Rorty, Critical Theory, and the Fate of Philosophy*. Boulder, CO: Westview.

Norris, Christopher. 1990. *What's wrong With Postmodernism?* Baltimore, MD: Johns Hopkins University Press.

Norway Times. 1994. "Norway Calls on the US to Take Action against Whaling Activist Group." *Norway Times* 104 (6):1–2.

Novotny, Patrick. 1994. "Race, Ethnicity, Class, and the Politics of the Environmental Justice Movement." Paper presented at the annual meeting of the Western Political Science Association, Albuquerque, New Mexico, March 10–12.

O'Brien, Conor Cruise. 1989. *God Land: Reflections on Religion and Nationalism*. Cambridge, MA: Harvard University Press.

O'Brien, Robert M., Michael Clarke, and Sheldon Kamieniecki. 1984. "Open and Closed Systems of Decision Making: The Case of Toxic Waste Management." *Public Administration Review* 44 (July/August): 334–40.

O'Keefe, P. 1988. "Toxic Terrorism." *Review of African Political Economy* 42: 84–90.

O'Riordan, Timothy. 1977. Environmental Ideologies. *Environment and Planning* 3:3–14.

———. 1979. "Public Interest Environmental Groups in the United States and Britain." *Journal of American Studies* 13: 409–38.

———. 1981. *Environmentalism*. 2nd ed. London: Pion.

Oates, David. 1989. *Earth Rising*. Corvallis: Oregan State University Press.

Oelschlaeger, Max. 1991. *The Idea of Wilderness: From Prehistory to the Age of Ecology*. New Haven: Yale University Press.

Offe, Claus. 1985. "New Social Movements: Challenging the Boundries of Institutional Politics." *Social Research* 52: 817–68.

Ole Parkipuny, M. S. 1988. "The Ngorongoro Crater Issue: The Point of View of the Indigenous Maasai Community of Ngorongoro." In *Paper for the International Congress on Nature Management and Sustainable Development*, December 6–9. University of Groningen, the Netherlands.

———. 1990–1991. "So That Serengeti Shall Not Die." Unpublished manuscript.

Omvedt, Gail. 1993. *Reinventing Revolution: New Social Movements and the Socialist Tradition in India.* Armonk, NY: M.E. Sharpe Inc.

Ophuls, William. 1976. *Ecology and the Politics of Scarcity.* San Francisco: W. H. Freeman.

Oxford Earth First! 1993. "Twyford Down but Not Out." *Earth First!* 13 (6):1, 13.

Pacey, A. 1983. *The Culture of Technology.* Cambridge: MIT Press.

Paden, Roger. 1992. "Nature and Morality." *Environmental Ethics* 14: 239–51.

Paehlke, Robert C. 1989. *Environmentalism and the Future of Progressive Politics.* New Haven: Yale University Press.

Pandam, Rafael. 1994. "Statement of the Confederation of Indigenous Nationalities of Ecuador." In *Rights Violations in the Ecuadorian Amazon.* New York: CESR.

Parkin, S. 1991. *Green Futures.* London: Fount.

Parlow, Anita. 1991. "Worlds in Collision." *The Amicus Journal* 13 (Spring).

Pearce, Fred. 1991. *Green Warriors: The People and Politics behind the Environmental Revolution.* London: Bodley Head.

Pele Defense Fund. 1994. "Pele Victory." *Earth First!* 14 (5):13.

Peluso, Nancy Lee. 1992. *Rich Forests, Poor People: Resource Control and Resistance in Java.* Berkeley: University of California Press.

———. 1993. "Coercing Conservation: The Politics of State Resource Control." In *The State and Social Power in Global Environmental Politics,* ed. Ronnie D. Lipschutz and Ken Conca, 46–70. Ithaca: Cornell University Press.

Penan leaders. 1993. "Malaysian Army Attacks Penan." *Earth First!* 14 (2):1, 25.

Pepper, David. 1984. *The Roots of Modern Environmentalism.* London: Croom Helm.

———. 1985. "Determinism, Idealism and the Politics of Environmentalism: A Viewpoint." *International Journal of Environmental Studies* 26:11–19.

———. 1993. *Eco-Socialism: From Deep Ecology to Social Justice.* London: Routledge.

Pezzoli, Kieth. 1993. "Sustainable Livelihoods in an Urban Milieu: A Case Study from Mexico City." In *In Defense of Livelihood*, ed. John Friedmann and Haripriya Rangan, 127–54. West Hartford, CT: Kumarian.

Pineda, Rafael. 1993. *Interview by author* (San Salvador, El Salvador, June 23).

Piven, Frances Fox, and Richard A. Cloward. 1992. "Normalizing Collective Protest." In *Frontiers in Social Movement Theory*, ed. Aldon D. Morris and Carol McClurg Mueller, 301–25. New Haven: Yale University Press.

Plant, Christopher and Judith. 1990. *Turtle Talk: Voices for a Sustainable Future*. Philadelphia: New Society Publishers.

Plato. 1971. *On the Trial and Death of Socrates*, ed. Lane Cooper. Originally published as *Apology*. Ithaca: Cornell University Press.

Porritt, J., and D. Winner. 1988. *The Coming of the Greens*. London: Fontana.

Porritt, Jonathon. 1985. *Seeing Green: The Politics of Ecology Explained*. London: Basil Blackwell.

Postel, Sandra. 1992. *Last Oasis: Facing Water Scarcity*. Washington D.C.: Worldwatch.

Potter, Van Rensselaer. 1988. *Global Bioethics*. East Lansing: Michigan State University Press.

Poulsen, C. 1984. *The English Rebels*. London: The Journeyman Press.

Project for Ecological Recovery. 1993. *Survey Report for the Pak Mun Area*. Bangkok: Project for Ecological Recovery.

Ramblers Association. 1992. *Annual Reports and Accounts 1992*. London: Ramblers Association.

Ramirez, Isabel. 1993. Interview by author, General director of CONAMUS, National Coordinating Committee of Salvadoran Women; San Salvador, El Salvador, June 7.

Ramphal, Shridath. 1992. *Our Country, the Planet*. Washington, D.C.: Island Press.

RAN (Rainforest Action Network). 1988. "Crackdown in Malaysia." *Earth Island Journal* 3 (1).

———. 1989. "With the Penan at the Last Blockade." *Earth Island Journal* 4 (1).

―――. 1990. "Biggest Demo in Hawaii's History Protests Puna Destruction." *World Rainforest Report* 6 (2):5.

―――. 1991. "Ecuado: ARCO, UNOCAL Drilling in Amazon." *World Rainforest Report* (January/March).

―――. 1993. "Thanks to Musicians." *World Rainforest Report* 13.

Rangan, Haripriya. 1993. "Romancing the Environment: Popular Environmental Action in the Garhwal Himalayas." In *In Defense of Livelihood: Comparative Studies in Environmental Action*, ed. John Friedmann and Haripriya Rangan, 155–81. West Hartford, CT: Kumarian Press.

Ranger, Terence. 1985. *Peasant Consciousness and Guerrilla War in Zimbabwe*. London: University of California Press.

Rasmussen, David. 1985. "Communicative Action and the Fate of Modernity." *Theory, Culture & Society* 2:133–44.

Reed, Peter, and David Rothenberg, eds. 1993. *Wisdom in the Open Air: The Norwegian Roots of Deep Ecology*. Minneapolis: University of Minnesota Press.

Rennie, Frank. 1993. "The Electronic Crofter and the Impact of High Technology Developments." *Scottish Affairs* 3 (Spring):40–47.

Rich, Bruce. 1994. *Mortgaging the Earth: The World Bank, Environmental Impovershment, and the Crisis of Development*. Boston: Beacon.

Richards, Audrey I. 1939. *Land, Labour and Diet in Northern Rhodesia*. London/ New York: Oxford University Press.

Richards, P. 1975. "'Alternative' Strategies for the African Environment: 'Folk Ecology' as a Basis for Community Oriented Agricultural Development." In *African Environment: Problems and Perspectives*, ed. P. Richards. London: International African Institute.

―――. 1985. *Indigenous Agricultural Revolution*. London: Hutchinson.

Rickwood, P. W. 1973. "Public Enjoyment of the Open Countryside in England and Wales, 1919–1939." Unpublished Ph.D. thesis, University of Leicester.

Ricoeur, Paul. 1974. *The Conflict of Interpretations*. Evanston, IL: Northwestern University Press.

Ridgeway, J. 1980. *Who Owns the Earth*. New York: Collier.

Rifkin, Jeremy. 1991. *Biosphere Politics*. New York: Crown.

Rirash, M. A. 1988. "Camel Herding and Its Effect on Somali Literature." In *Camels in Development*, ed. A. Hjort af Ornas. Uppsala: Scandinavian Institute of African Studies.

Roberts, A. J., C. Russell, G. J. Walker, and K. J. Kirby. 1992. "Regional Variation in the Origin, Extent and Composition of Scottish Woodland." *Botanical Journal of Scotland* 46 (2):167–89.

Robinson, Mairi, ed. 1987. *The Concise Scots Dictionary*. Aberdeen: Aberdeen University Press.

Rogers, B. 1980. *The Domestication of Woman*. London: Tavistock.

Rolston, Holmes. 1988. *Environmental Ethics: Duties to and Values in the Natural World*. Philadelphia: Temple University Press.

Rootes, C. A. 1992. "The New Politics and the New Social Movements: Accounting for British Exceptionalism." *European Journal of Political Research* 22:171–91.

Rorty, Richard. 1979. *Philosophy and the Mirror of Nature*. Princeton, NJ: Princeton University Press.

———. 1989. "Solidarity or Objectivity." In *Anti-Theory in Ethics and Moral Conservatism*, ed. S. Clarke and E. Simpson, 167–84. Durham, NC: Duke University Press.

Rose, C. 1990. *The Dirty Man of Europe: The Great British Pollution Scandal*. London: Simon & Schuster.

———. 1993. "Beyond the Struggle for Proof: Factors Changing the Environmental Movement." *Environmental Values* 2:285–98.

Rosenau, James N. 1990. *Turbulence in World Politics: A Theory of Change and Continuity*. Princeton, NJ: Princeton University Press.

———. 1993. "Environmental Challenges in a Global Context." In *Environmental Politics in the International Arena*, ed. Sheldon Kamieniecki, 257–74. Albany: State University of New York Press.

Roszak, Theodore. 1992. *The Voice of the Earth: An Exploration of Ecopsychology*. New York: Simon and Schuster/Touchstone.

Rothenberg, David. 1993. *Is It Painful to Think? Conversations with Arne Naess*. Minneapolis: University of Minnesota Press.

———. 1994. "Individual or Community: Two Approaches to Ecophilosophy in Practice." In *Ecological Prospects*, ed. Christopher Chapple. Albany: State University of New York Press.

Rothman, B. 1982. *The 1932 Kinder Trespass*. Altrincham: Willow Publishing.

Rowbotham, S., L. Segal, and H. Wainwright. 1979. *Beyond the Fragments: Feminism and the Making of Socialism*. London: Merlin Press.

Rucht, Dieter. 1989. "Environmental Movement Organizations in West Germany and France." In *Organizing for Change*, ed. Bert Klandermans. Greenwich, CT: JAI Press.

———. 1994. "Ecological Protest as Calculated Law-Breaking: Greenpeace and Earth First! in Comparative Perspective." In *Green Politics Three*, ed. W. Rüdig, 66–89. Edinburgh: Edinburgh University Press.

Rüdig, W. 1990. *Anti-Nuclear Movements: A World Survey of Protest against Nuclear Energy*. Harlow, England: Longman.

———. 1992. "Editorial." In *Green Politics Two*, ed. W. Rüdig, 1–8. Edinburgh: Edinburgh University Press.

———. 1994. "Maintaining a Low Profile: The Anti-Nuclear Movement and the British State." In *States and Anti-Nuclear Movements*, ed. H. Flam, 69–99. Edinburgh: Edinburgh University Press.

Rüdig, W., L. G. Bennie, and M. N. Franklin. 1991. *Green Party Members: A Profile*. Glasglow: Delta Publications.

Rüdig, W., M. N. Franklin, and L. G. Bennie. 1993. *Green Blues: The Rise and Fall of the British Green Party*. Strathclyde Papers in Government and Politics, no. 95. Glasglow, Department of Government, University of Strathclyde.

Rüdig, W., and P. Lowe. 1986. "The 'Withered' Greening of British Politics: A Study of the Ecology Party." *Political Studies* 34:262–84.

Rüdig, W., J. Mitchell, J. Chapman, and P. D. Lowe. 1991. "Social Movements and the Social Sciences in Britain." In *Research on Social Movements: The State of the Art in Western Europe and the USA*, ed. D. Rücht, 121–48. Boulder, CO/Frankfurt am Main: Westview Press/Campus.

Ruether, Rosemary Radford. 1992. *Gaia and God: The Ecofeminist Theology of Earth Healing*. New York: HarperCollins.

Ryan, Charlotte. 1991. *Prime Time Activism: Media Strategies for Grassroots Organizing*. Boston: South End Press.

Ryberg, Erik. 1993. "Are We Mere Banner Hangers?" *Earth First!* 13 (3):3.

Ryle, M. 1988. *Ecology and Socialism*. London: Century Hutchinson.

Said, Edward. 1978. *Orientalism*. New York: Pantheon.

Sale, Kirkpatrick. 1985. *Dwellers in the Land: The Bioregional Vision*. San Francisco: Sierra Club Books.

Sallach, Ariel. 1984. "Deeper Than Deep Ecology: The Eco-Feminist Connection." *Environmental Ethics* 6:339–45.

———. 1992. "The Ecofeminism/Deep Ecology Debate: A Reply to Patriarchal Reason." *Environmental Ethics* 14:195–216.

SAM (Sahabat Alam Malaysia). 1988. "Malaysia: Appeal by the Orang Ulu to Protect Their Lands, Forests and Resources." *IWGIA Newsletter* 53–54(May/August): Copenhagen, Denmark.

Sandbach, F. 1980. *Environment, Ideology and Policy*. Oxford: Blackwell.

Sanderson, J. 1974. "The National Smoke Abatement Society and the Clean Air Act (1956)." In *Campaigning for the Environment*, ed. R. Kimber, and J. J. Richardson, 27–44. London: Routledge and Keegan Paul.

Sanitsuda Ekachai. 1990. *Behind the Smile: Voices of Thailand*. Bangkok: Bangkok Development Support Committee.

Sargent, Caroline, and Stephen Bass, eds. 1992. *Plantation Politics: Forest Plantation in Development*. London: Earthscan.

Scarce, Rik. 1990. *Ecowarriors: Understanding the Radical Environmental Movement*. Chicago: Noble.

Scarrow, H. A. 1972. "The Impact of British Domestic Air Pollution Legislation." *British Journal of Political Science* 2:261–82.

Schelling, Andrew. 1991. "Jataka Mind: Cross-Species Compassion from Ancient India to Earth First! Activists." *Tricycle* 1 (1):10–19.

Schmink, Marianne, and Charles H. Wood. 1984. *Frontier Expansion in Amazonia*. Gainsville: University of Florida Press.

———. 1992. *Contested Frontiers in Amazonia*. New York: Columbia University Press.

Schneider, Stephen, and Penelope J. Boston. 1991. *Scientists on Gaia*, ed. Stephen Schneider and Penelope J. Boston. Cambridge, MA: MIT press.

Schubert, Louis. 1993. "Environmental Politics in Asia." In *Environmental Politics in the International Arena*, ed. Sheldon Kamieniecki, 239–55. Albany: State University of New York Press.

Schumacher, E. F. 1973. *Small Is Beautiful: Economics as if People Mattered.* London: Blond & Briggs.

———. 1976. *Small Is Beautiful.* London: Sphere.

Scott, J. C. 1985. *The Weapons of the Weak.* New Haven: Yale University Press.

———. 1990. *Domination and the Arts of Resistance: Hidden Transcripts.* New Haven: Yale University Press.

Seed, John. 1990. Funds Needed to Save PNG & Solomon Islands Rainforest. *Earth First!* 11(2): 18.

———. 1994. Report to the Foundation for Deep Ecology Re. John Seed Directed Grants, 8 May.

———. 1994b. "I Cover Myself with Leaves: Excerpts from a Ram Dass Interview with John Seed." *Earth First!* 14 (6):28.

Seed, John, Joanna Macy, Pat Fleming, and Arne Naess, eds. 1988. *Thinking Like a Mountain: Towards a Council of All Beings.* Philadelphia: New Society.

Selcraig, Bruce. 1994. "Native Americans Join to Stop the Newest of the Indian Wars." *Sierra Magazine* 79 (3).

Sellars, Wilfrid. 1963. *Science, Perception and Reality.* London: Routledge and Kegan Paul.

Sen, G., and C. Grown. 1987. *Development, Crises, and Alternative Visions: Third World Women's Perspectives.* New York: Monthly Review Press.

Sessions, George. 1974. "Anthropocentrism and the Environmental Crisis." *Humboldt Journal of Social Relations* 2:71–81.

———. 1987. "The Deep Ecology Movement: A Review." *Environmental Ethics* 11:105–25.

———. 1993. "Deep Ecology and Global System Protection." In *Environmental Philosophy*, ed. Michael Zimmerman, et al., 233–50. Englewood Cliffs, NJ: Prentice Hall.

———. 1993. "Introduction [to Deep Ecology]." In *Environmental Philosophy*, ed. Michael E. Zimmerman, et al., 161–70. Englewood Cliffs, NJ: Prentice-Hall.

Setterberg, Fred, and Lonny Shavelson. 1993. *Toxic Nation: The Fight to Save Our Communities from Chemical Contamination*. New York: John Wiley & Sons, Inc.

Shah, Ashvin. 1993. "A Technical Overview of the Flawed Sardar Sarovar Project for a Sustainable Alternative." Unpublished Manuscript, Scarsdale, New York.

Sharma, Pranjal. 1994. "Muddying the Waters." *India Today* (February 15).

Shea, Cynthia Pollock. 1989. "Doing Well by Doing Good." *World Watch* 2 (6), (November/December).

Shiva, Vandana. 1988. *Staying Alive: Women, Ecology, and Survival in India*. New Delhi: Kali for Women.

————. 1988. *Staying Alive: Women, Ecology and Development*. London: Zed.

————. 1991. *Ecology and the Politics of Survival: Conflicts over Natural Resources in India*. New Delhi: Sage Publications.

Sikorski, Wade. 1993. *Modernity and Technology*. Tuscaloosa: University of Alabama Press.

Simon, Thomas W. 1990. "Varieties of Ecological Dialectics." *Environmental Ethics* 12:211–321.

Singer, Paul, and Vinicius Caldera Brandt Brandt, ed. 1980. *Sao Paulo: O Povo Em Movimento*. Petropolis, Brazil: Vozes.

Smart, Bruce. 1992. *Beyond Compliance: A New Industry View of the Environment*. Washington, D.C.: World Resources Institute.

Smith, Iain Crichton. 1987. *Consider the Lilies*. Edinburgh: Canongate.

Smout, T. C. 1991. "The Highlands and the Roots of Green Consciousness, 1750–1990." *Proceedings of the British Academy* 76:237–63.

Snow, David, and Robert Benford. 1988. "Ideology, Frame Resonance, and Participant Mobilization." *International Social Movement Research* 1:197–217.

————. 1992. "Master Frames and Cycles of Protest." In *Frontiers of Social Movement Theory*, ed. Carol Mueller and Aldon Morris, 135–55. New Haven: Yale University Press.

Snow, Donald. 1992. *Voices from the Environmental Movement*. Washington, D.C.: The Conservation Fund.

Snow, Keith. 1994. "Dateline Toyko: No Presence for the Penan." Unpublished manuscript.

Snyder, Gary. 1990. *The Practice of the Wild.* San Francisco: North Point.

Southhall, A., ed. 1979. *Small Urban Centres in Rural Development in Africa.* Madison: African Studies Program, University of Wisconsin, Madison.

Spretnak, Charlene, and Fritjof Capra. 1986. *Green Politics.* Santa Fe: Bear and Company.

Starke, Linda. 1990. *Signs of Hope: Working toward Our Common Future.* New York: Oxford University Press.

Steller, Tim. 1992. "Ecuador's Rain Forest Natives Struggle for Lands." *The Circle* 13 (5).

Stephenson, T. 1989. *Forbidden Land: The Struggle for Access to Mountain and Moorland.* Manchester: Manchester University Press.

Stevenson, J. 1992. *Popular Disturbances in England, 1700–1832.* 2d ed. London: Longman.

Stock, R. 1988. "Environmental Sanitation in Nigeria." *Review of African Political Economy* 42:19–31.

Stott, Philip. 1991. "Mu'ang and Pa: Elite Views of Nature in a Changing Thailand." In *Thai Constructions of Knowledge,* ed. Manas Chitkasem, and Andrew Turton, 142–54. London: University of London.

Strong, David. 1992. "The Technological Subversion of Environmental Ethics." *Research in Philosophy and Technology* 12:33–66.

The *Sunday Times* Insight Team. 1986. *Rainbow Warrior: The French Attempt to Sink Greenpeace.* London: Hutchinson.

Sundkler, B. G. M. 1961. *Bantu Prophets in South Africa.* London: Oxford University Press.

Surplus People Project Report. 1983. *Forced Removals in South Africa.* Vol. 1. Cape Town: Surplus People Project.

Survival International. 1987. "Ecuador: Indians Kill Bishop as Oil Companies Invade." *Urgent Action Bulletin* (August).

Swimme, Brian, and Thomas Berry. 1992. *The Universe Story: From the Primordial Flaring Forth to the Ecozoic Era: A Celebration of the Unfolding Cosmos.* San Francisco: Harper San Francisco.

Switkes, Glenn. 1989. "Amazon Indians Movement Broadens." *Earth First!* 9 (5):12.

Sylvan, Richard. 1984. "A Critique of Deep Ecology." *Radical Philosophy* 40, 41:2–22.

Tambiah, Stanley Jeyaraja. 1984. *The Buddhist Saints of the Forest and the Cult of Amulets*. Cambridge: Cambridge University Press.

Tandon, Yash. 1993. "Village Contradictions in Africa." In *Global Ecology: A New Arena of Political Conflict*, ed. Wolfgang Sachs, 208–23. London & Halifax, Nova Scotia: Zed & Fernwood.

Taylor, Bron. 1991. "The Religion and Politics of Earth First!" *The Ecologist* 21 (6) (November/December): 258–66.

———. 1993. "Evoking the Ecological Self: Art as Resistance to the War on Nature." *Peace Review* 5 (2):225–30.

———. 1994. "Earth First!'s Religious Radicalism." In *Ecological Prospects: Aesthetic, Scientific, and Religious Perspectives*, ed. Christopher Chappel. Albany, NY: State University of New York Press.

———. 1995a. "Resacralizing Earth: Pagan Environmentalism and the Restoration of Turtle Island." In *American Sacred Space*, ed. David Chidester and Edward T. Linenthal. Bloomington: Indiana University Press.

———. 1995b. "The Wildlands Project." In *Encyclopedia of Conservation and Environmentalism*, ed. Robert Paehlke. New York: Garland.

Taylor, Bron, Heidi Hadsell, Lois Lorentzen, and Rik Scarce. 1992. "Grassroots Resistance: The Emergence of Popular-Environmental Movements in Less Affluent Countries." *Wild Earth* (Winter): 43–50.

———. 1993. "Grassroots Resistance: The Emergence of Popular Environmental Movements in Less Affluent Countries." In *Environmental Politics in the International Arena: Movements, Parties, Organizations, and Policy*, ed. Sheldon Kamieniecki, 69–89. Albany: State University of New York Press.

Taylor, Charles. 1985. "Interpretation and Ethnocentricity." In *Interpretation and Human Sciences*. Cambridge: Cambridge University Press.

Taylor, Dorceta. 1992. "Can the Environmental Movement Attract and Maintain the Support of Minorities?" In *Race and the Incidence of Environmental Hazards: A Time for Discourse*, ed. Bunyan Bryant and Paul Mohai, 28–54. Boulder: Westview Press.

Taylor, Paul W. 1986. *Respect for Nature: A Theory of Environmental Ethics*. Princeton, NJ: Princeton University Press.

Thomas, John. 1990. "Lewis Mumford, Benton MacKaye, and the Regional Vision." In *Lewis Mumford: Public Intellectual*, ed. Thomas and Agatha Hughes. New York: Oxford University Press.

Thomas, K. 1984. *Man and the Natural World: Changing Attitudes in England, 1500–1800*. London: Penguin.

Thompson, E. P. 1976. *William Morris: Romantic to Revolutionary*. New York: Pantheon.

Thompson, Francis. 1984. *Crofting Years*. Ayshire, Scotland: Luath Press.

Thompson, Janna. 1990. "A Refutation of Environmental Ethics." *Environmental Ethics* 12:147–60.

Thurston, Harry. 1991. "Power in a Land of Remembrance." *Audubon Magazine* (November/December).

Tilly, Charles. 1978. *From Mobilization to Revolution*. New York: Random House.

———. 1981. *Class Conflict and Collective Action*. Beverly Hills/ London: Sage.

Tiwari, Rajiv. 1986. "India: Undermining the Himalaya." *Inter Press Service* (November 6).

Tokar, Brian. 1988. "Exploring the New Ecologies." *Alternatives* 15:30–43.

———. 1988. "Social Ecology, Deep Ecology and the Future of Greenpolitical Thought." *The Ecologist* 18:132–41.

Toulmin, Stephen. 1970. *An Examination of the Place of Reason in Ethics*. Cambridge: Cambridge University Press.

Tovey, Hilary. 1993. "Environmentalism in Ireland: Two Versions of Development and Modernity." *International Sociology* 8 (4): 413-430.

Toynbee, Arnold. 1972. "The Religious Background of the Present Environmental Crisis." *International Journal of Environmental Studies* 3:141–46.

Tracy, David. 1978. *Blessed Rage for Order*. New York: Seabury.

Trenchard, E. 1987. "Rural Women's Work in Sub-Saharan Africa and the Implications for Nutrition." In *Geography of Gender*, ed. Janet Momsen and Janet Townsend, 153–72. Albany: State University of New York Press.

Trout Unlimited (Wolf River chapter). 1994. Mining policy statement.(January).

Tuan, Yi-Fu. 1976. "Geopiety: A Theme in Man's Attachment to Nature and to Place." In *Geographies of the Mind*, ed. David Lowenthal and Martyn J. Bowden, 27–28. London/New York: Oxford University Press.

———. 1990. *Topophilia: A Study of Environmental Perception, Attitudes, and Values*. Englewood Cliffs, NJ: Prentice Hall, 1974. Reprint. New York: Columbia University Press.

Turner, Bryan S. 1990. *Theories of Modernity and Postmodernity*. Newbury Park, CA: Sage.

Turner, Frederick Jackson. 1932. *The Significance of Sections in American History*. New York: Henry Holt and Company.

Turner, Ralph H. 1969. "The Public Perception of Protest." *American Sociological Review* 34 (December): 815–29.

Turner, Terry. 1991. "The World Struggle to Save James Bay." *Northeast Indian Quarterly* 8 (4).

Turner, Wallace. 1972. "A.E.C. Dismantles Aleutian Test Site of Controversial '71 Underground Blast." *New York Times* (August 5).

Tyme, J. 1978. *Motorways versus Democracy*. London: Macmillan.

Ueltzen, Stephan. 1993. *Como Salvadorena Que Soy: Entrevistas Con Mujeres En La Luncha*. San Salvador, El Salvador: Editorial Somrero Azul.

UNES (Unidad Ecologica Salvadorena). 1990. *Propuesta Del Cerro Verde*. San Salvador, El Salvador.

———. 1987. *Toxic Waste and Race in the United States: A National Report on the Racial and Socio-Economic Characteristics of Communities with Hazardous Waste Sites*. Charles Lee project director. New York: UCC Commission on Racial Justice.

———. 1992. *The Proceedings of the People of Color Environmental Leadership Summit*. New York: UCC Commission on Racial Justice.

United Nations. 1989. "Universal Declaration on the Rights of Indigenous Peoples." Draft. Geneva, Switzerland: Working Group on Indigenous Populations.

U.S. Environmental Protection Agency. 1992. *Environmental Equity: Reducing Risk for All Americans*.

U.S. General Accounting Office. 1983. *Siting of Hazardous Waste Landfills and Their Correlation with the Radical and Economic Status of Surrounding Communities.*

———. 1985. *Assessment of EPA's Hazardous Waste Enforcement Strategy.*

———. 1986. *Hazardous Waste: EPA Has Made Limited Progress in Determining the Wastes to Be Regulated.*

Urban Environmental Conference, Inc. 1985. *Taking Back Our Health: An Institute on Surviving the Threat to Minority Communities.* Washington, D.C.: Urban Environmental Conference, Inc.

Urbino, Moises, and Jorge A. Santamaria. 1989. "Un Pais En Guerra." In *La Situacion Ambiental En Centroamerica Y El Caribe,* ed. Ingemar Hedstrom. San Jose, Costa Rica: Editorial Departament Ecumenico de Investigaciones (DEI).

Vasquez, Isabel. 1993. Interview by author, a member of CONAMUS, National Coordinating Committee of Salvadorna Women; San Salvador, El Salvador, June 22.

Veldman, M. 1994. *Fantasy, the Bomb, and the Greening of Britain: Romantic Protest, 1945–1980.* Cambridge: Cambridge University Press.

Vennm, Jr., Thomas. 1988. *Wild Rice and the Ojibway People.* St. Paul: Minnesota Historical Society.

Verhovek, Sam Howe. 1992. "Cuomo, Citing Economic Issues, Cancels Quebec Power Contract." *The New York Times* (March 28).

Vidal, J. 1994. "The Real Earth Movers." *The Guardian* (7 December).

Vogel, D. 1986. *National Styles of Regulation: Environmental Policy in Britain and the United States.* Ithaca: Cornell University Press.

Vogel, Steven. 1991. "New Science, New Nature: The Habermas-Marcuse Debate Revisited." *Research in Philosophy and Technology* 11: 157–78.

Wald, Matthew. 1990. "Guarding the Environment: A World of Challenges." *New York Times* (April 22).

Wall, D. 1990. *Getting There: Steps to a Green Society.* London: Green Print.

Walzer, Michael. 1987. *Interpretation and Social Criticism.* Cambridge: Havard University Press.

Ward, C. 1974. "Say It Again, Ben!: An Evocation of the First Seventy-Five Years of the Town and Country Planning Association." *Bulletin of Environmental Education* 43:5–19.

Ward, D., ed. 1994. *Green History: A Reader in Environmental Literature, Philosophy and Politics.* London: Routledge.

Warford, Jeremy, and Zeinab Partow. 1989. "Evolution of the World Bank's Environmental Policy." *Finance and Development* 26 (December).

Warren, Jennifer. 1990. "Bikers Challenge U.S. Action Closing Desert Race Routes." *Los Angeles Times* (November 22).

Warren, Karen. 1987. "Feminism and Ecology: Making Connections." *Environmental Ethics* 9:3–20.

———. 1990. "The Power and the Promise of Ecological Feminism." *Environmental Ethics* 12:125–46.

Watson, Paul. 1992. "Letter from a Friend." *Earth First!* 13 (2):3.

———. 1993a. "Goodbye to Greenpeace" and "Raid on Reykjavik". In *Radical Environmentalism: Philosophy and Tactics,* ed. Peter List, 169–75. Belmont, CA: Wadsworth Publishing.

———. 1993b. "An Open Letter to Norwegians." *Sea Shepherd Log* (First Quarter): 5–11.

Watson, Richard A. 1983. "A Critique of Anti-Anthropocentric Biocentrism." *Environmental Ethics* 5: 245–56.

Weale, A., T. O'Riordan, and L. Kramme. 1991. *Controlling Pollution in the Round: Change and Choice in Environmental Regulation in Britain and Germany.* London: Anglo-German Foundation for the Study of Industrial Society.

Weiner, D., and R. Levin. 1991. "Land and Agrarian Transition in South Africa." *Antipode* 23 (1):92–120.

Wellmer, Albrecht. 1985. "On the Dialectic of Modernism and Postmodernism." *Praxis International* 4: 337–62.

West Highland Free Press. 1993a. *West Highland Free Press* (April 30).

West Highland Free Press. 1993b. "Crofting Development Plan Drawn Up to Secure Future." *West Highland Free Press* (October 8).

Weston, Anthony. 1985. "Beyond Intrinsic Value: Pragmatism in Environmental Ethics." *Environmental Ethics* 7:321–39.

———. 1992. "Before Environmental Ethics." *Environmental Ethics* 14:321–38.

Weston, J., ed. 1986. *Red and Green: The New Politics of the Environment*. London: Pluto Press.

Whaley, Rick, and Walter Bresette. 1993. *Walleye Warriors: An Effective Strategy against Racism and for the Earth*. Philadelphia: New Society.

White, Benjamin Jr. 1989. "Kararao: A Dam Called War." *Earth First!* 9 (4):15.

White, Lynn. 1967. "The Historic Roots of Our Ecologic Crisis." *Science* 155:1203–7.

White, Stephen K. 1987. "Justice and the Postmodern Problematic." *Praxis International* 7:306–19.

———. 1988. "Poststructuralism and Political Reflection." *Political Theory* 16:186–208.

Whitebrook, Joel. 1979. "The Problem of Nature in Habermas." *Telos* 40:41–69.

Wiener, M. J. 1981. *English Culture and the Decline of the Industrial Spirit, 1850–1980*. Cambridge: Cambridge University Press.

Wild, H. E. 1965/66. The Manchester Association for the Preservation of Ancient Footpaths." *The Manchester Review* 10 (Winter): 242–50.

Wildavsky, Aaron. 1991. *The Rise of Radical Egalitarianism*. Washington, D.C.: American University Press.

Williams, R. n.d. *Socialism and Ecology*. Pamphlet. London: Socialist Environment and Resources Associtation.

———. 1973. *The Country and the City*. London: Chatto and Windus.

Williams-Ellis, C., ed. 1938. *Britain and the Beast*. London: Readers' Union.

———. 1975. *England and the Octopus*. Portmeirion: Penrhyndeudraeth.

Wisner, B. 1988. *Power and Need in Africa*. London: Earthscan.

Wisner, B., and P. Mbithi. 1974. "Drought in Eastern Kenya: Nutritional Status and Farmer Activity." In *Natural Hazards*, ed. G. White, 87–97. New York: Oxford University Press.

Witte, John. 1993. *Deforestation in Zaire: Logging and Landlessness*, ed. Marcus Colchester and Larry Lohmann. Penang, Malaysia: World Rainforest Movement.

Wolke, Howie. 1987. "Thoughtful Radicalism." *Earth First!* 10 (2):29.

Wood, Harold W. 1985. "Modern Pantheism as an Approach to Environmental Ethics." *Environmental Ethics* 7:151–64.

Woodruff, David, Walter Rainboth, George Davis, and Srisuwan Kuankachorn. 1993. *Recommendations for the Pak Mun Project*. Washington: Bank Information Center.

World Bank. 1981. *Accelerating Development in Sub-Saharan Africa*. New York: Oxford University Press.

———. 1989. *Sub-Saharan Africa: From Crisis to Sustainable Growth*. New York: Oxford University Press.

World Commission of Environment and Development. 1987. *Food 2000*. London: Zed Press.

———. 1987. *Our Common Future*. New York: Oxford University Press.

———. 1987. *Our Common Future*. Oxford/New York: Oxford University Press.

WRM (World Rainforest Movement). 1989. "Declaration of the World Rainforest Movement." *IWGIA Newsletter* 59: Copehagen, Denmark.

Wuthnow, Robert, James D. Hunter, Albert Bergeson, and Edith Kurzweil. 1984. *Cultural Analysis: The Work of Peter Berger, Mary Douglas, Michel Foucault, and Jürgen Habermas*. London: Routledge and Kegan Paul.

Yachir, F. 1988. *Mining in Africa Today*. Tokyo: University Nations University Press.

Yenchai Laohavanich. 1989. "A Thai Buddhist View of Nature." In *Culture and Environment in Thailand*, ed. Michael Shari. Bangkok: Siam Society.

Young, S. C. 1993. *The Politics of the Environment*. Manchester: Baseline Books.

Zakin, Susan. 1993. *Coyotes and Town Dogs: Earth First! and the Environmental Movement*. New York: Viking.

Zald, Mayer N. 1992. "Looking Backward to Forward: Reflections on the Past and Future of the Resource Mobilization Research Program." In

Frontiers in Social Movement Theory, ed. Aldon D. Morris and Carol McClurg Mueller, 326–51. New Haven, CT: Yale University Press.

Zald, Mayer N., and John McCarthy, eds. 1987. *Social Movements in an Organizational Society*, ed. Mayer Zald and John McCarthy. New Brunswick, NJ: Transaction.

Zimmerman, Michael E. 1983. "Toward a Heideggerian Ethos for Radical Environmentalism." *Environmental Ethics* 5:99–131.

———. 1987. "Feminism, Deep Ecology, and Environmental Ethics." *Environmental Ethics* 9:21–44.

———. 1993. *Environmental Philosophy: From Animal Rights to Radical Ecology*. Englewood Cliffs, NJ: Prentice Hall.

Zuercher, Melanie, ed. 1991. *Making History: Ten Years of Kentuckians for the Commonwealth*. Prestonberg, KY: Kentuckians for the Commonwealth.

Contributors

Vikram K. Akula is Fulbright Scholar at Osmania University in Hyderabad, India, where he researches participatory rural development. He has worked as a community organizer with the Deccan Development Society and as a researcher with the Worldwatch Institute. He holds an M.A. in International Relations from Yale University and a B.A. in philosophy from Tufts University, and has done graduate work in religion at Harvard University.

S. Dulaine Coleman is a Ph.D. candidate in Political Science at the University of Southern California. Her main research interests lie in radical grassroots movements and the distribution of resources in urban environments.

Daniel Deudney is Assistant Professor of Political science at the University of Pennsylvania. For many years he was senior Researcher at Worldwatch, and he has written and lectured widely on issues of international politics, security, and the environment.

Bob Edwards, Ph.D., is an Instructor in the Department of Sociology and Research Associate in The Life Cycle Institute at The Catholic University of America in Washington, D.C. His dissertation compares the organizational styles of lower-class and middle-class social movement organizations. He has been a community organizer and low-income housing administrator and has served on the boards of several community organizations in Washington, D.C. He continues a collaborative analysis of changes between 1988 and 1992 among U.S. peace-movement organizations and is beginning a national study of local groups in the grassroots environmental movement. His articles have appeared in *The American Sociologi-*

cal Review, Sociological Forum, and *Nonprofit and Voluntary Sector Quarterly.*

Rachel Freeman is pursuing a Ph.D. in the School of Scottish Studies and with the Center for Human Ecology at the University of Edinburgh. Her dissertation examines the connection between folklore and land use in the Hebrides.

Al Gedicks is Associate Professor of Sociology at the University of Wisconsin, LaCrosse, author of *The New Resource Wars: Native and Environmental Struggles against Multinational Corporations,* and a longtime environmental/native solidarity activist in the upper Midwest. He has served as the director of the Center for Alternative Mining Development Policy and as the executive secretary of the Wisconsin Resources Protection Council.

Heidi Hadsell is professor of Social Ethics, Dean of the Faculty, and Vice President for Academic Affairs at McCormick Theological Seminary in Chicago, Illinois. She spends a great deal of time engaged with and writing about Latin American popular movements, especially in Brazil.

Brenden Hill is an English ecologist and former television producer living in Scotland. He is working on a Ph.D. in the psychological relationship between humans and nature at the Department of Psychology and the Center for Human Ecology, University of Edingurgh. He edits *Reforesting Scotland.*

Sheldon Kamieniecki is Professor of Political Science and Director of the Environmental Studies Program at the University of Southern California. He is the author of *Public Representation in Environmental Policymaking,* coauthor of *Environmental Regulation through Strategic Planning,* and editor of *Environmental Politics in the International Arena.* He is also editor for the SUNY's Series in International Environmental Policy and Theory.

Larry Lohmann studied philosophy at Cornell and Princeton universities and spent most of the 1980s in Thailand, teaching and working with nongovernmental organizations. He is coeditor of *The Struggle for Land and the Fate of the Forests* (with Marcus Colchester), and currently is Associate Editor of *The Ecologist.*

Lois Ann Lorentzen is Assistant Professor of Social Ethics at the University of San Francisco and is writing *The Production of Life: A Feminist Theology of Work.* She writes regularly on ecofeminism, Central American environmental movements, and feminist theology, and is an accomplished mountaineer. The research for the article was made possible by a Faculty Development grant from the University of San Francisco.

Alastair McIntosh directs the Msc postgraduate human ecology degree at the Centre for Human Ecology, University of Edinburgh, and is a trustee for the Isle of Eigg land restitution trust. He has engaged in ethnograpic research in Papua, New Guinea, and was involved in teaching and establishing the Pacific Regional Sustainable Forestry Programme.

Emma Porio is Associate Professor of Scociology at Ateneo De Manila University. She also serves as coordinator of the social science track of the Environmental Science Program and as chair of the Research Committee of the Philippine Social Science Council.

David Rothenberg is Assistant Professor of Philosophy and director of the Program in Science, Technology and Society at the New Jersey Institute of Technology. He translated and edited Arne Naess's *Ecology, Community, and Lifestyle,* and he is the author of *Is It Painful to Think? Conversations with Arne Naess, Hand's End: Technology and the Limits of Nature,* and *Wild Ideas.* Rothenberg is a noted composer and jazz clarinetist, and his recording *Nobody Could Explain It* is available on the Accurate label.

Wolfgang Rüdig is Senior Lecturer in Government at the University of Strathclyde, Glasgow, Scotland. He is the author of *Anti-Nuclear Movements: A World Survey of Protest against Nuclear Energy* (1990) and editor of *Green Politics One* (1990), *Green Politics Two* (1992), and *Green Politics Three* (1994) (all Edinburgh, Scotland: Edinburgh University Press). He is currently completing books on the British Green party and the comparative politics of global warming.

Jerry Stark is a Professor of Sociology at the University of Wisconsin, Oshkosh, and is Director of both the University Scholars Program and the University Learning Community. His central interest is critical social philosophy, an interest which unites his teaching and research. His most recent publications focus on critical pedagogy and the critical empirical analysis of puclic discourse. He is cotranslator of Jurgen Habermas' *On the Logic of the Social Sciences* (1988). His current research examines, both theoretically and empirically, the ideological structures underlying attitudes about the environment, politics, gender, and religion.

Yash Tandon works with the Southern Africa Non-Governmental Development Organizations Network (SANDON) and is editor of *Sustainable Development: Two Perspectives, Two Practices.*

Bron Raymond Taylor is Associate Professor of Religion and Social Ethics at the University of Wisconsin, Oshkosh, and author of *Affirmative Action at Work: Law, Politics and Ethics* (Pittsburgh: University of Pittsburgh Press, 1991). He has written numerous articles about the religion, politics, and ethics of radical environmentalism, and is currently completing *Once and Future Primitive: the Spiritual Politics of Deep Ecology* for Beacon Press.

Robert O. Vos graduated Summa Cum Laude with an A.B. (Program in the Environment and the City) from the University of Southern California in 1992. Currently, he is pursuing a Ph.D. with research focused on urban and environmental politics. His research has won awards from Phi Kappa Phi and the Western Governmental Research Association. In addition to his scholarly activities, Mr. Vos is an award-winning concert cellist.

Paul Wapner teaches international environmental politics at the School of International Service, at the American University. He is the author of *Environmental Activism and World Civic Politics* (Albany: State University of New York Press, 1995).

Ben Wisner is Henry R. Luce Professor of Food, Resources and International Policy at Hampshire College, Amherst, Massachusetts. Formerly, he taught geography at the Universidade Eduardo Mondlane, Maputo, Mozambique (1978–1980) and Community Health for the Faculty of Medicine at Dar es Salaam University, Tanzania (1972–1974). He is author of *Power and Need in Africa* (London: Earthscan, 1988), and co-author (with P. Blaikie, T. Cannon, and I. Davis) of *At Risk: Natural Hazards, People's Vulnerability and Disasters* (London and New York: Routledge, 1994).

INDEX

A

a luta, defined, 184
Abbey, Edward, 13, 27 n. 4, 208, 217
Abram, David, 347
Achary, Thankappan, 139
Ackley, Fred, 105
Acosto, Rosario, 59, 61
Adams, W., 180
Akula, Vikram, 317, 322, 325, 333, 337, 338, 339, 340, 343
Alegria, Claribel, 58–59
Allan, William, 184
Alliance for a Paving Moratorium, 17
Alvarado, Elvia, 57, 63, 65–66
Amte, Baba, 137
Anarchism and ecology, 17, 271; in green parties, 234–35; rejection of, 341, 351 n. 15. *See also* Hierarchy
Animal rights: in Britain, 239–40 n. 6
Anthropocentrism, 1, 64, 114–15, 119, 124, 126, 260, 264, 294–95, 322, 335; anti-anthropocentrism, 262; causes of, 16; defense of, 322; defined, 16

B

Anti-humanism, of earth religion, 295, 298. *See also* Misanthropy
Aquina, Sister, 163
Arjuna, 208
Arctic to Amazonia Alliance, 24
Association of Zimbabwe Traditional Ecologists (AZTREC), 169

Bahaguna, Sunderlal, 133, 134, 144. *See also* Chipko movement
Ball–Rockeach, Sandra J., 328
Banuri, Tariq, 346
Bari, Judi, 28 n. 11, 326, 327, 344
BCCs (Basic Christian Communities). *See* Liberation Theology.
Berglund, Axel–Ivar, 168
Betsworth, Roger, 11
Bhatt, Chandri Prasad, 133
Bingham, Mary Beth, 48
Biocentrism, 16, 114, 119, 124, 129, 133, 144, 235, 320, 328, 335; as litmus test of greenness, 235–36
Biological diversity (Biodiversity), 12, 15, 18, 113, 185; political commitment to, 345, 353 n. 28

Biodiversity Legal Foundation, 17, 28 n. 6
Bioregionalism, 213, 271, 289–90, 291–94, 299; and the state, 291; and the U.S. Constitution, 292
Bishnoi sect, and Chipko, 145 n. 3
Blumer, Herbert, 311
Bohlen, Marie, 305
Bonifaz, Cristobal, 102
Bonifaz, Diago, 101
Bookchin, Murray, 267, 273, 340
Bourassa, Robert, 90
Bradford, George, 273, 275
Bremer, Paul, 207
Broad, Robin, 346
Brower, David, 310
Brundtland, Gro Harlem, 201
Bruno, Giordano, 295, 296
Burke, Edmund, 288
Burns, Robert, 248
Bush, President George, 201, 324

C

Callenbach, Ernest, 292
Campbell, Angus Peter, 251
Canas, Mercedes, 62
Capercaillie, 252
Carballo, Alma, 60, 62, 65
Carlton, Jaspar, 28 n. 6.
Carlyle, 226
Carney, J., 181
Carson, Rachel, 232
Carter, N., 201
Cash crops. See Monocultures
Castells, Manuel, 325
Causes of ecogical resistance movements. See Ecological resistance movements–causes of
Cavanagh, John, 346
CCHW (Citizens Clearinghouse for

Hazardous Waste), 39, 44, 49, 54 nn. 15–16
Celtic culture, 245; and cultural renewal, 4, 255; and ecological resistance, 4, 255
Centro Salvadoreno de Tecnologia Apropiada (CESTA), 61–62, 64–65
Chabata, Lydia, 169
Chambers, R., 180, 188
Chavis, Ben, 42
Cheney, Jim, 263
Cherney, Darryl, 28 n. 11, 326, 327
Chief Victorio, 18
Chipko movement, 115, 133–36, 141, 144, 145 nn. 3, 4, 316–17, 350 n. 5
Chong, Dennis, 319, 325
Civic (civil) religion, 290
Civil disobedience. See Tactics; Earth First!; Greenpeace; Friends of the Earth
Civilization, Western. See Western civilization
Clinton, President Bill, 201, 215, 333 n. 3
Coalitions, 24–25, 143, 253, 325–27, 333 n. 5; James Bay, 92–93; obstacles to, 142–44, 156, 331; power and importance of, 77, 144, 145 n. 5, 326–27, 331–32, 347
Coalition for Nitassian, 24
Cohen, D., 189
Collective action frames, 41, 45
Commisao Pastoral da Terra (CPT—Pastoral Land Commisstion), 76–83
Commoner, Barry, 232
Commons Preservation Society, 222–23

Commons, the: defense and/or restoration of, 122, 133, 168–70, 222–23, 340, 342, 350–51 n. 9, 352 nn. 18&20; definition of, 222, 350 nn. 7–8; enclosures (clearances) of, 245–47, 249, 255, 339–340; examples of, 120–22, 153–55, 168–69; rationale for, 173

Coon–Come, Matthew, 92

Coordinadora Nacional de la Mujer Salvadorena (CONAMUS), 60–61, 67–68

Copernicus, 295

Cultural Survival, 100, 352 n. 34

Cuomo, Mario, 92, 93

D

Dams: impacts of, 12, 90–91, 109–11, 113, 118–19, 123, 113, 131, 134, 136–37, 138–39, 179, 197 n. 5, 339, 149; resistance to, 19, 24, 90–94, 110, 118, 136–38, 142, 144, 149–50, 354 n. 29

Darling, Sir Frank Fraser, 254

Darwin, Charles, 296

Deep ecology, 2, 13–16, 115, 153, 201, 202, 204–06, 208, 212–13, 221, 256, 259–281, 315; in Britain, 235; criticisms of, 124–26, 259–81, 315–16, 331; definition of, 202, 260–62; Gandhi's influence on, 206–11, 218; misanthropy of, 294–96; Naess's contributions to, 31 n. 30, 201–03, 205, 208, 218, 260–62; and non-violence, 206–11, 217–18; philosophy and spirituality of, 202–06, 217–18, 260–62, 273, 283, 287, 299, 321,

336, 347; and science, 268–74, 289, 296, 298; in Scotland, 256. See also Earth religion; Earth First!

Deforestation: impacts of, 60, 94–96, 130, 133, 148, 152–53, 191, 241, 315; in India, 127, 133, 142, 145 n. 4; resistance to, 94, 150. See also Reforestation efforts

Delors, President Jacques, 245

Deudney, Dan, 347–48

Devall, Bill, 261, 273

Dick, Chief Robie, 92

Dickson, David, 102

Direct action. See Tactics; Earth First!; Greenpeace; Friends of the Earth

Dobson, Andrew, 274

Donne, John, 188

Durning, Alan, 32 n. 38.

E

Earth First!, 92; celebration of natural disasters, 333 n. 4; criticisms of Greenpeace, 304, 314 n. 1; and Deep Ecology, 204; direct action campaigns (in Britain) 231, 237–38, (in Scotland), 242–43, 254, (in the U.S.), 3; ecological analysis, 16; and ecotage, 207; ethics of, 15–17, 269–70; journal, 20; moral claims, 15; political analysis 16–17, 51, 270–75, 317–18; spiritual dimensions, 16, 282, 287, 321, 353 n. 27; violence against, 343, 352 n. 21. See also Deep ecology; Earth religion; Radical environmentalists; Road building; Tactics

Earth Liberation Front (ELF), 24
Earth night, 329
Earth religion, 282; dangers of,
272–74, 285–86, 299; natural
basis of, 282; positive aspects of
290–91; scientific plausibility of
295–98; and the separation of
Church and State, 284
Ecocentrism, 114–15, 119, 124–26,
262, 276; defined, 16. See also
Biocentrism
Ecofeminism, 4, 29 n. 17; in Britain,
239 n. 5; in Scotland, 256; and
misanthropy, 294; in Central
America, 58–61, 62, 66
Ecological resistance movements:
causes of, 45, 106, 147, 153,
166–67, 169, 173, 178–79, 180,
183–84, 221, 231–32, 322,
335–36, 346, 350 n. 6, 354 n. 31;
definitional issues, 2;
anti–war/nuclear move-
ments–continuity with, 221,
229–30, 241–42; democracy
movements–continuity with,
180, 182, 196; independence
movements—continuity with,
130–31, 162–64, 173, 179,
183–84; future of, 143–44,
237–38, 346–47; in Thailand, see
chapter 6; impacts of, 344–47,
353 n. 28; obstacles to, 142; religious motivations/dimensions,
77, 106–07, 156–57, 166–72,
175–76, 282, 287, 290, 336–37;
equity/access to resources objective, 342; return to traditional
lifeways objective, 57–58, 61, 64,
70, 175–76, 342; successes (e.g.
logging bans), 107, 118, 136, 144,

145 n. 5, 151, 152–53, 170, 223;
sustainability objective, 71, 251,
317, 342; women's move-
ments–continuity with, 165,
182–83, 192, 196; See also
Women and Ecological Resistance; Popular Analysis; Tactics
Ecologist, The, 30 n. 23, 232, 339
Ecopsychology, 29 n. 13, 256, 261,
269
Ecotage, 147, 303; defined, 14; criticisms of, 30 n. 22; examples of,
21, 140; mistaken examples of,
112; rationale for, 14, 16–18,
310; as public ritual, 354 n. 29
Ecoterrorism, 207–08, 330
Edwards, Bob, 7 n. 3, 335, 337, 338,
344–45, 354 n. 31
Ehrlich, Paul, 232, 234
Enclosure process. See Commons,
enclosure of
Enlightenment: narrative of, 12;
philosophy of, 262–64, 270, 274,
280 n. 13, 286, 291. Compare
Postmodernism.
Environmental decline, 1; perceptions of causes, 2, 146, 190–91;
prescriptions to reverse, 2;
species extinctions, 3, 16, 254,
305, 308, 344; and sustainable
development, 70
Environmental justice movements,
2, 44–45, 35–55, 178, 333 n. 3,
351 n. 17
Environmental laws: enforcement–lack of, 44–46, 153–55
Environmental justice movements,
35–55
Environmental racism, 41–42, 53 n
7, 103; defined, 54 n. 13

Environmentalism: establishment, 219; radical, 2; militant, 2, 117, 300–04; Popular, 1–2. *See also* Ecological resistance movements; Radical environmentalism

Environmentalists: populist, 2; pagan, 29 n. 14; violence against, 343; women, 66–69

Extinction of species. *See* Environmental decline

F

Factoran, Fulgencio, 151, 152

Faker, Daniel, 58

Fauntroy, Walter, 40, 53 n. 10

Federal Bureau of Investigation, United States (FBI): and Earth First!, 332 n.1

Fishing: depletion of fish resource, 139, 153–55; defense of fish resource, 103–04, 72–76, 83, 139–40, 154–55; impact of mechanized fishing, 139, 153, 155; laws versus mechanized trawlers, 140; lack of enforcement of fishing laws, 153–55; loss of livelihood, 123

Foreman, Dave, 15, 27 n. 4, 332 n. 1

Forest Peoples Alliance, 19

Foucault, Michel, 185

Foundation for Deep Ecology, 21, 31 n. 30

Fox, Warwick, 261, 264, 268, 269. *See also* Ecopsychology

Freire, Paulo, 248

Friedman, John, 335, 351 n. 14.

Friends of the Earth (FOE), 96, 100, 228–30, 243, 319

Frodeman, Robert, 275

Fundamentalism: religious 286–87

G

Gadgil, Madhav, 129

Gaia, 280 n. 19, 282, 294, 348; hypothesis, 280 n. 19, 297; and politics, 282; and science, 295–98; term, 299

Galileo, 295–96

Gandhi, Indira, 134, 142

Gandhi, Mahatma, 131, 144, 206, 208, 209, 216, 339, 340; and India's independence; and sustainability, 349 n. 4; movements, 130–31.

Gedicks, Al, 318, 336, 337, 338, 339, 343, 345, 346

Geopiety, 288

Gerlach, Luther, 290

Gibbs, Lois, 38, 48, 185, 324

Goldsmith, Edward, 232, 234

Gore, Vice President Al, 324

Green Party: in Britain, 234–35, 239–40; and spirituality, 234, 243

Greenpeace, 92–93, 100, 316, 319; criticisms of-by militants, 300–04; defense of, 300–14; history of, 305–07; direct action strategies, 307–09; in Norway, 213; in Britain, 230, 231, 236, 238 n. 2; in Scotland, 243; international politics and tactics, 300–14

Grounded theory, 6

Guha, Ramachandra, 64, 129, 335,

340; criticisms of 352 n. 27, 354, n 30

Gusfield, Joseph, 311

H

Habermas, Jurgen, 267, 277
Hadsell, Heidi, 86 n. 20, 317, 318, 322, 323, 336, 338, 340, 345, 346
Hanbury–Tenison, Robin, 95
Hardiman, David, 130
Haswell, Margret, 184
Hayes, Randall, 18
Hedstrom, Ingemar, 64
Hegde, Pandurang, 134
Hierarchy, 17
Hill, Brendan, 4, 318, 336, 339
Hobbes, 290, 291
Howard, Ebenezer, 226
Human Rights Commission of El Salvador, 66
Hunger strikes. See Tactics; hunger strikes
Hunter, Robert, 305, 309

I

Ideology: bioregional, 289; and Christian stewardship, 156; defined, 85, n. 11; and extremism, 207; as motivation, 38, 71, 76, 82, 186, 219; and nationalism, 287; oppressive, 66, 68; political/ecological, 233–35, 239 n. 5, 261–64; struggle against economism, 166–68; Western, 295, 338
Independence movements. See Ecological resistance movements,

independence movements—continuity with
Indigenous Environmental Network (IEN), 24, 105–06
Indigenous peoples: and ecological resistance, 2, 4, 19–25, 89–108, 148, 156, 158 n. 3, 177; 244–45, 318; environmental organizations, 18–19, 24–25, 30 n. 25, 105, 156; knowledge, 251; lands claimed or controlled, 30 n. 24, 161. See also Spirituality, indigenous
Indigenous Peoples Union, 30 n. 25
Institutes for Deep Ecology, 24
International solidarity actors. See Solidarity efforts

J

James Bay Defense Coalition, 92
Jay, John, 293
Jharkhand Movement (and "Liberation Front"), the, 141–43
Juma, Calestous, 185, 186

K

Kamamba, Chief, 169
Kamieniecki, Sheldon, 344–45, 347
Kant, Immanual, 205
Kelly, Fathe, 150
Kimerling, Judith, 101
Kocherry, Tom, 139
Koenen, Bill, 106
Kohn, Joseph, 101
Krishna, 208
Kvaloy, Sigmund, 207, 213
Kwandu, Alex, 170
Kyle, Danny, 255

L

Lafollette, Douglas, 106
LAMBAT, 154–55
Land invasions/recoveries, 62–63,
    70, 183, 194–95, 343
Land rights, 94, 100, 351 n. 16. *See*
    chapter 9
Lawsuits: *See* Tactics, litigation
Leopold, Aldo, 15, 28 n. 8
Lewis, Martin, 323, 330
Liberation theology: and BCCs,
    148–49; and base community
    movements, 148–50; ideas of,
    64, 67–68, 77, 149–50, 153, 156;
    as ideological resource within
    popular movements, 77, 153,
    156
Liberationist Catholicism. *See* Lib-
    eration theology
Litfin, Karen, 344
Litigation: against popular move-
    ment participants, 116, 150–51;
    as movement tactic, 46, 48
Livelihoods: threats to, 55 n. 19, 79,
    95, 112–15, 123, 127–28, 131–33,
    135, 141, 144, 216, 335, 337–39,
    342
Lochhead, Liz, 251
Locke, John, 284
Lohmann, Larry, 328, 331, 336, 338,
    344, 345, 346
Lone Wolf Circles, 347
Lopez, Maria Mirtala, 63
Lorentzen, Lois Ann, 317, 318, 336,
    337, 339, 340
Love Canal, 38, 39, 41, 52 n. 6
Lovelock, James, 232, 297

LULUs (locally unwanted land
    uses), 37, 41, 44
Lyotard, Jean–Francois, 264

M

MacLeod, Norman, 244
MacLean, Dougie, 252
Macy, Joanna, 28 n. 7, 33 n. 43
Maddy, Lauri, 47, 48
Mainstream splinter organizations:
    examples of, 316, 319
Manes, Christopher, 27 n. 4, 294,
    326
Mannheim, Karl, 265
Manzer, Bruno, 22, 32 n. 35
Marcos, Fernando, 147
Marglin, Frederique 346
Marx, Karl, 267, 301, 302
Masuka, David, 163
Matriarchal (matristic, maternal)
    society, 294
Mbilinyi, M., 181
McAdam, Doug, 319
McPhee, Catriona, 249
Mephenaij Phaton Youth Associa-
    tion (MPYA), 153–54
Militant environmentalism. *See*
    Environmentalism, militant
Mining: impacts of, 103–07,
    140–41; resistance to, 47–48, 89,
    112, 135, 140–41, 339
Misanthropy (and anti-humanism),
    294–95, 335, 320, 322, 326;
    pseudonym Miss Anthropy, 294,
    326
Monkeywrenching. *See* Ecotage
Monocultures, 12, 110, 130, 136,
    175, 338–39
Montesquieu, 290

Morris, William, 226
Morse, Bradford, 137
Motivations for ecological resis-
    tance. *See* Ecological resistance
    movements, causes
Motorway construction. *See* Road
    building
Muir, John, 287, 304, 310, 320
Mujeres por la Dignidad y la Vida
    (DIGNAS), 62, 65, 67–68
Mukash, Matthew, 92
Mumford, Lewis, 292
Murdoch, John, 250
Murray, Dr. Donald, 251
Murton, Brian, 128
Mutendi, Bishop Samuel, 163
Myers, Norman, 98

N

Naess, Arne, 16, 29 nn. 13&16,
    201–03, 205, 208, 213, 217,
    260–61, 264, 268, 269, 274
Nagpakabanang Katawhan sa San
    Fernando (NKSSF), 151–53
Narrative(s), 42, 45; evolutionary,
    15; and natural science, 295–96;
    outsider stories-value of, 11–14;
    Earth First!'s, 14–15; options,
    348–49
Nash, Roderick, 267
Nation (and state) power: challenge
    to, 93–94, 217; erosion of, 344,
    353 nn. 24, 25; and the natural,
    287–89, 293, 299
Native American environmental-
    ism: *See also* Indigenous peo-
    ples—ecological resistance;
    Indigenous Environmental Net-
    work
Native Forest Network, 24, 33 n.
    47, 93

Navarro, Ricardo, 64
Nehru, Jawaharlal, 131, 144
New Age movement, 29 n. 15
Newanda, Mbuya, 171
Ngau, Harrison, 96
NIMBY (not in my backyard), 41,
    43, 45, 49, 228, 290
Nobel, Alfred, 207
Nonviolence, 128–29, 239 n. 6; and
    Gandhi's views, 209–11
NOPE (not *or* nowhere on planet
    earth), 43, 45, 49, 290
Noss, Reed, 29–30 n. 18

O

O'Riordan, Timothy, 271
Odhiambo, E.S. Atieno, 189
Oelschlaeger, Max, 262, 267, 347
Omredt, Gail, 139, 142

P

Palacios, Rebeca, 66
Paganism, 354 n. 29
Pantheism, 129. *See also* Paganism
Parizeau, Jacques, 93
Parkin, Sara, 234
Passmore, John, 267
Patriarchy, 17, 66, 68, 294, 298, 311
People of Color Environmental
    Leadership Summit, 40, 42, 44
Pilapil, Perfecto (Jr.), 154
Planterose, Bernard, 254
Popular analysis: summary of,
    337–41, 342–43; basis in every-
    day experience, 147, 166–67;
    theft/displacement/outsider
    expropriation of land, 173–74;
    commons–enclosure of, 121–22,
    247, 249, 252, 339–40; economic

growth–critique of, 166–67, 339–40, 351 n. 10, See also Ecological resistance movements, causes of; Commons, the Popular ecological resistance movements. See Ecological resistance movements

Porio, Emma, 336, 343

Porritt, Jonathon, 234

Postmodernism: and deep ecology, 262–64, 266–69, 282, 331; as metatheory, 264; rejection of subjectivity and objectivity, 263–64, 280 n. 21

Putnam, Hilary, 114

Q

Quayle, Vice President Dan, 324

Queen Victoria, 223

R

Radical environmentalism: constraints on (in Britain), 221, 227, 234, 237–38; criticisms of, 185, 353 n. 27; definition–types, characteristics, problematics of, 6, 19, 25–26, 33–34 n. 48, 61, 147, 172–76, 177, 313–14, 319–20, 337–43; effectiveness and impacts of, 315–33; Greenpeace as, 309–14; philosophy of and antecedants to, 232–33; in Scotland, 241. See also Deep ecology; Earth First!; Ecological resistance movements

Rainforest Action Network (RAN), 18, 20, 31 n. 31–32, 96, 97, 102, 319

Rainforest Information Center (RIC), 18

Ramblers Association, 224

Rangan, Haripriya, 145 n. 4, 335

Ranger, Terence, 162

Reagan, President Ronald, 35, 50, 201, 296, 324

Rearguard mobilization, 316; avoiding, 329–30

Reforestation, 138, 195, 254–55

Rennie, Frank, 252

Resource mobilization theory, 83 n. 2, 85 n. 12, 318

Ribeirinhos (river dwellers), 71–83

Richards, Audrey, 184

Rights: civil, 39–40, 36, 42; and community, 81, 168, 273; exploitative, 63; as movement resource, 74–75, 107, 253; people's bill of, 54 n. 14; violation of, 157, 248

Road building: resistance to (in Britain), 99, 228, 231–32, 237–38, 241, 350 n. 9; (in Scotland), 242, 254–55; (in India), 127, 140

Robin Wood (Germany), 22

Roselle, Mike, 18

Roszak, Theodore, 348

Rothenberg, David, 4, 317

Royal Society for the Protection of Birds, 219, 225

Royal Society for Nature Conservation, 225

Rousseau, 290

Rubber Tappers. See Seringueiros

Rücht, Dieter, 340

Rüdig, W., 317

Runrig, 252

Ruskin, 226

S

Sacred animals: whales, 215–16

Sacred places: 129, 169, 347–48, 354
nn. 29, 30; the sea as, 139;
defense of, 20, 23, 139–40, 169,
298; destruction of, 103; Mt.
Apo in Philippines as, 145 n. 5,
158 n. 3
Saganash, Romeo, 93
Sahara Club, 330
Sale, Kirkpatrick, 292
Sanjour, William, 48
Sargent, Caroline, 119, 121
Satyagraha, 131, 141; defined, 145
n. 2. See also Gandhi, Mahatma
Savimbi, Jonas, 179
Schellenberg, Keith, 253
Scherr, Jacob, 101
Schumacher, E.F., 232, 351 n. 10
Sea Shephard Conservation Society,
4, 28 nn. 9–10, 31 n. 27, 216–17,
302, 314 n. 1, 319, 327
Seed, John, 15, 18, 20–22, 28 n. 7, 32
n. 34
Seringueiros, 19, 145 n. 5
Sessions, George, 28 n. 4, 29 n. 13,
261, 273
Sheik Mohammed bin Rashid al
Maktoumm, 253
Shiva, Vandana, 132
Shoko, Andreas, 163
Shoniwa, Johane, 163
Smith, Iain Chrichton, 252
Snow, David, 327
Snyder, Gary, 18, 28 n. 7, 30 n. 22,
287, 347
Sobrino, Jon, 64
Social ecology, 17, 29 n. 17, 267
Social movement theory, 5
Socialist ecology, 221
Socrates, 295
Solidarity efforts: on behalf of peas-
ants and indigenous peoples,
18–19, 24, 76–83, 92–93, 97,

100–02, 107, 144, 157, 192–96,
352 n. 23; importance of, 76–83,
115, 126, 144, 288, 347
Soren, Shibre, 142
Spirituality: as movement resource,
107, 163, 168–70, 171–72, 209,
260–61; and deep ecology, 269,
271, 273–77; and green politics,
234; indigenous forms, 20–21,
22–23, 106–07, 166–68, 169–70,
175–76, 187, 245–46; and ritual,
17, 24, 106, 167, 185, 335–36.
See also Ecological resistance
movements, religious dimensions; Earth religions
Stark, Jerry, 347
Stivell, Alan, 255
Strategies. See Tactics
Subversion: accusations against
ecological resistance movements, 149, 155
Successes. See Ecological resistance movements, successes;
Radical environmentalism,
effectiveness of
Sundkler, B.G.M., 163
Survival International, 97, 352 n. 23
Sustainability: 72; and economic
development, 60, 180, 195, 232,
349 n. 4; as movement objective, 69, 317, 342, 347, 351 n. 17;
and post–modernism, 262; and
society, 251, 290, 332, 336, 337,
352 n. 18
Sustainable Development: defined,
70–71, 83 n. 1; as goal, 135, 141,
195; as ideological resource,
79–80, 84 n. 7, as influential
idea, 313
Sylvan, Richard, 275

T

Tactic(s): banner hanging and social change, 309–13; bearing witness, 305–09; civil disobedience, 15, 40, 47, 128, 131, 137, 145 n. 2, 214, 229–31, 235–36, 238; declining novelty/efficacy of, 231; disseminate ecological science, 308–09; diverse examples of, 14–15, 17–18, 19–22, 45–50, 107, 117, 127–28, 133, 151, 229, 253, 305–09; hunger strikes, 133, 137, 152; litigation strategies, 14–15, 28 n. 6, 46, 223; media strategies, 307–09, 327–29; music and storytelling, 242, 245; 251–52; non-revolutionary premises, 340–41, 351 nn. 13, 14; and non-violence, 206–11, 217–18; promotion of ecospirituality, 335–36; religious ritual as, 106, 134–35, 354 n. 29; rude and crude confrontation, 44, 47–50; strategic rationales, 14–15, 45; violent civil disobedience, 208. *See also* Ecotage; Road building; Spirituality and ritual; Vigilante action
Tandon, Yash, 179, 184, 322–23, 331, 336, 339, 340, 346, 347, 352 n. 18
Tasmania (Australia), 341
Taylor, Bron, 318, 321, 333 n. 5
Thatcher, Margaret, 220
Theology of Liberation. *See* Liberation Theology
Thompkins, Doug, 31 n. 31
Thompson, Janna, 270
Thompson, Governor Tommy, 106
Thoreau, Henry David, 320
Tilly, Charles, 83 n. 2, 85 n. 12

Timber harvesting, 122; bans on, 97, 110, 133–34; exploitive, 94–96, 98, 143, 149–51
Topofilia, 288; and national identity, 288–90; and earth religion, 299
Transpersonal psychology/ecology. *See* Ecopsychology
Trask, Mililani B., 32 n. 39
Tuan, Yi-Fu, 288
Turner, Fredrick Jackson, 293

U

United Church of Christ (UCC) Commission for Racial Justice, 40, 42
United Nations, 62, 67, 89, 201, 237; and its Commission on Environment and Development (UNCED) 83 n. 1; and its Educational, Scientific and Cultural Organization, 99; and its Universial Declaration of the Rights of Indigenous Peoples, 107

V

Vahini Uttar Khand Sangharsh, 133
Vamegas, Nora, 62
Van Lennup, Erik, 33 n. 46
Van Zile, Frances, 104–105
Vasquez, Isabel, 64–65, 67
Vigilante action: enforcing environmental laws, 154, 217
Violence: and cultural invasion, 248; against Earth and women, 59; against participants in popular environmental movements, 28 nn. 10–11, 29 n. 12, 98, 107, 141, 143, 150, 155, 158, 343–44,

352 n. 21; future prospects for, 143, 346–47; necessity of, 286; threatened by anti–environmentalists, 329–30; threatened or carried out by popular movement participants, 19–20, 23, 30 n. 26, 93, 96, 136, 142, 154, 239 n. 6, 352 n. 22, 154; versus non–violence, 209, 217; and zealots, 207–08. See also Rearguard mobilization
Viteri, Leonardo, 100

W

Wapner, 318, 328, 336, 344
Watson, Paul, 15, 216, 217
Watt, James, 296
Weber, Max 265
Weiner, D., 180, 225, 337
Western civilization, 1, 206, 282, 283, 299; criticism of, 174; and the environment, 189, 197, 197 n. 6; and environmental degradation, 264; model of development, 132, 338; rejection of, 61; resistance to, 131, 164, 171
White, Benjamin, 19
Wild Earth, 20

Wildlands project, 17, 29–30 n. 18, 31 n. 30.
Williams Ellis, Clough, 226
Wilson, Larry, 46
Wisner, Ben, 339
Wollock, Jeffrey, 92
Women and ecological resistance: contributions to, 38, 51, 107, 140, 174–75, 181, 239 n. 5, 311, 322, 337; reasons for participation/prominence in, 107, 132, 165–66, 172, 181–82, 322, 337, absence of men, 66–67
Wong, James, 95
Wordsworth, 226
World Bank, 109, 113, 135, 137, 144, 168, 179, 181, 196, 331, 332
World Rainforest Movement, 18, 30 n. 23, 97
Wright, John Kirtland, 288

Y

Yeloo Creek Concerned Citizens (YCCC), 46

Z

Zakin, Susan, 27 n. 3, 28 n. 4, 319
Zimmerman, Michael E., 261

8848